I0198495

THE LINDSLEYS
OF WESTOVER

FROM FIRST LUTHER LINDSLEY TO OUR LUTHER

Luther m. Nancy Lacy

Mahlon m. Mary Campbell

Luther C. m. Hannah Lamb who m. 2nd George Johnson

Robert E. Lee Johnson
Minnie Josephene (Aunt Minnie)
Maud Minton m. Gus
Willis L.
Ralph V. m. Musie

Bessie Marshall 1st m. Ernest m. 2nd Lillie Marshall

Virgie

Luther (of Westover)
William d. 3-4 months

MARSHALL FAMILY WHO ARE IN OR WROTE LETTERS

William Hanson Marshall m. Fannie Melvina Davis

Elizabeth (Bessie)	**Lula**	**Lillian (Lillie)**
m. Ernest Lindsley	**d. 1891**	**m. Ernest Lindsley**
Sept 23, 1880		**December 30, 1886/87**
d. December 1, 1885		**d. March 29, 1892**
One Child: Virginia		**Sons: Luther**
		Willie (died at 3 mos)

The three above sisters had three brothers:
John Davis
Samuel (Sammie) Hanson
Willie Edward
  We think:
  Father of Edgar of the letters

MYRICK FAMILY TREE

This is not a complete listing of Lillas's cousins.

Tip had three children, Fullie two.

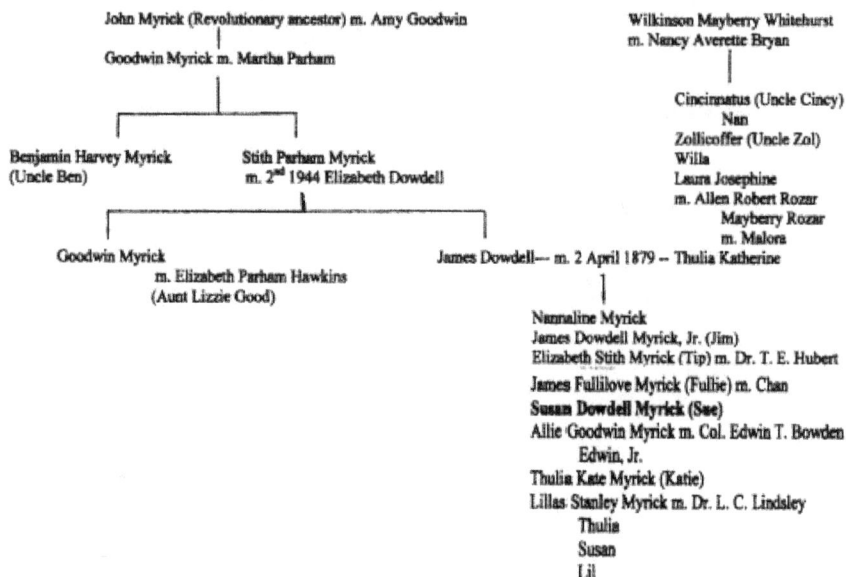

John Myrick (Revolutionary ancestor) m. Amy Goodwin

Goodwin Myrick m. Martha Parham

Benjamin Harvey Myrick
(Uncle Ben)

Stith Parham Myrick
m. 2nd 1944 Elizabeth Dowdell

Goodwin Myrick
    m. Elizabeth Parham Hawkins
    (Aunt Lizzie Good)

James Dowdell— m. 2 April 1879 -- Thulia Katherine

Wilkinson Mayberry Whitehurst
m. Nancy Averette Bryan

Cincinnatus (Uncle Cincy)
Nan
Zollicoffer (Uncle Zol)
Willa
Laura Josephine
m. Allen Robert Rozar
    Mayberry Rozar
    m. Malora

Nannaline Myrick
James Dowdell Myrick, Jr. (Jim)
Elizabeth Stith Myrick (Tip) m. Dr. T. E. Hubert
James Fullilove Myrick (Fullie) m. Chan
Susan Dowdell Myrick (Sue)
Allie Goodwin Myrick m. Col. Edwin T. Bowden
    Edwin, Jr.
Thulia Kate Myrick (Katie)
Lillas Stanley Myrick m. Dr. L. C. Lindsley
    Thulia
    Susan
    Lil

THE LINDSLEYS
OF WESTOVER

Susan Lindsley

ThomasMax

Your Publisher
For The 21st Century

Copyright © 2018 by Susan Lindsley, all rights reserved. No portion of this book may be reproduced, stored or transmitted in any form or by any means without written permission from Susan Lindsley and/or ThomasMax Publishing.

ISBN-13: 978-0-9972920-1-5

ISBN-10: 0-9972920-1-6

First printing, May, 2018

Published by:

ThomasMax Publishing
P.O. Box 250054
Atlanta, GA 30325
www.thomasmax.com

ACKNOWLEDGMENTS

The front cover picture of Westover and the painting of the Blount House on the back cover are the work of Sterling Everett, artist from Macon, Georgia. Sterling also helped me with defining some of the architectural details of Dad's rebuilt Westover.

My sisters Lil James and Thulia Bramlett have been of limitless assistance with remembering many events and details that I had forgotten, as well as writing their memories of our parents.

The many articles from the *Macon Telegraph* and *Macon News* are included with the permission of today's *Telegraph*.

Random House kindly granted permission for me to use the extensive quotes from the book *Midnight in the Garden of Good and Evil* (authored by John Brendt), in which Jim Williams discussed Luther.

The story of Westover from *Ghosts of Grandeur* is reprinted with permission of the author, Michael W. Kitchens.

I owe thanks to Mary Purcell who selected Luther as the subject of her history research paper and thereby led me to many heretofore unknown resources.

Many of my sources were the special collections of libraries in colleges and universities my parents attended. My thanks to the Special Collections Research Center, Earl Gregg Swen Library of the College of William and Mary, and to Eileen O'Toole of W & M for her long-term dedication to my project; Josh Kitchens, Nancy Bray and Gordon Thomas of the former Georgia State College for Women (now Georgia College and State University); Elaine D. Engst and Eisha Neely of Cornell University; Tom McCutchon, Jocelyn K. Wilk and Matthew Bolton of Columbia University; Sarah Johnson of University of Minnesota, and Ashley S. Thacker of Eastern Kentucky University

Scott Parham, volunteer at the Prince William County Courthouse, researched many of the deeds and land records for this book

My high school buddy Pat Blanks faced the difficult task of typing much of this material from handwritten pages that had yellowed with age. She also sketched the layouts of Dad's Westover and of the Dovedale house, and the family truck.

This book would never have been possible without the ongoing support and patience of my life partner, Gail Cabisius.

And of course, thank you, Lee Clevenger, for your as-always careful formatting and producing my books.

For

Jamie, Rebecca, Elizabeth and Victoria

Because an index would be prohibitive, this table of contents lists headings with pages and the general contents of that section, some without page numbers, but in sequence.

TABLE OF CONTENTS

THE LINDSLEYS

OF WESTOVER

On the Anvil of Life, our Souls are laid

Struck blow after blow until they are made

Stronger and brighter and tougher, until

They are tough enough to do God's will

Unafraid.

Luther C. Lindsley

INTRODUCTION

My dad was proud of being a Virginian. He used to tell about how Virginians in slavery times would punish a slave by selling him to a Georgia plantation. We would respond by asking how come he married a Georgia girl and stayed here. He would say that after he found Westover and decided to stay, he couldn't resist the charms of the Georgia lady. Looking back, we see the answer: He loved her deeply.

He said when you meet someone new, you need not ask where he was from. If he was a Virginian, he'd tell you in the first five minutes; if he was not a Virginian, it didn't matter where he was born.

But Dad was more than a Virginian. He was a chemist, a researcher, a philosopher, a writer, a historian, a lover of nature, a seeker of knowledge and an educator.

From childhood, he dreamed of owning a home with tall white columns, and eventually his dream became reality—twice. He purchased Westover Plantation (house and acreage) in 1929, and in 1945 he purchased the Blount House, another house designed by the same architect, Daniel Pratt. Both houses had the tall white columns and stood before Sherman charred the landscape so severely that a crow had to carry its food if it flew over Georgia.

He taught at Virginia high schools, and some of his students stayed in touch with him. Elizabeth Storm sent us girls Christmas gifts until we were adults. After Dad's death, I wrote her and she sent me her memories of Dad.

Some of my strongest memories involve my father's writings. He had bound copies of the *William and Mary Literary Magazine*, which contained the stories and poems that he wrote while a student there. I would sit in the living room, with one of those volumes, and read.

Many of his stories had a touch of the mysterious. When I was young, he told me of his childhood readings, especially the science fiction stories of Jules Verne, and that Verne had known the speed necessary for a space ship to leave the earth's orbit more than a half-century before space flight was considered, and thus had me reading Verne's stories. In his own stories, Dad references authors of his childhood, such as Dumas who wrote the *Count of Monte Crisco*. His college writings also showed his interest in the classics of English literature as well as those of other nations.

In later years, I realized how much his stories and poetry revealed about his childhood. Death, mysticism, and loneliness pervade his works. Separation from his older sister and the deaths of his parents and baby brother cast sadness on many of his writings.

The loss of the family farm shadowed the rest of his life, and he often reminded me that I should never mortgage the land, never sell it, never go on anyone's bond against the land. Protecting ownership of land became a major theme in his life.

Although we never visited his father's home, Douglas Hill, my father often spoke of it—the home his own father lost because he went on his friend's property bond. At least his step-grandfather, George Johnson, bought Douglas Hill. Luther spoke highly of the generosity of George Johnson, who also helped rear him and paid for his education at William and Mary. Johnson was Dad's grandmother's second husband.

Reared on their farm, Dad developed a love of the land and of the farm animals. One of the topics at breakfast and at supper was what was new on the plantation. He always tried to treat an ill animal, although most times the animal died. Christmas, as well as other holidays, meant an extra bale of hay at each barn for the cattle and horses.

His love of and respect for animals extended to wildlife. He often spoke of the fox squirrels, larger than the common gray squirrel and varicolored. Some were gray with black heads; some black with gray heads; some entirely black. Dad said that he brought them into Georgia. He told his son-in-law, John James, that he had brought them in, but not from Virginia as I had thought. He had purchased three pair through an ad, from someone in Arkansas, and released them at Westover. The population is still low, and we are always excited to see one.

Although he was highly educated and was a college professor, he loved farm work. He pitched hay, milked the cows for household milk, cream and butter, and fed the livestock himself in the winter. When the cattle herd numbered more than 100, he could describe every cow and bull that fed at any of the barns.

His workload was too heavy for him to do all he wanted to. We had many tenant houses on Westover lands which were occupied in my early years, but when the tenants moved out for "better pay" in town or "up North," he seldom was able to keep the houses up. We often laughed about one tenant house—the tenants tore off the inside paneling to use for firewood. When they moved out, the house remained empty. Some of these empty tenant houses became hay barns.

At one time, his workload included tending to some of the Dovedale lands that belonged to Mother's siblings: Jim Myrick, Fullie Myrick, Allie M. Bowden, and Katie M. Lowerre. Including the Dovedale lands, he had 20 miles of fences to keep up.

He and his hired man Emanuel Bryson were walking different sections of the fence between the "big pasture" and the State Farm land when Dad apparently had a heart attack or stroke. He woke up on the ground, unsure of where he was, and heard Manuel calling him. In a few minutes, everything cleared up for him, but when he told me about the incident, he insisted that I promise not to tell my mother. He did not want her to worry every time he went out of the house.

He had probably worried about Pattie Love, his first wife, every time he went out of the house because of her bad health. When he spoke of her, it was with love in his voice. He told of her love of Westover and the Nicholson House, their historic home in Williamsburg, Virginia. When she was hospitalized with cancer at Emory Hospital, he would drive to Atlanta after he finished teaching his chemistry classes in Milledgeville, sit with her awhile, and drive back to Milledgeville for a little sleep and to prepare for classes the next day. At the time, he must have had enough tenants and hired people to tend to the livestock.

One story he told about the roads into Milledgeville always caused him to laugh. The "Macon Road" (now Georgia Highway 22) was paved only a short distance, and the asphalt ended on a curve. He was driving into town when another car came out of town, going too fast for the muddy road it was approaching. It hit the end of the pavement and spun all the way around in the mud, and continued on its way.

When the county decided to pave Highway 212, and later the road in front of Westover, he balked at giving away land. Land was precious to him, especially Westover land. The agreement with the county was that it replace fences, but also that in front of Westover, the county would have land only to the ditch on the house side, and take the footage on the other side of the road, to have its forty feet. He protected the yard.

Ironically, however, he did not own anything. When Thulia was born, he deeded all of his land to "the mother of my daughter." The deed was one page and handwritten.

When I received the deed to the land known as the John Myrick Place, he also wrote it out in longhand.

Sometimes his gifts to us were handwritten. He gave us each a horse for Christmas one year, the gift written on a counter check (a blank check that had the name of the bank and its town, with no account information; at the time, the customer list was small enough that all checks were cleared by hand). The bank's name had been struck out and above it written "the bank of love." On the "to line" would be our names, and on the "amount" line was the name of the horse.

His handwriting was elaborate. The summer that the three of us children went to a week-long camp, at which Mother was also a parental counselor, the camp leader could not read the addressee on a letter and asked other adults for help. Mother laughed; it was addressed to her, from Dad.

Having been reared almost on the Manassas Battlefield itself, he had a child's natural interest in The War. This interest was heightened by the influence of his paternal grandmother, who lost her first husband in the War Between the States and had married another Confederate veteran a few years later.

My father grew up hearing about his own father, who was still a child, going with his own mother to the battlefield to get the soldier's body and take it home for burial. Dad's grandmother's second husband was also a Confederate soldier, and the battlefield friendships he made continued after The War. When these fellow soldiers would visit and share stories of The War, Dad would sit at their feet and soak up the stories. As an adult, he could map out the battlefields of The War on the dining room table and use the salt shaker and silverware to show battle lines and troop movements.

So no wonder he wrote about Robert E. Lee and Manassas. His interest in history, however, was not limited to The War, but also to the early years of America and the history of Greece, Rome and Persia. He passed this love of history on to his daughters—who often received nonfiction books relating to the Incas or Toltecs or America's westward movement, or the two major wars (Between the States and the Revolution) as birthday and Christmas gifts.

He often told the story of walking by the courthouse in Milledgeville when an auction was going on. He bid on a safe and a bell, and won the bids. Both items, he was told, came from the capitol building. The safe was supposed to have come to Georgia on a ship with James Oglethorpe and used by the colony leaders in Savannah and eventually moved to Milledgeville. The bell was supposed to have rung out secession. (Thulia has researched these items but has no proof of either background story.)

Dad bought copies of many books about the War: *Lee's Lieutenants*, for example. And other books by Douglas Southall Freeman, a fellow Virginian who was a student of the War Between the States. His desk was always stacked with War books and with cross sections of pine trees, which were labeled with information about the location where the tree had grown.

These cross-sections were part of the work Dad did with Charles Herty, the scientist who developed paper from pine pulp and began the pulp wood industry in the South. Dad established the annual Herty Day celebrations to honor not only Dr. Herty but also other chemists who contributed to the economy and advancement of the South. The celebrations brought national attention to the Georgia State College for Women in Milledgeville.

Dad often spoke of the difficulties he faced at GSCW. One of his classes would always be scheduled for 8 a.m., and a lab would be scheduled for 3 or 4 p.m. In winter, he would leave school in the dark and feed the livestock in the dark.

He and Guy Wells, the president, did not get along. In later life, I learned that "Doctor" Wells had not earned his doctorate; it had been conferred by Mercer University as an honor since he was a college president. I think he was simply jealous of Dad and his reputation.

Dad's reputation was international because of his research and his book. He had done qualitative as well as quantitative analysis for the Metropolitan Museum of Art and for numerous industries. He had taught at several high-level universities. He taught his students what steps were necessary to split the atom long before the Manhattan Project actually did so. Two of his students and one of the teachers under his supervision were called by the Department of Defense to work on the Project. He was in touch with the major scientists and chemists in the South, and he founded Herty Day. Dad retired at sixty, at the request of Guy Wells; he had wanted to continue teaching. He had already given up his research at the demand of Wells, whereas today, research is strongly encouraged in colleges.

The college discontinued Herty Day at some point after Mother's death, and the event moved to Savannah. GSCW lost its greatest claim to fame, for Herty Day events had put GSCW on the world map. Herty Day is "alive and well" in Savannah today. Few southern chemists know the history of the gathering or that the college in Milledgeville "discarded" its most prestigious event.

Dad paid for the gold medal. He paid for the tea held at Westover on Saturday afternoon. He paid for the barbecue supper. He paid for the breakfast held at Westover on Sunday morning.

He often spoke of the hardships of school in his childhood. He walked six miles from "Gamma's" to his school. When working on his doctorate at Cornell University, he took a job in the school's agricultural department and in winter his pathway to the barn sometimes was a channel cut in six-foot snowdrifts.

The "country" never left my dad. When he came to Georgia for a year's teaching, he saw Westover Plantation house—the house he promised himself when, as a child walking to school, he had passed a two-story white house with tall columns With the house came 795 acres of land.

That property grew in acres for a number of years, reaching some 2,500 by the mid-1950s. With the Dovedale lands included, he managed about 3,000 acres. Cattle and horses roamed over the 2,500 acres. Pigs had a sty just across the road from the main house. Chickens and turkeys roamed the yard, sometimes roosting in the tree box; some roosted in the hen house. Hawks and foxes would sneak a meal when they could.

He never thought a job was too difficult, in spite of his limitations. Many times I watched Dad limp across the yard or to the barn, yielding to the pain in the knee he sacrificed to football at William and Mary College. I would see him flex his fingers on cold days, as if to get his hands back to working after being exposed to the cold metal handles of the pitchfork. But he never complained about pain.

He was big-chested for a short man, standing only 5'8". Football wasn't his only athletic interest in college. He boxed in secondary school, and when he got to college he continued boxing, but only for his freshman year. Dad knocked out the school champion, and the boy lay unconscious for three days while Dad sat by the boy's bed, praying for him to live. The boy lived, and Dad never boxed again.

When we stopped for water at the spring one day, I became aware that my father was aging and stiff. We'd had our drink and stretched out for a few minutes of rest before returning to work, but when the break was over, Dad didn't just stand up. He sat up, turned to get onto his hands and knees, and pushed himself up, butt first, then walked his hands up his legs to push his upper body erect.

In his retirement, he stayed involved in chemical matters. One such was to help a Milledgeville friend, a local physician, who went to his country estate, the home he had bought for retirement, and couldn't get onto his own property. He had restored the old farmhouse into a mansion, but the U. S. Army stood guard at his driveway and refused to allow him onto the property.

He hired an attorney and then came to Dad, to determine why the government seized his land without warning. Dad went to investigate. When he arrived at the gate, the guard asked him if he were a U. S. citizen. Without cracking a smile, Dad said, "No, I'm a citizen of the Confederate States."

Smiling, the guard drawled, "Go right on in, Suh."

Equipment visible on the flatbed railcars told Dad the government planned to use the property for a hydrogen bomb plant.

He found a spring flowing with naturally heavy water; that is, the hydrogen atom had an electron and both a neutron and a proton, ideal for splitting the hydrogen atom. Naturally flowing heavy water is very rare.

He also found an area of sand. From samples, he made a diamond-like glass. Once cut, the refraction was so high that only a jeweler could tell that glass from a diamond. The Woodmen of the World heard about the jewels Dad made and came to him, offering a contract to purchase several thousand, at a guaranteed price, the total reaching into several million dollars. But Dad didn't want to tie up his time. I did not know then that he had become a member of the Woodman when he lived in Virginia.

I drove Dad and the doctor to Augusta for the trial, a tribunal of three judges. Dad spent two days testifying, but the chief judge declared that the chemicals had no value to anyone except the federal government, and they struck all of Dad's testimony from the records.

And so our friend lost the case.

Dad enjoyed collecting; he collected porcelains and coins, and often purchased from a young man from Gordon, Georgia. Jim Williams later became famous for being tried for murder four times before being found not guilty; Jim credited his final verdict to Dad, who had told him that a bird can tear down a house. His account of how conversations with Dad influenced him is given in the chapter titled "Remembrance."

He kept his porcelain collection in the "brick house," which had been the overseer's office in plantation days. In the picture below, he is holding a goblet purchased from Jim Williams and said to be one of many objects Napoleon had sent to Louisiana when he planned to escape from exile and move there. The family has since been told that the goblets are fake. In the bookcase behind him he has displayed capodimonte plates, each with a different coat of arms; these have been divided among his daughters. The bird plates hanging from the ceiling bear the N and crown emblem similar to that of capodimonte, but probably are not. The goblets on the top shelf are crystal with gold decorations are now in possession of his daughter Susan.

Luther holds one of the "Napoleon" goblets
that we learned were probably fakes.

One day he went into the brick house and discovered several items missing and a window broken. Local and state law enforcement came out, but after several days, they had no clue. Dad suggested that they go on the radio with the news, and perhaps someone would have seen the items.

Someone had. Teenage boys had stolen the items for a Mother's Day gift. When the parents heard the description, they returned some of the items. Dad said he "let it go" since he got back the more valuable pieces.

He could be persistent. When he discovered that someone had broken into the Blount House, he did not depend on law enforcement. (Another lesson he taught me.) He followed the tire tracks in the dirt road that fronted the property, interviewed the local sit-abouts, and followed the roads until he found someone who knew the driver of the truck loaded with furniture.

The local Jones County sheriff was no help—the items had been moved into Baldwin County. The Baldwin County sheriff was no help—the burglary occurred in Jones County. The Georgia Bureau of Investigation was no help—the agent could not find Westover.

Dad held a casual discussion with the known culprit, and the items "appeared" down the driveway, behind the house, the next day. (See *Blue Jeans and Pantaloons in Yesterplace* for details.)

No matter the challenge, Dad faced it with determination to win. Defeat was not an option. When Westover burned, he rebuilt. When the land eroded, he stopped the washing. If a rabid fox attacked the livestock, he called the vet and saved the horses. Any disaster simply called for extra energy.

Truly, for Dad, the child was the father of the man.

The Why Of Many Things

In working with family papers, newspapers and legal documents, I have seen facets of my father that were invisible to me as a youngster. I see now how he longed for security that he saw in land and real estate, which his father had lost. He spent ready cash for more acreage, for a downtown business site and lots. He had morning classes and afternoon labs, and countless laboratory exercises and other papers to grade. Eventually, as the acreage and number of livestock grew, he did not have enough time in a week to do the other necessary chores such as repair fences, gather in the hay, feed the livestock, tend to repairs on all of the tenant houses and the Liberty Street house, operate a furniture store, and restore the Blount House. He had no time to return to Virginia to tend to his real estate there. Cattle got out and managed to get killed on the railroad tracks; empty tenant houses became hay barns that eventually leaked and became dilapidated.

But he gathered together acreage that fed the livestock and grew pines. Timber, not the livestock, generated enough funds to put his children through college and to provide them with a secure future.

He had faced childhood with only a grandmother's affection and guidance, his Aunt Minnie's love for security, and his own dreams for his future. But he left his family financially secure for generations to come.

Dad's Good Judgment

The quality of person's judgment sometimes can be measured by the person he chooses to marry. Dad's judgment was excellent. He selected a woman of intelligence, education, devotion to science and chemistry, and one heck of a good mother and wife, who had no fear of the hardships to be faced in the country.

Although this book began as my father's biography, we must not forget the contributions Mother made. She left her teaching position and her research behind when she married. She managed the Herty Day events at Westover, which took days of planning and preparation.

Her children became her students. She had them reading before they entered school. She subscribed to children's publications such as the "Weekly Reader," and held classes every summer to keep her children ahead of their peers and constantly interested in learning. She turned her interest in nutrition into a game for her children—who ate what vitamins and minerals each day? Diet determined how far you could move your "man" on the game board.

She was a devoted mother in many ways. She not only taught her children, but she played and competed with them. She turned solitaire card games in multiple solitaire, and gave no quarter to the children; everyone fought heartily to win, and the competition brought laughter, not stress.

Chicken did not come from the grocery store. She herself, and later her children, chased down and beheaded the chickens. She plucked and cleaned them. She picked vegetables from the garden and canned them. I came home from school one day to find Mother and Aunt Tippie scraping vegetables off the kitchen ceiling—the pressure cooker had blown up.

She went out to the pastures to pick apples and blackberries to make jellies. When peaches ripened, we would go to Haddock to get them by the bushel to can. Then, one year, Dad went to Haddock to get a bushel of peaches, and instead of buying peaches he bought another house of his childhood dream—the Blount House.

Mother did complain a few times. She said we were "land poor." All our cash seemed to go to the land, for taxes, for fences, for feed for the livestock. I remember going with Dad to a track of land off what is now Highway 22, a place he had recently purchased, but it turned out the seller, a local leader, did not own it. When he had a chance to buy the land now known as Andalusia, Mother did put her foot down against that expenditure. She had children and was going to be sure they had the same educational opportunity she and her siblings had. Money spent on land could not pay for a college education, and the family was paying taxes on about 2500 acres.

She gave up a life of bridge games, tennis matches, teas, and parties, and party dresses. She gave up a self-supporting job, the satisfaction of financial independence and the camaraderie of other professional people for the isolation of Westover and the day-to-day chores of a housewife in the country. She gave up the comfort of city life to run a plantation home with no central heat, only fireplaces, which she had to stoke on winter days to stay warm. She gave up city water for a well, operated by a pump—she had to go outside and across the yard to turn on the pump when she wanted water. There was no running water when freezing weather came or the power went off. She gave up the consistency of a city stove for the inconsistency of country electricity—a strong wind would put a limb down on the power lines. Breakfast was often cooked on an open fireplace.

Every vehicle that went down the unpaved road out front sent a wave of dust into the house during the warm months, when windows were held up by removable screens that did not keep out the dirt daubers. Wooden doors, with no screens, stood open to catch the breeze, and also to allow entrance for various wildlife: Bees that lived in the front porch columns and upstairs porch flooring; snakes that entered in search of whatever might be hiding within; stray cats that entered soundlessly and found an open drawer to have a litter of kittens; bats that entered before dark and couldn't find a way out. And forever, mosquitoes and dirt daubers.

When she married my father, my mother gave up town comforts to return to the country life she did not remember from her childhood, for she had left the country when she was only 10 years old. But I never heard her complain about living conditions.

Aunt Allie, however, once said that she wondered how my mother managed life under the conditions she faced after her marriage.

Mother had many adages of advice. Two remain in my mind constantly as reminders to keep my attention on whatever I'm doing. Others are plain and simple directions for behavior.

A sorry workman blames his tools.

What you lack in your head you make up in your heels.

The gum-chewing girl and the cud-chewing cow, seems to me there's a difference somehow—Ah, now I know. It's the thoughtful look on the face of the cow.

Fools' names, like monkeys' faces, always appear in public places. (Referring to the "Joe loves Sally" comments painted on walls and bridges.)

Better to remain silent and be thought a fool than to speak and remove all doubt.

Pride knows neither heat nor pain.

PART I

LETTERS FROM THE LINDSLEY

FOREBEARS

FAMILY BACKGROUND

Hannah Lamb Lindsley Johnson saved many family letters and documents. Her daughter, our Luther's Aunt Minnie, gave them to Susan Lindsley, fortunately after Westover burned or they would have been lost. The letters here were written by family members in our Luther's paternal Lindsley line and his maternal Marshall line, as well as by family friends.

Details of the family lines are given in Appendix I, but a brief outline is here to help determine "who's who" among the writers. See Appendix II-A for photographs of Lindsley family members.

Luther Lindsley, writer of the first letter, was owner of the family Bible and married Nancy Lacy. At the time of his death, he and Nancy lived in Ohio.

Their son Mahlon moved to New Jersey; his wife Mary Campbell gave her last name as middle name to their son Luther Campbell Lindsley (the second Luther, referred to here as Lt. Luther Lindsley) who fought in and was killed in the War Between the States. This Luther married Hannah Lamb. After Lt. Luther's death, Hannah married George Johnson.

Luther and Hannah's son Ernest L. Lindsley (we don't know if that L was for "Lamb" or "Lacy" or "Luther") had two wives: The first, Elizabeth (Bessie) Marshall, gave him a daughter Virginia (Virgie). After Bessie's death, Ernest married Bessie's sister Lillie, who became the mother of Luther of Westover.

After our Luther was orphaned at the age of five, Grandmother Hannah and her husband George Johnson reared Luther.

LUTHER'S LINDSLEY ANCESTORS

These letters are given with no editing (to retain the flavor of the written language of the time) and in chronological order. Some were written by either friends or cousins, whose relationship we do not know; these are included because of the picture they present of the time period.

The first-named Luther who married Nancy Lacy lived in Carroll Township, Ottawa County, Ohio, at the time of his death.

The earliest letter we have was written in Ohio, where many of the Lindsleys lived.

* * *

From the first-named Luther

Carroll Aug 16, 1857

Dear Grand Children
 I write to inform you at this time of my health which is quite poor at present I wrote to your Father a month or 2 ago & as yet have Received no answer my Daughter Nancys Husband has written 1 or 2 letters to your Father that Remain Unanswered or if they have they have never been Received. the crops look well for the season Wheat has come in good corn will be an average crop in this country this year Oats were never better than they are this year Wheat is worth $1.00 per bushel corn 50 cts Oats 40 cts Potatoes 62 1/2 cts per bushel Well Luther I have Sold my place and am at present boarding out I am boarding with my daughter Nancy & now perhaps you would like to know how much I got For it I Sold it for $400.00 Dollars & I have other Property and notes to the Amount of $700.00 Dollars there is 20 Acres in the farm I sold Elihus wife is married again & living on Elihus Estate
 I sold my place to Nancys husbands son by his first Wife I would like to have your Father and yourself come and See me for I am so feeble I don't think I shall come to see you though I should like to if my health would permit it is a General time of health in

this Country at present and now I would like to know whether you are coming out this fall or not for I have a disire to See you once again before I leave the World and I know in all Reason that I have but a few more months or years at most to live here in the World & it would give me Joy to great you once more while on Earth

Please write whether you are coming this fall or not So that I can be looking for you when you come Come to Pittsburg then to Cleveland to Sandusky Port Clinton where you will find me or my friends No more at present But I remain your Father Grandfather & Friend

Luther Lindsley

To Luther C. Lindsley Junior & Wife
N. B. Please write as soon as you get this
Without fail.

Note: Luther Lindsley married Nancy Lacy (see Family Bible, possession of Thulia Lindsley Bramlett; see also *The History of the Lindley, Lindsley, Linsley Families in America 1639-1930* by John M. Lindly). The son of Luther and Nancy, Mahlon Smith Lindsley moved to Virginia, and our Lindsley line descends from him.

* * *

To Mahlon from his sister Elizabeth Lindsley Green, Locust Point, Ohio.

Uncle Clossen Lacy refers to the brother of Mary Clawson (note various spellings). Mary was the wife of Jacob Lacy, whose daughter Nancy married the first Luther Lindsley in the family Bible.

Emily and Eliza (Elizabeth) are Mahlon's daughters.

I have been unable to find information on Wilham Russell.

Uncle Jepthy Odden (Ogden?) may be a brother of Charles Ogden who married the first Luther's sister Sarah.

The Lindsley family Bible shows Elizabeth, Mahlon and sister/brothers born in New Jersey; Lindly's book shows their father Luther moved to Ohio after 1808. Elizabeth refers to a "New Jersey settlement" in Ohio.

Addressee: Mr. Mahlon S. Lindsley
Dumfries, Prince William County, Virginia

February the 7th 1867

Dear Brother this is the second letter I have wrote to you and haint had any answer and I thought I would write another and see if we would here from you Wilham Russell has wrote you a letter and he haint had any answer and we are getting uneasy about you. we are all well as (illegible) I hope when you get this letter it may find you all the same we are Anxiously waiting for the time to roll around that you was comeing to see us you must bring all of your family we will make a big dinner for you. the way we do here when our friends come to see us we kill a hog and make a fuss Uncle Clossen Lacy and his wife is in Green Village a visiting and I dont no but what they will be out here before they go home Uncle Jepthy Odden and his wife is a living. and lives one mile from our house Aunt Marriah Gorden is well we have got a New Jersey settlement out here and I wish your family was in our midst we talk of building a church forty rods from where we live I have got all the letters that you ever wrote to father and some that Luther wrote it does me good to set down and read them over but it would do me more good to read a letter from you now I want you to write how you all are getting a long and how Emily (Mahlon's daughter) has done a getting Married. and how far she lives from you. whare do you direct your letters to her for I would like to write to her. Give my respects to Eliza and Luthers wife and kiss the little boy for me we are getting long pretty well it is getting pretty heard times but I guess we can stand it. we having not much news to write but I want you to write back And I will try and do better the next time we have got us a good place and out of debt and got horses and cows sheep and hogs and wheat enough in our grainery to last us two years so if you come you wont eat us out of house and home you needent be a fraid well Dear Brother I cant think of any more to write only for you to write as soon as you get this for we are getting so uneasy about you

> I will have to close and here is a letter
> stamp for you to send me back

from your sister Elizabeth Green

to Smith Lindsley

write soon Good by

Direct your letters
   Locust Point
   Ottawa County
   Ohio

* * *

The next letter is from Alfred Pierson, probably to Mahlon, since Lt. Lindsley is dead. Hannah has not remarried, and Alfred says to give respects to Hannah and Earnest.

"Mary" is probably Mary Pierpoint, Mahlon's adopted daughter.

Clossen Lacy is probably Nancy Lacy Lindsley's brother since Nancy's mother was a Clawson.

Odgens are mentioned in two letters. Here, and in her letter (dated February 7, 1867) to her brother Mahlon Lindsley, Elizabeth Green refers to "Uncle Jepthy Odgen." He and Catherine are probably of the same family. We have been unable to determine Catherine's relationship to either the Lacys or Lindsleys. We have no information on Lowisa.

Locust Point Ohio
February 15th 1867

Dear Brother sister and friends,

  this being a rany day I thought I would write to you. we are all well at present except bad colds we have had 6 weeks sleighing but its use up now. well we heard from N. J. last weeke and Clossen Lacy and wife are out there on a visit. well Brother Bill and me got home all wright. well I suppose you ar a climbing up those hills and you must be sure to put on the britching when you go down to the Spring. hurraw for Johnson and the constitution

Well Mary says I must write the price of produce and so here it goes. wheats 2.42 pur bushel. corn 75 cents Potatoes 1.00. pork 8.00 pur 100 Pounds. we had a fire in our neighbourhood night before last it was a Store that belonged to Catharine Ogdens husband it was insured for 1500 Dollars.

Well I expect you are thinking of coming out to Ohio and making us a visit well I want you to put your thoughts into action. come and see us if you do not stay more that 6 months and when you do come I want Hannah and all the rest to come I want to sea you all.

Now I want you Southern people to Stand up for your rights under the Constitution. I am opposed to Negro Sufrage. this is a white mans government. now give my best respects to Hannah and Earnest and tell Mary that I have not forgotten hur. tell Lowisa that She nead not go to much trouble about Supper. write soon so no more at present but remain your Brother untill Death.

Alfred Pierson

* * *

Emma Lindsley Mann was daughter of Mahlon and sister of Lt. Luther C. Lindsley, CSA. Mahlon and his wife moved to Texas and he died there. The reference to the "son of my brother" is to Ernest Lindsley.

Troup County
State of Texas

Know all men by these present that I Emma Mann formerly Emma Lindsley of Prince William County Virginia at present a resident of Travis County Texas - That about the year 1858 in Prince William County Virginia that my brother Luther C. Lindsley gave me a note for one hundred dollars interest to be made payable or to urn from the date of my marriage. the said note being lost or mislaid I do hereby agree that should the son of my bother Earnest L. Lindsley who is the heir pay to and furnish my Father & Mother with 1st class passengers ticket by Rail Road from their home in

Prince William County Virginia to Austin Texas and money in addition to pay their necessary traveling expenses to Austin, then I hereby acknowledge the said note principal and interest fully paid and discharged and fully release my nephew Earnest L. Lindsley from all farther liability in connexion. Otherwise to be and remain in full force and effect until all interest and principal due me are paid.

August 20, 1883
Emma Mann

State of Texas
County of Travis
Before me Ed Summenow a Notary Public in and for said County and State this day personally appeared Emma Mann known to me to be the person whose name is subscribed to the foregoing instrument of writing who acknowledged to me that she executed the same for the purposes and considerations therein expressed.

Witness my hand and official Seal at Manchaca (seal) Texas on this the 23rd day of Aug A D 1883

Ed Summenow
Notary Public
Travis Co. Texas

This letter to Lillie is from Ernest, whose wife Bessie Marshall, Lillie's sister, had died December 1, 1885. Bessie was the mother of Frances Virginia Lindsley.

May 6, 1886
Dumfries Prince Wm Co. Va.

My dear Lillie

I received your kind and welcome letter today words fail to express the pleasure it afforded me it was like a ray of sun shine after weeks of rain I have not been to Manassas yet I may go in the morning if it is not raining. I wont be gone long if I go, only a day or two We had a terrible hail storm in this neighborhood to day about two oclock The hail fell from 3 to 4 inches deep and some places where the water ran and washed it up it is 3 to 4 feet deep it has ruined all the wheat and grass crops wheat is all cut and mashed down to the ground the storm was twice as hard as it was last summer it dont seem possible but it was all the fruit is cut off of the trees. I am more discouraged to night that ever Fate is against me and what is the use of a man trying to fight against it. I have been fighting against it for the last five years and it comes off victorious every time. The day I was married there came a dove and sit all the morning in the locust tree at my window a little white tame dove. And Grandma saw it, she was out in the yard She went in to the house and sit down and cryed for hours she said it was a bad omin, I was not-at-all supersticious and am not now, but how offten I have thought of it since. I never told Bettee but some one did and how offten she ust to speak of it when fate served against us. that was the first tame dove I ever saw here, and the last one. But all that day and all that night my Grandma words were in my mind. I have never looked at the tree where the dove sit since that I did not think of it.

I hope you will continue to Answer my letters, for they are the only sun shine that finds its way here.

I do not see how your Ma could be so unkind as to Forbid you answering them, After I had given up to her all that was der on this earth to me. She little knows what it cost me to part from Virgie if only for a short time.

Some think I suppose that it is ridiculos in me, to ever think of wanting Virgie, or ever Seeing her. She is the forbidden fruit I must taste not, touch not handle not, but can stand at a distance and look with longing eyes and driping heart, while others receive the caresses which by right are mine before all others.

I know what it is to be motherless or Fatherless. no one can tell better than I. After the Father or Mother is gone no one can fill the place of the missing one so well as the remaining one I have lost a parent when I was just Virgies age. I just can remember him and with what prid have I listened to his praise falling from others lipse I ust to want to grow up and be a man just like him a man that every one loved and Respected. how well I can remember sitting on my mothers lap every night after we had gone to our room to bed, while She told about my father and how she wanted me to grow up and be a good man like him. and with that respect have I obeyed my mothers whishes.

After I left my mother I did not hear so much about my father so I went astray. if I had paid more attention to my mothers words I would be an happier man to day and a better one. I never had a evel thought in my life, and my fathers memory came up before me but what -- the evel thought -- did not vanish. Virgie will be hoping for a time where she is but when she is grown if she can remember her Happyest thouts will be of her <u>Mother</u> and father.

E. L. Lindsley

* * *

Date on this letter from Ernest to Lillie is November 22, either 1886 or 1888. It is written on the back of a bill from Gaylord Watson, Map Publishers, dated Jan 19, 1886. Luther of Westover was born in February 1888, so if the year of this letter were 1888, there would have been a reference to him.

According to entries in the Marshall Family Bible (Susan Lindsley has a copy of the relevant pages), Lillie and Ernest were married December 30, 1887. This letter is not clear as to where he was to take her "home," but the implication is that "home" is their home and that they are married. Other letters, however, are signed "your devoted husband."

Lee is Ernest's half-brother, son of Hannah and George Johnson.

Douglas Hill
Nov 23/86

Dearest Lillie

I am sorry indeed that I could not get over last night to see you. it was nine oclock when I got home Darling it is impossible for me to carry you home today. And realy I do not know whether I can carry you before Sunday if I can I will. I am going to start soon this morning so I can get home in time to come over to night.

Sammie was in Dumfries last night waiting for you until dark he said you promised to meet him there. I begged him to come home with me last night and take you home this morning but he would not do it. Lee and Papa will be down today or tomorrow and maybe I can get Lee to take you home if that will do.

I will get one of Burke's boys to deliver this for me And if you wish to answer it, you can do so by him. You need not be in a hurry to go home Sammie said your Ma was not going to Washington

As ever your own
E. L. Lindsley

Ernest wrote this letter sometime after their marriage.

Dumfries Va Monday night

Dear Lillie

I have some news to tell you, alice broke in the house last Friday and got some flower—and I don't know what else I cant tell untill you come home. she got in the window up stairs in the room where I sleep you know the ladder was at the well handy for her to get, I never would of known any one had been in the house if had not been for one thing I had not touched the cake you left for me, and it was just as you left it Friday Morning and that night it was gone.

I have got plain proof that she did it Shall arrest her tomorrow. if you know where her Mother is you had better see her at once and tell her She got about twenty pounds of flower And I dont know what else. Cant know what is gone untill you come home be sure and come home Sunday I have had the ruffest time this time I have ever had

Your devoted husband
E. L. Lindsley

OUR LUTHER'S CHILDHOOD

We have little information about our Luther's childhood, other than stories he told his three daughters, most often the story of walking to school from the farm and the mansion he dreamed of owning.

His first cousin William **Edgar** Marshall was a childhood playmate, and after years of lost contact, they reconnected in the late 1950s.

Pictured below is the house in which he was reared. On the back of the original photograph was written: "House, white; chimney red; barn red, Mrs. Hannah Johnson, Manassas, Va."

In Luther's handwriting, below the words of his grandmother: "L. C. Lindsley was raised here by his Grandmother Hannah Johnson from about age 5 until he finished college. L. C. Lindsley."

Home of Hannah Lamb Lindsley Johnson and George Johnson

Luther's biological grandfather, Lt. Luther C. Lindsley, was killed in the War Between the States. All official records show that he died at the Battle of Cedar Creek (Appendix III). His widow, Hannah Lamb Lindsley, sent a map to her grandson, Dr. Luther C. Lindsley (my father) with a note:

> **My dear Luther**
> **This old map is the one your grandfather picked up on the Battlefield of "Seven Pines" & carried until he was killed at the battle of "Fishers Hill"; before he was buried Major Thornton took it from his pocket & after the Surrender, sent it to me.**
> **Grandmother**

The Battle of Cedar Creek was October 19, 1864. The battle extended from Fisher's Hill (south of Strasburg) northward to about three miles south of Middletown. Hannah's reference to Fisher's Hill implies he was killed at or near there during the battle. The battle called "Fisher's Hill" occurred on September 20, a month before Lt. Lindsley was killed. The map and note are now in possession of Russell Myrick (Rusty) Bramlett.

The family story, told by Dr. Luther to his girls, is that Hannah harnessed up the mule and, with only her eight-year-old son, Ernest, rode some sixty-five miles, crossed the Yankee lines to the battlefield, dug up his body, and drove home to bury him. Her husband's sergeant wrote to let her know where to find the body:

> **about a mile from Middletown, on the Pike toward Strasburg on the Battlefield of Cedar Creek or Bellgrove, Across the Pike from the first fortifications. At the head of a "gully" running from the Pike and nearly opposite a piece of woods, & from the woods about (struck out) between ¼ & ½ a mile.**
> **T. S. Chancelor**
> **The above is the escact (sic) location where we buried Lieut. Lindsley, Oct 19th, 1864.**
> **T. S. Chancelor, Serg, Co.B. 49th Reg. Va.**

About a mile from Middleburn
on the Pike towards Strasburg
(on the Battlefield of Cedar Creek
or Bellgrove. Across the Pike from
the first fortifications.
At the head of a "gully" running
from the Pike & nearly opposite
a piece of woods, & from the woods
between a 1/4 & 1/2 a mile

       J. J. Chancelor

The above is the exact
location where we buried
Lieut Lindsley, Oct 19th 1864

J. J. Chancellor Sergt
Co. B. 49th Reg. Va.

This note was written on the back of a page torn from a small publication released by the American Tract Society, apparently the only paper available to the soldier at the time. A poem on the other side is entitled "Him that cometh to me, I will in no wise cast out."

A few days later, Hannah obtained this statement, which she must have needed for legal reasons, especially to obtain war-widow's pension. Prince William County had the marriage on record, but copies at that time were handwritten. She apparently did not have a copy of the entire certificate, which is given in Appendix I.

This is to certify that I solemnized a marriage between Luther C. Lindsley and Hannah M. Lamb, both of Prince William County Virginia, on the 10th day of January eighteen hundred and fifty Six. John Clark, Minister of the Gospel, 18 Nov. 1864.

On January 7, 1868, she married George W. Johnson, a Confederate veteran; many of his friends, as well as friends of Lt. Lindsley, visited the Johnson home in Manassas. The veterans would sit around and talk about The War.

Living with his grandmother Hannah after age five, our Luther could be said to have been "weaned" on War stories. His deep interest in The War never faded. He read constantly about the battles and the military leaders. His children joked that if you asked him anything about the War Between the States, you better be prepared to sit for an hour and learn details of the relevant battle and the biography of the relevant officers.

His college writings also reflect his interest in the War, and his later writings show his knowledge of war throughout history, from before recorded history through World War II.

The rest of these letters were written after our Luther's birth. Note especially those from his father Ernest L. Lindsley, and the "contract" with his (Ernest's) mother, in which he gives his two children, Luther and Virginia, to her.

Luther's childhood was a series of losses. His baby brother died at the age of about three months in 1890, when Luther was not quite three.

His mother died March 29, 1892 (Lindsley Family Bible entry) at home at Douglas Hill, and shortly thereafter Luther and his sister Virginia were sent to live with their Lindsley grandmother, Hannah Lamb Lindsley (Mrs. George) Johnson.

A month later, Ernest was arranging the sale of his property to pay the bond for a friend. The "friend" skipped town before his trial, and Ernest had no funds so he lost the farm. He then moved to Washington, D.C., where he died October 22, 1893.

George Johnson bought Douglas Hill before it went to auction, but we don't know why Ernest did not remain at the home there. We don't know who lived at Douglas Hill thereafter.

Luther was only five when his father died and he and Virginia were orphaned. These letters provide the only information we have for the years before Luther left home for college.

* * *

From Sammie's mother, Fannie M. Davis Marshall, our Luther's grandmother

Sammie is brother of Lillie, who is mother of our Luther.

Minnie is a daughter of Hannah Lindsley and George Johnson. She was about sixteen when Luther of Westover was born, and they became close. Aunt Minnie became a sort of substitute mother as well as an older sister. She was the one relative that Luther spoke of often to his children.

July 24th 1889

My Darling Sammie

I just got your dear letter this morning and will answer at once as I expect Ernest will go to Brentsville tomorrow & will mail it for

me. I was so glad to hear from you & to know that you are coming to spend some time with us. Lillie & Ernest are both delighted that you are coming & so is Virgie; If you could be here a few days & see what little time I have to devote to writing you wouldent blaim me for not having written before this for dear little Luther has been sick ever since I came & takes most of Lillies & my time to attend to him. then Virgie was sick in bed for Several days soon after we came & last week She hurt her foot very bad & couldnt walk for 5 days & you very well know she courned ALL of my time during those few days & yesterday I was sick in bed myself. all together I have had quite a ruff time since I came to the country. Lillie & Ernest both look dreadful, have nearly worked themselves to death & for that reason I try to take as much off of her as possible which goes VERY hard with me. Oh! the horred old country I wouldent live in it again under any consideration if I could help myself; I have been here 3 weeks yesterday & haven't been off the place but once & no one has been here but Mrs. Branner and every boddy too busy to write. Ernest has a splendid crop but his horses look dreadful; so poor can hardly get along but he will soon be through with his busy work then they will pick up & he will get himself a new suit for the Association which is the 27 of Aug; you must stay here & go with us as we will go in the big waggon & have plenty of room. Lillie will go home with me & stay 4 weeks after the Association. Will you go to Salem before or after you come here; how I would love to be there with you & Spence a week give my love to them & tell them if I can araing it I will make them a visite before I go home; tell them to send me some of those nice Salem peaches by you Sam cant you bring me about 3 or 4 of my half gallon glass cans from out of the wood shed or the clarred for me to put up some peaches while I am here I have made one gal of black berry wine & it is grand (the best I ever made & Lillie gave me 1/2 gal cans of nice black berrys for a birthday present; Mrs. Branner has the greatest quantity of peaches you ever saw. Willie Chapmans wife is comine to Mr. k--- next Saturday for the rest of the summer; Lil & myself want to go over there tomorrow to spend the day; will go again when Minnie comes; give yourself no uneasiness I will not mention it to anyone about her coming; Dont disappoint us for we ALL will love to have you come & want to see you SO bad I told Lillie you sent Luther the whiskey I brought to him so don't give me away but let her still think so for she was so proud of it & tells everyone how sweet it was of you. Pleas bring Virgie & Luther a bundle of _____ I must stop as my sheet is full & I must write to Willie & your Pa & _____ tomorrow also as I dont know when I will have another oppertunity; All join in much deep & tender love & hoping to see you the tenth I am your true & loving

      Ma
Virgie wanted to write to you but I haven't time to wait for her.

* * *

The next letter is undated. Luther is mentioned as a toddler, trying to take the pen from "Ma" as she writes. He was perhaps 18 months or so. This letter was probably written after the one just above.

From Fannie M. Davis Marshall, mother of Lillie Marshall Lindsley. Sammie is our Luther's uncle.

Sunday Evening

My Darling Sammie

This time last Sunday you were here; but now so far away; which makes it seem twice as lonely here as it did before you came; Ernest as well as myself seem to miss & wish fur your dear presence but I will build sweet communication for a few moments though the medium of the pen if I cant in person with you, if Luther will allow me; but he is pulling at my pen so that I can scarcely write attal, or think of what to write; Lilli sais Ernest as well as her shed tears after you said good by & left them at the Association but she is consoling herself on the thought of seeing you next Sunday & Ernest building his hopes on having you spend one week with him this fall during hunting season sais how he would love to have you come & how he will enjoy hunting with you; Well my Darling, they both were there at the Association to meet me the next day; Ernest went to see Mr. C. that same evening asking him about the wagon & he declaired he niver said any thing of the kind & that he was welcome to it untill after the Association had closed. so Minnie and Maud (daughters of Hannah Lindsley and George

Johnson; aunts of our Luther) **came home with us that night and Pens wife the next; She even complimented you to the Skyes; said she had never seen Such an improvement in any one in her life as she saw in you last winter at her house both in appearance, manners & in every way & never had a more plesant & aggreable Surprise that when she found you standing at her door that night. teased Pen conciderable & in praising you in Such extravigant terms; You dont know what you missed by not Staying untill the Association was over; Smoot withdrew from the others carrying the Quantico & Occoquan Churches only & only part of their membership remained with him Mr & Mrs Chapman left him & now have no church & the same with Jim Barby but his wife is still with Smoot they seem terable grieved; an friday morning the Preachers had a big quarel in the pulpit almost fought; it was quite an exciting time never saw so many tears shed to me Smoot will have quite a lonely old time of it; Ernest sais you never left our Address with him but I think I have it if I have I will send this letter to your NO if not will be compelled to send to my NO! You must write to him and tell him about the carriage he will appreciate it so much seems to think <u>so</u> much of you**

Well Sam we will be home this time next week without fail unless it rains & you must be sure & come around to see us for we will all be anxious to see you; Virgie wants to write to you but she will see you so soon that I have persuaded her to wait until then & tell you all instead of writing; but dont say she aint happy because the time is so near at hand for her to get back & leave the dull country she does nothing but sing & and rejoice & I can say ditto,

   from your loving Ma

All send love & sigh for your presence.

* * *

From Lillie (our Luther's mother) to her mother, Fannie M. Davis Marshall. Lula, Lillie's sister, died in February 1891. John (Davis Marshall) is her brother. "Red flag" maybe refers to having her monthly period.

Douglas Hill
March 1st 1891

My Darling Ma

I have just received your dear letter was so glad to hear from you & that you all was well Oh if you will continue to improve Ernest is still feeling badly could not eat any supper last night he and Luther both have bad coles if Luther does not get better I will send for Bouan Ernest is look a little better but far from being well. I was sorry to hear that the Measel (measles) was so near you hope if it is God's will our loved ones will not take them. am afraid Luther is going to have them he showed every sine last night but seems much better this morning I am well have not been sick since I came home feel as well as I ever did in my life my back feels a little bad today on a count of the red flag as John sais ant you glad I told you I was all right did I not. Ma, Alar has a baby boy.

Please ask Pa to have my garden seeds sent at once or as soon as he can attend to it for me. **Minnie** (Johnson, her sister-in-law; Hannah's daughter and Ernest's half-sister) **is hear comes home every night when she is feeling well & it is not storming She gave Ernest a beautiful suit of clouth, hat and all & he looks splendid in them he is as kind and sweet as he can be only a little jelous Sends love to all of you so does Minnie; Mrs. Bronners son is hear came last night said he saw Pa the other day & would have spoken & told him he was coming but did not reconise him untill he had past him he is conducker on the Cabble carr Mrs. B has been real sick I was up to see her last week; Ma I would be glad if you could send Luther's Picture to Texas as soon as you can I think they are waiting to get that before they write. if I get those I told you about from there I will give you one you Pa John & Ella must have some taken as soon as you can & I will send you the money to help to have Virgies taken I am going to have mine & Ernest taken as soon as possible. tell Virgie to be good & her Pappa sais he will take her and Luther to Sunday school every Sunday when she comes home.**

Give my love to Miss Rearie Gurtie and all our kind good friends kiss all our dear ones for us all. think of me when you all visit dear Lula's Grave how I would have loved to have gone out there again before I left **Mrs Johnson** (Ernest's mother, Hannah) **will send the rose bush I expect she had already done so sad she would send it as soon as She could get it up without killing it**

good by please take care of your dear selves & I insure you I will do the same. God bless you all tonight and watch for each & every of you is my night and daily prayer.
   Lillie

*   *   *

From Ernest L. Lindsley, to his wife Lillie's father.

Dumfries Va March 12th 1891

Mr. W. H. Marshall

Dear Sir

I have done as you advised me in regard to my place that was what I had first thought of but Lillie did not like it but after I got your letter she thought better of it.

I sold to Geo. W. Johnson for nine hundred dollars part in money and His note for the balance. And the deed is reckorded now Lillie and Virgie can by it back any time, at once if neccery and hold the deed and not have it Recorded for Some little time. now can I advertise my personal property and sell and get one or two friends to by it in and keep the property on the place and be safe. the sale list would show who bought the property. I dont think it would be any bodys business if they choosed to let the property stay on the place. If they were put on the witness Stand they could swear they bought it I do not like to ask those lawyers in (illegible)ville to much about it. unless I could see E. E. (illegible) and I can't see him untill after court. I thought of giving E. Nelson a deed of Trust on my personel (property) but he advised to wait a while. thought it was best not to be in too big a hurry about it not to let the deed of trust and the deed for the place go on reckord at the same time. there is bound to be trouble there is no help for it. I don't know whether I told you whos bond I was on or not Jns N. Tolson is the man. The two first years he settled up with Kincheloe ever cent I have found out for a fact he is $18.00 behind for the last year and it is impossible for him to Ketch up now. And all proberbility he will be more than that behind for this year. I and Willie Williams are the only ones that Kincheloe can make anything out of and he can't make much out of Williams. The other Bondsmen are as follows: Jns R Fick James H. Reid James Barbie Dr. Leary and Jns Laiber. Tolson property would not pay more than $1,000 and I would have to foot the balance Kincheloe new all of these men just as well as I do, and he must of took the bond on my name alone, and it looks as if he let Tolson get just enough behind to brake me up now if I can get out of it all clear Kincheloe will be the looser as he cant get anything out of the other securities. I want to outwit him if I can. and if I can handle my personal property all right I think I will have him.

Lillie is not very well. Luther is well. Give my love to all.
Yours affectionately

E. L. Lindsley

Note: Luther, my father, often spoke of the family's loss of the land, and he stressed that we should **never go on anyone's property bond, never mortgage the land, and never sell, for the land can always provide an income.**

* * *

In this letter to Virgie, Ernest refers to his second wife (Luther's mother) as "Aunt Lillie" to Virgie since Lillie's older sister Bessie was Virgie's mother.

Dumfries Va Jan 11 1892

Dear Virgie

I received your letter the other day and would of answered it sooner but I have been sick and am not well yet. the boy I had stay with me is real sick. so you can see I am all alone. you must hurry up and grow big so you can stay home and cook for me when Aunt Lilli (our Luther's mother) goes away visiting you must be a good Girl and learn your books and mind your teachers. Virgie that cat of yours is the meanest thing I ever saw. it skims the milk every morning for me it (is) a great big cat now just as fat as can be
Goodby for this time. Kiss Luther for his Papa--
From Your loving father

E. L. Lindsley

* * *

From Lillie to Fannie M. Davis Marshall, her mother. References to
Minnie and Minnie's parents Hannah and George Johnson.

**Douglas Hill
Jan 24, 1892**

My dear Ma,

I wrote to you from Manassas the day I got there & Mrs.
Johnson wrote the day I left & I have not received a word from you
you said I wrote to Ernest 2 or 3 times a week but you knew I
would not write to you once a month when I got home and I have
done all the writing Mr and Mrs J came down last night. Ernest is
much better was able to go to Dumfries last evening got me a nice
fig and such nice cabbage.

Monday Mrs and Mr Johnsom have just left and Ernest has
gone to Potomic and I feel real lonely as this is the first evening I
have been hear alone with no one but Luther and the boy I have 2
Girls now one is _____ and the other one is Jones one 16th, the
other 19th but will not take latter one until their four month is up
& then perhaps Ernest will have a chanch to see the Wate Girl or I
would rather have her than eather of the others. It seems real good
to be at hom Ernest is so kind and sweet gets me everything I want
tell Sam & Willis he sent for a barril of Oysters will be at Potomic
tomorrow tell them if they come down MON I will feed them on
Oysters

Luther & I are well. I never felt better in my life Ernest sais I
am all right and he meens to help me somme he seems happer than
I ever saw him although he has such a bad cole & feeles verry bad
at times.

how are you all I feel so worried about you all please write and
let me hear I have been home a week tomorrow and have not heard
one word tell me if you have moved and all the news; I was going to
Church Sunday but Mr. and Mrs Johnson, Minnie & Mrs Bronner
spent the day hear of course I could not go

Ernest will not let me go as far as the woodpile for fear I will get sick. I made some apple & lemon pies today the best I ever made wished you all had been hear to help us injoy them I will send Virgie the money to get her skirt with as soon as I can get it and will sent her the 10 cents I borried from her in this letter if Ernest has it tell her she must write to me and her Papa to she is plenty large enough to write if you have not time please write some of you this is 3 times you have heard from me since I came home & I have not heard one word from you & I feel so worried

I will say good night as it is bedtime what a beautiful day we have had it looked like spring kisses for you all Ernest & Luther send much love please write soon & try to come down soon some of you & as many as can come Kiss the children goodby Luther is sleepy

> your loving child
> Lillie

* * *

From her father Ernest

Dumfries Va Jan 30 1892

Dear Virgie

As Aunt Lillie has written to Grand Ma I will answer your letter. I am glad you are well again. And going to School. You must be a good Girl and learn fast, so you can come home. aunt Lillie is well and so is Luther but I am Still Sick. dont get much better some days I have to stay in the house all day. Luther is having a big time to night hooking Arkey up to his waggon and playing with his tittle winks and dominos.

I must stop writing for this time will write a longer letter next time. Write Soon and tell me all the news.

> Give my love to all I am your devoted Papa
> E. L. Lindsley
> Dumfries Va

* * *

From Lillie to Fannie M. Davis Marshall

Ma what ar eggs
worth in town now
Douglas Hill
March 1st 1892
My Darling Ma.

I recied your dear letter last week but did not ansire because I did not know when I could have a chanch to mail it but Ernest is going to Dumfries today & I will write you a few lines

we are all well I dont think I ever Saw Luther look so well he is as fat & beautifull as a child could be & the best thing I ever saw he dresses himself evry morning before I am up & I could not tell the day when I heard him cry. Ernest got Luther & I a beautifull pair of shues mine ar fine shus the prettis I have had for a long time Luthers are evry day Shoes but his little foot looks so swet in them have 8 buttens on them & he got me a lot of cotten to line my quilts with he is so good has got a man to come & build me a new henhouse & is going to have Steps put in the kitchen & a closit under so I can have the use of the kitchen stair. I have had my yard all cleaned & the Grave yard they look beautiful Covard the graves all over with moss; I was so sorry to hear of Aunt E death did the children seem to take her death hard give my love to them all & kiss Cousan G tell them they have my deapest simpty I know to well those feelings for I hav past through it so often.

We have a new Dr in Dumfries he is friendly he came last week & will stay a while & if he likes will bring his family. Ma, Charly was hear this morning and sais he wrote to Mr. Thomson for a place on his farm but would like to get a place in town on one of his waggain do you think Thomson would like to hav him I think he would be a good han for Thomson tell her Pappa will write to her and latter send her a pair of shoes -- or the money to get them with Sais he can get her beautifull fine shoes in Dumfries like mine for 1.25 I do not know which he will do he was proud of the notes she sent she must be a good girl & get nice reports & send to him he loves to see that his little Girl thinks of him. I will say goodby as he

is ready to start

write soon & tell me all the nuse if Ella is there & all. Luther sais come if you have to bring Bank Oh do come if you can; love and kisses to you all E & L send love to all L akes every morning if dear Ma is coming today; good by dear Ma

Lillie

This letter from Lillie is apparently her last communication with her mother.

* * *

Our next letter is from Ernest to his mother-in-law Fannie M. Davis Marshall. It was written only five days before Lillie's death on March 29, 1892. Baun is probably the local physician.

Douglas Hill
March 24 Tuesday Morning

Dear Mrs. Marshall

Lillie is verry sick with Pneumonia Buan was here last night. And will be here again this morning.

Luther was sick week before last and She worried herself to death about him and took cold jumping up waiting on him.

Yours in Hast
Ernest

* * *

Envelope addressed to Mr. S. M. Marshall. 31236 Union St. SW, Washington D.C. He was Lillie's brother.

Dumfries Va. Apr the 11th, 1892

Dear Sam

I wrote you last week and told you what day my Sale would be.

it will be on Thursday next the 14th of Apr. And if it is so you can't come down won't you write to E. Nelson and Ask him to send me a deed of releise by that day but if you are here yourself it does not matter. your presence at the Sale is surfiscent. And the deed of releise can be attended to after. And if you do not come down write me and let me know what I must do with your waggon must I sell it or let it remain here.

give my love to all I hope the children are well. in hast

your friend

E. L. Lindsley

* * *

From Virginia Lindsley, our Luther's older sister. Undated. Probably sent with the above letter from Ernest, her father.

My Dear uncle Sam

I am so glad you are coming to see us. for we all do want to see you so bad. we will have some nice ripe peaches for you

Your darling
little Virgie

* * *

The year was not given in letter below from Hannah Lindsley Johnson. It was probably 1892 since the children were staying with her then, after the Douglas Hill property was lost. The events of this letter fit the time frame. A few months later, their father contracted for their Marshall grandmother (Lillie's mother) to care for them. Maud and Minnie are Hannah's daughters and Lee is her son.

Lillie Marshall Lindsley had died March 29, 1892, and apparently Ernest felt he was unable to care for the children since he had lost the farm.

Manassas Aug 3rd

My dear Mrs. Marshall—

Virgie has just received your letter. We are all quite well—and was terribly disappointed by your not coming Saturday. You have written for the children to go home Saturday (the 6th) but as I can not let them go by <u>themselves</u>, they will have to wait untill next week, as I cannot <u>possibly</u> spare Maud until Minnie comes home; I look for her Saturday or Monday. Virgie says please excuse her for getting "Gamma" to write for her (she is learning a new Song & is too figity to write)—that she will write and let you know when she is coming; the children are both well, & hearty. they both send much love, & Luther says "tell Ma the girls are all 'stuck' on me; but some are blind—some cannot see."

Hastily yours,

H. M. Johnson

P. S. Tell Ernest Luther was much disappointed because he did not send <u>him</u> a letter by Lee.

* * *

With this contract, Ernest practically gives up his children:

This contract or agreement made and entered this 27th day Dec 1892 between Mrs. Fannie Marshall, my mother in law and myself E. L. Lindsley in regard to my two children Virgie and Luther Lindsley Mrs. Marshall does agree to board clothe same for the amount of Tenn Dollars per month untill I may see fit to take them away. The money to be paid in weekly or monthly payments. I am to have the priveledge to come to see them ever I wish.

Given under our hands this 27th day of Dec 1892.

F. M. Marshall
E. L. Lindsley

* * *

Ernest Lindsley left the farm (Douglas Hill) for Washington the year before his death. He was the representative or Supervisor for Cole's District of Prince William County, Virginia. He died in Washington on October 22, 1893. The letter below is about Luther C. Lindsley (of Westover) and his sister Virginia. Fannie Marshall, their maternal grandmother, reared Virginia, while Hannah and George Johnson reared Luther.

From George W. Johnson, husband of Hannah Lamb Lindsley Johnson (our Luther's grandmother).

Manassas Va
Nov 9th /93
Mrs. Fannie Marshall

Dear Madam

I write to inform you what has been done in regard to Ernest's affairs. The Court has appointed me his administrator and Mrs. Johnson and I guardians of the children; this had to be done, in order to protect what there is, the things that are here will be appraised (by three disinterested men appointed by the Court) all but the books, pictures, relics & (which come under the _____ of mementoes) but nothing will be SOLD but the <u>horse</u>, as it was his wish that these things should be kept for the children.

The farm will be made over to the children by a Deed of Gift. Luther we shall keep, as we know what his father's intentions were concerning him. Any time Virgie chooses to come to us, we will do the best for her we know how, and we shall never charge the Estate for anything we do for them. So if you keep Virgie you will have to maintain her at your own expense.

Very Respectfully

Geo W. Johnson
 Manassas
 Va

* * *

From employees of the Railroad

Brightwood, Dle
Dec 1st 1893

Mr. G W. Johnson
 Manassas Va.

Dear Sir

 Enclosed please find check for twenty one Dollars on West End Bank of this city—which was contributed by the employees of this Co as a mark of their esteem of their deceased friend Ernest Lindsley, & hope it may be used for the benefit of his children— both of whom have our deepest sympathy.

 Very Respectfully fr

 Employees of the Brightwood R.R. Co;

 by A. W. Harrison

* * *

This letter was found in an envelope addressed to Emma Mann in Austin, Texas, undated, and signed "your loving grand Daughter." The reference to Luther as the writer's brother and the greeting line to "Gamma" can leave no doubt that the letter was written by Virginia Lindsley.

It was not to Hannah Lindsley Johnson. Virgie was probably barely into her teen years, which would explain some of the incomplete thoughts in the letter.

Virginia mentions her strong distrust of the Johnsons, but her grandmother Hannah was married to one. And was also in Manassas. This letter, therefore, had to have been written to Virgie's great-grandmother Mary Louisa Campbell (b. 1810, wife of Mahlon) Lindsley. Mahlon and Mary Louisa (parents of Ernest Lindsley) had moved to Marcos, Texas. Their daughter Emma Lindsley Mann was sister to Lt. Luther C. Lindsley and sister-in-law to Hannah L. Johnson.

My Dear Dear Gamma Lindsley

How I would love to see you this lovely spring evening. I can remember you and Dear Gauer (as I used to call him) perfectly. do you remember the lovely day in Aug I think it was, just before you went to Texas that Mama and I walked up to Gamma's and I led dear Old Gauer & Pa said it reminded him of that passage in the bible that he dear Pa always talked to me so much about that I feel that I remembered it as distinctly as if it were yesterday & it is stamped on my memory so heavily that & many other times with he & you that I shall never forget. Oh! those dear old times how I wish we could have them back again how lovely it would be, but Alas so many are gone to that happy home beyond the Skys. My dear Mama, Papa, Aunt Lil (Luther's mother), **Laura Pat Gauer** all gone & you & I separated by thousands of miles perhaps will never meet again on this earth but it is a happy thought to have that we will meet each other there where there is no more parting & no sorrow nor pain & where those Johnsons can never harm me more for they are the only enemys I have ever had but they have made my heart ach constantly ever since the death of my dear Papa but I have just received a letter from Congressman Meredith (who will be my (illegible) after this affair is settled) & he sais I shall soon have my dear little brother now & all of my dear Mama's things then I will be so happy but I will always be afraid to trust myself with them again for I know they are my enemies; I thank dear Aunt Emma for her kind feeling & assistance for Luther & I; & I trust some day to have it in my power to praise & reward her for all she has done which has proved to be much. As I am very busy with my studies preparing for our examination as I have been transferred to the 6th grade (I tell you this because I know you are interested in me) I must say good by for the present with love for your dear sweet self, Aunt Emma & girls

I am your loving Grand Daughter.

(unsigned)

* * *

Virgie was fifteen when she received this next letter dealing with any possible inheritance from her father:

Sinclair & Lion
Attorneys-at-Law
Manassas, Va. March 24, 1896

Miss Virgie F. Lindsley
1344 Emerson St. N. E.
Washington
D.C.

My Dear Miss,

Your favor of the 6th inst to hand and noted, I will answer by stating that I have seen Mr. Geo. Johnson, and he informs me that he has no funds in his hands belonging to you and your brother. He tells me that Douglas Hill was sold and bought by himself before your Father's death. Therefore as he claims there would be no income for me to receive from him to hand to you. If the above is not in accordance with your understanding of this matter, let me know and I will make a further investigation. Mr. Johnson also states that he has one feather bed, two pillows, one (illegible), three quilts, your Mother's marriage certificate and pictures, which he will deliver to you at anytime you desire, If you wish I will receipt for these articles and ship to such address as you direct.

It looks as though (if Mr. Johnson's statement of this matter is correct) there is nothing here in Mr. Johnson's hand for you, that I can see. I wish it were in my power to find something here in the shape of funds to send you.

Your friend,
Thom Lion

P.S. Your letter would have been answered earlier but have been unable to get the above information until Sunday last.

* * *

No date, no return address, no addressee and no signature.

Dear Friend

Did that trial against V & L come up last Oct & if it did how was it decided? in their favor I hope, for it is so horrible to think of it going against them & leaving those dear little orphans pennyless I cannot see how Kinchlow could be so heartless as to do such a wicked thing for he has children him self & they may suffer the same (torn) just retribution for his sin, so could you not make him show mercy by talking to him in this way? the more I think about it the more dreadful I think it & the more miserable it makes one so my dear friend if you have any influence with him I hope you will use it in their behalf for my sake as well as for their own & another favor I must ask of you. it is that you will never betray to <u>any one</u> the confidence I placed in you an yours   <u>write</u> here concerning Virgie & a young Gentleman in Va for I would not have any other person know that I confided to you for worlds & the only reason I confided in you as I did neither she nor I knew anything of his family & I felt sure I could trust you and you would enlyten me if I told you the exact circumstances so I feel very thankful to you for telling me all that you did concerning him & his family as V- thinks just as much of him as he could possibly think of her (torn) she was affrad to let him know it as she (knows) nothing of his family   so trusting my secret will never be divulged I am still your very true friend
    No signature

"Kincheloe" is the spelling given by Ernest in a letter dated March 12, 1891, to his farther-in-law. Kincheloe was involved in the bonding of Jns. N.Tolson, which cost Ernest Douglas Hill.

* * *

Several letters from friends—one who migrated to Oregon and one who was stationed in the Philippines, are included in Appendix IV for their historical interest. As far as we know, those writers are not related to us.

* * *

From her brother Luther

>   **Manassas, Virginia**
>   **Feb. 11, 1902**
> **Dear Virgie,**

   I received your long looked for letter nearly two weeks ago and was glad to hear from you. Mr. C. E. Ruffner, my teacher, gets the report of the Weather Bureau, and Joseph Gulick and I put up the weather signals on the flag pole which is on the top of the house. The ground is covered with snow and ice and it is very difficult to stand up on our feet, and more than that the report says more snow tomorrow. Mrs. Twiman and her sons stay up at Cousin Edgar's now, and she and her younger son have just been here to spend a few minutes. She looks as if she was about eighty but I do not think she is more than fifty eight.

   During the last week there have been sleighs running up and down the road day and night. You could not turn your head away from the window five minutes without hearing a jing-a-ling and you drop your work and rush to the window only to see a young gallant going down the road in his cutter with his best girl beside him.

   Mary Julian Hutchinson got badly burned several weeks ago. While she was asleep her bed caught on fire and she had a narrow escape with her life but she is now doing very well.

   Aunt Maude is up to (her sister) Aunt Minnie's quilting but I expect she will be home tomorrow. As Gamma is going to write some thing I will close, love to all, not forgetting yourself,

   I remain your loving Brother

   Luther

Good morning Virgie. I wish you a lovely day, this 14th day of February. Luther invited me to write you in his letter last night. I put it off till this morning & now I have not time.

Gamma

* * *

We do not know what year Luther sent this card to his sister, but Virgie saved it and the card found its way back to Luther in the papers saved by his Marshall relatives and sent to him in the early 1960s.

* * *

From her brother, Luther C. Lindsley

**Manassas, Va.
Aug. 5, 1902**
Dear Virgie,

Why! in the name of common sense don't you write to me; or why in the name of common sense don't you come up here? What are you staying down there in that hot, suffocating village, which is called Washington by all pious Americans for? What's the matter with you? Are you sick? Are you dead? Or have you completely forgotten that you have a little baby brother 5 ft 8 or more in existence.

We looked for you the fourth of July, you did not come; we looked for you every day since and still you haven't come; again, I ask you Madam what is the matter?

You are down to Cousin Gerty's; please tell her for me that, "she is not the only pebble on the beach," and likewise rack your brains and see if you did promise me some time ago to spend the summer with some clod-hopper who resides in the vicinity of the great city of Manassas, which you have seen and heard so much of, as one of the greatest cities of the world.

I know you are getting tired of this foolishness so I will now take the time to make a more lengthy inquiry as to the state of your health which I fear is in a bad state; I mean it is in a bad condition and in a bad State for I expect it is in Maryland. If you are still at work tell F. that I will be down there and pull him out of the shop by the hair. You said you were going to surprise us and you have; not in the way <u>you</u> meant, but by not coming.

There is a whole lot of news to tell you but I'm going to make you wait till you come, and come you must I implore I beseech; love

to all & you too. (In haste)
Your loving Brother
Luther C. Lindsley.

* * *

From her Aunt Maud, youngest child of Hannah L. Lindsley and George Johnson

Buck Hall, Va
Feb. 17th

Dear Virgie,

For some time I thought of writing you a little bit, but have not done so as you see. however, I do better than you—is it not so?

Miss Linstrong and I have company to-night. two of her girls are here and are apparently much surprised at the antics of their two Old Maid instructors Well you know dignity will relax <u>some times</u>.

Luther was very angry at R. H. for telling him you were married—and I don't blame him. I thought I would tell you that when you get ready for that you might let me know--and I will do the same by you. By the way I want you to come up and stay a week or two this spring "special" can't you? I particularly want you, but you are not to tell any one that I wrote to you in this strain, not even Luther for he doesn't know "just yet." This is a dead secret please, "tween you and me" Ask your "boss" if you cannot have a holiday this spring. I have five more weeks to teach, and possibly more. Friday we have a holiday but have to attend a teachers meeting Friday and Saturday. If my present companions knew the contents of this they would mob me. Last night one of them said something, and I spoke of my beau. one of them said "why has Miss Johnson got a beau," perfectly astonished they were, "why really <u>has</u> Miss Johnson got a beau? <u>I</u> did not know it."

They evidently doubted it altogether. Well what are you going to do about this. write to me about it but please do not talk to <u>any</u>

that's a good girl.

Now I must rest up for my labors tomorrow. I hovered over the stove to-day and taught just one scholar!!

A week ago to-night Beta and I gave a dance—don't be surprised, Beta was to teach some of them how to waltz, and it turned out quite a dance, as they all came.

Good bye, write real soon—but what nonsense for me to ask you, you just won't do it, I am afraid. With lots of love.

   Maud

PART II

LUTHER CAMPBELL LINDSLEY

of

WESTOVER

at

THE COLLEGE OF WILLIAM AND MARY

1903-1908

WILLIAMSBURG

O Williamsburg

Twas end of June we took a trip.
It was 19 of 89.
We travelled many many hours,
not knowing what we'd find.

A long and turning gravel road --
it took us to a place
where plantation land and water met.
Westover was its name.

Tall and splendid were its walls,
brick aged with time and wear.
If only trees and shrubs could talk,
the history they could share.

Down Highway 5, that river road,
the James does wind around.
To stately places life it brings.
Williamsburg life abounds.

The birds (the wren and robin) I dare
to think of what they'd say.
If only we could understand
their tales of yesterday.

O Williamsburg, your thoughts so high.
Your presidential style
brings millions to you every year
to look at you and smile.

To walk upon your cobblestone
and gaze upon your stature,
brings to mind those days of old
when England sought your capture.

Those guns and ammunition stored
for future generations.
Those courts of law and congress seats
preserve a mighty nation.

O Williamsburg, your streets so clean.
Twas York, the one we sought.
For there we saw where Granddad lived
when at the school he taught.

O Williamsburg, your college grounds
brought radiance to our eyes.
The alma mater of my grandfather -
a place that made him wise.

In the ole Swen we spent a day
looking at leaves of old.
Page after page we turned and read
not knowing what we would be told.

And there we saw on pages yellow
a poem, a story, a token.
As we read, we smiled and cried.
Luther C. Lindsley had spoken.

Lindsley & Sandra Bramlett

WILLIAM AND MARY

The College of William and Mary was the first American college with a royal coat of arms, issued on May 14, 1694 by the College of Arms in London. The First Seal was used from 1694 through 1783, when the Second Seal was adopted. It was used while Luther was at the College.

Luther attended the College of William and Mary from the fall of 1903 through the school year ending in 1908, at which time he had completed all but one course for his master's degree.

His expenses were borne mostly by his step-grandfather, George W. Johnson, but Luther earned some money. His cousin Edgar wrote in a letter to Luther many years later:

I have a vague recollection of the trials, tribulations and hardships you endured to get through school. I remember very well Virgie telling me about you getting up long before dawn to clean out the school and to build the fire in order to earn money for your college education.

Luther performed other work, and one job was to peddle a musical instrument, a "lap harp." After his graduation, his demonstration harp was left with family members in Virginia, and in the 1960s, his Aunt Minnie (Hannah's daughter) sent it back to him by his daughter Susan, whom they all called by her first name, Virginia.

In his college writings, he quotes the words of "My Old Kentucky Home," which makes us believe that it was one of the songs he sang when he demonstrated the harp to potential customers. It is now in the possession of his great-grandchildren Rebecca and Victoria Bramlett.

Photograph by Sandi Bramlett

Luther not only carried an exceptionally heavy load of lectures, but also participated in many extra-curricular activities. He played on the sub-varsity football team in 1903, on the sub-varsity baseball team and served on the Athletic Executive Committee in 1904. For the rest of his life, he suffered the long-term effects of athletic injuries. As the smallest man on his team, he was the quarterback. Luther told his daughters that in those years, instead of passing the football the team passed the quarterback—he received the football from the center, stepped onto the center's back, and the men in the backfield threw him over the heads of the opposing linemen. The defenders would reach up, grab the quarterback by the foot, and often twist as they pulled him down. Luther limped.

Luther, standing, in hat at baseball game.

Postcard mailed from Williamsburg, VA to Mrs. G. F. Hoxton, 1405 51/2 Street, NW Washington, D. C. Luther C. Lindsley of Westover is far left, under the X. William and Mary football team, 1906. Mrs. Hoxton was his sister Virginia.

He was best known among his fellow students for his intellectual achievements. He earned the James Barren Hope scholarship award in 1905 for his poem "Dawn," the Orator's Medal in 1907, and the prose medal in 1907 for his article "Arabian Poetry." He served as editor-in-chief of the *Literary Magazine* 1907-1908 and contributed heavily to both it and to the *Colonial Echo*, the college annual, by writing poetry, editorials, short stories and nonfiction. He told his daughter that he had to write most of the material for the *Magazine* since other students were reluctant to submit their works.

He earned diplomas in Latin, Mathematics, Philosophy and Pedagogy. For him, however, his greatest achievements were his membership in the Philomathean Literary Society, for which he served as vice-president and as president; and his membership in the Flat Hat club, an honor society that pre-dated the Phi Beta Kappa, and in which Thomas Jefferson had been a member.

Fortunately, his grandmother saved many of his letters written while he was at William and Mary. These letters, as well as a few of his college documents, tell us of his college years.

I have deliberately shown the inconsistencies in layout of the letters' return addresses and dates.

COLLEGE OF WILLIAM AND MARY.

CHARTERED 1693.

—AND—

State Male Normal College of Virginia,

ESTABLISHED 1888.

The Session begins the 1st Thursday in October, the Half-Session the 14th of February and closes the 4th Thursday in June.

Report of the Scholarship and attendance of Mr. *L. C. Lindsley*

at the College of William and Mary, for the Quarter ending *March 20* 190*4*.

STUDIES.	CLASS GRADE.	STUDIES.	CLASS GRADE.
English,	*Very Good*	Psychology,	
History of Virginia,		Ethics,	
History of the United States,	*Very Good*	Logic,	
History, General,		Civil Government,	
History,		Political Economy,	
History,		Physics,	
Mathematics,	*V. Good*	Chemistry,	*V. Good*
Latin,	*V. Good*	Botany,	
Greek,		Physiology,	
French,		Physical Geography,	*V. Good*
German,	*Good*	Pedagogy,	
		Teaching,	

NOTE.—Grades: Excellent, Very Good, Good, Fair, Tolerable, Poor. The attention of parents or guardians is respectfully invited to the above Report.

REMARKS:

Fine Student

J. A. Strubk Sr _____ Secretary to the Faculty.

From Luther to Hannah L. (Mrs. George) Johnson, his paternal grand-mother.

Williamsburg, Va,
June, 15, 1904

Dear Gamma,

Received your welcome letter a few days ago, will answer and put this in the invitation envelope. I got the cheque all right. The day after I wrote my last letter to you someone stole my pocket book from my coat pocket and everything in it. I was about to borrow 2 cents to write to you when I got your cheque. You may know I have been worried about it. I have two more exams. they are 1 & 2 Math. I must close this to grind like a grist mill upon Plane and Solid Geometry. Will see you again in little over a week. I have plenty of money so don't worry. Give my love to everybody and tell them I will soon be in old Pr. Wm. again.

lovingly,

L C Lindsley

Note: Pr. Wm. stands for "Prince William County," location of Manassas and Dumfries.

* * *

From Luther. Edgar is probably Edgar Marshall, the cousin who visited and authored many letters in the section "After the Children Left Home."

Ewell Building
Oct. 1904

Dear Gamma,

I was about to write to you the very night that I received your letter for your delay caused me to think that some thing was the matter, but when I received your letter and found that everything was all right I have kept putting off answering your letter for these reasons.

The only time I have is at night and after I get up my lectures it is after 12 o'clock and by that time my eyes are so tired that I HAVE to go to bed. I caught cold in my head about a week after I got here and it is only now that I am getting control of it. You know how a severe cold in ones head feels, ("and" struck out) especially if your eyes are watering and aching too.

I will have to take a good many lectures this year in order to get my degree (A. B.) next year.

I am taking 27 lectures a week all of them are 2nd and 3rd year classes and are (CORKERS). If I more than make all of them I will be indeed lucky but I am going to try. If I make them all I will have 9 Distinctions and 1 Normal Graduation. So do not look for all Excellents and V. Goods in my reports. I cannot perform miracles. (Yes it was during that cold snap that I and many others caught cold. We did not have any fire whatever in our rooms.)

Am so sorry that I was not home when Edgar came. I would have liked very much to have seen him. Am glad Aldine is so much better. Did Uncle Ralph cut all the corn by himself? If he did he certainly did hustle it through. Am glad he has gotten practically over his sickness.

I received a letter from A. Mann the same time I received yours but haven't answered yet. I guess I will do so the first chance I get.

Mars so far is studying fine. He is the only one of the Manassas crowd that is studying at all. I tell the boys that I am from Pr. Wm. not from Manassas.

Fred has gone to Manassas as a witness in some suite VS R. R. My roommate is C. Douglass & he is from Durham, N C.

Oh. yes I kept out of hazing ring <u>entirely</u> & did all I could against it. Yes there is something I want you to do. Aunt Emma told me that you could not sleep at night for worrying about me, fearing that I might get sick or something. I want you to <u>stop</u> <u>worrying</u>. Of course it is nice to know that you have people who love you so well, but please do not get so worked up on my account. This is all that you can do for me now and THAT will save ME from a lot of worry.

Jessie Ewell is going to West Point Christmas & he wants me to coach him in Geometry as that does not come until after Christmas here. I told him that I would & so I will have <u>some</u> pin money and it will help a little. Well, as the lights will go out in about five minutes I must close this for this time. Hoping to hear from you in a few days, requesting you to give my love and regard to everyone who may inquire after me I remain your loving Grandson,

      lovingly,

      L. C. Lindsley

P. S. Enclosed find lecture schedule, my lectures enclosed by an oval ring. There are 27 of them.

LECTURE SCHEDULE, 1904-1905.

	9—9.45	9.45—10.30	10.30-11.15	11.15-12	12-12.45	12.45-2	3-4	4-5	5-6
MON.	1 Math. 2 Ped	1 Eng. 4 Math. 3	1 Ped. Sr. Ger. Sr. N. S.	Psych	Jr. Ger	1 N. S. Sr. His.	2 Lat.	Literature 1 Latin	
TUES.	1 Math Sr. Phil	2 Math Sr. Ped.	Am. His. 3 Lat. Sr. N. S.	G. His	Politics	2 N. S.	1 Lat. Jr. Fr.	2 Latin. Jr. Phys. Cul.	Jr. Phys. Cul.
WED.	1 Math 2 Ped	2 Math.	Am. His. 3 Lat. Sr. N. S.	2 Eng	Politics	1 N. S.	1 Eng.	2 Latin.	Sr. Phys.Cul.
THURS	1 Eng. 3 Math	2 Math. Sr. Ped.	1 Ped. Sr. Ger. Sr. N. S.	Lit.	Jr. Ger	2 N. S.	1 Lat. Jr. Fr.	Psych Jr. Phys. Cul.	Jr. Phys. Cul.
FRI.	1 Math. Sr. Phil.	2 Math.	Am. His. 3 Lat. Sr. N S.	G. His	Politics	1 N. S. Sr. His.	1 Lat. Jr. Fr.	2 Latin.	Sr. Phys. Cul.
SAT.	1 Eng. 3 Math	4 Math.	1 Ped. Sr. Ger. Sr. N. S.	2 Eng.	2 Ped. Jr. Ger	Sr. Ped. 2 N. S. 4 Eng.		Jr. Phys. Cul.	Jr. Phys. Cul.

Ewell Hall dormitory (from W&M archives)

From Luther

> **Williamsburg, Va.**
> **Dec. 4, 04**

Dear Gamma,

I would have answered your letter again Sunday but expected to get one from you Monday or Tuesday but I did not, so will scribble you a few lines to let you know that I am getting on alright.

Have you had any rain yet? We have had several days of it and it is raining yet.

This morning I wrote an essay for Dr. Hall. My subject was the Poetry of E. A. Poe. I began it at nine o'clock and finished at one o'clock.

Has Uncle Ralph gotten all the corn in yet? How are the horses colts cattle calves hog and chickens likewise all of the "kids."

I have a big job on hand now. It is to prepare a debate for the open meeting of the Philomathean Society 2 weeks after College opens after Christmas.

The subject is: Resolved that ("Canada" struck out) **the annexation of Canada would be beneficial to U. S. I am on the aff.**

Examinations begin on the 12th of December and last until the 23 which is Friday.

College reopens 12 days after, on the Tuesday following New Year.

What is everyone doing up there at Manassas now. I have not seen the latest paper. Fred takes it and I have not had time to see it.

What is Johnnie doing now. I have not heard of him for some time. Is Hendley still on the farm? Is Emma coming home Christmas?

How are Uncle Lee & Aunt Emma getting on? What is he doing now?

Douglass has just crawled in bed and pulled the covers up over his head and informed me that <u>he</u> was going to sleep. I wish I had time to do so also but I have not. I have got to write an Essay for Prof. Payne on the "Waste in our present Education," and to review Analytics and everything else. Hoping this will find ALL of you in good health, with no crowd of company brethren and hoping you will write soon to your devoted grandson I remain lovingly,

L. C. Lindsley

COLLEGE OF WILLIAM AND MARY.

CHARTERED 1693.

—AND—

State Male Normal College of Virginia,

ESTABLISHED 1888.

The Session begins the 1st Thursday in October, the Half-Session the 14th of February and closes the 4th Thursday in June.

Report of the Scholarship and attendance of Mr. _____

at the College of William and Mary, for the Quarter ending _____ 190__.

STUDIES.	CLASS GRADE.	STUDIES.	CLASS GRADE.
English,	Very Good.	Phys. Culture	good
History of Virginia,		Psychology,	
History of the United States,		Ethics,	
History, General,	Very Good	Logic,	
History,		Civil Government,	
History,		Political Economy,	
Mathematics,	Very Good	Physics,	Very Good
Latin,	V. Good +	Chemistry,	
Greek,		Botany,	
French,		Physiology,	
German,		Physical Geography,	
		Pedagogy,	Very Good
		Teaching,	

NOTE.—Grades: Excellent, Very Good, Good, Fair, Tolerable, Poor. The attention of parents or guardians is respectfully invited to the above Report.

REMARKS:

_____ *Secretary to the Faculty.*

From Luther

> Williamsburg, Va.
> Dec 30, 04

Dear Gamma,

I suppose you are wondering where I am and what I am doing. Well I am doing business at the same old stand and doing it in the same old way except I go out for an hour or so sometimes and shoot an old rabbit or something of the kind.

Tomorrow four of us start at sunrise on a hunting expedition to Jamestown Island. Game of every kind is here, rabbits, squirrels, partridges, snipes, ducks, turkeys and deer, to say nothing of foxes, coons and opossums. Do Uncle Joe and the boys hunt much now? (Uncle Joe is Luther's great-step-uncle, brother to George Johnson.)

Well I think I made all of my examinations although some are a little doubtful. Have you gotten my report yet. I guess it is a sight, completely marked up with "tolerables" and "fairs." I will send the receipt for December board in this letter if I can think of it.

I got a Christmas box from V. and G. (Virginia and her husband) the other day. She sent me a beautiful white shirt with "ruffles" & "tucks" I don't know which is front, also a box of paper and a lot of "goodies."

Uncle Gus and (his wife) **Aunt Maude** (Hannah's daughter) **sent me a pair of cuffs and a collar and a beautiful necktie.**

Santa Clause has been mighty good to me.

Are Uncle Willis (Hannah's son) and Aunt Maude at Home now? I'll risk it and send their letters in this package of letters.

How is Grandpa? Better I hope. This beautiful weather is enough to make anyone feel good and joyful. How are you feeling? I hope you didn't work too hard over the dinner Monday did you? Who was there? Did (his great aunt, Mahlon's daughter) **Emma come home during the holiday? If she did this is the first time for three years. It seems only yesterday. If I am away next Christmas I will surely be there the Christmas after. How fast time flies. A few more years and the little red-headed boy will be out in the great wide** world just as he is now in the minnie world.

I creased and pressed my old gray suits this morning and they looked much better when I finished than when I began. I have put on my heavy grey suit and thick underwear.

Did you get the *Magazine* that I sent you? Your red-headed grandson wrote "Eventide" by Robin Adair.

I wish I could write more to you but indeed I don't know what to write. I have so much writing to do that I sometimes think I will never get through. I must write next to Aunt Maude.

Give my love to everyone in Prince William old and young alike and write soon to your

loving grandson,

L.C. Lindsley

* * *

From Luther.

Lee is one of Hannah Johnson's sons. Emma Lindsley Mann had gone to Texas before 1905. Luther's reference to Uncle Lee and Aunt Emma indicates Lee either lived with his sister or married an Emma. I could not find a record of his marriage.

Williamsburg, Va.
Jan. 22, '05
Dear Gamma,

How are you and everyone this dreary evening?

How is Uncle Lee? I certainly do hope he's better. It must be very hard on Aunt Emma.

I would have answered your last letter sooner but I have had an enormous amount of extra work to do in the shape of a debate. It was held last night over in the Chapel at Philomathean open meeting. The meeting was quite a success.

I am glad it is over with for it was a great worry.

(A page is missing.)
I am in splendid health.

Every morning I take a 3/4 hour walk before breakfast and this makes one feel fine. It is a help to my lungs to breathe the pure country air.

As I would like to answer Aunt Minnie's letter this evening I must stop this scribble for I have told you all there is to tell and it is fast growing dark.

Hoping He will bless you and quickly raise Uncle Lee from the bed of sickness I remain

your loving grandson

L. C. Lindsley

* * *

From Luther. Uncle Joe is brother of George Johnson, Luther's step-grandfather.

Williamsburg, Va.
Feb. 12, 1905

Dear Gamma,

How is Uncle Joe? I saw in the paper that he had fallen on the ice and had sprained his shoulder badly.

Yes I knew Grandpa had been appointed assessor. I saw it in the *Journal*, I sympathize with you.

I received a letter from Aunt Maude (Johnson, Hannah's daughter) **Friday. She sent a couple of dimes for the 10th.** (Luther's birthday)

Did you get the last *Magazine*? I did not put anything in that one. I did not have time to write anything. "Berch" and "due" were spelt so by the printer in "Eventide" and it was not my fault.

Well I am to read an original poem over in Cameron Hall at a joint open Meeting of the Phoenix and Philomathean Literary Societies.

I will do what I can to uphold the "rep" of the Philomathean

Society and Pr. Wm. Co.

"Eventide," I forgot to mention, was "clipped" by Washing-ton and Lee Univer. and put in their Lit mag.

What is Uncle Ralph doing now? Is Uncle Willis still in Prince Wm.?

What has happened in and around home since you last wrote? The *Journal* does not tell us anything.

How are affairs over at Clover Hill? Do they ever mention my name, or have they completely forgotten me?

Has Uncle Lee recovered from his illness?

Tell Aunt Emma to write to me if she has a chance.

What are the "kids" doing now? By the way how is Aunt Minnie? Has her malaria attack worn off yet?

How is Grandpa's patent coming on? Has he had any offers yet?

Has the purchaser of Douglas Hill "ponied up" yet?

This is all the news that I can think of so will have to close I guess. Give my love to everyone & everybody and a full share to Gamma.

Lovingly,

L. C. Lindsley

Note: Searches of the records in Prince William County, by two attorneys and a volunteer at the courthouse in Manassas have resulted in no information about the sale of Douglas Hill in 1904 or 1905.

* * *

COLLEGE OF WILLIAM AND MARY.

CHARTERED 1693.

—AND—

State Male Normal College of Virginia,

ESTABLISHED 1888.

The Session begins the 1st Thursday in October, the Half-Session the 14th of February and closes the 4th Thursday in June.

Report of the Scholarship and attendance of Mr. ~~S. C. Lindsley~~

at the College of William and Mary, for the Quarter ending ~~March 18~~ *190~~2~~*

STUDIES.	CLASS GRADE.	STUDIES.	CLASS GRADE.
English,	*Good*	Psychology,	*very good*
History of Virginia,		Ethics,	
History of the United States,		Logic,	
History, General,	*Excellent*	Civil Government,	*very good*
History,		Political Economy,	
History,		Physics,	*Very Good*
Mathematics,	*Good*	Chemistry,	
Latin,	*Very Good*	Botany,	
Greek,		Physiology,	
French,		Physical Geography,	
German,		Pedagogy,	*Good*
		Teaching,	

NOTE.—Grades: Excellent, Very Good, Good, Fair, Tolerable, Poor. The attention of parents or guardians is respectfully invited to the above Report.

REMARKS:

~~T. J. Stubbs Jr.~~ ....Secretary to the Faculty.

COLLEGE OF WILLIAM AND MARY.

CHARTERED 1693.

—AND—

State Male Normal College of Virginia,

ESTABLISHED 1888.

The Session begins the 1st Thursday in October, the Half-Session the 14th of February, and closes the 4th Thursday in June.

Report of the Scholarship and attendance of Mr. *L. C. Lindley*

at the College of William and Mary, for the Quarter ending *June 23* 190*4*

STUDIES.	CLASS GRADE.	STUDIES.	CLASS GRADE.
English,	Good	Psychology,	
History of Virginia, 3.	Good	Ethics,	
History of the United States, 3.		Logic,	
History, General,		Civil Government,	
History,		Political Economy,	
History,		Physics,	
Mathematics,	I. Pint	Chemistry,	
Latin,	Good	Botany,	Good
Greek,		Physiology,	
French,		Physical Geography,	
German,	Good	Pedagogy,	✓ Good
		Teaching,	

NOTE.—Grades: Excellent, Very Good, Good, Fair, Tolerable, Poor. The attention of parents or guardians is respectfully invited to the above Report.

REMARKS:

Good student.

J. A. Stubbs Secretary to the Faculty.

JUNIOR CLASS.

From the college annual *Colonial Echo*, 1905, page 34.
Luther, right front.

Luther's picture enlarged.

COLLEGE OF WILLIAM AND MARY.

CHARTERED 1693.

—AND—

State Male Normal College of Virginia,

ESTABLISHED 1888.

The Session begins the 1st Thursday in October, the Half-Session the 14th of February and closes the 4th Thursday in June.

Report of the Scholarship and attendance of Mr. *L. C. Lindsley*

at the College of William and Mary, for the Quarter ending *March 1st* *190*2.

STUDIES.	CLASS GRADE.	STUDIES.	CLASS GRADE.
English,	Good	Psychology,	very good
History of Virginia,		Ethics,	
History of the United States,		Logic,	
History, General,	Excellent	Civil Government,	very good
History,		Political Economy,	
History,		Physics,	Very Good
Mathematics,	Good	Chemistry,	
Latin,	Very Good	Botany,	
Greek,		Physiology,	
French,		Physical Geography,	
German,		Pedagogy,	
		Teaching,	

NOTE.—Grades: Excellent, Very Good, Good, Fair, Tolerable, Poor. The attention of parents or guardians is respectfully invited to the above Report.

REMARKS:

T. J. Stubbs Jr Secretary to the Faculty.

From: His sister, Virgie. Mrs. Hoxton is her mother-in-law, Grover her husband, and Willis her Johnson uncle.
Postmark: Washington, D. C., Aug 15, 1905

Aug 14, 05

My dear Luther:

Both of your letters received. when the first one came Mrs. Hoxton was very ill (Typhoid Fever) You know when a person her age has this disease it most always proves fatal. It was so in her case. she died Friday week. her daughter and I were the only ones she would let nurse her she was devoted to me loved me as though I was her own child. and I cannot express how I miss her, she was so good and kind to me. she often said "Virgie you are the only one who can fix my pillows and give me medicine right." she was a good Christian and I am sure she is much happier than those left behind.

The day Maud came to see me I had been out to Mrs. Hoxton's a part of the night before and had only been at the office a few hours when Marie telephoned me that her mother was much worse and had asked for me. I was compelled to go home first. I found a dress suit case, and a few packages. also papa's picture my first thought was you.

The land lady told us a lady and gentleman from the country had called and had gone to the office to see me. I left word for them to wait until I got back I would not be gone long. it was then about 2 p.m. at 5 p.m. I was back home again. Maud had gone—left a card on the table stating she had gone to look for quarters. I am very sorry she did not wait for I could have arranged to make them comfortable. she did not say where she was going or how long she intended staying so I could not look her up. am very sorry that I did not see her.

I found Mrs. H very much worse but after a while she got a little better. it was this way all through her illness. I am feeling very well considering what I have been through.

I am delighted to hear of your success. I would love so much to see old Douglas Hill. I always thought it a pretty place and my happiest days were spent there. I often think how I would love to play under the locust trees and make mud cakes like I did there with you. would be willing to step on a thorn occasionally.

Is Mrs. Brawner still living?

You can tell by the beautiful writing how sleepy I am and I want to write Gamma a little note and enclose in this so will ask you to excuse me for this time.

Give my love to Willis and tell him I hope he and the preacher are still good friends.

With lots of love for you and wishing you much success

    I am your own devoted sister

       Virgie.

Enclosed with Virgie's letter to Luther was one **"For Gamma"**

    Aug 14- 05

Dear Gamma:

I want to thank you for the picture you sent me of Papa it is splendid. Cousin Gertie thinks you had better "put out your shingle." I have a large picture of Mama so will have Papa's framed and hang with her.

I miss them more as I grow older. just think I am twenty-four years old. Grover lost his mother last week. I miss her so much. she was so good to me. and loved me, as if I were her own child. I was devoted to her. when Maud was here I was at her bed side. am so sorry I did not see her.

Will put this note with Luther's letter am sure you will not mind.

Write to me some times. I would love to hear direct from you.

    Lovingly,

      Your granddaughter
      Virgie.

* * *

From Luther

> **Williamsburg, Va.**
> **Oct.29, '05**

Dear Gamma,

I guess you think I am sick or something else as horrible has happened to me, but such is by no means the case.

I have never felt better in my life and if it were not for the Model School I would feel to use the Slang expression, like a two year old.

Mr. Thornton came down last week to a meeting of the Board of Visitors. J. B. Terrell and I got up a petition among the boarders at the Hotel for better board and I am glad to say so far we have been getting it.

Our class (Senior Class) organized the other night. Wigglesworth was elected Pres. They wanted me to be the Class Poet but as usual I threw the "golden apple" away for the sake of a degree.

Yesterday our boys played V. M. I. in Lexington. Two of our best players were sick and our team was really in no condition to play. The score was as expected 23 to nothing in favor of V.M.I.

Saturday we play Maryland Agr. College. R. H. Ruffner is going there now and I expect he will make the team. We play here and if he does I will see old "Bob" again.

At the Model School I am teaching the History of Williamsburg and Colonial Virginia. I am taking up the history of each of the old buildings in succession.

This evening (Sunday) I called on the Miss Garretts and for three hours they told me the histories of the different buildings and showed me some real Willow Ware. If Aunt Maude could see the room I was in today she would go crazy.

The picture on the Willow Ware is something like this. On a hill on one side of a great river is a cottage in which lives a poor young man. On the opposite side of the river is a magnificent castle in which lives a young lady and her father. Her father wishes her to marry an old, yet rich man whom she detests.

She and this young man have met and love each other. She tells him that her father is going to make her marry this old man. They plan for an escape. On a dark night he rows across the river and tosses a pebble against her window pane, which is the signal. She hastens down the back way to meet him, and as she goes out of the outside door it slams. This awakens her father who follows them. They push off just in time, and the father is left standing on the shore. But a storm has come up and the wind has lashed the waves to fury. They look back and they hear faintly the father's voice. He is begging them to return and he will forgive them, but they cannot hear him for the roaring of the wind. The boat is capsized and they are both drowned, and as their spirits are wafted up to heaven they are transformed into two doves which fly away together to the willow trees upon the bank.

Is this not a pretty old story?

Have you ever heard it before? Lord Ullin's Daughter is something like this.

I received the cheque all right and thank Grandpa for me. I do not know what I would do if it were not for him.

Give my love to everybody at home and abroad and accept a good night's kiss from,

Luther.

L. C. Lindsley
Williamsburg Virginia
463 H. St- N. W.

* * *

From Luther

Williamsburg, Va.
Nov. 12, '05

Dear Gamma,

I guess you have been worrying yourself to death about me, fearing I am sick or something. For one day I was feeling too bad to attend lectures but am practically all right now. There has been an unusual amount of sickness here this winter. First, lead poison in the water, due to fixing the new pipes with white lead. Next came the "Diphtheria" but that was soon worked out. Next came the measles and about forty fellows are now lying flat of their backs besides those who have recovered. And now there are four cases of typhoid fever in the hospital. You see I am perfectly plain with you. It is better for you to hear it from me than out of a newspaper.

While the Science Hall was being completed all of Prof Garrett's machines acids etc. were piled up in the Gymnasium. Consequently we could get practically no exercise unless we played foot-ball. Those of us who did, have not suffered except with the measles and I have had them you know.

But the measles got into our football team and has I fear ruined it.

A few weeks ago we played Richmond College and we "licked" them nicely. They could not even score. Yesterday we played them, our championship game. Some of our boys had not shed the measles scales and three got out of bed to play. In spite of this during the first thirty minutes we had licked them worse than before. But then our men weakened—they could not stand the strain in their weak condition and in thirty more minutes Richmond had made 4 touchdowns and kicked 3 goals making the score 23 to 5 in their favor. It certainly was heart rending.

I saw in the *Journal* where Cousin Fora and Cousin "Sank" have tied "a true lovers knot" and was indeed surprised to hear that Uncle Ralph and Miss Dora had followed suite. Please write me particulars and extend to them my heartiest congratulations and tell Uncle Will not to let any more of us beat him.

Well, thank heavens I've taught one half of my time at the Model School. It has conflicted with several of my classes and I have had to cut them on that account. (The Model School always has the preference). It certainly is a strain on one's nerves. If I can last for five more weeks it will be over with.

Well, I believe this is all there is to say except I was ashamed to send you our first *Magazine* for this year.

Hoping this will find you all well and happy and sending love to "Aunt Dora" and everybody—Uncles, Grandpa and Grandmother.

I am as ever your loving Grandson
    L. C. Lindsley

*   *   *

From Virgie. Grover is her husband.
Postmark: Washington, D.C., Nov 27, 1905

Sunday Night

My dear Gamma:

As I did not hear from you, we telephoned to Mr. Tyler at Wm and Mary college last night at 8 p.m. talked direct to him. he said "Luther Lindsley has a slow fever not typhoid. he has not been near so ill as the others boys. is better tonight." this was Saturday night! We asked for more information, but were cut off. we could have talked longer but it would have cost 50 ¢ a minute and after hearing he was better, I felt satisfied to wait until Monday to hear more. Please let me know as soon as you hear his condition and I will do the same. Appreciating any information I am as ever your loving granddaughter

Virgie

Grover joins me in love.

* * *

The student in the next letter had to be Luther Lindsley, but the letter was addressed to Mr. Lindsley. Apparently, the minister did not know Luther's family situation. The letter must have been delivered to the Johnson's address since Luther himself received mail there from Virgie.

Postmark: Williamsburg, Va, (Month and day illegible) 1905
On envelope: "If not delivered in 3 days return to Dr. Merritt, Williamsburg, Va"

Williamsburg, Va. Dec 2ⁿᵈ

My dear Mr. Lindsley,

It was my privilege today to visit your son who has been sick with fever but is now improving. He is cheerful and has every medical attention. two physicians who constantly see him and trained nurses who are very careful and tending.

Everything possible is being done for his speedy recovery of health which we expect in due time.

It is my pleasure to be associated with the students as chaplain in the college and pastor of the Methodist church. If I can be of any service to you don't hesitate to call on me

Sincerely,

Dancie (?) T. Merritt

COLLEGE OF WILLIAM AND MARY.

CHARTERED 1693.

—AND—

State Male Normal College of Virginia,

ESTABLISHED 1888.

The Session begins the 1st Thursday in October, the Half-Session the 14th of February and closes the 4th Thursday in June.

Report of the Scholarship and attendance of Mr. *L. C. Lindsley*

at the College of William and Mary, for the Quarter ending *June 13th* 190_5_.

STUDIES.	CLASS GRADE.	STUDIES.	CLASS GRADE.
English,	*Good*	Psychology,	*Good*
History of Virginia,		Ethics,	
History of the United States,		Logic,	
History, General,	*V. Good*	Civil Government,	*Good*
History,		Political Economy,	
History,		Physics,	
Mathematics,	*Gmt*	Chemistry,	
		Botany,	
Latin,	*V. Good*	Physiology,	*Good*
Greek,		Physical Geography,	
French,		Pedagogy,	*Very Good*
German,		Teaching,	

NOTE.—Grades: Excellent, Very Good, Good, Fair, Tolerable, Poor. The attention of parents or guardians is respectfully invited to the above Report.

REMARKS:

Excellent student

T. J. Stubbs, Jr. .... Secretary to the Faculty.

COLLEGE OF WILLIAM AND MARY.

CHARTERED 1693.

—AND—

State Male Normal College of Virginia,

ESTABLISHED 1888.

The Session begins the 1st Thursday in October, the Half-Session the 14th of February and closes the 4th Thursday in June.

Report of the Scholarship and attendance of Mr. *L. C. Lindsley*

at the College of William and Mary, for the Quarter ending *Dec. 15, 190 2.*

STUDIES.	CLASS GRADE.	STUDIES.	CLASS GRADE.
English,	Good.	Psychology,	
History of Virginia,		Ethics,	Good
History of the United States,		Logic,	
History, General,		Civil Government,	
History, *Roman*	Excellent	Political Economy,	
History,		Physics,	Very Good
Mathematics,	Fair	Chemistry,	
		Botany,	
Latin,		Physiology,	
Greek,		Physical Geography,	
French,	Good	Pedagogy,	Good
German,	Good	Teaching,	Good

NOTE.—Grades: Excellent, Very Good, Good, Fair, Tolerable, Poor. The attention of parents or guardians is respectfully invited to the above Report.

REMARKS:

We hope he will return after Christmas.

H. S. Louthan ....*Secretary to the Faculty*

From Luther, re a summer job.

Washington, D.C.
July 5, '06

Dear Gamma,

I am going to work to-day. I have found a very good position here paying between fifty and seventy five dollars. Has it been warm enough for you during the past week? The heat here has been terrific but during the last day or so it has been cooler and this morning it is quite cool. Has Uncle Ralph started getting in his hay yet? Has he any help or is Uncle Will still over to Uncle Joe's?

Last night Virgie and I went over to Emerson Street. They seemed very glad to see us.

Virgie expects to take her leave this morning if Miss Kate Flannery comes back to the office. Virgie has lost several pounds during this hot weather.

Two young fellows were around to see me the other day but I was not at home. I guess they must have been the Gulick boys.

It is time for me to go to work now so goodbye for this time. Hoping to hear from you in a few days

I remain,

your loving grandson

L. C. Lindsley

* * *

From Luther

Williamsburg, Va
Sept. 28, '06

Dear Gamma,

Here I have a few moments to spare before I go down to the Model School. I would have written Sunday but had nothing to write except of myself and I get tired of doing that.

Yesterday another young fellow came in from Pr. William Co. Guess who it was. It was Mr. Calhoun Colvin's son. From what I have seen of him he is a fine young fellow and is going to do well I believe.

Saturday an old farmer stopped in front of Ewell building selling apples. While the boys were gathered around buying them some "ducks" slipped into the wagon from behind and stole about twenty. Saturday night we arrested them holding them without bail and late Saturday night tried them for petty larceny. We convicted them. The jury inflicted their penalty, which was to "set up" the Judge, lawyers jurymen and witnesses to 1/2 bushel of apples.

The *Magazine* this year is "bum." Terrell J. B. our best fiction writer swears he is not going to write a <u>line</u> for the "Mag." I am the only one here now that can write poetry and I have "cut it out." Rotten Politics put a lot of Editors on the staff who are not only inexperienced but have never written a line for the "Mag" in their life. In fact can't write a decent letter. They are "frats" you know, shoved in at the first meeting of the Phoenix when only a few of our fellows were there. You see they expect us to write up the "Mag" for them and when the year is ended <u>they</u> will have the credit for the fine magazine published by <u>them</u>. They have worked that "gag" on us once too often and this year those of us who supported it last year have decided to let the reputation of the magazine go to the "dogs" rather than to "cuss."

Well it is time for me to go down to the Model School so must close. Give my love and best wishes to everyone and write soon to your

loving grandson

L. C. Lindsley

*   *   *

From Luther

Williamsburg, Va.
Oct.28, '06

Dear Gamma,

Has it rained any in Pr. Wm during the past few weeks? For two whole weeks here we did not see the sun. Some thought that it was mildewed but after it did come out, after careful consideration they concluded that it had escaped that dire calamity. To-day the air is crisp and cool the wind is blowing from the N. W. and the warm steam radiator feels very good indeed.

Every Professor seems to be making his course twice as hard as he did last year. The number of lectures they allow a student to take is about fifteen now. I am taking twenty six but they don't know it. It is more that anyone in College is taking I have it to do in order to make sure of my degree. I am feeling fine though and as yet not in the least discouraged. I have gained about ten pounds in the last two weeks.

I suppose you are nearly done seeding if not quite and that the corn is being pulled off. How is it turning out? Well, I hope, although fellows from all over Va & N.C. say the ears are not filled out like they should be. You have several fresh cows now haven't you? There is a dairy farm near College and it furnishes us with milk. The training table has a large pitcher full on it and my glass makes frequent visits to it. They also feed us on "Force" and Egg O See. Did you ever try any of it? Egg O See is the better of the two. I like it far better than oatmeal and it is really better for you. Get some sometime and try it! I am confident you will like it. I certainly do. That's what is making my weight gain.

Monday is my easiest day. I have Pedagogy, Latin and Math. I have quite a lot of English to translate into Latin and 115 lines of Horace to translate. This is the hardest Latin written I think. You know we have a new Prof. of Latin. I have an oration to get up for Saturday night, forty examples in Calculus to work for Monday. Three poems and one story to copy by the 3rd of Nov. So you see I am quite busy and will have to pardon my short letter. I certainly hope you will take care of yourself and make Grandpa do likewise.

I am worried about you all of the time fearing you will catch cold this rough weather. Hoping to hear from you soon and sending much love to each and every one I remain

   Your loving Grandson

   L.C. Lindsley

P.S. Yes Geves received your letter

     * * *

From Luther
     Williamsburg, Va.
     Dec. 2 06

Dear Gamma,

 How are you all feeling this beautiful weather? Isn't it ideal? This evening Wigglesworth and I strolled down to College creek and back. It was rather dusty but we did not mind that very much. On our way back we stopped at Miss Mary Garrett's. Now don't get frightened and think I am taking a course in "calico" for I'm not. She is Dr. Garrett's sister and she is about fifty years old. She is the one who has so much willow-ware if you remember. She is a beautiful character and is mother to all of us William and Mary boys. She keeps us straight.

 About a week ago Dr. Coffey announced to us Senior Pedagogy fellows that he wanted us to attend the Richmond Teachers Conference. Every member of the Faculty joined him in urging us to go. It was the largest Conference ever held in Richmond. Thousands of people, teachers from all over the State were there and discussed the problems of teaching and related their experiences. The fare was $1.70 round trip (special rates). Joseph wrote me to come and stay with him during my stay and so I did, my board and lodging costing me nothing. We all went, and I do say that I got as much instruction and training by listening to and discussing the problems of Education as I have gotten during my entire three years course in Pedagogy here. It was the practical from beginning to end and when I came back I felt that I had never in my life spent $2.00 to such an advantage. Joseph is thinking something of spending Christmas with me here. I certainly wish he could. I could show him a merry time. Model School work has begun to pile up on me now so good-bye to studying on my lectures. Everything has to be neglected for that. I don't know how I could ever catch up again if I fell behind if it were not for the Christmas holidays.

It is getting right late now and as I will have to write to Virgie to-night I must close. Hoping every one is well—and that all the farm work is progressing nicely, and sending love to everyone especially yourself, I remain,

> Your loving Grandson
>
> L.C. Lindsley

P.S. Yes, I'd be so glad if the Van Suden's could settle up and have it over with.

* * *

From Luther

> Williamsburg, Va.
> Dec. 16, '06

Dear Gamma,

Yours of the 9th was duly received and I was so distressed to find you were suffering so with your eyes. I'll bet you had been exposing yourself to all kinds of weather. You must be more careful of yourself. I certainly hope that by the time this reaches you you will be quite well.

Did you get the *Magazine* I sent you about two weeks ago? You did not mention it in any of your letters.

Give my congratulations to Grandpa upon the success of his pig "industry." This turned out fine, was even better than I expected.

The weather here is warm as a day in June. The fellows are walking around with their coats off. No indeed I do not need the overcoat. Not as yet anyway.

I began teaching at the Model School two weeks ago. They put me in the Kindergarten. The very hardest place, and the most costly. I have to buy a great quantity of material to work with. I have fallen off from 158 lbs to little over 140. I am nearly over with it though. If I can make it by Christmas it will be a Christmas gift such as I can appreciate as I have never before appreciated anything. It has thrown me back so in my work that I shall have to "grind" all during the holidays to catch up. Sometimes I have to "cut" my classes. Since I began teaching I have in truth done nothing else whatever.

Last Monday week the Phi Beta Kappa had its annual Celebration here. On Wednesday morning I walked up to my room about 12 o'clock and started back in astonishment. There propped back in a chair looking perfectly at home sat Mr. George C. Round of Manassas Va. Well I was surprised. He told me he was a member of the Phi Beta Kappa and had come down to its celebration. He invited me to dinner with him at the Hotel and also to ride with him to Jamestown. I accepted both and can truly say I got something out of Mr. G. C. Round once.

Thank Grandpa for cheque. I'll pay up my board in the morning. Give love to everyone and keep a large share for yourself from

   your loving Grandson,

   L. C. Lindsley

COLLEGE OF WILLIAM AND MARY

CHARTERED 1693

...AND...

State Male Normal College of Virginia

ESTABLISHED 1888

The Session begins the 3rd Thursday in September; the Half-Session the 1st of February, and closes the 2nd Thursday in June.

Report of the Scholarship and attendance of Mr. *L. L. Lindsley* at the College of William and Mary, for the Quarter ending *Dec. 21* 190*6*.

STUDIES	CLASS GRADE	STUDIES	CLASS GRADE
English	Very Good	Logic	Good
History of Virginia		International Law	
History of the United States		Civil Government	
History, General		Political Economy	
History		Physics	
History		Chemistry	
Mathematics	Fair	Botany	
Latin	Very Good	Zoology	
Greek		Physiology	
French	Fair	Physical Geography	
German	Fair	Pedagogy	Good
Psychology		Drawing	
Ethics		Manual Training	
		Teaching	
		Physical Culture	

NOTE.—Grades: Excellent, Very Good, Good, Fair, Tolerable, Poor. The attention of parents or guardians is respectfully invited to the above Report.

REMARKS:

_____ Secretary to the Faculty.

From Luther

Williamsburg, Va.
Feb. 3, '07

Dear Gamma,

No, I **never** (never is struck out) **received the letter you mentioned. For the last three weeks I have not even been to the Post Office. My last letter written to you I think will explain why I have not answered it sooner. I owe Virgie three letters but she did not feel hurt because I have not answered. She understood that I was in the midst of examinations and one month's work in everything to make up. When one has had to sit up until four o'clock in the morning for three weeks getting only three or four hours sleep one does not feel very much like sitting up an extra hour writing letters and if you feel hurt as the tone of your letter suggests I wish to convince you it was in no degree for lack of affection, Gamma, but overwork. I have come near doing what no one in the history of the college has ever done, obtaining an A.M. degree in three years, taking all introductory classes the first year. I lack only 8 points for it.**

Oh! I hated to give it up but I could not quite make it. I am taking twenty-five lectures now, seven more than one is really permitted to take and more than any Senior has taken for years. Since the first of January I have written only two letters and they have been written to you.

Last night the Philomathean Society held its first meeting. We had adjourned the Saturday before examinations until after examinations. Neither the President nor Vice-President was present so they elected me President "pro tem."

We had an exceptionally good meeting, especially the debate. The question read something like this. Resolved that egoism is a greater motive power than altruism. One tall lean awk-ward fellow from the Southwest rose on the affirmative. For a few minutes he appeared very awkward. It was his first attempt. Soon however he forgot himself and became enthused. His eyes shone and fairly blazed. His tall form towered and almost trembled. He won his side. His name is Compton and is about thirty years old.

No, Joseph did not come down Christmas. I certainly was disappointed.

Yes, I found my blanket all right.

Yes, I received a letter from Virgie in the same mail in which I received your letter. She mentioned the $165 check. She is in fine health now, weighs 117 pounds. A few months ago she was quite sick and had a large Drs. bill to pay. I certainly was glad to know she could get the money. I know it was a Godsend.

Where is Uncle Will now? I want to write to him.

The State is constructing a "macadam" road from here to Jamestown and have about twenty-five convicts at work upon it. Twice a day, going and coming, they pass beneath my window in their striped suits and at every step I can hear their chains clank. Two guards stand over them with loaded Winchesters ready to kill them if they make the least suspicious movement. It is horrible. I have gotten so that I shudder when I hear the measured tread as they go marching by with their clanking chains.

Gamma, you can not imagine how I felt when I read your letter telling about the kindness of Governor Swanson. Wiggles-worth was watching me as I read it. He said my eyes grew moist. I don't know whether they did or not but I felt a choking sensation in my throat. Do you think it would be proper for me to write him a little note of thanks?

How is everything on the farm? Have Grandpa's little pigs kept up to the record of previous pigs? Do you make as much butter now as you used to? Both milk and butter are very high here as are also, eggs.

I received a letter from Wheatley a few weeks ago. He and Hendley are contemplating walking home in June.

By the way I believe I half-way promised Bessie to send her our *Magazine* and I have not sent her as yet a single copy. You might ask her if she wishes to see them and if she answers in the affirmative you might let her read the one I sent you. Write me, if she wishes still to read them and I shall send her one hereafter. Yes I have had several things in the magazine. In Nov. Mag I had "Sunset in the Hills," "Alone" & "In the Land of the Rising Sun." In December Mag "Memories," and in January the story, "Sir Bayard."

You were speaking of remittances   my board has been due

some little time, but as I have remarked in my last letter, I shall endeavor to relieve you of other incidental expenses. When my photographs come I will send you one immediately. I guess you are getting tired of this long letter so will close. Give my love to Grandpa and everybody and also keep a large share yourself from your loving grandson

   L. C. Lindsley

                              *   *   *

From Luther
                    Williamsburg, Va
                    March 3, '7
Dear Gamma,

   Your letter of the twenty-fourth was received on the twenty-fifth and was indeed glad to hear from home but was very sorry to hear you were feeling so badly. I have been enjoying very good health indeed this winter so far not even ever having a serious cold

   Well, I have some more work on my hands now. Last night the Philomathean elected me for final orator. I came near refusing but when I remembered that this was the only time a Manassas student, so far as I knew, had been so honored, I accepted and this of course means an hour or so extra every night for awhile. It also means I will have to confine myself in letter writing to four pages.

   It seems so hard for some people to understand. Some think a person here has nothing whatsoever to do but to write letters and if I put off writing I get such letters as I got the other day from Loudoun making some sarcastic remarks about the size of the hat band it would take to go around my hat (a delicate way of putting the thought, swell head). I am glad Aunt Mamie and the children are well. I get letters from Maurice occasionally and always endeavor to answer them as soon as possible.

   Our basketball team is making a record. It has not been beaten this year. Now no team in the State will play it. All are afraid. (illegible) played a game here in the gymnasium last night and beat Hampton 33 to 8. I did not see the game. I was president of the

Philomathean and consequently could not go. My board last month was about two weeks behind and will be due again in a little while. I thought I would mention it because it is better to be right on time. I had deprived Col Lane the treas. of his clothes agency and he is not in a very pleasant humor. Well Gamma, goodbye until next Sunday when I shall start you a few more lines. Hoping you are all well and that everything is prospering on the farm and giving love to all I remain,

Your loving grandson,

L. C. Lindsley

* * *

From Luther

Williamsburg, Va.
March, 17, '07

Dear Gamma,

To-night I thought I would have an opportunity to write you a long letter but it seems the Fates are against me. Just as I sat down to begin writing some one called me saying Gilliam wished to see me and knowing he had the mumps I dropped my pen and went down to his room on the second floor. His roommate had gone to Church and the electric light was turned off. I switched it on and spoke his name but he did not answer so I spoke still louder, and bent over the bed but still he said nothing. I took hold of him and shook him, rolling him over, and as his face became turned toward the light I saw that it was covered with sweat—and when his eyes opened they were wild and rolling. I placed my hand on his head and found it burning hot. He began to murmur something about the Jamestown Exposition and the Chesapeake Bay. He was delirious. I went over and "phoned" for Dr. Hawkins. He came and doctored him up. In addition to the mumps he had a bad attack of the chills. He is much better now but I have wasted half of the night.

Gamma, you certainly must take care of yourself. You must

remember you are not as strong as you used to be and that it is time you were being taken care of instead of being the support of others and rest assured that that time is not far off.

I certainly am sorry the farm is not as prosperous as it might be, but still there is much to thank God for Gamma, for things might be worse and if you could see some of the poor farmers of this section you would truly thank God.

The same storm you mentioned struck here about the same time and in exactly the same manner—snow, rain and thunder. For the past few days we have had beautiful weather. Spring has truly opened and fellows who were shivering with the cold a week ago were today mopping their faces with handkerchiefs.

Poor Bessie (I mean Bessie horse). She has a time of it. I certainly sympathize with her and all of you. I hope she is better now and will suffer no permanent injury. It is a pity.

O, yes that was sufficient money   please tell Grandpa. I have three more months to pay for. I have heard that College will not close until the 20th of June on account of the Exposition. Is Grandpa or Uncle Will coming to the exposition?

There has been quite a lot of stealing going on here. About seventy-five dollars have been stolen so far and we have not been able to catch the thief yet but are hoping to have him in a few days. A few of us seniors had a meeting and talked it over but could reach no definite conclusion as to the proper methods of procedure and the conference wound up by leaving it entirely in my hands to ferret out, which I intend doing if it is possible. I have quite a few clews and the net is slowly closing upon a certain young fellow and when all is ready I shall draw the mouth of the net as I have done several times before.

Well Grandmama, Goodnight and may God keep and pro-tect you from all sickness and unhappiness is the desire of
   your loving grandson

    L. C. Lindsley

COLLEGE OF WILLIAM AND MARY

CHARTERED 1693

...AND...

State Male Normal College of Virginia

ESTABLISHED 1888

The Session begins the 3rd Thursday in September; the Half Session the 1st of February, and closes the 2nd Thursday in June.

Report of the Scholarship and attendance of Mr. *L. C. Lindsley* at the College of William and Mary, for the Quarter ending *Mch. 31* 190*3*

STUDIES	CLASS GRADE	STUDIES	CLASS GRADE
English............	Very Good	Logic................	
History of Virginia.........		International Law..........	Very Good
History of the United States...		Civil Government...........	
History, General............		Political Economy..........	
History....... Eng......	Excellent	Physics..............	
History................		Chemistry...............	
Mathematics...............		Botany................	
Latin..................	Excellent	Zoology................	
Greek.................		Physiology..............	
French................	Fair	Physical Geography.........	
German................	Fair	Pedagogy.... Begin......	Fair
Psychology...............		Drawing.. Ed. E.	Good
Ethics.................		Manual Training...........	
		Teaching...............	
		Physical Culture..........	

NOTE.—Grades: Excellent, Very Good, Good, Fair, Tolerable, Poor. The attention of parents or guardians is respectfully invited to the above Report.

REMARKS:

H. L. Bridges _____ Secretary to the Faculty.

From Luther

1045 1/2 5th St. NW
Williamsburg, Va.
Apr. 15, 07

Dear Gamma,

Old Governor Spottswood's cannon which for years has stood upon the campus, its end pointing down the Duke of Gloucester St., has just given two deep roars, shaking the window panes of the dormitories and startling the entire city. To-day our baseball team defeated our old rival Randolph Macon, and our boys are celebrating the victory by shooting off old "Spottswood." The score was five to two in our favor.

I guess it is about time for the quarterly reports to go out. By the way, Dr. Bishop does not mark like the rest of the professors. <u>Good</u> is his highest mark and corresponds to the others excellent.

In a few days will be decided who is going up against Richmond College in debate on the 26th. There are about six trying. My Roommate, Douglas, is one of the contestants. So also must decided who is going up to represent us in the state oratorical contest held in Roanoke the third of May. I am not trying for either. I have all the work I can do. Thank Grandpa for the "cheque" for me and tell him and Uncle Will that college closes the 11th in order for the boys to be present at Virginia Day at the Exposition. If either come try to come during the finals and so take in both. The lights have flickered and I am mighty sleepy as you can judge by the numerous mistakes in this letter so thanking Grandpa again for his kindness and sending much love to all, I remain,

Your loving grandson,

L. C. Lindsley

*   *   *

From Luther

Williamsburg, Va.
Apr. 29, '07

Dear Gamma,

I would have written you yesterday but I was employed nearly all day in copying off my oration for Miss Christian, the librarian, to typewrite for me. I finished about four o'clock and was so tired that when Freeman came up and asked me to go walking I could not refuse. We walked down Lover's Lane to Queen's Creek where Blackbeard and the pirates were hung. In going down there we had quite an amusing adventure. The road is closely lined on one side with huge cedars whose bows hang down about six feet from the ground. Anyone looking back to see who may be coming behind them would have to step out from underneath the branches. Well to make a long story short, Freeman and I as we turned the corners saw before us about half a dozen girls of about eighteen years of age. Wishing to have some fun and feeling perfectly secure they had taken off their shoes and stockings and were walking along in the deep dust or splashing in a huge mud puddle. I was seized with a sudden fit of coughing. Such terror stricken faces I have never beheld. In a moment however they had recovered and with shrieks of horror made for their shoes and laughing, shrieking and screaming plunged into the woods which border the road. And what did we do? Well, we stopped and gave three "rah'rah'rah's!" for shoes and stocking and laughingly continued our walk.

Now I shall tell you the news. First, Richmond College won the debators cup from us Friday night. The speeches were limited to twenty minutes and before our debators could prove their points time was called upon them. Next, our baseball team has inflicted two heavy defeats upon Randolph Macon and Saturday held the Univ. of N. Carolina down to four runs. We are quite proud of our teams. When we beat R. M. the boys shot old Spotswood's cannon off eight times. They shook the town.

I have ordered some more photographs but as yet they have not come. I have (illegible) left over now and if they do not, I shall send them to you.

The invitations have not yet come out. When they do I shall

send you one. College closes on the 11th of June. I will make an estimate of what I shall need in regard to settling up and let you know soon. Miss Davis, the principal of the Model School, has each member of the Ped. class make a basket out of raffia. I made a demijohn. I wove the raffia around a beer bottle. It was the first time anything like that was ever undertaken and she was delighted. That and some other raffia works are exhibited at Jamestown Exhibition. Saturday night she and Miss Stillwell her roommate gave a party to the three regular teachers: Gilliam, Krontz, and Miss Elizabeth Morecock (& myself) who was so kind to me when I had the fever. We had a delightful time as we always have when we spend an evening there. I have just time enough to mail this before going to Sr. Ped. So good-bye. Give my love to everyone and write soon to your loving Grandson,

Luther Campbell Lindsley

* * *

From Luther

**Williamsburg, Va.
May 25, '07**

Dear Gamma,

The Annuals have just come. The art in it is fine but the literary matter is nothing in comparison to the Annuals last year. I am somewhat disappointed. I have gotten rid of four examinations. I am a little doubtful on International Law. Pres. Tyler has a way of putting up just enough of unimportant, insignificant questions to pull a fellow's percentage down. I have six more examinations to take. I have paid up all dues and have $3.00 which will pay for my class gown and cap. Twenty-five dollars would be very near enough but I do not know how much I shall have to pay for my degree. Not more than $10.00 I don't think. I may not have to pay anything, I may fail. Thirty-five dollars would be sufficient, yes ample to pay up everything and land me in Manassas.

Is Uncle Will or Grandpa coming down to Williamsburg when they come to Richmond? I would be glad to quarter them here with me for awhile.

Today has been very warm. This evening however a cloud came up and it began to rain steadily about seven o'clock and has not stopped yet and it is now nearly ten. The road to Jamestown is being completed rapidly. It is of stone and will last centuries. Last week I had the <u>pink eye</u> and was in the Infirmary with orders not to open a book. I remained there for over a week doing practically nothing and in two days after I came out examinations began. If I had been "a cussing man" I would have cussed roundly but as it is I shall have to make the best of it. I have some Logic to get up for examination, so good bye 'till I see you. I hope Grandpa and Uncle Will will come down. Give my love to everybody and keep a large share for yourself from

your loving grandson

Luther Campbell Lindsley

LUTHER'S SENIOR CLASS

In 1907 Luther was a senior at the College. The *Colonial Echo*, the annual, provides information about the senior class:

Motto: "Homines summus: humani nil a nobis a'ienum putamus"

Colors: black and maroon

Flower: Forget-me-not

Yell: Hi, yi, yip!
           Hi, yi, yap!
           Seniors, Seniors!
           Rip, rip, rap!

Class Poet: Luther C. Lindsley

The annual also included the futures of various class members as seen by the Class Prophet, who wrote in part:

Instantly, as if in answer to my question, I was projected into another city, which was alive with "the hurly-burly" of business and people rushing to and fro, as only people of a great metropolis do. Not knowing just what course to pursue, I stationed myself against the wall of a great edifice and gazed down what appeared to be the main thoroughfare of this magnificent city. While I thus stood, excited and bewildered with numerous things that came before my vision, I cast my eyes across the street and saw, posted in front of the Dome Theater, New York, an advertisement: "'The Heart of An Indian,' the greatest drama of modern ages, by L. C. Lindsley."

Burning with desire to see the play of my poet classmate, I went immediately toward the ticket office, to secure a seat in the great auditorium. Just as I entered the door, someone clapped me on the back... .

Note: The story continued about another student.

* * *

GRADUATION: 1907

LUTHER CAMPBELL LINDSLEY
Manassas, Virginia
"Let other mouths speak my praises."

GRADUATION PROGRAM 1907

The graduation program was leather-bound and tied with a leather string.

The Faculty and the

Phoenix and Philomathean

Literary Societies

of the

College of William and Mary

request the honour of your presence

during the

Exercises of Commencement Week

June 7th to 11th 1907

Williamsburg, Virginia

Calendar

Friday, June 7th

8 P. M.—Celebration of Philomathean Literary Society

Saturday, June 8th

8 P. M.—Celebration of Phoenix Literary Society

Sunday, June 9th

11 A. M.—Baccalaureate Sermon

8 P. M.—Sermon Before the Y. M. C. A.

Monday, June 10th

11 A. M.—Senior Class Celebration

8 P. M.—Oration Before the Alumni Association

Hon. Richard Evelyn Burd, Winchester, Va.

Tuesday, June 11th

11 A. M.—Awarding of Degrees, Diplomas, Medals and Scholarships

9 P. M.—Final Ball

The Philomathean Literary Society

"Praesto et Persto"

President, G. Livious Hoddon Johnson
Secretary, Alfred Thomas Hope

Orators

Luther Campbell Lindsley
John Holivid Dowen

Debaters

William Edgar Roach
Hiram Petty Wall

Executive Committee

Coleman Bernard Ransone, *Chairman*

Grover Thomas Somers

Micajah Oliver Townsend

Cecil Cooper Bell

Herbert Heldhruf Young

Marshals

Clarence Edgar Koontz, *Chief*

J. Arthur Parsley

Rosco C. Young

Ernest William Koontz

William Hatcher Croswell

The Philomathean Literary Society's page. Luther is orator.

The Phoenix Literary Society

"Invictus Resurgam"

President, George Oscar Ferguson, Jr.
Secretary, Robert Francis Terrell

Orators

Edwin Francis Shewmake

Grover Ashton Dovell

Debaters

Guy A. B. Dovell

Channing Moore Hall

Executive Committee

Kendell Palmer Brickhead, *Chairman*

Jack Marye Davis   William Sale Terrell

Marshals

Stephen Ashley McDonald, *Chief*

Malcolm Peel Dillard   Blake Tyler Newton
Bailey Jett Locker   James Garland Unruh
Charles Albert Taylor

Master of Arts Class

Robert Beverley Dade	.	Airmont, Loudoun Co., Va.
William R. Wrigglesworth	.	Chula, Amelia Co., Va.
John Tyler . .		Williamsburg, James City Co., Va.
John Baynham Terrell	. .	Essex Co., Va.

Officers of the Class
of 1907

President

George Oscar Ferguson, Leesburg, Va.

Vice-President

Alfred Thomas Hope, Hopeton, Accomac Co., Va.

Secretary

Coleman Bernard Ransone, Port Haywood, Mathews Co., Va.

Treasurer

Grover Thomas Somers, Bloxom Accomac Co., Va.

Historian

James Fitzgerald Jones, Alexandria, Va.

Poet

Luther Campbell Lindsley, Manassas, Va.

Prophet

C. Livius Haddon Johnson, Unity, Southampton Co., Va.

Valedictorian

Herbert Heldhruf Young, Aquasco, Prince George Co., Md.

Note that Luther is class poet.

GRADUATE STUDENT: 1907-1908

Luther returned to William and Mary for one more year for postgraduate studies and continued his extra-curricular activities. He left William and Mary after the school term ending in spring 1908 to begin teaching.

LUTHER'S ORGANIZATIONS

The William and Mary Literary Magazine, 1907-1908.

L. C. LINDSLEY
EDITOR-IN-CHIEF

From the *Colonial Echo*:

Member, Philomathean Literary Society
        Corresponding secretary, 1903-04
        One of four co-presidents of the Society, 1907
        Orator, 1908

Luther
***Colonial Echo*, 1908.**
From a group picture of the Philomathean Society

Member: The Spottswood Club
        Organized December 1907
        Motto: "Sic juvat transcendere montes"

Member: Fiends Club

Motto: "Hitch Your Wagon to a Star"

Motto: "Hitch Your Wagon to a Star"

THE FIENDS
L. C. Lindsley—the "Mag" Fiend

Vice-president of the Class of 1908, from the *Colonial Echo*:

Motto: Prudens futuri

Prophecy: Hæc olim meminisse juvabit

Yell: Whew-i-y-y-y-y!!!!

THE CLASS

HERBERT HELDRUF YOUNG...President
LUTHER CAMPBELL LINDSLEY....................................Vice-President
ALFRED LORD TERRELL...............................Secretary and Treasurer
GAIUS LIVIOUS HADDON JOHNSON...........................Biographer and Poet

QUOTES: From the *Colonial Echo*

Be It Resolved:

That if I should search the world over, I should not find my equal.
L. C. Lindsley

That Senior French is a snap. L. C. Lindsley

Greater men than I may have lived, but I do not believe it.
L. C. Lindsley

None but himself can be his parallel.

The lunatic, the lover, and the poet are of imagination all compact.
L. C. Lindsley

HONORS

Fratres Honors College

This honor, together with others, was listed by Luther, but W&M has no record of this college. Many colleges and universities have internal "honors colleges" that vary over the years.

Voted by the Students in 1908

Most Intellectual Man: L. C. Lindsley
Best Poet: L. C. Lindsley
Best Prose writer: L. C. Lindsley
Most Intelligent man: L. C. Lindsley

Flat Hat Society

A Latin honor society of William and Mary, the Flat Hat Society predated Phi Beta Kappa by about twenty years. Membership remained secret; the only evidence of Luther's membership is his medal, in possession of daughter Susan. The 1920 *Colonial Echo* gave a bit of information about this secret honorary club. There is no record at the College of membership in this organization, and the organization itself has no rolls from previous years, although secrecy was relinquished in the early 1920s.

When I attempted to verify his first year of membership, I was informed "due to the fact that it was and remains a secret society, we do not have any list of membership of the Club."

I was also informed that The Club was "discontinued" in the 1800s, so that Luther would not have been a member, that it was not officially re-founded until the 1920s.

Apparently, however, the organization went totally "under-ground" and membership continued to remain secret, for Luther's Flat Hat Club medal verifies his membership during his college years: 1903-1908.

Luther was especially proud of his membership in this organization. When Westover burned, this medal was high on the list of items looked for when the family sifted through the ashes. Ownership of your medal was your only "proof" of membership since there were no rolls.

The Flat Hat Club is the oldest living college organization in America, having been founded at the College of William and Mary on November 11, 1750, thus antedating the Phi Beta Kappa Society by twenty-six years. On its rolls may be found the names of Jefferson and others of the college's famous alumni, including the long list of notables in the Spotswood Club of Old Virginia.

In spite of all efforts to attract the Society into other colleges, it has consistently maintained a policy which is opposed to expansion, preferring to remain local and retain its tradition.

Luther's medal

Note initial FHC

He received the Orator's Medal of Philomathean Literary Society of William and Mary College in 1907. This medal, too, survived the fire at Westover, although it is badly damaged.

COLONIAL ECHO (COLLEGE ANNUAL)

LUTHER C. LINDSLEY......................*Manassas, Virginia*
  B. A. Degree 1904; Editor-in-Chief William and Mary Literary Maga-
zine 1905; Poet's Medal 1902; President of Philomathean 1904; Vice-
President of Philomathean 1905; Final Orator's Medal 1904; Sub Varsity
Football Team 1903; Senior Class Poet 1904; Diplomas in Latin,
Mathematics, Philosophy, and Pedagogy; Athletic Executive Committee
1904.
  DREAMY JIM. A human paradox. Has a good mind, but he knows it.
Born in the Objective Case. Bears a versatile pen. Writes sweetly of
women, but no one ever saw him speak to one. Wants to be a lawyer,
but lost his first case before the Board of Visitors. Is kind to his
friends. Is extremely radical in his nature. He was seen *once* at church,
but didn't tarry long. He has no special faith, but a Christian Scientist
in sentiment. Claims to be self-made, and, with a few discrepancies,
made a pretty good job of it.
          "None but himself can be his parallel."

This entry in the annual contains numerous errors as to dates. From his graduation program and his letters to his grandmother Hannah Johnson, we know he received his B.A. in 1907, was Editor of the "Mag" in 1907-08, won the James Barren Hope award for poetry in 1905; was Senior Class poet in 1907; served as president of the Philomathean Society in 1907; was Final Orator for the Philomathean Society and received its Orator's Medal in 1907.

HIS TRANSCRIPT:

COLLEGE OF WILLIAM AND MARY
OFFICE OF THE REGISTRAR
WILLIAMSBURG, VIRGINIA

February 5, 1935

Official Record of: LUTHER CAMPBELL LINDSLEY

1903-1904

Arithmetic
Elementary Algebra
Plane Geometry
Latin, Caesar, Cicero, Vergil
Botany and Chemistry
Introduction to English

1904-05-06

Algebra	Latin, Horace, Livy
Pl and Solid Geometry	Physics and Physiology
Advanced Algebra	Psychology
Spherical Trig	German
Theory of Equations	Junior English
General History	Amer. History and Political Science

1906-07

Logic and Ethics	4
English History	2
Latin V - VI	6
English	
French I - II	6
German I - II	6
Political Science III	2
Dif. Calculus	3

1907-08

Greek I - II	3
Physics III - IV	
Physics, Graduate	
Greek History	2
Philosophy VII	
Senior French	

Degree Conferred: Bachelor of Arts
Date: June 2, 1907

REGISTRAR

The College of William and Mary

PART III

LUTHER

FROM

WILLIAM AND MARY

TO

MILLEDGEVILLE

IN 1929

HIGH SCHOOL TEACHING YEARS

Luther left William and Mary in the spring of 1908 and began his teaching career. He sometimes took a one-year contract with a community and then moved on to another location.

His students were no longer kindergarten but high school level, his subjects, agricultural chemistry and animal husbandry. He continued to teach high school or college for the rest of his professional life.

In June 1913, he wrote a check to his step-grandfather, who never cashed it, and the check came back to him many years later. Since it is dated only two months before Luther's marriage to Pattie Love Jones, possibly George Johnson considered the coming event and therefore decided not to cash it.

See the letter from his cousin Georgia Embry in the chapter of letters written to and by him and his wife Lillas in "After the children left home."

Pattie Love's parents sent out a notice of the wedding, and the local newspaper carried the wedding in its social column:

Mr. and Mrs. Daniel Hicks Jones

announce the approaching marriage of their daughter

Pattie Love

to

Mr. Luther Campbell Lindsley

on Tuesday, August the twenty-sixth

nineteen hundred and thirteen

Boydton, Virginia.

We do not know what newspaper ran this announcement:

SOCIAL AND PERSONAL

On Tuesday, at high noon, in Boydton, the marriage of Miss Pattie Love Jones, of that place, and Luther Campbell Lindsley, of Manassas, was quietly celebrated at the home of the bride's parents, Mr. and Mrs. Daniel Hicks Jones. Only near relatives of the bride and groom witnessed the ceremony, which was performed by the Rev. Charles W. Sydnor, rector of St. James' parish. The wedding marches and selections from Dvorak and Engelmann were played by Mrs. Hanie Stokes Edmonson, and the parlors were decorated with ferns and wild flowers and lighted with many candles. The bride, who was given away by her father, wore a blue traveling gown, with a modish hat to match, and carried a white prayer book with markers of lilies of the valley. She was met at the improvised alter by the groom and his best man, Henry Jones.

Following the ceremony, Mr. and Mrs. Lindsley left for the mountains of North Carolina, where they will spend their honeymoon. After September 8, they will be at home in Norton, where the groom holds the position as principal of the Norton schools.

*   *   *

Luther kept no diary, and we have few records of where he taught or served as principal of high schools for those ten years. We do know he was in Chase City in 1916. We have his copy of his membership card for the Woodmen of the World:

Form 23¼

DEPUTY HEAD CONSUL'S RECEIPT

MODERN WOODMEN OF AMERICA
BY AUTHORITY OF THE HEAD CAMP

RECEIVED of Mr. *J. C. Lindsey* ....this....*7*......day

of....*Oct*........., 19*16* at *Chase City* { State } of *Va.*
{ Prov. }

the following fees to cover his application for membership in Camp No. *12012*

Modern Woodmen of America, Located at....*Chase City*......, *Va.*

Adoption Fee, $5.00 Local Physician's Fee, $ *1.25* Sup. Med. Director's Fee, $.25 TOTAL, $ *6.50*

It being understood that if the applicant is rejected by the Camp this membership fee in full shall be refunded; if rejected by the Medical department. adoption fee only of $5.00 shall be refunded by the undersigned. In case applicant is adopted pending issuance of benefit certificate, such temporary adoption shall not deprive him of the right to withdraw from the Camp as a social member and demand refund of adoption fee in case his beneficial application is rejected by the Medical department. If the Deputy fails or refuses to refund said fee upon request. and application is then made for refund. accompanied by this receipt to A. R. Talbot. Head Consul. Lincoln. Nebr., within four months from date hereof, said fee will be refunded by the Society, but not otherwise.

$ *6.50*

......................*J. C. Evans*......................
Deputy Head Consul.

His friendship with one of his students, Elizabeth Storm, was life-long, and even after his death, she stayed in touch with one of the daughters. She wrote this about Luther in the mid-1960s:

I think Mr. and Mrs. Lindsley came to Chase City, Virginia in the fall of 1915 (or 1914). The school at that time consisted of an elementary school, grades one through seven, and a four-year high school, with one principal for both schools.

In the fall of 1916, the state organized one-year extension courses as preparation for teaching in several areas of the state. Chase city, which had a fully accredited high school, was one place selected. I had hoped to study medicine but due to my father's illness I had to abandon the plan. I enrolled in the "Normal Training course" the following year, your father honored me by asking that I be given a place on the elementary school faculty. So my first year of teaching was done under the supervision and direction of the finest teacher I have ever known, your father.

I do not have any knowledge of your father's military service. I remember hearing your father and Mrs. Lindsley speak often of a school in the mountains of western Virginia, as I remember it was called Tazewell in Tazewell County, but I am not sure I remember correctly. At any rate, your father had been very active in this community as principal of the school.

I think your father left Chase City in the fall of 1919 and went to William and Mary College.

During the years I have lost touch with most of the people I knew in my "teens" so I know little of my classmates now with the exception of one, a dear friend all though the years, who recently visited me. She says your father did some teaching at William and Mary before coming to Chase City.

You asked if I went directly from high school to graduate work. No, but due to your Dad's letter of recommendation and my records from his fine school, I entered the Johns Hopkins undergraduate school without difficulty.

Your father's first wife was Miss Pattie Love Jones (from Boydton, Va., I think). Her sister Miss Lois Jones taught in Chase city.

I often heard your father speak of his grandmother's farm in Manassas, Va. He told how every stone wall on this place had been razed during the War Between the States. I don't know whether or not his grandmother reared him.

Your father was a remarkable teacher. He exercised a great influence for good on his pupils. In our little town we had no public library. Your father had many books. He never locked his front door and he invited his older pupils—whether he was at home or away—to stop in and make use of his library. I never heard of anyone who abused this privilege.

Another thing I remember well was how he obtained a chemistry laboratory for the high school. It seemed there was no money for this—so your father secured some lumber, just how I don't know. However, I do know that he carried all of the material to the third floor (attic) of the school and during his summer vacation built a chemistry laboratory. After he had finished he carried Mrs. Lindsley, who was ill, up the stairs to see his work. Difficulties never kept him from achieving his goals.

When our little class graduated, your Dad gave each of us a little "fairy stone cross." These are found only in Patrick County, Virginia, I think. I had mine mounted in gold and I still have it and occasionally wear it. I always felt that your father was deeply religious.

**Two examples of the fairy crosses. Because these are natural
formations, the shapes varied a lot.**

On June 5, 1917, he registered for the draft in Mecklenburg
County, Virginia, as required by law of all men between the ages of
eighteen and forty-six at that time. He served in the horse-drawn
artillery, but we do not know if he ever saw action in Europe. He told
his youngest daughter Lil that he was supposed to be commissioned,
but when the Army learned that he could not raise his hand high over
his head, he was not commissioned. An officer in the artillery had to be
able to raise his hand to signal the cannon man when to fire. We have
no other information about his service. The picture of him with his
grandmother Hannah in Appendix II shows him in uniform.

In our childhood, when Thulia would play the piano and we stood around singing, one of Dad's favorites was the official Army song, which fitted his service well since he was in the artillery:

U.S. Field Artillery (1918)
(Music by Gruber, arranged by Sousa, copyright and published by Carl Fischer)

Over hill, over dale,
We will hit the dusty trail,
And those Caissons go rolling along.
Up and down, in and out,
Counter march and left about,
And those Caissons go rolling along,
For it's high high he,
In the Field Artillery,
Shout out your "No" loud and strong,
For wher-e'er we go,
You will always know,
That those Caissons go rolling along.

The words Dad taught us varied slightly: Line 5 was "—and **right** about" and line 9 was : Shout out your **slogan**"

A copy of his registration papers and his draft card are shown below.

REGISTRATION CARD 570

1. Name in full: *Luther Campbell Lindsley*   Age: 29
2. Home address: *Manassas Va*
3. Date of birth: *Feb. 10th 1888*
4. Are you (1) a natural-born citizen, (2) a naturalized citizen, (3) an alien, (4) or have you declared your intention (specify which)? *Natural Born Citizen*
5. Where were you born? *Dumfries Va USA*
6. If not a citizen, of what country are you a citizen or subject?
7. What is your present trade, occupation, or office? *Principal of School*
8. By whom employed? *State Bd of Education* Where employed? *Chase City Va*
9. Have you a father, mother, wife, child under 12, or a sister or brother under 12, solely dependent on you for support (specify which)? *Wife*
10. Married or single (which)? *Married* Race (specify which) *Caucasian*
11. What military service have you had? Rank *No Com___*; branch *Artillery* years *3*; Nation or State *State*
12. Do you claim exemption from draft (specify grounds)? *Dependent Wife*

I affirm that I have verified above answers and that they are true.

45 · 1 · 29 A

REGISTRAR'S REPORT

1 Tall, medium, or short (specify which)? *Medium*   Slender, medium, or stout (which)? *Medium*

2 Color of eyes? *Brown*   Color of hair? *Brown*   Bald? —

3 Has person lost arm, leg, hand, foot, or both eyes, or is he otherwise disabled (specify)? — *No*

I certify that my answers are true, that the person registered has read his own answers, that I have witnessed his signature, and that all of his answers of which I have knowledge are true, except as follows:

Jas D Bryson

(Signature of registrar)

Precinct **Chase City, Va.**

County **Mecklenburg Va**

State

JUN 5 1917

(Date of registration)

REGISTRATION CERTIFICATE.

To whom it may concern, Greetings:

THESE PRESENTS ATTEST,

That in accordance with the

No. 5B

(This number must correspond with that on the Registration Card.)

proclamation of the President of the United States, and in compliance with law,

J. C. Lindsley   Chase City, Va.

Precinct Chase City, County of *Mecklenburg* State of *Virginia*

has submitted himself to registration and has by me been duly registered this

day of JUN 5 1917 1917,

Jno. D. Bugg
Registrar

*   *   *

His notes on the back of the picture (below) of "Mac," his bulldog, tells us that at one time he was in Norton, Virginia.

CORNELL

In 1917, the Smith Hughes Act passed Congress; it made funds available to states for teacher training in specific vocational areas, including agriculture.

The next summer (1918), Luther attended the College of Agriculture at Cornell to take "the emergency course for teachers of agriculture under the Smith-Hughes Act." He had a strong letter of recommendation from the College of William and Mary. (See the first letter in Appendix V.)

He returned to his position as principal of the Charlotte County Agricultural School, where he earned the highest salary paid a high school principal in Virginia. But he saw no future advancement there.

That summer at Cornell, however, had peaked his interest in chemistry, and Dr. Dennis, his supervisor in the agriculture department, had him slated for an assistantship, for him to return to Cornell, but World War I had caused a change of plans.

On June 13, 1919 he wrote the president of Cornell and asked about admission to graduate school and the availability of any job on campus, "no matter how humble, from an assistantship on down to day laborer, that will enable me to finish my chemistry course under Dr. Dennis."

He stated that he had only about one thousand dollars and to "make out nicely" would need to earn at least eight hundred a year.

His letter of the 13th was answered on the 18th. His William and Mary degree and his years of teaching qualified him for admission to graduate school. An application was enclosed.

In October 1919, he was officially accepted as a candidate for Ph. D., with inorganic chemistry his major subject, organic chemistry his first minor subject and agricultural chemistry his second minor subject.

He found work. He often spoke of his job in the agriculture department. We don't know if these jobs were during his first (Smith Hughes) time at Cornell in 1918 or later, when working on his Ph. D. Today, he might be called a "teaching aide," for he gave practical exams to the students. One such exam required the student to select a hen from the chicken pen, to feel of her abdomen, and to determine how many eggs she would lay in a year. Luther would later laugh about the hen no one ever selected, the hen that was the best layer in the flock: She looked like a rooster.

Another job was to milk the world's champion milk-giving cow. When a cow's bag is full she must be milked or complications can occur which will decrease her milk-giving. Her supply of milk was so great she had to be milked four times a day (not two, as dairy cows are milked). A cow must be milked when her bag gets full or she can go dry or her bag can get inflamed.

Luther often spoke of his winter there, when the snow was so deep that he walked to the barn on a path with snow higher than he was tall. He was five-nine.

He was first author of a paper on double selenates, co-authored with Dr. Dennis, who served as chair of his doctoral committee. His publications while at Cornell are given in Appendix VI.

A prerequisite for the doctoral program was "a working knowledge of French and German." Luther demonstrated a reading knowledge of both languages to his Special Committee. In later years, his children realized that he also had a working knowledge of both Latin and Greek.

When Luther received credit for his post-graduate work at William and Mary he had met all requirements for entrance into the doctorate program.

His records show steady progress toward his doctorate, especially in the first months of 1922. He submitted the topic for his thesis in February and it was accepted. On March 22, 1922, his thesis was approved, and by June 5, he had turned in the thesis and taken the exams proffered by his three committee members.

Luther's doctoral thesis is given in its entirety in Appendix VII, together with the published version released a year later: "Some New Double Selenates."

He received his doctorate on June 21, 1922; his diploma reads "in the 146th year of the Republic and the 54th year of the University." The diploma is in the possession of his grandson Lindsley Bramlett.

From the Flat Hat publication at the College of William and Mary came this announcement about the publication of his doctoral thesis. Date of the newspaper is not available:

PROF. LINDSLEY PREPARES INTERESTING PAMPHLET

An interesting pamphlet on "Some New Double Selenates," by Professor L. C. Lindsley of the chemical department of the college has just been published. It is based on a thesis presented by Mr.

Lindsley at the graduate school of Cornell University for the degree of doctor of philosophy, in 1922. The work is purely technical and would not appeal to anyone not interested in chemical research, but to the student of that science it will prove of value.

BACK TO VIRGINIA

He returned to the College of William and Mary as an associate professor of chemistry for the school terms of 1922-23. From 1923-25 he was a full professor and held the chair once held by William Barton Rogers before he became president of the Massachusetts Institute of Technology (M. I. T.).

While in Williamsburg, he and his wife purchased a home, known as the Nicholson House, now at the edge of the historical area, the fourth structure from the beginning of York Street. His teaching took him to other localities (e.g., Columbia University), but his chemical research could have been carried out at home. We do not know how long they maintained the house as their residence.

The William and Mary Alumni newsletter gives us a chronology of his work from teaching at his alma mater until his arrival in Milledgeville:

Coincident with his post-graduate work, Dr. Lindsley was Associate Professor of chemistry at William and Mary. From 1923 until 1925, he was head of the department of chemistry in this institution. In 1926, following this period of teaching, he was chemist for the Royster Guano Works, Norfolk. From 1925 until the past year he has held the chair of Professor of Industrial Microscopy, Department of Chemical Engineering in the Summer School of Columbia University. Besides these activities, Dr. Lindsley has specialized in industrial and research problems since 1927, doing special research for the Royster Guano Company and acting as research chemist for the Archeological Department of one of the world's largest museums. Dr. Lindsley has won an international reputation in the field of archeological chemistry.

The reference to "one of the world's largest museums" was to the

Metropolitan Museum of Art. One of his projects for the Metropolitan Museum was to determine the chemical composition of a glaze or paint on a piece of Chinese porcelain that dated from many years B.C. It turned out to be a chemical that had to be heated to thou-sands of degrees to turn that color. Luther told his children that China reached high levels of science, art and civilization long before Western Europe.

While in Norfolk, Virginia, working with Royster, on February 21, 1926, he wrote his state senator in hopes of becoming a member of the William and Mary Board of Visitors:

Addressed to Senator W. H. Jeffreys in Richmond, the letter read in part:

The terms of five members of the Board of Visitors of the College of William & Mary expire in March. I do not know if the present Governor plans to make any changes. In case he does there is nothing that would please me more than to be a member of the Board.

William and Mary records indicate that he did not receive this appointment.

A requirement for his classes at Columbia was for the student to already have a doctorate in chemistry. He taught in summer school at Columbia for four years 1925-1928, in the department of chemical engineering. His subject: Microscopy.

Luther's files contain a record of several tests he ran for the Pillsbury Flour Company of Minnesota. He was asked to test rat hairs for arsenic, and many of the samples he tested did contain arsenic.

Here we have one of several letters from a company asking him to research for them.

ALL AGREEMENTS SUBJECT TO DELAYS OF CARRIERS, STRIKES, ACCIDENTS OR OTHER CAUSES BEYOND MY CONTROL

J. C. GRINNAN
BUILDING MATERIAL :: CLAY PRODUCTS
INSULITE COMPOSITION FLOORING
305 ARCADE BUILDING
NORFOLK, VA.   May 11, 1927.

Dr. L. C. Lindsley,
Marshall College,
Huntington, W. Va.

My dear Dr. Lindsley:

I am sending you another sample of
"KAPAC".

I would suggest that you analysize this too.
It is not the real Elaterite, though it does contain a large
percentage of Elaterite and Gilsonite.

Yours truly, Grinnan

G/M

Luther not only performed research for hire after he left William and Mary; he also continued to teach. The May 18, 1926 *Parthenon*, the student newspaper for Marshall College, stated:

Dr. L. C. Lindsley, a member of the faculty of Columbia University, will become professor of chemistry at Marshall College after June 1. --- Dr. Lindsley is also on temporary leave from Columbia and will report back there next summer when the university's new chemistry engineering building is completed.

Dr. Lindsley obtained his A. B. and M. A. degree from William and Mary College and his Ph. D. from Cornell University.

The Marshall College catalog for 1926-1927 shows that he had a bachelor's degree and a doctorate in its listing of faculty.

The September 26, 1926 *Parthenon* reported:

Dr. L. C. Lindsley, professor of chemistry, has been extracted from the faculty of Columbia University and will serve in the place of Professor Campbell, who is on leave of absence. Dr. Lindsley was formerly with William and Mary College.

Luther served as professor of chemistry at Marshall College (now Marshall University) for the school term 1926-27.

He saved the catalog for the year 1922 and a flyer issued by the Real Estate Board of Huntington, West Virginia. He probably obtained these when he became interested in teaching there.

I suspect that his interest developed because the college was named for John Marshall. A portion of the flyer reads:

THIS INSTITUTION was founded by private agencies in 1837 and named after the distinguished Virginia jurist, John Marshall. In 1867 it was taken over by the State of West Virginia. It has served as an academy, normal school and college. It now comprises—

> A State Teachers College;
> A College of Arts and Sciences; and,
> Pre-Medic, Pre-Engineering and Pre-Law Departments.

The Bachelor of Arts Degree is conferred upon graduates of the Teachers' College and the College of Arts and Sciences. The work of these colleges is standard and is accredited by leading universities and professional schools.

A large variety of courses are now offered by the institution, among which may be enumerated the following:

Agriculture	French	Mathematics
Art	General Science	Music
Bible	Geography	Nature Study
Biology	Geology	Physical Education
Botany	German	Physics
Chemistry	Greek	Political Science
Commerce	History	Psychology
Economics	Home Economics	Sociology
Education	Latin	Spanish
English	Literature	Zoology

Though the College may boast of years and honored traditions, it is so new in its modern development that few people realize the extent of its present facilities.

It is our pleasure to call attention to the fact:

That Marshall College has the largest attendance of any educational institution in the State with the sole exception of the State University;

That it has the largest teacher training school in the State;

That it has the largest summer school in the State;

That it has the largest woman's hall in the State;

That it has the largest number of graduates in the public school service of the State;

That it maintains the only psychological clinic in the State.

All the work offered by Marshall is of college grade. To be eligible for admission students must have completed a standard four-year high school course.

For the school term 1927-1928, he may have devoted himself entirely to his research, for we have no record of where he taught, if he did. A later catalog for GSCW shows his professorial years, but omits that school year.

For the term 1928-1929, he was professor of chemistry at East Kentucky State College. Thereafter, he was at the Georgia State College for Women, in Milledgeville, Georgia.

INDUSTRIAL MICROSCOPY: LUTHER'S BOOK

In 1929, Luther published 1,000 copies of his book, *Industrial Microscopy*, which became an internationally sought-after book in 1929. Dr. E. M. Chamot of Cornell, who had been on his examining committee, had begun a study of microscopic analysis, but used only sketches as illustrations. (See Appendix VIII for Chamot's comments on Luther's work, and Appendix IX for flyers Luther prepared as advertisements.)

Luther used photographs. His book was the beginning of the microscopic analysis now routine, and seen constantly on the television "cop shows" such as "CSI." A sample could be analyzed microscopically rather than chemically; chemical analysis would destroy the sample. Microscopic viewing preserved the sample.

American buyers of his book included many colleges and universities (e. g., Harvard, Cornell, University of Georgia, M. I. T., Duke) and organizations such as the American Chemical Society, Department of Commerce (Bureau of Standards), Bell Telephone Laboratories, various booksellers, and even the publisher D. Van Nostrand Company.

He often said that the Russians and the Germans bought the majority of copies. The American chemistry industry was still in its infancy in the 1920s, in spite of the efforts of his friend Charles Herty to strengthen the industry. Luther said that Herty had encouraged President Wilson to seize German chemical patents during WWI and lease them out to the budding chemical industries in the United States, and to use the incoming funds to split the atom.

The May 1929 issue of *Isotopics*, a regional bulletin of the Ohio, Michigan, Lexington (Kentucky), Kanawha Valley (West Virginia) and Erie (Pennsylvania) sections of the American Chemical Society, carried a brief story about Luther on page 13 in the Lexington segment:

Dr. L. C. Lindsley of Columbia University spoke on "Industrial Chemical Microscopy." Dr. Lindsley has spent many years in developing this material and illustrated his lecture with lantern slides. This was an opportunity to learn something of the progress being made in this somewhat unfamiliar field.

Luther at his lab. Note photography equipment to the left rear.

The Flat Hat Society had been "re-founded" in the 1920s at William and Mary, and it issued a newsletter that soon became the student newspaper. In the October 18, 1929 issue, page 3, it reported:

INDUSTRIAL MICROSCOPY

Dr. L. C. Lindsley has just published "Industrial Microscopy" which will be a great aid to industrial chemists and students. Besides presenting systematic procedures for the identification of most of the elements, the text included the procedures as applied to common starches, alkaloids, industrial woods and pulps, papers and textiles, minerals and rocks.

Dr. Lindsley's clear and concise treatment of the subject based upon varied experience in the classroom and in the industrial field makes the work invaluable as a textbook and laboratory manual for schools and colleges. The price is $4.00 and is sent on ten days

approval. Copies may be obtained from the author at Williamsburg, Virginia.

Here is a copy of the catalogue card for the book at the William and Mary library:

record 1 of 1 for search **words or phrase "L. C. Lindsley"**

Item Information	Catalog Record

Industrial microscopy
Lindsley, Luther Campbell, 1888-

Author: Lindsley, Luther Campbell, 1888-
Title: Industrial microscopy, by L. C. Lindsley ...
Publication info.: Richmond, Va., The William Byrd press, inc., 1929.
Physical description: 2 p. *., [vii]-xv, 286 p. illus. 24 cm.
Note: Contains bibliographies.
Subject: Microscopy.
Subject: Microchemistry.

Holdings

Offsite Stacks Facility	Copies	Material	Location
578 L64	1	Unknown material	By Request from Offsite Stacks

Industrial Microscopy was still held in 104 libraries worldwide in 2015.

The November 15, 1929, issue, page 3, in the section of News and Announcements of The Alumni Association, carried this column.

LINDSLEY, '07 OUTSTANDING IN SCIENTIFIC RESEARCH

Dr. Luther C. Lindsley, '07, brings to the subject of Industrial Microscopy a fund of practical experience acquired in the field, as well as the theory of the classroom. Since he graduated at William and Mary, he has alternated between research work in the field and teaching appointments.

In preparation for his degree of Doctor of Philosophy at Cornell University in 1922 it was the author's privilege to be a student under Dr. E. Chamot, who more than anyone else is responsible for the development of chemical Microscopy in this

country.

During the past decade Professor Lindsley has devoted much of his time and thought to experiments with the microscope, building up step by step the data contained in this work, making over five thousand experimental preparations.

LUTHER'S RESUME: 1927

COLLEGE OF WILLIAM AND MARY
FOUNDED IN 1693
OFFICE OF THE DEAN
WILLIAMSBURG, VIRGINIA

December 23, 1925

To Whom It May Concern:

Dr. L. C. Lindsley was professor of chemistry at the College of William and Mary from 1922 to 1925. Part of his work included the inorganic chemistry which is given in our Freshman year. When Dr. Lindsley took charge of this work it was in need of reorganization. His success in accomplishing this task had a very benficial effect on the entire Department of Chemistry.

In my judgment Dr. Lindsley is a strong teacher. He knows, and maintains, good standards of instruction, and is successful in arousing and continuing the interest of students in his subject. His point of view towards the whole subject of science is particularly modern. During his stay as a professor at this institution I did not hear from any of his students a single criticism of his work; on the contrary, a great many things came to my office from the students which were commendable. I cordially recommend Dr. Lindsley as an efficient and progressive teacher of chemistry.

Yours very truly,
K. J. Hoke
Dean

MARSHALL COLLEGE
HUNTINGTON, W. VA.
OFFICE OF THE PRESIDENT

September 30, 1927

To Whom It May Concern:

For a year Dr. L. C. Lindsley filled the vacancy of our Professor Campbell who was on leave of absence and it is a pleasure to testify of the excellence of the service rendered. Dr. Lindsley may rightfully claim to be something of an authority in the field of industrial chemistry and as an instructor and worker he is unusually effective. His personal interest in his students adds materially to the value of his services and his consistent faithfulness for the work in which he is engaged results in worth while advantages to the institution with which he is connected.

In addition to all this, both he and Mrs. Lindsley are valuable social additions to an institution.

Yours very truly.
M. P. Shawkey
President

COLUMBIA UNIVERSITY
IN THE CITY OF NEW YORK
DEPARTMENT OF CHEMICAL ENGINEERING
Nov. 23, 1927

Prof. L. C. Lindsley
Williamsburg
Virginia
Dear Prof. Lindsley:

The two courses which you gave during the Summer Session this year were very favorably commented on and I consider the work of very excellent character. I hope that you will be able to repeat these courses the coming summer.

With kindest regards, I am
Cordially yours,
D. D. Jackson
Executive Officer,
Department of Chemical Engineering.

This resume was perhaps used as a part of his application for his position at Eastern Kentucky State College, where he taught chemistry in the 1928-29 school term. He came to the Georgia State College for Women (GSCW) in the fall of 1929.

He continued to sell his book after his move to Georgia. Note that in 1929, the postal service did not need a street address for Milledgeville residents:

A few copies left of

$4.00 **Industrial Microscopy** Write

L. C. Lindsley, Ph. D., Milledgeville, Georgia

30 DAYS APPROVAL

Two hundred and eighty-six pages with 148 illustrations and photomicrographs of tests for the elements, acids, alkaloids, and many materials.

Used in 48 states and 15 foreign countries. It is the first edition of such a book so illustrated in the English language. A part of the essential equipment of every Industrial and University laboratory.

The book cost $4.00 in 1929. Its price has been as high as $250 on internet rare book sites in 2014.

PART IV

MILLEDGEVILLE

AND

WESTOVER

LUTHER COMES TO MILLEDGEVILLE

Luther came to GSCW for a one-year teaching contract, but shortly after his arrival, he saw Westover Plantation House. He didn't mind that the house was in bad shape, that goats had roamed throughout the building, and that windows were broken out. All those little problems would be solved with work, one little job at a time.

The house had been empty for a number of years and local residents would stop by to see the house. Ruby Farr (aunt of Pat Blanks who was a classmate of Susan Lindsley's) wrote in her diary:

Friday—July 23. Dear Diary, This morning Dot and I went on a little adventure out to Merieweather (sic) to spend the day.... Spent the day with a Mrs. Stiles.... On way back stopped at old historic Jordan home and went inside to see the old furniture and beautiful spiral stairway. It is a beautiful place.

Watercolor by Frank Herring about mid-1920s

Luther bought the house and the adjacent 795 acres of Westover Plantation in 1930. (About 65 acres of the original 850 acres owned by Benjamin Jordan had been sold to the Huff family, which still lives on their lands; see maps in Appendix X.)

Luther never again thought of moving to another community or another teaching position. He had found home, and he remained at GSCW until his retirement. He continued life at Westover Plantation until his death.

His love for the house and the land oozed into his children by osmosis, and in their retirement years they all three have stayed close to the land. As he added daffodils, so do they. As he cared for the domestic livestock, so they care for the wildlife. As he pursued the cattle rustlers, so they pursue the men who poach deer, turkey and fish. As he cared for the "thrown-away" pets, so do his daughters.

Dad with our last thrown-away dog.

Our last throw-away dog came to us as a puppy and earned the name "Danny-might" because he might bite but probably would not. He stayed with Dad every day as he rebuilt Westover.

As the daughter who spent the most time on the land as an adult, I can walk the paths in my mind, see the creek crossings, the meadows, the oaks and persimmons. Today, however, instead of hearing the hounds from the possum hunts I hear the coyotes that run in packs in the night.

I can see the bookcase that replaced the outside door from the ballroom. It reached to the ceiling and held books whose leather covers cracked with age and whose pages, crisp with the years, held secrets of the past that lured me. The ballroom stretched the length of two rooms, its floor covered with a 30-foot-long rug. The Myrick dining table, opened to seat sixteen, extended more than half the length of the room. It bore the candlestick that Dad gave Mother for a wedding anniversary gift, now in possession of Lindsley Bramlett's children. Two windows on the north side of the room opened into the parlor; these had been outside windows when the house was built in 1822, and became "inside" when the ballroom was added in 1852.

We know the date of the addition only because of the fire. When Dad rebuilt after the fire, we found the date carved into the masonry of the southeastern chimney, just above ceiling height of the room.

Another window was closed when the ballroom was added. Rather than plaster over the window opening, however, the architect who handled the addition inserted behind the glass a painting of a sailboat drifting beneath a cloud; the cloud was the silhouette of Benjamin Jordan, the original owner of Westover.

Dad told us Jordan originally built the house as only a part-time residence, that his major objective was to provide a location for the members of the State Legislature to go to for quiet contemplation and conversations about the state's affairs. The gardens were laid out in such a way to invite casual strolling.

The Peachtree Garden Club of Atlanta, Georgia, published *Garden History of Georgia 1733-1933* in 1933, and the Westover gardens were among those selected. A copy of the diagram of the garden was framed and lay on a table just inside the front door, to the left, alongside a guest book that recorded all visitors since Luther had lived in the home. Thulia, his oldest daughter, has one of the guest books.

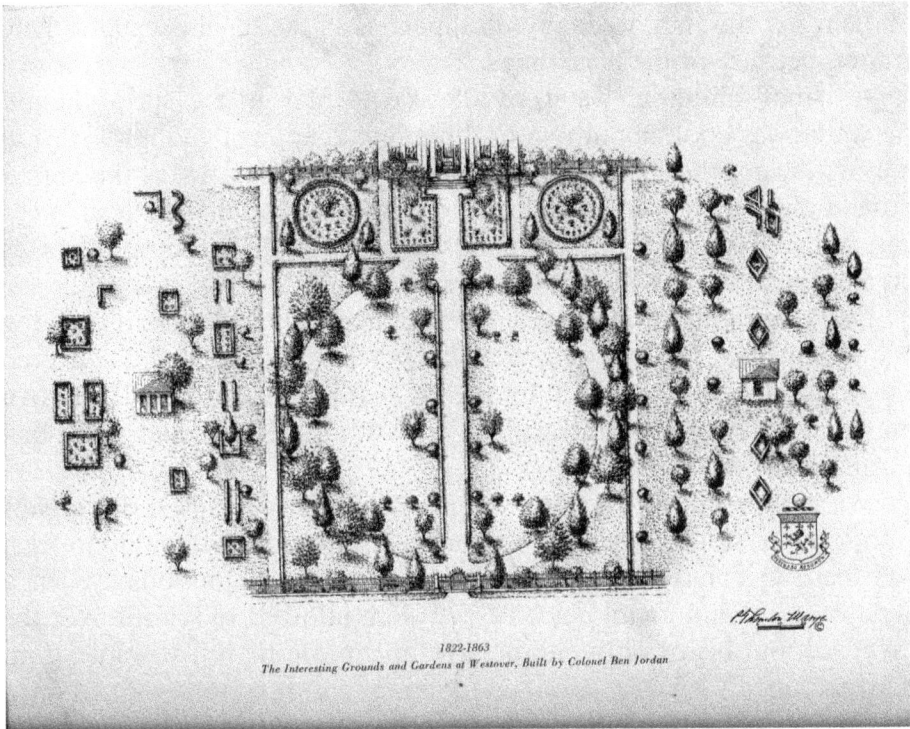

1822-1863
The Interesting Grounds and Gardens at Westover, Built by Colonel Ben Jordan

When Dad bought Westover, the boxwoods had been trimmed to about knee height by the resident goats. By the 1950s the hedges had grown to more than six feet in spite of the chickens that scratched out a nest or a dusting site at the roots.

Someone had planted wisteria on the east side of the house, and it had grown wild, rising into the trees and threatening the boxwood on that side of the yard. Wisteria draped the trees in the spring, and periwinkle ran over the ground. The area behind the wash house and smokehouse was a danger to bare feet, with rose bushes as tall the smoke house. One of the elms at the other (western) end of the yard carried a yellow rose vine into its upper limbs and spread gold onto the ground.

He had planned to have two small lily ponds in the back yard, between the house and the site of the original kitchen, and in our youth the two dug-out areas were clearly visible. We never saw them filled with water or flowers, however. But at the bottom of the hill, where the spring ran into the brick building for storage of milk and butter, he had dug out several fish ponds. We would take oatmeal down to feed the goldfish; but the fish gradually disappeared as the tenants caught them for food because of the hard times.

As small children, we were allowed to play in the spring house. The water was cool, about two or three feet deep, just enough for us to cool off during the heat of the summer. A few years later, the spring house replaced the yard well as our source of water, and lead pipes stretched across one of the fish ponds and up the hill, exposed in places that froze and burst in the hard winter freezes.

Dad often told of buying the plantation and shortly thereafter going back to Virginia. He told no one of the whiskey still he had discovered in the old kitchen. On his return, the kitchen had been burned, and two new graves had appeared in the slave graveyard. He did not share that information with the sheriff.

We wondered if all of the graves were those of slaves, or perhaps some Yankee soldier lay underground with those he had come to free. Was there a Yankee sword there? Maybe coins or buttons. When a friend came with a metal detector, we were allowed to scan it over the graveyard, but heard only one beep—for a piece of foil wrapper from chewing gun.

Dad said that the Yankees had not burned Westover because they camped there on their way from Atlanta to Savannah. Dad had closed up the bashed-out wall at the top of the stairs; he left a small opening to show that the Yankees were supposed to have knocked out the wall to get into the attic to look for the family's silver. That opening provided a door for the cats to go exploring, and one fell into a well in the wall. It landed at floor level under the stairs and yowled. It couldn't climb up, so a hole had to be bashed in the wall to get the cat out.

A slice out of the banister was supposed to have been made by a Yankee who wanted a souvenir from the house. The cut-out would have easily fit into a pocket.

Much of the original fencing still stood. Dad always said it had come from around the capitol building, but Thulia's research has been unable to confirm that as fact. After Bill Banks purchased the Blount House and moved it to Newnan, Georgia, he obtained Mother's permission to copy the gates to place in front of the house in Newnan. Later, unknown to the family, he shared these blueprints with the owners of Westville, a reproduction of an antebellum plantation home site in Lumpkin, Georgia. We discovered these copied gates when Thulia and Susan visited Westville in the 1980s. The Westville operators have since changed their gates.

Westover gates

On the east side of the yard stood the commissary, the wash house and the smoke house. Hog hams hung from the rafters in the smoke house, and the large salt box was used to cure other pork. Mother's canned goods lined the shelves, their sugar and/or salt keeping them from freezing. The dirt floor was a threat to bare feet because of broken glass that lay half-buried in the loose dirt.

Behind that row of buildings, at the edge of the hill, stood the outhouse, large enough for a "family gathering."

Under a shed on the south side of the smoke house was the generator that kept electricity flowing before the Rural Electric

Administration came to our county. Dad let it go to disrepair after we had the juice from the REA some twenty miles away.

Behind the old kitchen, the hillside was a jumble of red gullies. Beneath one of the slave houses, a mound of ground shows that the land around it has eroded almost three feet of topsoil since the house was built.

Luther and his help filled in a ditch he said was deep enough to bury a mule standing up. The land never saw a bulldozer. He then planted daffodils, the upper ten feet or so in rows; the rest of the area is a field of gold in spring. We call it "Wordsworth's Acre" in honor of the poem about the dancing daffodils.

Dad in Wordsworth's Acre. He always wore a hat outside.

To the south of Wordsworth's Acre lay more gullies, and these he worked on for many years, with the help of his children and at times a hired man. Mostly, however, he did the heavy work himself. He built terraces, planted azaleas in and along the gullies, even transplanted some of the Spanish bayonet that was a common yard plant on plantations. In the twenty-first century, these gullies are no more—they are a maze of flowers and shrubs, and the land is stable.

In 1948 (or 1949; the children aren't sure of the year), he damned up the creek that flowed from the Spring House and made a lake of about two acres. His love of flowers and history let him to plant five water lilies and five Egyptian lotus. Over the years, the lotus choked out the lilies and eventually, together with beavers, "killed" the lake.

But the children had a swimming hole to go to when their mother said "go jump in the lake," and because Lillas so loved frog legs, the daughters would go frog gigging and learned how to clean the frogs for her. After Luther's death, when Lillas was alone, it served as a source of recreation for her and her sister Susan Myrick on Sunday afternoons. Lillas learned to handle a fly rod as well as a "casting" rod, and she and Susan would catch dinner.

About 1933 Luther had a telephone at the house. We found the 1933 date in a letter from Dixon Williams who claimed he and C. S. Winn owned half of the "Meriwether telephone line" and offered to sell his interest for $25.00. Dad's reply (we have only his handwritten draft) stated that he would investigate at the courthouse how Williams had the right to run the line on one-fourth mile of his land and what judgments were against the line or the owners. "If there is no such record (of an easement) it will be difficult to judge to whom the line in the field in front of the house belongs." I found no record in the Baldwin County courthouse for any Meriwether Telephone Company or line, nor any record of an easement for such a line.

The line ran alongside the railroad, where years later we would find the glass connectors that, together with the poles, had fallen. Luther discontinued the telephone line because he said everybody in the neighborhood came to him to use the phone. Few of the neighbors respected his time—some knocked on the door in the middle of the night.

The Milledgeville-Eatonton train still runs at the foot of the hill, today carrying wood scraps and sawdust from the lumber mills, where it once carried passengers and later coal to the power plant. When the first railroad was to run from Milledgeville to Eatonton, Ben Jordan was a stockholder of the company, and he had his slaves lay the tracks on his land. He never deeded the land to the railroad, but the railroad seemed to think it owned the land, and Dad had to fight with the railroad to keep them from encroaching onto the land. Some eighty-five years later, daughters Thulia and Susan, through an attorney, had to remind the then owners that the property was never deeded to the railroad, as shown in this letter:

CENTRAL OF GEORGIA RAILWAY COMPANY
OFFICE OF LAND AND TAX COMMISSIONER

Ɔ. HORNE,
LAND AND TAX COMMISSIONER.

SAVANNAH, GA., October 26, 1960   dch-c-f

Dr. L. C. Lindsley
Meriweather Road
Milledgeville, Georgia

Dear Dr. Lindsley:

We refer to your letter of October 19, 1960, concerning title to Railway right of way through property of your ownership on the Covington District.

From Mile Post S-189 through Mile Post S-192, we hold title by prescription and claim to the toe of the fill or top of cut on the south side and to the overhang of the telephone poles on the north side, or to the toe of the fill or top, which ever may be farther from the center of the track.

From Mile Post S-192 through Mile Post S-194, our title is by prescription; however, in 1908, we set rail monuments 50' from the center line of the track on each side, and no question has ever been raised on this issue.

From Mile Post S-194 through Mile Post S-195, our title is the same as to Mile Post S-189 through 192.

We trust that this information will suffice.

Very truly yours,

Land and Tax Commissioner.

In his years, livestock had the right of way—be it horses on the road or cattle on the tracks. The train's "cattle catcher" did not "catch" the cattle; it kicked them off the track, usually fatally. The railroad paid for the cattle.

Appendix XI contains three parts. Articles about his purchase and future plans for Westover are reproduced in Appendix XI-A. Appendix XI-B is a bibliography of other articles and books about Westover. Appendix XI-C provides copies of records from the Library of Congress.

During the Great Depression, President Roosevelt's Historic American Building Survey hired architects to go around the states to blueprint and photograph historic homes and buildings. Westover was one of the homes selected. The pictures show how much work Luther had undertaken to restore the house.

**Westover, 1930s. We think the figures
on the porch are Lillas and daughter Thulia.**

Westover House   1822

Date of this snapshot is unknown.

PART V

LILLAS STANLEY MYRICK

LETTERS FROM OUR MYRICK FOREBEARS

From: Rebecca Lily Dowdell, sister-in-law of Stith Parham Myrick. (She married Rev. A. O. Stanley.) Perhaps Lillas's middle name Stanley came from this Great Aunt Lily.
To: James Dowdell Myrick, son of S. P. Myrick
Thulia is James's wife. Kate is probably Katie M. Barron.

Nov 30, 1901

1739 N. Meridian St.
Indianapolis

My dear James,

I returned to Indianapolis yesterday—so direct your letter hereafter to this place.

I rec'd dear Thulia's letter and appreciated it so much. And tell her I will write to her before a great while.

I am just writing now about a little business.

I want you to straighten out Mr. Chapman's note. Read it carefully and you will see it is made out for two (2) thousand lbs to give me an increase in 1903 and 1904, of 250 lbs in addition for each year. Do you know whether he gave me 1000 or 2000 for 1902? He calls it a 2 horse farm and you will know what one gets from that size farm. I wrote to Mr. Herring that I would send the note to you to get it fixed all right.

I would write more but I'm pushed for time just now but will write to Kate soon. Love for each of the dear family

Affec – Your Aunt Lily

* * *

The next letter, from Thulia Kate Whitehurst Myrick to her younger son Fullie, reveals the difficulties facing her after the death of her husband the previous year. The now-all-female family was living in town, and Dovedale was a long twelve miles away. Georgia produced a record crop of cotton in 1922, and the price per pound dropped. The volume produced at Dovedale, however, did not increase. Cotton was the major income from Dovedale, but the family was far from destitute.

In *The Story of the Myricks*, Allie wrote of James Dowdell Myrick's death "he left sufficient estate, without the sacrifice of the Myrick lands, to support his family and send the five younger children through college." This estate provided the funds for the move to town and the purchase of the house on Liberty Street.

Susan had begun her first teaching job, as a "scholarship teacher" at Georgia Normal and Industrial College in Milledgeville and lived at home. Jim lived and worked in Baltimore and the wedding was probably planned for there. Fullie had dropped out of Georgia Tech to help out at home when his father died, but returned to school the next fall.

"Miss Kate," however, was thrifty, and Allie referred to her as "an astute business woman."

Oct 24, (19)11

Dear Fullie,

I am heart sick today and not feeling very joyous or brave. The price of cotton depresses me with so many expenses to meet. The poor quality of cotton the negroes here brought in for rent is terrible and Bob Nullis brought a bale today that brought 6 ¢.

Jim and I went out home Saturday. Almost every negro told us how bad the conditions of their houses and Geo Scogins and his wife are about to part and give up their farm.

Well, I'll not tell you all these unpleasant things, still I know you wish to be in touch with finances at home.

Susan's salary will about pay for her shoes and hats, and the rent may or may not bring 6 ¢; I am holding for a while any way.

Jim has decided not to have any of us at the wedding—just have a very private affair; so if you can wait till Spring for your good clothes, do so. The grey suit that Papa wore is here. I want you to see if you can use it when you come home.

I am sending check for $20.00.

I am glad you are busy if you can be well and do good work. Any thing you can do that will help your fellow man (illegible) may be a part of your work.

If you can get home to the YM Association we shall be glad.

> Your loving
> Mother

*   *   *

All other letters are to Lillas from her mother Thulia Katherine Whitehurst Myrick:

To Lillas Myrick, 955 Pleasant St., Boulder, Colorado

Postmark Jun 27, 1928

Dear Lilla,

It has been more than a week since Sue mailed you the Certified check—Surely you have rec'd it or else we will notify the bank & mail or telegraph you another.

Also, as soon as you reached Col. I mailed your entire mail (Gen. Delivery) containing a G.S.C.W. envelope supposed to be a check.

We were thrilled over the tel. announcing "Big Brother's" arrival (probably James D. Myrick, Jr., Lillas's older brother) last Sat.

Allie has plans to spend Aug. at Camp near Lake Erie with her husband at wonderful rates.

Rumors are prevailing that Scott is in line for Pres. Dr. Beeson is in the dark & still thinks "not Scott," but what does he know?

Sue is still at home. She is "crackers" over reporter's work & would love to quit her profession & take up journalism.

You must be in need of cash unless it has arrived. My summer school roomers are quiet, well behaved women. No such luck, I fear, next year.

**Sue enclosed the pictures so you can have a good laugh.
Love,**

Mother

*   *   *

June 24/28

In the same envelope, a second letter from her mother to Lillas, also
dated June 24, 1928. "Big Boy" probably refers to her older son James
Dowdell Myrick, Jr.

Dear Lil,

  **A tel(egraph) announces the coming of "Big Boy" on June 12!
We were in the midst of a party that Sue was giving to the visitors
in town when received. The Allen's had three guests. Marguerite
Parks is here & Frances Herring still at home. Cat Beeson here for
the summer, Florence Andrews at home.**
  **It rained "cats and dogs" and they had to be provided with
komonas, dresses, shoes to get to cars. The party was a success, but
ended in a mess.**
  **Sue is ready for any emergency & thus everybody laughed &
enjoyed the worst of it.**
  **I have "Merry & Cherry" with me. (These were Dicken's
characters & made it funny). Merry Roadhouse, Mrs. Cherry are
their real names. No trouble & $4.00 for one room together.
Everybody (is) trying to rent rooms. It must be wonderful to see
Pike's Peak. Mr. Scott was conferred Dr.'s degree by University
which makes him eligible for Pres. The wind may blow any way.**
  Write soon,

Mother.

Dr. Beeson was named president of GSCW in June 1928, probably about the time that Thulia Kate wrote this letter.

* * *

Nov 29, 1929

Dear Lil,

Liz Gwinn is back for Thanksgiving & came in to see me this morning. Also, Estelle Carnes & Cornelia Chappel came in for a little visit. Miss Rogers asked me to room two old girls and they are here for the week end. But never again! They have beaux from Gray Ga and the whole business is tacky. Besides it has turned cold & they keep two fires.

Would you like me to make the green satin dress longer (& how much longer). It does not look so bad. I would not mind to fix it longer.

Allie and I went to Macon to buy me a coat, but did not find one I really liked. She found a brown one for herself.

Clare and Louise Green are at home for the holidays. (They are daughters of Cousin Ella Green, often called "Cousin Ella" or "Kunella.")

Mr. Massey, out at (the) country store, was buried Thursday. The services were <u>very</u> early so that everybody could go to the Foot Ball game. How is that for (an) "up to date" town?

Old Mr. Stembridge is critically ill.

Poor Miss Barnett has decided to give up work till after Xmas & stay at Minnies. She has a horror of being deaf.

No further news from John Key. He will have to do better if he stays on. Sol sold the cows & brought me some money.

No tenant for home place.

I am sending Al & Katie's letters.

I hope you will not let your ears or feet freeze. And you are wise in deciding not to stay for 12 weeks summer school, and you can get French and German at Emory or Mercer. Six weeks. And please do not plan to teach here unless you really wish to do so. I miss you of course, but I get along fine.

Look out for the best you can get & look forward to home & vacation.

Love
Mother

*   *   *

Dec. 16/29

My dear Lilla,

I am sending your Christmas gift first of all—you know that old saying about the "one that is fartherest away" that is you. (She told her children that she loved best the one that was fartherest away.)

I've wrapped it in a nice piece of paper so it will not look like just an ordinary enclosure. It might turn out to be a dinner dress longer than your pink one—or it might turn out to be anything that you wish more than a dress. Any way, I hope it will help make you a Merry Christmas. Of course I shall buy Sue a goblet and Al is giving her one too.

You will have to settle down so as to start your own hope chest of silver by another year.

Miss Tuttle continues very ill at hospital with no chance of recovery though she may last some time partly paralyzed. She told me she had an old friend at Minneapolis City. Miss Brown in Home Ec Dept, teacher.

Miss Barnett improves slowly at Minnies. Her ears are involved & she fears a throat operation.

All trade is dull here, and no sale for (illegible word Brucer?) yet.

With you and Miss Barnett away I do not get much College news. Mrs. Lucas has been removed to Parks Memorial, there being no room at City Hospital.

Frances Bell is coming home next week. In fact the whole family is expected. Another baby house party as you may recall a former one.

Lots of love and please do not get out in zero weather without plenty of wraps.

Fondly,
Mother

*   *   *

Capt Bowden is Allie's husband.
Josie is her sister, Josephine Whitehurst Rozar. Lillas and her children referred to her as "Aunt Josie."

From her mother:

Sunday night, Jan 12, 1930

Dear Lilla,

I reached home on the bus from Augusta tonight after a week's visit to Allie.

Capt (Bowden) came over, he said for a day's hunting, but really to take me over for a little visit since we failed to get over for the holidays. He also drove over to Augusta this morning and I came from there on the bus. Sue could not get over as her work carried her elsewhere.

Your letter was forwarded there and I enjoyed it. The tray and teapot will certainly be used for my very much beloved and longed for <u>special visitor</u> this summer. I do not really think you should work 12 weeks this summer! Too much work is not the fastest way to get a Ph.D.

Poor Mrs. Tuttle seems to improve physically somewhat at City Hospital but no hope of mental activity and as she has no family will probably land at State Sanitarium in (the) near future. I enjoyed every minute at Allie's. The boys at Bailey are much like GMC (boys). Allie took me to her Episcopal tea and a banquet at Bailey for the College girls in town. All of it enjoyable.

Excuse this paper and pencil. I know you wanted to hear from me & I have not written in so long.

I'll be writing again soon & jotting down some news items. You see I am writing very disconnected after the trip & supper with Josie. She sends love & says will write you soon.

Worlds of love,
Mother

* * *

Katie is seventh child
"Cat" is Dr. Beeson's daughter. He (Dr. B) was president of GSCW
Walls and Hall couple, friends
Merry, the maid/cook
Edwin Jr., Allie's son
Lena is wife of her elder son Jim
"Jessie" probably another local friend
Tippie, her second child
Stella, Tippie's daughter
From her mother

Aril 25/30

Dear Lil,

    Katie had dinner (6 o'clock) with the Beesons yesterday. Cat is home. Also the Walls, Frances Hall & her husband. Dr. B related with great delight your attainments. Hurrah for Lil! The children are darling. Of course (illegible) for their happiness, about 5 meals per day which takes up most of the time. Merry cooks & a little girl comes after 3 in the afternoon to keep them.

    Edwin Jr. is the best boy in Ga! He is never cross or unruly & played with the children like a big boy should. The plan for sale of Brucer fell through but I am on another try. "Never say die" is my motto.

    Lena is returning to Bal(timore) for hospital observation. She evidently has something bad the matter.

    Jessie's father died suddenly at supper table.

    "Hassie" comes back as head of Dept. Miss Barnett still under treatment for ears. Miss Thrash ill with stomach trouble. Tippie much better. Stella went home with Al for week end. The "Bailey boys" gave her the rush.

      Love
        Mother

LILLAS STANLEY MYRICK PHOTOGRAPHS

Lillas, about age three.

Lillas Myrick, the flapper

Lillas, several pictures as a gad-about

Lillas and friend at GSCW campus

Lillas, the farmer, in front of the house on Liberty Street

Lillas, the future mom, in front of the family home on Liberty Street. The doll is now in possession of Thulia Bramlett. It is one of two that traveled with Lillas when she left home for college.

Lillas Myrick models the dress worn by Benjamin Harvey Hill's mother. Lillas's great-grandmother was twin sister to the dress's owner. Hill was a State Senator (Georgia), a U. S. Representative, a U. S. Senator, and a Confederate Senator. As a State Senator, he had opposed secession. Hill is one of the Myrick family's favorite relatives who is not in the direct family line.

Lillas was born on Dovedale Plantation, in northwest Baldwin County, Georgia, on November 11, 1900, the youngest of eight children. (See Appendix II-B for family portraits and family buildings.) Like her siblings, she ran barefooted across the plantation.

Much of her early life is given in **Susan Myrick of Gone With the Wind** by Susan Lindsley, and the Myrick genealogy in **The Story of the Myricks** by Allie Myrick Bowden.

After the death of James Dowdell Myrick, his widow Thulia Katherine moved to Milledgeville where she reared the four daughters still at home. After a few months in a temporary home, she purchased the house on Liberty Street still known as the Myrick House.

On her thirteenth birthday, young Lillas wrote an "illustrated letter" to her brother Fullilove. Note that she dated the letter October 11 rather than November 11. She often mentioned that her birthday was a national holiday—the country celebrated Armistice Day, the end of World War I.

*   *   *

Uncle Good is Goodwin Myrick, brother of her father James Dowdell Myrick. Lizzie is Goodwin's wife.

Uncle Cincy is Cincinnatus Whitehurst, brother of Lillas's mother. Nan is Cincy's daughter who lived with Lillas's family for several years.

Milledgeville, Ga.
Oct. 11, 1913.

Dear Jullie,

As I have no studying to do I thought I would write you a short little letter.

Aunt Lizzie and Uncle Good were here to 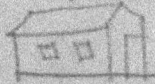 Fri.

Uncle Lucy sent  last mon. They put the  under the 🏠. and we play 👧 🧑 in it.

we have fun playing in it. but

Katie and Nan think they are most two old to play.

I'm sewing we have made a and a . We have just started on a .

Mr. M. S. Bell was shot at last night in the . The think it was a (notice the eyes)

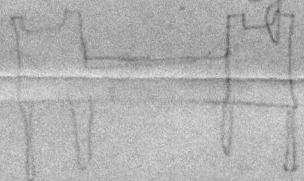

Cousin Sophy sent us some by aunt Sithy

Sat. night we had a hard
wind and just lots of ⬭ fell.
Sun. morning we had a little
snow. We were coming from sunday
school when it began.

The circus was here 31st
they gave us half holiday. When
the

came by we got to see it but
after it over we had to come
back and go on with our
lessons. We went over and sat
on the ~~porch~~ over at the
mansion. The parade was
not very good, I did not
go the circus but miss Barne
did she said, It was fine,
at (J) Sat miss Tait said,
she had an announce to
made. She told us if we
would stay 10 min longer
we would not after come
back that evening because
of the rain.
Constance Day is
going to have a

3.

partywed, I aw evvited,

came

to see us Sun might, mamma was at church, He is, going to take allie to Gordon to spend Thanksgiving.

I am 13 t day. Yestaday Katie and I made some birthday candy. While

 and  played tennis. I and eating same now.

Caro is at aunt Paulines. She is coming to see us wed.

mamma said, she wonders
why you dont write.

Hope 2 C U B 4 L ___
Your sis,
Lil.

P. S.

How do you do ?

At some point in her youth, she wrote a short story (in long hand), which is given in Appendix XII.

Lillas appears to have been a "sight for the sore eyes of the boys," because of the letters she received at different times. The earliest one we have is from Harvey Jones:

U.S. Barracks.
Sept. 24, 1917
Dear Lillas: --
How are you enjoying your school days at dear old GNJ? (GNIC: Georgia Normal and Industrial College, Milledgeville) **Know you are having some grand time. I <u>shore</u> am (Exercise slang.)**
Saw you on the street this afternoon sure did want to stop and

talk to you, but knew there was nothing doing. I go to town every day just to see you. Know I can't talk to you but it does me so much good to see you. You just can't imagine how much good it does me to see you.

Say, can't you send me a little picture of yourself so I can put it in my watch? I will certainly appreciate it and also a nice letter.

Respectfully,

Harvey Jones

Lillas entered Georgia Normal and Industrial College (GN&IC) in 1917 as a student in the teachers college and graduated in1920. She remained at GN&IC for two more years and was a member of the first class to receive a degree in 1922.

In her papers are three letters from a gentleman—student probably—at the Georgia Military College. Even town girls attending GSCW were not allowed to date or associate with "boys."

These three letters are on GMC letterhead notepaper.

Feb 2, 1920

Dear Miss Myrick—

For goodness sake stop looking at me so. Girl, don't you know a boy can't stand those be-witching looks. I'm no exception either. When you look at me that way I want to talk to you so bad I don't know what to do. Isn't that natural???

Listen, I'd like to know you better. I want to write to you and come to see you some time if you'll let me. I'd like it <u>very</u>　<u>very</u> much. Can that be possible? Here's hoping I can have a chance to become acquainted better.

It already seems that I know you but that's not enough "C."

Listen won't you write me real soon and tell me?

Be sweet,

　　Lovingly,

　　　　Oliver Montgomery

* * *

Feb 8, 1920

Dearest Lilla,

I sure was charmed to get your letter. It's the kind that I like to get from girls.

Well, now to begin with, I'm going to plainly state a fact. I'm coming to your house Fri night, where ever it is, provided I'm not in the casualty list (delinquent). That will be alright won't it. I'll find out somewhere where you live. I've just <u>got</u> to come to see you, "C."

It was a case of love at first sight in this case. I guess we'll know each other better next Saturday morning won't we.

Girl, the thought of you has been with me ever since I first saw you and I'm simply <u>crazy</u> to see you. I mean where we can talk. Those smiles just run me <u>crazy</u>. I can't explain it at all.

You know it's a shame we haven't ever met before isn't it. I believe I'll love you more the more I see of you. So let's hurry and become better acquainted, hear?

I guess I'll see you at the game Tuesday night, won't I?

I'll have to close.
> Yours
> Oliver

Be sure to tear this up just as soon as you read it.
> ORM.

* * *

Sunday night

My <u>dearest</u> friend,

I sure was disappointed when I got your letter saying that I could not come to your house Friday night. I wanted to come <u>so</u> bad. But listen, may I come next Friday night. If I can't come then, when can I? I passed by our house this afternoon but didn't see you anywhere. Wish I could have been in the car this afternoons with <u>you</u>. Wouldn't we have spread joy. In my opinion we <u>would</u>.

The girl that I was looking at at church today is my sister. I guess you know her don't you?

You bet I wish I could have been with you when you made that candy. I'm a pretty good hand at making fudge myself. I'm sure both of us <u>together</u> could make some <u>mighty</u> <u>good</u> candy.

Listen, Lillas, we've just <u>got</u> to arrange some way whereby we can meet. I've gotten to where I love you even tho I don't know you personally. You know I'm in a fix. Can't you suggest some way to meet.

I can just see those <u>eyes</u> now. You have such enchanting eyes.

Well sweet dreams (about me). I'm going to dream of you tonight. I just feel that way.

Lovingly,
Oliver.

She spent the 1920-1921 term at Columbia and then came home to Milledgeville and GSCW where she earned her B.S. degree in 1922. She became an instructor in chemistry at GSCW that fall and continued at that position though 1924.

On January 1, 1924, another possible "boy friend" wrote her. We don't have a name other than John, Johnnie and Jack, which he entered into the letter itself. The letter is not "romantic," but is very chatty about friends and their "doings," and the writer refers to Ithaca. We do not have the complete letter. He may have been a friend from Columbia who later attended Cornell, and their friendship led her there in 1925.

A poem she saved was hand-written on a sheet of notebook paper. It was apparently from one of the men she dated. We have no info about when it was written or the individual who wrote it.

ILLUSIONS

I made her whom I loved to be a tree
And round its splendid towering
I twined a vine of hope whose leaves were faith.
So I of human frailty did make entirety.
But when the bitter wind of need blew hard and merciless

Then with the crashing of my tree, my heart was crushed.
My soul lay hurt, a wounded thing hurt by her dreams.

I made her whom I loved to be a sea
A deep, storm-tossed, tempestuous sea.
So I of human shallowness did make the deep.
Thus when the black, o'erwhelming storm of huge despair
Seized pitiless on my heart and conquered all her strength,
When I would fain seek out my sea,
Its endless depth to drown my hurt within
I found it surface waves and all inadequacy.

Summer months found her away at graduate schools: Columbia (again), Cornell (1925), Colorado (1928), and University of Minnesota (school term 1929-1930).

She returned to Columbia University in 1924-1925 as a senior. She was awarded a Bachelor of Science on February 25, 1925. She stayed on at Columbia through the summer session and was awarded a Master of Science degree on October 28, 1925. Her major field of study was "Practical Science."

Luther was teaching summer school at Columbia in 1925, while Lillas was a student there, and we can only wonder if perhaps they did meet and she told him about GSCW and the potential vacancy there for the head of the chemistry department.

While at Columbia, she attended social functions at some of the Ivy League colleges, especially Yale. And fell in love with a Yale man named "Rex." We have no last name for him, but we have correspondence. She visited Yale, and he visited her in New York.

The first two poems her were on Yale Graduate Club stationery.

SHY LILLAS

She's blithe and gay,
And sweet and neat,
And has a sparkling eye;
She's not effete
But quite petite
And oh! So very shy!

She bobs her hair
And tints her cheek
And casts a roving eye;
She's never late—
Quite up-to-date
But oh, So very shy!

She wears the latest
Things in hose—
Things that make me sigh.
Silk underthings
Of blue and gold.
Would you say she's shy?

She doesn't mind
To bum a ride
From the city's rim through Rye
And on thru Stamford
Clear to Yale
Oh how very shy!

She dances in
The Pirates Den,
And makes the minutes fly;
But don't forget
And don't regret—
She's shy, oh <u>very</u> shy.

In the envelope with the poems to her was this draft of a letter. Maybe she typed it, or maybe she never sent it.

I'm glad you think me cute! But what did I unconsciously answer in my last letter before I received your letter—you do so get my curiosity aroused—

Please don't plan on my coming in August. It really is too good to be true. I'm coming if I can. I've written Duke about taking work there and if I can get what I want I'll try it out. I can't make any definite plans yet.

I'm afraid (two illegible words) report the girls field day and the po' things are having a terrible time. I'm not letting anybody know I was there.

This poem was untitled.

When Lillas said she loved me
The harp that, muted, lay
Abandoned by the lonely way
Was swept by love-winds
From afar. And strings that knew
The silence of despair, attuned
To whispers from the heart of her
Now pulsed with life and breathed
The Song of Songs: the hymn
That drew Leander through the waves
To clasp Hero, his love; the hymn
That touched the aching heart
Of Abelard and thrilled poor Heloise.
But can the lover's tongue supply
The word the poets seek in vain?
Or is the song too mighty?
Oh, if to human lips Love's Deity
Can give the power, tell me the Secret,
And let my cloven tongue convey
Love's melody. Oh, let me learn
To be the troubadour.

The next poem was hand written on paper stock that appears to be the same as that on which the two previous poems were written. The handwriting is the same, but the paper lacks the Hartford Graduate Club letterhead.

COMING TO YOU

Coming to you! You cannot know
How much it means to me!
Between us lie so many things—
Fields of corn, parched by the sun,
Forests, roads and bridges

Tunnels piercing mountains—
Rivers winding endlessly
Across and though them all
The steel rails push their way,
Signals flash and whistles warn,
And mighty engines throb and sway
Through sleeping towns and villages,
Bringing me to you!

Coming to you! Three little words
That mean so much to me!
For days with you are golden days,
Brightened by your nearness;
And nights with you are starry nights
Though every star be hid.
Oh, let us love and strive to reach
Love's fullness! For love is life,
And life without it barren.
That's why through busy cities,
Through fields and waving forests,
The steel rails push their way
And mighty engines throb and sway—
I'm coming, Dear, to You.

"Rex"

The poem below was written on letterhead from the Department of History, Dartmouth College. So we wonder if "Rex" were a student, a teacher's assistant, or a professor of history.

ODE TO A DIMPLED KNEE

Well may I sing of ruby lips
And eyes of blue or brown,
Well may I sing of golden hair,
My true love's fairy crown.

But when the summer breezes blow

And waft o'er land and sea,
I 'most forget her other charms
And sing her dimpled knee.

O Muse, Awake and tune my harp!
Inspire a sweeter tone;
Fain would I sing a deathless song
When Lillas rolls her own.

For why lament with gobs of gloom
Dame Fashion's stern decree,
When I can see, if Fate is king,
My true love's dimpled knee?

UNTITLED

I asked of Love's muse that I might sing a song,
    A song that would thrill my True Love today.
But she wouldn't oblige—she's treating me wrong—
    The words sort of come—and then fly away!

But I have a scheme, and I hope it will serve;
    I'll send her the songs that <u>some</u> muse inspired;
They're really not mine—no praise I deserve;
    I'll have to admit that they're just kind of hired.

(signed) Rex

Rex appears to have been an artist as well as a poet. With these letters, Lillas kept two hand-drawn pictures, which are the same except for shading. Each is an original, but neither is signed.

Apparently the relationship began to fall apart. Lillas wrote this letter, but we don't know if she ever sent it. What we have is a draft, and a portion of it has a diagonal line struck through it.

Lest you forget me, I am writing this. I imagine that the realization that one was forgotten by one who means so much as you do to me would drive one to drink or maybe even worse. Then for the sake of being a law-abiding citizen I'll get to keep informing you that I'm still existing when I'm not near you and living some times, when I hear from you.

If you had been in M'ville and understood how not more than one event takes place in (the) course of 12 months you could rightly understand the wonderfulness of my knowing you. Here where I work all day for the pleasure of sleeping that night, I sometimes

forget that there are more glorious pleasures than sleeping until along comes a letter from you and wakes me to the realization that life can hold all the wonders of Paradise.

I know that you do not love me as much as I do you and never will, but you have come to mean so much to me that I am going to make one big effort and that is no complete loss, for I will have at least a memory that will be far sweeter than any realities most people know.

NOTE: Remainder of letter has a penned slash through it.

The divinity that gave the gift of abilities forgot to give me the ability to express a single thought of mine. But she did give me a double portion of heart to feel and could you read this heart of mine you'd find -----------(her blank) and nothing else there.

I'm wishing—not this day alone, but all future days, shall be jeweled with joy and that no cloud shall shut the sunshine from your view—mostly because I love you.

* * *

Lillas remained at GSCW for the fall-winter-spring quarters to teach chemistry.   She was an instructor 1922-1924, an assistant professor 1925-1927, an associate professor 1927-1931, and acting head of the chemistry department for the term 1928-1929.

She took a leave of absence for the term 1929-1930 to attend the University of Minnesota to work on her doctorate.

In a March 10, 1927, report to the Board of Directors of GSCW, Dr. Beeson, newly appointed president, stated:

It is not possible for me to teach my classes in Chemistry and do the administrative work of the College.—I gave Assistant Professor Lillas Myrick my classes. I had her especially prepared at Columbia and Cornell to do this advanced work in case the need should arise. Miss Myrick is carrying the work well, and I recommend that she be given additional compensation of one hundred dollars this year for this larger responsibility.

In the school year ending in 1928, she was acting head of the chemistry department at Georgia State College for Women in Milledgeville. As department chair, she added "Advanced General Chemistry" to the schedule of courses.

As a teacher and as an individual, she enjoyed fun. She wrote a poem as an invitation to a party on October 24, 3 p. m., to be held at Nesbitt's Woods, a picnic spot on college grounds (the area has been denuded of trees, paved, and is now a parking lot, a dorm, and a Center). It read:

> **Come, oh come where the cyanides silently flow**
> **And the carbonates droop on the oxides below.**
> **Where the rays of potassium glow on the hill**
> **And the song of the silicates never is still.**
> **Come, oh come, tumi-ti-tum**
> **Peroxide of soda and uranium.**

When one of her students fell asleep in class, she dismissed the others early and warned them to exit quietly, not to wake up the classmate. A student, in passing, poked the sleeper and woke her.

When she was helping a freshman student register for classes one fall term, she did as the student asked: "I have to take chemistry, but please schedule me for anyone other than Miss Myrick. I hear she's really hard." The next quarter, the student had to take her class, but Miss Myrick never mentioned that student's request.

Her youngest daughter, her namesake, was planning to attend summer school in 1955, but fell from the roof of the cottage where the family lived after Westover burned. She had climbed onto the roof to cover the old wood-burning-stove pipe. When asked why daughter Lil did not register for summer school, she told her friends at the college library (Virginia Satterfield and Betty Ferguson) that Lil had "fallen off the roof" (a Southern expression at the time for a girl having her monthly period). Betty and Virginia both looked shocked. "Was it the first time?" one asked. "Yes, and I hope it's the last," Lillas answered. After sitting on the steps of the library, laughing, she went back inside and explained what had happened.

We have two pictures of her from the ***Spectrum***, the GSCW annual, from her teaching years.

LILLAS BUILDS HER CAREER, HEADS NORTH

In response to a telegram from Lillas Myrick, J. F. McClendon, Professor of Physiological Chemistry at the University of Minnesota, wrote her on September 13, 1929. He wrote that teaching fellowships and assistantships were filled, and went on at length about other positions that were filled.

Perhaps the personal letter from the president of GSCW influenced him:

GEORGIA STATE COLLEGE
FOR WOMEN
MILLEDGEVILLE, GEORGIA

OFFICE OF THE PRESIDENT

August 5, 1929

COPY

Dean Graduate School
University of Minnesota
Minneapolis, Minnesota

Dear Sir:

I have your letter of August 1 relative to Miss
Lillas Stanley Myrick of Milledgeville, Georgia.

I have known Miss Myrick since her early childhood.
She is a young woman of unusual ability, reliable and depend-
able, and a fine young woman in every way. I am sending you
a college catalogue which gives you an account of her preparation and work. Miss Myrick has been acting head of the department of Chemistry since I vacated the headship two and one-
half years ago, and she has made a splendid success of the
work. If she had had the Ph.D. degree, I would have made her *permanent*
head of the department of Chemistry. This is the highest com-
pliment I can pay her as a woman, as an executive, and as a
chemist.

Miss Myrick is entirely worthy of a fellowship in
your institution, and I assure you that she would make good
use of her opportunities. She has been teaching Food Nutrition
Chemistry and is in need of the kind of work which you offer
in the Medical School of the University of Minnesota and the
Mayo Foundation.

Any courtesies which you may be able to show Miss
Myrick will be very much appreciated.

Very truly yours,

J. L. Beeson,

JLB:B   President.

Professor McClendon continued in his letter:

...the only reason we have vacancy now is that our research
assistant resigned last month in order to take another position. At
present there would be only $500.00 for nearly nine months but
you could help a little in the summer school and obtain $200 for
that work.

We have been working on the ovarian hormone besides doing a
little work on iodine analyses. We have a man applying for this

place but I would rather have a woman in this case for the work on the ovarian hormone. Furthermore, this man has not had quite as much training in chemistry as you have had.

...There are no formalities to be gone through except a letter in case you wish to accept the position and you would be paid $30 every two weeks and you could adjust your working hours to suit the schedule of your classes. Furthermore you can use some of the results obtained in this research for a thesis.

...In case you accept, let me know what train you will arrive on and I will meet you. Graduate students try to arrive about Sept 23 or soon after to arrange their work.

She left GSCW for Minnesota in the fall of 1929, when Luther Lindsley came to GSCW that fall to take over as chair of the chemistry department. Her students at GSCW in Milledgeville gave her a sendoff, as reported in the student newspaper, the *Colonnade*:

From The Colonnade

FAREWELL HIKE

An event of Monday afternoon was a farewell hike given in honor of Miss Lillas Myrick by the Majors in the Chemistry Department. For two years Miss Myrick has been acting head of the Chemistry Department. It was with much regret that these girls bid her farewell before work on her Doctor's Degree. Those attending the hike included the chemistry faculty of G. S. C. W. and the Majors in that department.

You didn't tell me you was honor guest —

In searching for information on her stay at the University of Minnesota, we have found only her listing in both faculty and student directories, and her transcript which shows course work for her doctorate and her credit hours and grades:

Fall 1929 courses:
>   **Physiology 103   Physiology 8 hours (illegible)**
>   **Physiology 201 Phys. Seminar   1 hr. A**
>   **Physiology 205   Phy. Ch. Research 10 hrs. A**

Winter 1930 courses:
>   **Ag. Biology 202 Seminar in biochem. 1 hr. auditor**
>   **Physiology 205 P. Ch. Research 10 hrs. A**
>   **Ag. Biology 116 Advanced Animal Nutrition   auditor**
>   **Physiology 100   Phys & Path chem. 5 hrs. A**
>   **Ag. Bio. 112 Biochemistry Auditor**

Spring 1930 courses
>   **Physiol. 205 Research 10 hrs. A**
>   **Physiol. 101 Physiol. Chemistry 5 hrs. A**
>   **Biochem. 202 Seminar 1 h. Satis.**

While in Minnesota, she performed research on ovarian hormone and metabolism, and her results were published in the *American Journal of Physiology* with her as second author and Professor McClendon (department chair) as first author. See Appendix XIII for the article. This research would have been the basis for her dissertation, which the memo below shows that her proposal had been approved.

UNIVERSITY OF MINNESOTA
GRADUATE SCHOOL
MINNEAPOLIS

OFFICE OF THE DEAN

May 14, 1930

Miss Lillas Myrick
Sanford Hall

Dear Miss Myrick,

the last meeting of the Executive Faculty your
Thesis was approved and the following Committee appointed Dean.

ain responsibility for the development of
the The of course, upon the Adviser, who is chairman.
I sugges ever, that when your problem is well in hand,
you talk r your aims, methods, and results briefly with
the other members of the Committee. You understand that it
is the rule of the Graduate School that the report of this
Committee must be unanimous, as to the acceptability of your
Thesis.

Guy Stanton Ford, Dean.
Committee. Profs. McClendon (chairman), Burr, Gortner,
Randall and Kendall.

Her work on iodine became the subject of a feature article, which is given in Appendix XIV.

We do not know why she had a copy of the graduation program for the October 1930 ceremonies at the University of Minnesota, for she had returned to GSCW in the fall of that year. Perhaps a friend was being graduated and sent her a copy. Because she saved it, we have saved it also and it is among the family papers at Georgia College and State University (formerly Georgia State College for Women) in Milledgeville.

GOING HOME FROM MINNESOTA

Lillas, in her typical fashion for fun, which she never outgrew, wrote of her trip home in the car she affectionately called Tinker Bell. We believe she returned to Milledgeville in the summer of 1930 and returned to the faculty of GSCW that fall. The story became a printed narrative that was sent to her family one Christmas. Her travel companions were two dolls and a hand-cranked record player that she swore played "backwards" when she made certain turns. See Appendix

XV for her tall tale of the trip.

LILLAS AT GSCW

When Luther came to Georgia State College for Women, Lillas Myrick had been acting chairman of the chemistry department. She left for Minnesota, and he was appointed department chairman and found Westover. He stayed in Milledgeville. In later years he admitted he'd rather have been teaching only, not worrying over the administrative duties that fell to him as chairman.

Lillas returned to Milledgeville and to the faculty of the college the fall of 1930. They expanded the chemistry courses from nine courses to sixteen.

When Lillas planned a trip to Virginia the summer of 1931, Luther wrote a letter of introduction:

GEORGIA STATE COLLEGE

DEPARTMENT OF CHEMISTRY   MILLEDGEVILLE, GA.   June 18, 1931

Dear Miss "Pinkie,"

This will introduce to you Miss Myrick, a member of my department of Chemistry who is on her way to the University, and who wants to see Williamsburg.

Can you arrange for her to meet some of our people and see their homes? She is one of Georgia's best.

Love to Everybody.

Sincerely,

L C Lindsley

In October 1932, when Lillas's mother died, Luther served as a pall bearer. A year later, Patty Love, his first wife, died in October, after a long illness. During that time, some of his academic work load had to have been picked up by Lillas.

Shortly thereafter, Luther listed his assets and potential disposition. The entire listing is given in Appendix XVI. His leaving supervision of his home and lands to Lillas Myrick showed his respect and confidence in her. He also recognized that she would care for his pets. The list reflects as well his deep affection for the college itself.

To Miss Lillas Myrick my 1932 Chevrolet and my dog Penny and my cockerel "Ripley."
The balance of the cash from insurance and from various kinds of paper, I leave in trust for the upkeep of the Plantation and for the purpose of Cancer Research (illegible) Lillas Myrick of the Department of Chemistry of the Georgia State College for Women cooperating with the Medical College at Augusta and the State Sanatorium.

This mutual trust and respect evolved, and Luther and Lillas were married in June 1934.

Unfortunately, Lillas ran into a salary problem. Although she was on a 12-month contract, that is, her pay was to be in 12 monthly installments although she was not scheduled to teach summer school, when she married, the salary checks stopped. (See Appendix XVII.) The State never paid her for those months (June-August). She and Luther fought for that income for years, doing battle with GSCW, the State Board of Regents, and even a couple of governors. But to no avail.

Luther often told the story of how he almost didn't make it to the wedding. That story is excerpted here from *Blue Jeans and Pantaloons in Yesterplace*, which contains much more information about Lillas Myrick. See also *Myrick Memories* for more information on Lillas, her love of laugher, and her devotion to Luther and his dreams.

PART VI

THE WEDDING AND LIFE TOGETHER

THE WEDDING

(**From** *Blue Jeans and Pantaloons in Yesterplace*)

The sun blazed into Russell Auditorium that June day as the faculty filed in, clad in caps and gowns more suited to frosty mornings than brinjin hot summer days in middle Georgia.

Dad was in the line, impatient for the commencement ceremonies to be over long before they began, for over at my Great Aunt Josie's, Mother waited. They would be married as soon as Dad escaped his professorial duties at the Georgia State College for Women. They had planned the wedding carefully, based on the time for faculty and students to march in, the time allotted to the speaker, and the time for the graduates to receive their diplomas. Mother did not have to march with the faculty since she was getting married, but Dad did. After all, the only thing he would have to do to prepare for the wedding was to take off the cap and gown. A gentleman always wore a full suit.

The speaker was allotted 30 minutes, but he droned on and on. The temperature rose, and with it Dad's impatience. Before air conditioning, being inside in summer was to suffer from the heat as if you were in a sweat lodge. Faculty members dripped sweat, their clothes soaked beneath the robes, the auditorium stifling. Everyone suffered except the speaker, who was generating much of the hot air floating into the audience long after his oration was to be finished. Dad would be forever grateful to the professor sitting beside him, for she seemed to know he needed help to get out of there. She fainted.

Hero and gallant that he was, Dad rose, lifted her up, draped her over his shoulder, and left the auditorium for his wedding.

For years, Mother laughed, saying she wondered why he even married her. The first time she cooked for him, while they were courting, he brought corn on the cob, which she dutifully scraped off to fix creamed corn, her favorite. He liked his corn left on the cob and boiled.

I never heard Dad complain about the food. Mother could fry

the corn, and he would eat it. When he mentioned wanting some 6-inch thick apple pie like his grandmother made, Mother stacked up a couple of her regular pies. Virginia cobbler was not on our Georgia menu in the 1940s.

Dad would upset Mother because when the sugar bowl wasn't on the table at breakfast time, he didn't say a word. He would just use blackberry jelly in his coffee rather than ask her to get the sugar. It became my duty to set the table when I was perhaps 6 or 7, but I never learned to run a mental list the way my Aunt Allie could: knives, forks, spoons, plates, napkins, water, coffee cups, salt, pepper, sugar, cream, jelly, jam, butter.

Mother frequently said that since Dad was late for the wedding, she should have known never to expect him to be anywhere on time. He often came in late to meals: to breakfast because of some situation he ran into while milking or feeding the livestock; to supper because of a late lab at school, or maybe a cow or two out on the road on his way home, or because he was off somewhere on the plantation, doing something, and just forgot the time.

Then she would turn her words around and say she knew how those commencement ceremonies went at GSCW in those days—she had been on the faculty herself and even been a student there at one time, back when it was Georgia Normal and Industrial College. Back when she had to wear a uniform. Back when the girls could not speak to the Georgia Military College cadets, and no student could go home for the weekend or have visitors. Students could not go off campus even with their parents back in the good ole days.

At the time they wed, Mother was still working on her Ph. D. but quit her nutritional research shortly after her marriage to attend to the responsibilities of motherhood and to manage a plantation household.

The newlyweds spent their honeymoon at the mountain cabin of Dr. Sam Guy, chemist, who headed the chemistry department at Emory University. He also served on the Herty Committee. From the mountains, the couple brought home a seedling white pine, which they planted near the spring house, down the hill from Westover. The children often would count the limbs, which grew in parallel circles, to count the years of the marriage.

The winter after Luther's death, an ice storm hit the area over the Christmas holidays and felled the tree. Lillas told her daughter Susan it was almost like losing her husband all over again, that she had treasured the tree so much.

NOTES LILLAS MADE ON THE BACK OF AN ENVELOPE

In her papers was an envelope, opened into a flat sheet of paper. Lillas had written on both sides, as if performing a "write-it-out-psychotherapy" treatment. The date is unknown, but we think it was before the children were born, a time when Lillas was facing the hardships of the change from town to country living. A letter to Lillas from her sister Katie after Lil's birth mentioned that Lillas had told her (Katie) that she wanted three children.

Her salary for 1932-33 was $2,400.

No great responsibility, a pretty frock, a fresh permanent and a friendly disposition, a girlish figure. I reached the age of 30 before I knew that honest people did not pay their debts.

When I inherited a house and small farm I learned more about people than the Prof. of Psychology could possibly know. I found that well-to-do people with responsible jobs in banks don't pay house rent unless they want to.

I married my boss and discovered I was more charming as an assistant than as a wife.

First as instructor and later as assistant professor, in a state college in the South for a happy, friendly 10 years.

My salary provided a comfortable living, a car, and a little for a raining day. There was always cash for a new dress, sheer hose and sensible heels. a permanent when...

Being a conscientious, efficient worker there was no complaint against my work and I was well prepared for my job; after 4 or 5 hours in the classroom my responsibility ended. That meant time for a game of tennis or a horse back ride, a hand of bridge or anything else interesting that loomed up. There were friends among the faculty, among the students and among the "town people."

Each morning before nine I was at the office, well dressed, with a smile and a cheerio for everyone.

Nan Whitehurst, a first cousin who lived at Dovedale when Lillas was a child, wrote to her in 1932:

What beautiful "finery" you must have bought in Atlanta! You bought enough for several days shopping—how you ever did it in so short a time I don't know. Five new dresses this spring—now all this. What's the big trousseau for?

At that time, the Nancy Hanks, a special train, ran from Savannah to Atlanta in the morning and returned in the later afternoon. Milledgeville ladies often drove to Macon, caught the Nancy to Atlanta to shop, and returned on the afternoon run.

Marriage brought many changes to her life, more than she had expected. Other ladies have said life does change quite a lot when a woman marries.

Mother had expected to live in the Westover mansion, but instead lived in the "cottage" that stood next door. It became home until the children were old enough not to write on the plaster walls of Westover or to tumble down the stairs, although Thulia did fall down the stairs and break her arm one afternoon, in a hurry to join her siblings and mother for a walk when a storm finally ended.

Mother had experience in the managing her 135 acres at Dovedale, and she had inherited one-half interest in the house on Liberty Street, but the responsibilities of managing a plantation were far greater, more time consuming, and more exhausting than those of teaching and looking after Dovedale and making some repairs as needed at Liberty Street. And having three children in four years tied her down as firmly as chains.

She also discovered that money was no longer available for a pretty frock, a new permanent, and gadding about here and yon. She had traveled to Yellowstone, where she worked one summer waiting tables. She had driven to Minnesota to go to graduate school. She had lived in New York City while attending Columbia University and working on her doctorate. But the state had refused to pay her two months salary the last year she taught, so she was short personal funds from the start.

She often laughed that Luther married her for her savings account, which was used to pay off the loan on Westover.

All available cash now was used to expand land holdings.

In wartime, with gas rationed, although they received extra ration tickets for farm travel—to gas the truck to haul hay, to pick up and take home the hired help too far away to walk, and for Luther's daily round trip to the college, ration tickets had to be used sparingly. Lillas walked from home to the grocery store, when necessary, in the afternoon, purchased what they needed, had it packed into a cardboard box, and toted it to the college where she would wait in the truck for Luther to finish classes and labs and drive her and the groceries home.

She owned her own car when she married, but when it "broke down" in the late years of World War II, spare parts were not available, and the car sat outside the small building known as "Woodall's Tool House," where axes were sharpened and the farm tools were kept, located between the "cottage" and the railroad. There it eventually rusted away.

New duties as the wife of a plantation owner probably included cooking a noonday meal for the hired help and also for the drifting hobos fleeing the depression.

Her first baby arrived on February 28, 1935, barely two months before Herty Day, so she had the baby to tend to while she made the arrangements for the afternoon tea at Westover house. See Appendix XIX for the guest list for a typical year.

After a childless first marriage, Dad was pleased to have a child when Thulia Katherine was born. He deeded all of his property to Lillas, "the mother of my daughter."

In her diary, Lillas's sister Susan Myrick mentions looking after the children so Lillas could get some rest when they had the whooping cough. Lillas's oldest living sister, Tippie (Elizabeth Myrick) Hubert, lived about four miles away and offered what help she could, but Tippie did not drive so could not just run down the road to Westover when she wanted to.

In a letter dated only "Sunday 11th," and apparently never mailed, Lillas wrote to her cousin Nan Whitehurst Ingram:

Dearest Nan,

   It was so nice to have your letter and especially when I was in bed. I spent about two weeks there after a fall from a horse. I would have stayed longer but two of the girls got the measles so I had to get up and hobble about. Everybody is well again now. And thank goodness the maid is back after having the measles too. ---
---------- I haven't done any riding since my fall for the weather has been too hot but I still love my horses. We have five colts about two months old and they are so cute. We bought recently a little two year old colt that had already been trained for the children to ride and mine have had such a good time. (Not only mine but all the friends'.) Thulia leads him while I hold Mill Lil and (illegible).
   Later
   Aunt Josie and her family came out and from the looks of this letter I think Miss Lil has been in trying to write you too.
   Must get supper for the kids and put them to bed. More another time.
      Much love to all but most for you.

She had to be nurse, even when she was sick herself.
They had no telephone.
Electricity often went out when the wind blew.
Heat was usually only a fireplace in one room.
When Allie came to stay with the older children at the birth of the third baby, it was January. Allie asked Lillian, the maid, where were the children's shoes. She replied "they ain't got none."
   If early life was hard on the babies, it had to have been harsh on the mother used to constant running water, to house-wide heat and a telephone. But in some of her papers, we found her comment about life:
   "I faced the world with a smile and didn't talk my troubles."

MONEY MATTERS

Somehow, a number of cancelled checks written by both Luther and Lillas survived the years. These checks reflect prices of the times as well as how both spent their ready cash. Some of these are listed in Appendix XVIII for the fun of seeing how much a hired man would be paid, how much a bed spread might cost, or the value of intangibles owned.

This check, however, creates a mystery that perhaps a future heir to my father may solve. It ran through banks in Williamsburg, Virginia, but I have been unable to locate Ashby property that he might have owned in James City County in 1928. A good excuse for a visit to Williamsburg and the courthouse records.

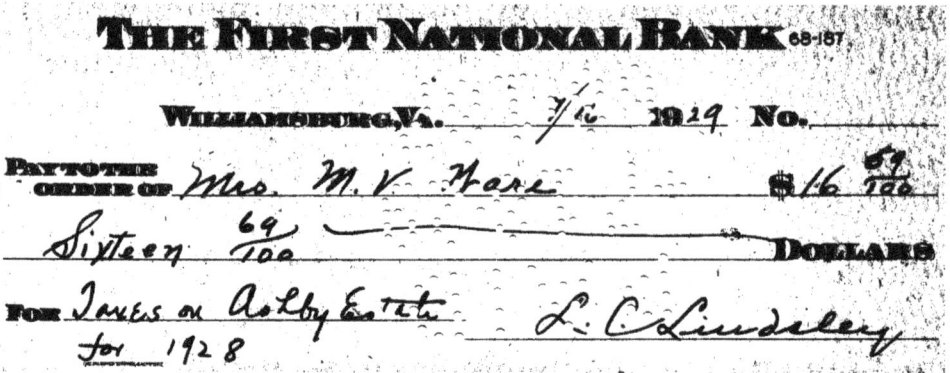

LEGAL MATTERS

Taking on the County Commissioners

Dad did not hesitate to take on city hall, and when he found the county chain gang cutting a road along the edge of our land, he jumped all over the county. We wound up going to court, and I joined Dad at the table in the courtroom. He was his own lawyer. Contrary to the slogan "he who is his own lawyer has a fool for a client," Dad won his case before a jury.

The existing road was originally a wagon road that just ran through private lands and eventually became used by the public. The county never owned the roadbed.

Sherman's troops had marched down that road and some had spent the night on the land Dad now owned. I reckon the officers had slept in the house, because they did not burn it.

Some soldiers tried to catch a chicken for supper, and when the chicken ran under the house, one of the soldiers tried to shoot it. He missed the chicken and got one of his fellow blue-coats. That Yankee is perhaps the soldier buried in the front yard.

Anyhow, those events gave Dad a good argument for the jury on why the land was extra special. In his summary, he compared the land to a coin. He had in his coin collection a shekel, and he brought it to court. He let the jurors pass it amongst themselves, and told them it was just an old coin, and it was worth so much. But, he said, suppose it had been one of the 30 pieces of silver given to Judas, what would its value be? History added value to anything.

Sherman's troops added value to the land in question.

The jury accepted his arguments, and put a higher value on the land than was usual. And since the county had no ownership of the old dirt road, the jury decided that the county should have to pay for the roadbed also.

The Shooting Incident

The *Union-Recorder* reported on January 16, 1936, that the Grand Jury indicted Dr. L. C. Lindsley, professor at the college, for shooting at and attempting to murder two white men, Sid Ross and Louie Johnson, the previous November.

He went before the judge on January 22, 1936, with a plea agreement, and the charges were reduced to misdemeanor. He paid a $250.00 fine.

Frank Bell was his attorney.

10 9

MINUTES Q, BALDWIN SUPERIOR COURT, JANUARY TERM, 19 36

THE STATE)
              :   No. 2711, Cri. Dkt. E, page 98
   vs.   )   January Term, 1936
              :   Assault with Intent to Murder
L. C. Lindsley)

     The Defendant waives copy of indictment, special presentment and list of witnesses; also waives being formally arraigned and pleads guilty to unlawfully shooting at another. Jan 22, 1936.

Frank W. Bell   C. S. Baldwin, Jr.
Defendant's Attorney.   Solicitor General.

STATE OF GEORGIA, BALDWIN COUNTY
THE STATE   )   Indictment in the Superior Court
v.   :   No. 2711, Minutes Q, Folio 88
L. C. Lindsley   )   For assault with intent to murder.

     The Defendant, L. C. Lindsley, having on the trial of the above stated case, plead guilty to unlawfully shooting at another and showing no reason why the sentence of the Court should not be pronounced against him:

     It is ordered and adjudged by the court, that the said L. C. Lindsley do work in the STATE PRISON FARM OF GEORGIA for the term of twelve months, to be computed from this date, or that he may pay into court at any time before the completion of the period of service, a fine of two hundred & fifty Dollars, including the costs:

     It is further ordered, that the said L. C. Lindsley be committed to the common jail of said county, there to be kept in close custody until he shall be demanded by the Superintendent of the State Prison Farm.

     Witness my hand and official signature, this 22 day of Jan. 1936.

                             Blanton Fortson, J. S. C. W. C.
                             Acting Judge Superior Courts,
                             Ocmulgee Circuit Presiding.

::::::::::::::::::::::::::::::

The family knows that, when pushed, Luther did have a temper, but we never knew him to resort to any physical reaction to another. A man who had knocked him up side the head with a rock went to prison, and when he was released, Dad hired him again. Dad did business with a man who had served time for rustling cattle. We have no idea what prompted him to shoot toward others, unless he thought they were committing some crime against him.

A search of the criminal docket books for both felony and misdemeanor charges for the names of both men showed neither name.

That year was mid-depression; cattle rustling was common in our area of the county. So was bootlegging, which often resulted in forest fires. Someone had illegally harvested timber off of Lindsley lands.

We learned of this incident while preparing the book, and have no details of the incident other than the legal document shown above.

Traffic Ticket

Luther had a previous "run-in" with the law six years earlier. On February 25, 1930, he wrote a check for $5.00 to R. T. Baisden to pay his fine for "driving over a stop sign in Milledgeville."

The Land Line Case

CLINE vs. L. C. LINDSLEY, Tenant in Possession
CASE # 2467
Filed July 12, 1943, Settled April 1951

The dispute was over what we called the "calf pasture," an area that extended the eastern line of the "barn pasture" downstream from the creek crossing behind Westover Pond.

The defendants were expanded to include Lillas M. Lindsley as the case progressed. The jury visited the site and the Lindsley girls went with the court and their parents to the fence line. There in the woods, Lillas was asked to raise her hand and swear to the truth. The children also raised their hands.

The case ended with a hung jury.

The Clines (the plaintiffs) appealed. When the case went back to trial in 1947, the plaintiffs, who were originally executors of an estate, became Regina O'Connor and her brother Louis I. Cline. In July, the jury found for the Clines.

There was a back and forth with attorneys to settle some of details of vacating the lands and payment of costs, but by April 11, 1951, it was over.

The land line was set as a straight line that followed land lot lines. Land Lots 275 and 276 were to be a part of the Jordan Place, and LL 301 and 302 a part of the Hall-Kenan Place, according to the survey by Calvin Rice in Deed Book 26, page 327, "this 11th day of April 1951."

The judge ordered Lindsley to vacate the premises and for the plaintive to pay court costs, as had been agreed by both parties.

In spite of the legal differences, the two families remained friends. Regina Cline O'Connor and Lillas Myrick grew up as neigh-bors, Lillas on Liberty Street and Regina about a half-block away on Greene Street.

Lillas often visited Andalusia, and Regina and her daughter Flannery O'Connor visited Lillas at Westover, and the friendship expanded to include Flannery and the Lindsley daughters as well.

Lindsley vs. Lowe

Luther and Jerry Lowe had a long-standing dispute over Luther's cattle and hogs that got into Lowe's crops at different times. Luther owned a long-horned cow that was given to him when Texan ranchers brought some of the herds from Texas to Florida and stopped off in Milledgeville to let the cattle recover from a part of their rail trip. Luther had pastured some the cattle for a few days.

He found the long-horn cow dead, shot, and was sure that Lowe had killed her.

In 1951, Lowe brought a court case against Luther for damage to his oat crops.

From Writ Book R, pp. 200-203:

Lowe leased land known as the Harper Place. During the years 1947-1951, he planted 206 acres of oats annually. He claimed that Lindsley cattle entered the land and ate or destroyed

1951: 500 bushels
1950: 400 bushels
1949: 200 bushels
1948: 200 bushels
1947: 75 bushels

at a value of $1.00 per bushel.

The judge found for Lowe. Luther appealed for a jury trial. The case was settled for $350.00 as full payment **and** court costs.

Of interest is that Lowe's attorney was Stephen T. Bivins, known as Pete Bivins. Pete was one of the two attorneys killed by Marion Stembridge when he went on a shooting spree during the Milledgeville sesquicentennial celebrations in 1953. (See *Blue Jeans and Pantaloons in Yesterplace* for details of the Stembridge shooting.)

L. C. Lindsley vs. Superintendent Of Schools

From Writ Book F, pp. 71-73

The school board ordered the bus driver to drive into Putnam

County and bring children from Putnam County to Baldwin, an extra 20 miles per day, an extra expense to the county and a hardship to the other children.

Luther's children were picked up at 6:30 a.m. and driven some 20 miles to reach school, then returned home some 12 hours later, which made an exceptionally long day for first graders.

But the case was decided in favor of the school board. Luther had to pay court costs, and the bus continued to pick up the Napier children.

A year or two later, however, the bus route was changed so that the Napier children were picked up earlier and the local children had a shorter ride. The Putnam County children attended school in Baldwin County until they were graduated from high school.

In those years, some of the Milledgeville people called Luther the Yankee from Virginia.

LUTHER, THE PROFESSOR

Luther arrived at GSCW in 1929, and became department head and retained that position until he retired in 1948. When he came to the college, nine chemistry courses were listed in the catalog. By 1931, the number had increased to sixteen.

Whether or not the students feared his tests, we don't know.   His exams were not just on paper; his students had to perform experiments to get the answers, as shown in a few samples from an exam.

Chemistry Test: Common Ion Effect

A FEW QUESTIONS

1. To a solution of MgCl-2 add NaOH. What is formed? Give the equation.

2. To a like volume of MgCl-2 add NH-4OH. Is this precipitate as large as in 1? Explain and give equation.

3. To a third like volume of MgCl-2 add NH-4Cl and then NH-4OH. Write ionic reactions and also equilibrium equation

explaining the phenomenon.

4. To a concentrated solution of BaCl-2 add concentrated HCl. Explain.

5. To a saturated NaCl solution add concentrated HCl. Explain.

His daughters Thulia and Lil remember the "final" that he gave all of his lab students. They were told to clean their lab sites and wash every beaker and flask and all other equipment so it would be perfectly clean for the next quarter's class.

When they declared that all was washed, he told them to each bring a beaker, and he poured in punch for them to drink.

One of his major achievements was to begin a chemistry club that reached beyond the college. The college did have a science club, as mentioned in the *Spectrum*, the college annual, in 1930. Two years later, the chemistry club was formed, with its purpose "to stimulate an interest in chemistry among the students of the college and to broaden their knowledge of chemistry as applied to everyday life."

Faculty listed as members of the club were Miss Jessie Trawick, Dr. Lindsley, and Miss Lena Martin, with Lillas Myrick as faculty advisor. Lena Martin was sought out by the Department of Defense to help on the Manhattan Project. (From Lena's niece Mary Martin Bowen to Susan Lindsley.)

In 1933, the club sponsored the first Herty Day events, and Herty Day became the major activity of the organization. In 1934, Luther became faculty advisor. Beginning in 1939, on the club's page the *Spectrum* showed the Herty medal and each year the information provided about Herty Day increased. (See section on Herty Day; also see *Blue Jeans and Pantaloons in Yesterplace*, which details the events of Herty Day.)

Each year, the club also held special programs, both for members and for the student body. In 1938, for example, the year's programs dealt with industries of Georgia, and the students made several field trips to plants in Middle Georgia. The club also brought several distinguished scientists to campus for their open meetings.

On December 29, 1933, *The Colonnade* reported that Dr. Burgin Dunn, instructor of physics at Emory University, spoke to the

Chemistry Club and "while in Milledgeville was entertained by the chemistry faculty and was the house guest of Dr. Lindsley of Westover."

Dr. Dunn apparently enjoyed the visit, for on December 11, 1933, he wrote to Luther:

The events of the past weekend are of course uppermost in my mind just at present and from the impression that was made they will be in that position for a very long time, especially when my mind turns to Milledgeville. Before I had ever been to GSCW I heard from all sides what amounted to the fact that there was almost no one there who was in any way human. I know that as far as the Chemistry Department is concerned everyone connected with it is human, not only that but (they) **delight in showing people that they are.**

In other words, Dr. Lindsley, I want you to know that our interest and the time you gave US was certainly appreciated (I take it that you understand that US does not stand for United States). I enjoyed every minute, and your hospitality and interest made that possible, to a large degree.

He added a P. S.:

I still claim that four-poster as my bed, so don't let it get away.

Luther's connections to the chemical industry helped bring such scientists as the head of the Herty labs and the dean of Emory University to the campus as guest speakers.

He was pictured in the GSCW annual, the *Spectrum*, in several issues:

1930

1934

Luther in 1935

Luther in 1936

From the 1938 *Spectrum*: Luther, H. Rogers, Jessie Trawick, M. Rogers

"Jessie Trawick and Dr. Lindsley discuss the strange lives and loves of molecules and atoms." From the 1946 *Spectrum*

1948 *Spectrum*: "Dr. Lindsley and Miss Trawick teach the future scientists of the atom era."

A LATIN SPEECH

The GSCW newspaper, *The Colonnade*, on May 22, 1945, carried a front page article about the college's honoring Dr. Francis Potter Daniels, former professor and head of the Latin Department at the college and the founder of the National Doctor's Academy.

Luther represented the Doctor's Academy at GSCW and presented the loving cup. He gave the presentation speech as a poem, with the title: "Summa Veritas at Scientia." Was the poem itself also in Latin? Unfortunately, his copy burned in Westover. His notes indicated that a former GSCW student Mary Burns had a copy, but we were never able to obtain one.

DR. "POSSUM HUNT" LINDSLEY

In 1944, the *Spectrum* stated: "Miss Jessie Trawick and Dr. L. C. Lindsley may be identified by their passion for burettes and beakers." In the cut-line for a picture of Luther (who had his back to the camera) and Jessie that year, the *Spectrum* identified him as "Dr. (Possum Hunt) Lindsley."

When Luther began his annual possum hunts at Westover for members of the chemistry club, the membership grew. Only members of the club could attend, and only officers of the club could take part in the Herty Day tea at Westover.

Such an opportunity was considered golden for the students. One of the restrictions at GSCW in the 1920s and into the 1930s was that no student could go off campus except under unusual circumstances, which did not include a visit from the parents or a date with one of the boys from the nearby military junior college.

So to spend an afternoon at the country mansion and to mingle with local society and visiting dignitaries on Herty Day, the students eagerly joined the organization and competed to serve as officers. But all members could attend the annual possum hunt and picnic.

When his daughters were old enough, they joined the hunt. The "Jessies," as the college girls were called, would watch over the younger girls. And the younger girls wanted to be up front with their father and the dog men. The dog owners knew from the sounds of the barks if the dogs were just trailing or if they had something treed. Silence meant they were searching for a trail.

A good possum dog would track only a possum or a raccoon.

The night would be chilly. As we busted our way though the brush we made too much noise to hear anything but ourselves. We heard owls sometimes, when we'd stop to listen to the dogs. We children did not have gloves, and our hands always felt the cold, even stuffed into pockets.

The dog men and Dad carried lanterns, and as they walked, the lanterns threw switching leg shadows along the bushes, as if a ghost walked black-legged beside us. Flashlights did not always find roots or sticks before feet did, but the unlucky stumbler would reach down and throw the stick aside. Creeks presented a barrier, but somehow everybody usually managed to cross without sinking into the muck or stepping into a cow patty on the pathway across.

When the dogs barked "treed" everyone would get excited, the giggling got louder, and the sense of urgency increased. We had to get to the possum!

What a disappointment to arrive at the tree, only to find no possum. Sometimes the fleeing animal would "mark" a tree, that is, dash a few feet up one side and then leap off the other side, leaving the dogs convinced it was up in the limbs.

But what a thrill to see a pair of eyes gleaming in the light. The dogs would be frantically trying to climb the tree. The hunters would be looking at tomorrow's supper. The Jessies were not squeamish and were thrilled when we did come home with supper.

With or without a possum, supper waited for us back near the spring house, where Mother and her help had a bonfire going, and a table covered with food—potato salad, slaw and other goodies, and of course hot dogs and marshmallows ready to burn over the fire on sticks.

I'm sure Mother would have preferred to be on the hunt instead of at the camp "kitchen."

Other faculty members and local friends sometimes went on these hunts, and the story Dr. Clyde Keeler wrote about one of the hunts appeared in the *Union-Recorder*, Milledgeville's weekly paper, on October 8, 1953, several years after the final possum hunt. Dr. Keeler, a genealogist and professor at GSCW, studied albino people in Latin America for a number of years. Lil Lindsley James worked with Dr. Keeler in his research shortly after completing her medical studies and internship.

Nature Notes

by Clyde Keeler

The annual 'possum hunt that Professor Lindsley inaugurated and maintained for many years was one of the most colorful and unique traditions that the Georgia State College for Women has ever known. It was one of the thrillers that packed enthusiastic students into the Chemistry Club. What was it like?

Come with me at dusk to the west end of Parks Hall on an appointed night about Halloween Time. The air is clear, and comfortably warm with jackets or light sweaters. The ground is dry. A moon of the first quarter is bright in a clear sky, in which a few white, fleecy clouds are lazily adrift. Yes, all the weather signs are auspicious and Parks Hall with its camellia shrubs, its abelia bells and its sweetly scented eleagnus is the rendezvous.

A score of happy, laughing girls, most of them in loud plaid lumberman's shirts and rolled-up, blue dungarees, are milling about excitedly and disappearing one after another into several automobiles lined up on the drive. These are driven by volunteer professors of the Chemistry Department.

Oh, yes, it is theoretically a Chemistry Club affair, but there are plenty of proselytes for the occasion who have chipped in their thirty cents for the "feed."

Twenty minutes ride in the moonlight and the cars pull to the side of the road. Here we join the first batch and wait for the cars to bring out the third and fourth groups.

There are stories, laughing and snatches of song. Groups of three are describing the thrilling, latest letter from a fiancé. There are heart rending pleas to the chaperoning professors not to grade this morning's quiz papers heavily, but just to toss them into the waste-basket and forget them.

Here we are cordially welcomed by our genial, khaki-clad Professor Lindsley, Head of the Chemistry Department, who is not only our Host but also Master of the Hunt.

When we have all arrived there is the testing, lighting and setting of old fashioned kerosene lanterns. Flashlights emerge from pockets and are focused on everybody and everything within several rods distance. The Master of the Hunt disappears into the darkness up a side road to a waiting automobile in the distance only to return a few moments later accompanied by two colored men and preceded by a couple of friendly, wagging, sniffing, droop-eared houn' dogs, of no particular escutcheon. The dogs run about extrovertly among the crowd pleading for attention.

Instructions are given to the colored men who start off plodding down the road with their active dogs and guided by Dr. Lindsley's twelve-year-old daughter who knows every branch, gulley and hollow where 'possum tracks have been seen this autumn. The crowd gives them a ten minute start and then follows by twos, threes, and half dozens in no particular order. But there is no hurry, and the conversations continue.

We cross fields and fences in the moonlight and at a ridge we sit down to wait until eventually the yelps of a hound on the trail reach our ears. Some minutes later the barking seems localized, and our host observes with the certainty of experience, "They've got one treed, all right. Let's go!"

So we follow the voices of the dogs down through the woods, the thickets, and briars, across gullies, and over barbed-wire fences. But before we arrive the barking stops. The colored men meet us in the darkness of the woods and grunt, "Dry trail." Then they start off up the hollow again with their hounds.

Again a track, again hounds yelping on the trail, again barking under a tree. Again a "dry trail." This disappointment has to be alleviated, but it is not very encouraging to be told that experienced 'possums especially black ones, frequently climb a tree, jump down and run away just to trick the dogs that sit patiently barking under the empty tree until relieved by their masters.

But the third strike is real! The trail leads to a small, slender, leafless persimmon tree and even before the flashlights are turned on it, one can make out a large, black furry lump high up in the branches. The tall, young negro climbs the tree while his stocky father stands below with an open croaker sack. The tree begins to sway. Faster and faster it moves until the heavy object in the top looses its hold and tumbles down, to be deftly caught in the sack. After everybody has had a chance to peep into the sack its opening is made fast with twine and it is swung about the tall man's shoulder.

The girls are all tired by now so we start back toward the

stately stand of tall pines on the hillside behind the Lindsley Mansion where a blazing camp fire beckons. And OH! oh! there are hot dogs, doughnuts, and steaming coffee ready in generous quantities.

It is so good to stretch one's tired body out before the comforting heat of a dancing, crackling, orange flamed fire and see the happy youthful faces of the girls as they are lighted up by its bright glow. But before the line has time to form for food, the dogs start yelping less than two hundred yards away and half the party rushes off through the woods again, working through thickets and scratching briars and carefully negotiating two barbed-wire fences.

Again a stately young permission tree. Again a heavy ball of fur. Again a violent shaking and a drop. But this time it missed the croaker sack, and the hounds seized it in an instant. Indeed they would have made short work of it had not the tall colored man dived in between them and swung the possum aloft by its tail, high above his own head, while the hounds jump and bark frantically in their efforts to retrieve their quarry.

Mile, the big, black hound with the brown ears, forgets all about 'possums when he smells food at close range, jumps the fence and grabs for the buns laid out on newspapers before the fire. Two gulps and two buns disappear before half a dozen girls fly to the protection of the food and chase the dog away until his master can catch him.

Food is served to the great circle of hungry girls about the campfire, and the colored men with their dogs, including the impetuous Mile, are not forgotten in the shadows

After the food, joyous college songs, story telling, conversation with your neighbors and just plain rest. The pleasure of lying quietly on your back and gazing up at the bright stars above the tall pine trees!

At length the Host and Master of the Hunts suggest that some of the girls may care to see the old, slave-days' mansion, and all retired through the moonlight to the top of the hill. There they inspect the beautiful, old, historical house with its stately columns, and its formal gardens.

The professors go to the crossroads for the cars and after much waving and many cheery goodbyes, the happy procession speeds back to Milledgeville and the dormitories.

The town clock strikes two.

Thus, another highly successful Annual Possum Hunt of the Chemistry Club disappears into history and enters the cherished, unique campus memories of the girls at the Georgia State College for Women.

Thirty years after the last possum hunt, DeWitt Avery told about one of the possum hunts he led. The college students helped shake the possum out of a tree, and it sulled up (curled up and played dead, or "played possum"). The girls carried it like a baby, turn about, all night, even back to the picnic supper grounds and tended to it while they ate. DeWitt, as the "dog man" was supposed to get the possum as part of his payment, but left for home without it. He didn't know what they did with the possum—they were still loving on it when he left.

Susan remembers some of the girls going over toward the Cline/O'Connor fence line from the picnic, and believes they went to release the possum.

* * *

Luther's students' respect for him is reflected in a column in the GSCW student publication *The Corinthian*. We don't have the date of the article; it was in the section "Personalities!" page 9.

THE CORINTHIAN

He addresses the bevy of bobby-soxers that crowd into his classroom on third floor Parks as "young ladies" in the gentlemanly fashion characteristic of the Old South. His brown eyes sparkle as he peers indulgently over horn-rimmed reading glasses, which, since one earpiece is missing, perch precariously on the tip of his nose. As he skillfully pours and mixes chemicals on the disheveled desk littered with his scientific treasurers, we feel a great admiration for the old man enveloped in the huge, rough, brown smock and with the bald spot thinly veiled with upright wisps of white hair.

Even having been at G.S.C.W. for many years, he had not become afflicted with the chronic pessimism of most of his fellow teachers about the mental capacity of his students. Rather than bemoaning the fact that the mind of the average Jessie is a sealed

vacuum completely impervious to intellectual stimuli, he laughs good naturedly at the amazing activity of our "forgetters." When every face in 102 assumed an expression of hopeless bewilderment over the formula for alum, he only admonished *himself* for not having had the foresight to rouse us in the middle of the night to repeat the formula, since he well knew that our "forgetters" rendered it impossible for us to retain information over a twenty-four hour period!

He does not use the classroom as a rostrum from which to launch into egotistic tirades about his illustrious ancestors and his domestic felicity. If he strays from the immediate subject, and he does it only rarely, it is always to instill in us a bit of his own joy of living. On a lazy afternoon, when our metabolism was at an unusually low ebb and we were sprawled listlessly in our seats, his brown eyes danced as he suddenly said: "Young ladies, you would get such a kick out of living, if you only had the energy to kick!"

Miriam Massey

* * *

A letter dated March 23, 1983, from a former student came to Dr. Ed and Mrs. Dawson, a former colleague of Luther's at GSCW, who forwarded the letter to the Lindsley family. The signature is illegible:

Thank you for sharing your memory of Dr. Lindsley's children and the crocuses. I'll have to share one of my memories, although it's not half so poignant.

When I think of Dr. Lindsley, I think of glowworms. There was this possum hunt, and there were glowworms among the grass roots as we stumbled about in the dark. I'd not seen them before.

My memory of the possum hunt, itself, is not a bit painful. We've come to understand that possums are terribly misunderstood, even by biologists. There are several reasons for this, the main one being that until they have learned to trust you, possums act like turkeys, and it takes months for a possum of any size to learn to trust you. Possums have all of these teeth, of course, but when they mistrust you, their main defense is being rude. Possums know how to be rude in a variety of ways. However, truly trusting possums come to "kitty, kitty, kitty," use sandboxes, and make fools of themselves over certain perfumes. Our possums are particularly fond of Revlon's "Intimate," Max Factor's "Mountain greenery," the man's cologne "Pole," and "Givenchy III." If you put a drop of any of these on a bit of paper towel, our possums will chew it into a spitball, and dab it on their fur.

But getting back to Dr. Lindsley; he had a capacity to appreciate sweetness and innocence in one of his students whether or not there was any hope that she would ever become a chemist. I think of a freshman named Lois.

She was open and absolutely innocent and had a face which perfectly reflected the fact. I believe that she found the chemistry lab to be a bit alarming. Dr. Lindsley already had students who were well on the way to becoming precise and disciplined chemists, but Lois was not one of them. As a matter of fact, I think that she tended to be accident-prone.

In any case, she had once burned herself, and the thing which I remember about Dr. Lindsley is the affection and amusement with which he described the incident. According to Dr. Lindsley, she had said not a word, but one big tear had formed in one eye, then slowly rolled down her cheek.

* * *

Another of Dad's students, Virginia Wood, a chemistry major, made a sizeable donation to the college in 2017 in Dad's honor.

She said about Dad:

"He was a true Southern gentleman. He told me that chances were I would get married and not spend my life as a chemist. I would need to be able to take part in various local activities, so at his recommendation, I took Music Appreciation and Art Appreciation. When I did get married, to Charles Alexander, I was able to mix and mingle in local activities as he had suggested."

She joined the United Daughters of the Confederacy. Like my father, she lost her Confederate soldier grandfather in The War. She organized a local UDC Chapter and later served as State President in Tennessee.

Dad would be very proud of this student.

HERTY DAY

Herty Day was the most significant event in GSCW history. It brought not only local recognition to the college, but also national exposure. Local and regional newspapers carried articles about the events. Unfortunately for GSCW, the college lost this prestige when it gave up the celebrations.

To honor both his friend Dr. Charles Holmes Herty and the chemists in the South who were contributing to the advancement of science, Luther founded Herty Day in 1933. He designed the medal, which shows Herty in profile and in Latin the words "For Science and Country." The medal was gold. Dad paid for it and all the costs of the Herty Day events.

After the first Herty Day, Luther received this letter from Dr. Herty:

DEPARTMENT OF FORESTRY AND GEOLOGICAL DEVELOPMENT

STATE CAPITOL, ATLANTA, GA.

COMMISSION

GOVERNOR EUGENE TALMADGE, CHAIRMAN
J. LEONARD ROUNTREE, SUMMIT
ALEX K. SESSOMS, COGDELL
MRS. M. E. JUDD, DALTON
J. M. MALLORY, SAVANNAH
ROBERT E. PRICE, KINGSLAND
L. L. MOORE, MOULTRIE
S. W. McCALLIE, SECRETARY

DIVISION HEADS

S. W. McCALLIE, STATE GEOLOGIST
ATLANTA
B. M. LUFBURROW, STATE FORESTER
ATLANTA
CHAS. H. HERTY, RESEARCH CHEMIST
SAVANNAH

DIVISION OF PULP AND PAPER RESEARCH
CHARLES H. HERTY, RESEARCH CHEMIST
510 RIVER STREET
SAVANNAH, GA.
June 3, 1933

Prof. L. C. Lindsley
Georgia State College for Women
Milledgeville, Georgia

My dear Prof. Lindsley:

Many thanks for sending with your letter of May 30th the clippings covering the exercises of last Friday.

Please forget about the expense account. I just had a jolly frolic on those two days and could not think of asking any reimbursement from the Chemistry Club. I was so grateful to them for all they did for me I wish that instead of sending an expense account I might send a real contribution to the Club.

We reached Savannah Saturday afternoon after a very delightful drive from Milledgeville. They were all delighted with the beautiful hospitality of the Milledgeville people, and you know what a joy it always is to me to get back among my home folks.

But I want to express to you particularly my deep appreciation of all the thought and interest you put into this whole meeting. Sam Guy was right when he said Friday night that you were the "mainspring".

With all good wishes and with renewed appreciation, I am

Sincerely yours,

CHH:C

The first Herty Day was to be the first and last for his wife Pattie Love. She died that October. The next year, 1934, Lillas Myrick helped Luther host the event. They married the next month.

An early Herty Day, with students and faculty on front porch of Westover.

A panel of chemists selected the Southern chemist who had contributed the greatest scientific advancements in the past year and the festivities were held in May. The date eventually became the first weekend, and the tea was then held on the same day as the Kentucky Derby.

On Saturday afternoon, Luther hosted the tea at Westover. The guest list included the entire faculty of GSCW, many of the local leaders, from bankers to politicians, and numerous out-of-town scientists. A list in his records showed more than one hundred guests. (See Appendix XIX for the guest list and for an excerpt from the local paper about the dignitaries who attended the 1936 celebration.) The tea lasted about two to three hours, and the guests spilled from the ball room through the parlor and into the gardens. Ladies who sighted the bay tree often left with springs to add to their herbal collection in their kitchens back home.

Officers of the college chemistry club served at the tea, and were happy to have a chance to "escape" the confines of the college campus.

The Colonnade, May 11, 1940

Dressed in pantaloons for the Herty Day ea at Westover, are left to right, little Misses Thulia Lindsley, Sue Lindsley, Helen Evers Long, and Polly Farr. Dr. Wells and Doris Satterfield pose with the young ladies.

Caption should read: Herty Day tea, 1940. Left to Right: Susan, Thulia Lindsley, Helen Evers Long, Polly Farr. In back, Doris Satterfield, and Guy Wells of the college.

As the tea ended, everyone went to the college campus for a barbecue supper, which Luther himself financed. The medal was presented in Russell Auditorium and the recipient would speak about his research.

Many of the out-of-town visitors were house guests at Westover, and the next morning, they were joined by the chemistry faculty and other notable visitors at Westover for a breakfast of eggs, bacon, ham, fried chicken, homemade biscuits, and numerous homemade jellies and condiments. By early afternoon, all of the visitors had headed home.

An article about the 1935 Herty Day stated in part:

Afternoon tea will be served from 4 to 8 p.m. in the home and boxwood garden at Westover, home of Dr. and Mrs. L. C. Lindsley. Dr. Lindsley is head of the department of chemistry at G.S.C.W. and it was he who originated the idea of the Herty Award which was given for the first time in 1933.

The actual selection of the recipient and the presentation of the medal are carried out through the Georgia section of the American Chemical Society in co-operation with other local sections of this society within the states of Virginia, West Virginia, Tennessee, North Carolina, South Carolina, Georgia, Florida, Alabama and Mississippi. The committee chairman for the selection of the recipient is Professor J. Sam Guy, Emory University.

Luther with Herty Day guests. Year unknown. Gentleman behind the ladies and facing right is believed to be Dr. Herty. They are in the front yard, just to the northeast side of the front porch of the house.

Herty Day, 1936. Left front, Dr. Sam Guy (Emory University) and Dr. W. H. MacIntire (metal recipient). Far left, Luther. Back row, Dr. Gilbert Boggs (Georgia Tech), Dr. Alfred Scott (University of Georgia). Far right, Dr. Herty. Below, Dr. Guy, Herty and Dr. MacIntire.

In this 1946 Herty Day photo taken at GSCW were (left to right) Dr. L. C. Lindsley, host for the occasion who is head of the department of chemistry at the college; Dr. Sam Guy of Emory University, chairman of the Committee on Awards for the Herty medal, Miss Barbara Lazier of Birmingham, AL, daughter of this year's medalist; Dr. Arthur Lazier, who received the Herty medal this year; Mrs. Lazier, and G. A. Lazier, of Rochelle, Ill, father of Dr. Lazier. Dr. Lazier worked at the Southern Research Institute. (Drinnon Photo)

Luther C. Lindsley, founder of Herty Day, stands with Virginia Brazel, Jo Miller, Mary Stubbs and Sara Betty Martin by the marker at the birthplace of Dr. Charles Holmes Herty in Milledgeville. At the time, it was placed in the center of pine trees. One of Dr. Herty's many accomplishments was the development of paper from pine pulp.

This undated article, probably from the *Macon Telegraph*, shows that guests did not limit conversation strictly to chemistry:

CHEMISTRY PARTY HELD AT BEAUTIFUL WESTOVER

Last Saturday several Macon people motored over to Milledgeville to attend the annual party the chemistry department of G. S. C. W. gives when it awards the Herty medal, held this year at Westover, the beautiful home of Dr. L. C. Lindsley, of the chemistry department, and Mrs. Lindsley, who is the former Lillas Myrick, sister of Susan Myrick of Macon.

Among those who went was Mrs. Ed Burke, who was keeping

her companions in gales of laughter with stories about Panama. ... Mrs. Burke was telling of shooting at a noise she heard in the yard. Dr. Charles Herty, of Savannah and Milledgeville, who was in the group, asked if she could hit anything with a gun. She said no, she guessed not, she never could see how anybody could hit anything with a gun because it was necessary for her to close both eyes when she shot.

LUTHER, THE RESEARCHER

Luther remained professional in his correspondence—he had his own letterhead when he lived in Milledgeville. Only one copy of that remains, and he retained it because he had written family history notes on it.

L. C. LINDSLEY, Ph. D.
INDUSTRIAL AND RESEARCH
CHEMIST

MILLEDGEVILLE, GEORGIA

A letter from Carter Poland, president of Poland Soap Works in Anniston, Alabama (August 16, 1937) states:

I received your letter of August 14th and the photomicrographs yesterday. I knew this was a hard job I was giving you. I am good at figuring out such jobs as that.

Most of the letter concerns technical aspects of Luther's work, and Mr. Poland asks for photographs of the "slender needles" that form when water is added to ECO and then allowed to evaporate. Mr. Poland ends with his hopes to come to Milledgeville in a few days.

C. G. Harrel, director of Products Control and Bakery Research Department, Pillsbury Flour Mills Company, Minneapolis, Minn., wrote on July 27, 1937:

We have a problem wherein we desire to determine from the hairs of a rat whether the rat died of arsenical poisoning.

We know that you are one of the outstanding authorities on microscopic analysis work and it is for this reason that I am presenting this to you.

I will appreciate your comments along this line, and if this work can be done would you be in position to run such a determination for us, and approximately what remuneration would you expect for your services?

Luther kept a booklet detailing all of his experiments for Pillsbury. We do not know what he charged.

He also kept his records of research for Columbia University in April 1940. Their letter ends with "trusting you have recovered from your illness" causes us to wonder if that were the time he had diphtheria.

Columbia University sent seven samples taken from an old Italian painting on a gesso base. The samples were taken from 1. blue sky, 2. forehead (flesh color), 3. red garment, 4. blue garment, 5. pilastro or column, 6. green garment, and 7. the gesso base.

Luther was to determine the pigments used and whether or not any impurities were present in the pigments. "For example, if the blue sky contains Prussian blue, we know pretty positively that Prussian blue was not known previous to the 15th or 16th century."

He sent interim reports, and a final report on May 3, together with microphotographs.

No. 1 Gypsum, trace of iron oxide, lead oxide, azurite
(Azurite particles covered with a trace of copper oxide gave the appearance of traces of indigo. A few particles were not soluble in ammonium hydroxide and these were probably lazurite. They were deep in the lead oxide and may have been protected from the solvent. I can duplicate the blue from samples of azurite in my possession.)

No. 2. Yellow lead oxide with small fragments of the blue scattered through. Gypsum.

No. 3. Yellow and red lead oxide. Trace of iron oxide.

No. 4. Azurite. Traces of malachite with traces of cuprite, a common impurity found in these minerals. There is some lead

oxide and calcium sulphate.

No. 5. Yellow lead oxide.

No. 6. Yellow lead oxide, gypsum, malachite, cuprite (impurity) trace of iron oxide.

No. 7. Gypsum, a small amount of carbonate, a protein giving Biuret, Millon and Xanthro-proteic reaction, starch (wheat), and oil (removed by ether) and some rag fibers of linen and wool, some of which are colored. These resembled materials used in old papers of 1450 made in Venice.

In 1940, he served on the Executive Council of the Georgia Academy of Science. Its annual meeting was held April 5-6, 1940, at Emory University, Atlanta, where his friend Dr. Sam Guy headed the chemistry department.

Eighteenth Annual Meeting

of the

**GEORGIA
ACADEMY *of* SCIENCE**

EMORY UNIVERSITY
ATLANTA, GEORGIA
April 5 and 6, 1940

OFFICERS

President, J. HIRAM KITE
Vice-President, R. B. HOLT
Secretary-Treasurer, GEORGE H. BOYD

EXECUTIVE COUNCIL

W. B. BAKER, ('40)   J. S. GUY, ('41)
W. H. VAUGHAN, ('40)   L. C. LINDSLEY, ('41)
          D. F. BARROW, ('42)
          O. R. QUAYLE, ('42)

EX-OFFICIO MEMBERS

J. H. KITE   G. C. WHITE
R. B. HOLT   GEORGE H. BOYD

LUTHER, THE SCIENTIST PUBLICIZED

Luther garnered headlines in the local paper with his speeches and his own writings. These articles are given in chronological order.

DAR Hears Talk by Dr. Lindsley

Milledgeville, March 20, 1942

Tracing the history of armament from the battle of Crecy to the present war, Dr. L. C. Lindsley, head of the department of chemistry at GSCW, told members of the local DAR chapter of the contribution chemistry has made in the development of explosives. The meeting was held at the home of Mrs. H. D. Allen, Sr.

The business session was conducted by the regent, Mrs. Stewart Wooten. Mrs. Harris Yarbrough and Mrs. Wooten were named as delegates to the National DAR Congress to be held in Chicago in May. Alternates named were Mrs. Frank Bone, Miss Elizabeth Napier and Miss Floride Allen.

* * *

The Macon Telegraph and News, Sunday supplement "Georgia Magazine" carried his speech to the DAR.

Through Blood to Peaks of Progress Man May March
By L. C. LINDSLEY

It has been said that victory in battle goes to the side which gets there first with the most men. It has not always worked out that way. The battle has more often gone to the side which had the most energy at its command, well directed. This is the fundamental principal upon which the past wars have been won and upon which all future wars will be won.

A handful of Normans conquered England. Robert Bruce won Bannockburn with 30,000 Scots against 100,000 English. Cortez, with a few hundred Spaniards, conquered the millions of Mexico. The English took India with only a few thousand troops. Jackson won his Valley Campaigns against almost unbelievable odds.

Wars have not always been the ruin of mankind. Some have been blessings in disguise. Instead of the race being set back a thousand years, mankind, in some instances at least, has marched forward through blood to peaks of progress that otherwise would not have been attained until centuries had passed.

At Crecy in 1346 the half-savage tribesmen of Wales and Ireland destroyed not only thousands of the knights of France and routed a much superior army but also destroyed a social order, feudalism. The barefoot footsoldier with the equipment then at his command proved himself superior to or the equal of the armored knight. No one can deny the end of feudalism was a blessing to mankind.

The wars between the Cavaliers and Roundheads, while bloody, settled forever the argument over the divine right of kings, and the taking of the Bastille was the beginning of the great Free France, the dream of Voltaire and the mother of Pasteur.

If the Arabs had not overrun Spain and the Near East, science would not have entered Europe, probably for centuries, and America would have remained undiscovered for many years.

Men die in battle, women mourn, one nation may seem to win, another seems to lose, but the great fundamental principles of human progress always survive. They are more eternal than the hills and more indestructible than matter. The nation that wins the war may lose the peace, and its economy; while a nation that loses the war may, by necessity, gain additional stamina through the trials and misfortunes of the conquered. Illustration of this is the rise of the New South with its mills of steel, textiles and paper, increasing annually at the expense of New England's people.

Courage is valuable in a war, provided human life is not squandered, but it takes more than courage to win wars. It may not even win battles. Pickett's charge at Gettysburg did not win Gettysburg; the Old Guard died at Waterloo, and Verdun did not win the war for France, nor lose it for the Germans, and the Persian army went through the pass at Thermopylae.

Energy properly directed and courageously used is necessary to win wars. A nation in a modern war that is outmanned and outgunned, outbombed and outgeneraled is apt to be overrun by superior energy more than at any time in the past history, because of the speed of the attack, the Blitzkrieg.

The Blitzkrieg is not a new idea. Washington employed it at Trenton. Jackson's Valley Campaign is better known in Germany than in America. His attack upon the rear of Hooker at Chancellorsville was his last. Stuart's cavalry rode around McClellan and Napoleon's Italian campaign made him famous.

These Blitzkriegs did not have tanks and airplanes but then neither did the opponents.

Good direction of energy in wars implies surprise, doing what the other fellow thinks is impossible, not only using new types and better weapons but also springing a new method of attack against which the opposing leaders have not been coached in the war college. These are the real high explosives in war when they are backed by a Home Front with high morale. The one who excels in these wins, and the actual shooting and bombing are a side issue. Those are used to drive home the argument and convince the enemy that he has lost. Sometimes the enemy is hard to convince, as was the case of Douglas MacArthur.

New implements of war are often decisive when other things are equal. The Steel Age won over the Bronze Age.

Damascus steel won over European in the Crusades. Toledo steel of Spain carried her armies of conquest over America and Europe. The English longbow out shot the continental crossbow. Wooden cannon of the Turks battered Constantinople and brought the Turks into Europe. The Confederate Merrimac retired the wooden navies of the world. The tank, an English product, and the Wrights' airship at Kittyhawk have made this war seem truly like an invasion from Mars.

In World War I, tungsten steel won over the German variety (of steel) because our tools used in making cannons were hardened with the tungsten, making it possible for us to produce three cannon to every one the Germans could produce.

The sling and the bow and arrow were the first weapons attempting to kill at a distance. By mixing sulphur, charcoal and saltpeter together, black gunpowder furnished the overturn of that social order whose downfall began at Crecy.

For about 500 years this explosive was the most important material for war, with saltpeter the most difficult ingredient to obtain. (Napoleon's garbage and Southern bat caves supplied the component.) Later, mineral deposits in Chile supplied the world market. While the English fleet ruled the waves England's enemies would have great difficulty in carrying on much of a war, and England felt secure.

In the lifetime of our fathers, Nobel united glycerine with nitric acid and made nitro glycerine, a very violent explosive. This material, soaked into fine sawdust or infusiorial earth and molded into sticks, made dynamite. Nobel devoted his life and his fortune to make war so horrible that nations would not fight. Our Nobel prizes are from the sale of dynamite. Wholesale killing of masses, from then on, became a science.

Cotton, nitrated with nitric acid and dissolved into a jellylike mass by ether and alcohol and molded into sticks, became widely used, but since England's fleet controlled the nitrates, England still felt secure even though the huge German fleet was being built. Germany's 1913 problem was nitrates for ammunitions; without it, she could not fight for a place in the sun.

At this time the German chemist, Haber, developed the method of making ammonia from the nitrogen in the air and hydrogen from water. That ammonia can be oxidized to nitric acid. This made it possible for Germany to fight in 1914. She was no longer dependent on nitrates from Chile. Her dye factories, busy making aniline dyes one day, could be changed to make TNT the next by reason of those nitrates.

Since then organic chemists have been busy developing better detonators and explosives which would produce greater concussion. There is still a wide field open for such compounds.

Ordinary corn starch mixed with an oxidizing agent and properly detonated makes a wonderful explosive. Ammonium nitrate, when detonated, makes one of the most powerful known. There are combinations of HN-3 which, if properly controlled could be used to shock even the Japs, and the nation which first learns to control it will probably rule the world. I have seen three or four drops of this material reduce many pounds of glass apparatus to a fine powder and partially wreck one end of a room. American chemists have won the chemical supremacy of the world during the past 20 years. When better explosives are made I am confident America will make them.

The time bomb that goes off in the ground after it has been dropped is very annoying but if you get it out in time before the acid has had time to be effective, it is not dangerous.

The isotope of uranium (135) has great possibilities if research can develop sufficient quantities. It has millions of times more energy than the same amount of coal. A handful of it could drive a battleship across the ocean and a bomber around the world. This is the weapon of the future.

There is stored, also, in the nucleus of all atoms, enormous quantities of energy beyond the conception of the human mind. All of the chemical energy we get from chemical reactions comes from the electrons in the outer shells of the atoms. This is probably less than a billionth of the energy enclosed in the nucleus of the atom, waiting for the right scientist to control, or to unloose, it upon the world. If I were that scientist and had such knowledge, the energy in a glass of water unloosed would detonate all matter in my vicinity, and this detonation could go onward in every increasing intensity until our earth would go out as a falling orb in space, as dust and minute fragments falling here and there, eventually as small meteors on the other planets.

Few war gases cannot be absorbed by masks. It is doubtful if it pays to use them. The dive-bomber gets more done by concussion.

Flame throwers are effective by subjecting the enemy and his equipment to such heat that the air he breathes burdens his lungs and the expansion of parts of his gun causes it to jam. Much thought has been given such things for use in specific instances for special jobs.

The most important war explosive which can be used on the enemy is morale on the home front.

When the man with the gun knows the home folks are just as willing to make the supreme sacrifice as he is willing to make, he can go on with a smile to victory or death. When he feels he is fighting and dying for John L. Lewis and his gang, he questions the value of democracy as a political institution. This is what placed France, a democracy, at the mercy of the Germans.

On the other hand, Russia, a communistic state, has so sold its people on service it can render by community working together and pooling their resources that a nation and a system despised by our democracies may possibly be the nation responsible for our winning the war. The most continuous explosion on the Russian front is the high morale. In their minds there is no doubt of the outcome. In Russia, there are no John L. Lewises. They would have been shot.

Russia has always belonged to the Russians. It always will. When we feel the same way about our own country, even though the Japs are invading our land, we shall have won the war.

LUTHER, THE PROPHET

The Macon Telegraph, on August 26, 1945, reported on Luther's predictions about the World War and the atomic bomb. Whereas some folks had kind of sneered at his predictions in 1942, the *Telegraph*, which had published the above article, was quick to recognize his foresight and reiterated it below. This published article duplicates much of his speech.

GSCW Scientist Foretold coming of Atomic Bomb

By Willa Beckwith

Nearly two years before the Emperor Hirohito accepted the surrender terms laid down by the Potsdam conference and almost two years before the atomic bomb was dropped upon Hiroshima to astound and awe the whole world, Dr. L. C. Lindsley, Professor of Chemistry at the Georgia State College for Women in Milledgeville, prophesied that properly directed energy would win the war against Japan. He prophesied that research would unloose the powerful energy that lay within the atom of Uranium 235.

Dr. Lindsley, speaking to the members of the Nancy Hart chapter of the DAR, said:

"It has been said that victory in battle goes to the side that get there first with the most men. It has not always worked out that way. The battle has most often gone to the side with the most energy, well directed, at its command."

He added that energy, properly directed and courageously used was necessary to win wars and pointed out the fact that new implements of war are often decisive when other things appear equal. The Steel Age won over the Bronze Age.

Damascus steel won over European steel in the Crusades; Toledo steel of Spain carried the armies to conquest over Europe and America; the English long bow outshot the continental cross bow; the Merrimac retired the wooden navies of the world; World War I tungsten steel won over the Germans, he pointed out.

The longbow, first effort to kill at a distance, was made obsolete by the appearance of gunpowder and for 500 years the nation that could secure the gunpowder ingredient, salt peter, was the leader. Salt peter was not easy to obtain and Chile supplied the world.

Then came the discovery of nitro glycerin, and with its magnificent fleet England controlled the nitrates until a German chemist, Haber, developed the method of making ammonia from the nitrogen of the air and the hydrogen of water.

"That ammonia can be oxidized to nitric acid made it possible for Germany to fight in 1914; she was no longer dependant upon Chile for nitrates," he said.

He told how organic chemists have developed better detonators and explosives to produce greater concussion and said the field was still wide open. Corn starch, he said, could be mixed with an oxidizing agent to product a powerful explosive; and ammonium nitrate, detonated produces a powerful explosive.

"A combination of HN-3, properly controlled, could be used to shock even the Japs and the nation which first learns to control it will probably rule the world.

"I have seen three or four drops of this reduce many pounds of glass apparatus to a fine powder and wreck one end of a room," he told the group.

But the most potent of all, the chemist said, was the isotope of uranium (235)—if research can develop sufficient quantities. It has millions of times more energy than the same amount of coal. A handful could drive battleships across the ocean and bombers around the world.

"This is the weapon of the future."

Though most of his audience smiled a little and considered Dr. Lindsley's ideas to echo from Buck Rogers or Flash Gordon, he told them of the powerful forces that lie with the atom.

"In the nucleus of the atom is stored enormous quantities of energy, beyond the conception of the human mind. All the chemical energy we get from chemical reactions comes from the electrons in the outer shell of the atom. This is probably less than one-billionth of the energy inside the nucleus of the atom, waiting for the right scientist to control it or loose it upon the world.

"If I were that scientist and had such knowledge and should

loose the energy in this glass of water, it would detonate all matter in my vicinity and this detonation could go onward in every increasing intensity until our earth would go out as a falling orb in space, as dust and minute fragments, falling here and there, eventually as small meteors on other planets."

Dr. Lindsley reported this week that one of his former students, a young woman who had majored in chemistry at GSCW, worked on the atomic bomb at the plant near Knoxville. She told him, the other day when she was on a visit to Milledgeville, of an experience at the plant.

Day after day she worked on a formula, doing only the thing she was told to do, "knowing nothing, seeing nothing, hearing nothing, telling nothing." But she couldn't help thinking and wondering.

One evening, after she had gone to bed, she lay wondering. Suddenly recollection of a lecture in Dr. Lindsley's classroom flashed upon her mind. She sat up in bed and exclaimed:

"But this sounds like the splitting of the atom!"

Next morning, reporting to work, the young woman asked permission to talk to the foreman; she told him about what she had thought.

In less than 30 seconds, that young woman was transferred to another department.

Two of Luther's students and his chemistry department colleague Lena Martin worked on the Manhattan Project.

* * *

Retired Chemist Tells of Russian Scientific Efforts Thirty Years Ago
Dr. Lindsley's Book May Have Aided Russians to Launch First Sputnik

By JERE MOORE, JR

That the Russian rise in the scientific world has not come exclusively from efforts of the last few years can be told by Dr. L.

C. Lindsley, retired head of the Chemistry Dept at GSCW.

Nearly 30 years ago, Dr. Lindsley had published a book on a new method of analysis using microscopes. It was titled "Industrial Microscopy." Of the 1000 printed, Russia immediately bought 600. Another 150 went to 26 other foreign nations.

Although the first and only edition sold out in 90 days, Dr. Lindsley refused to let any more be printed because he knew they would not be helping his country as much as he intended.

The method of analysis illustrated in the book allowed researchers to use microscope and polarized light, working with minute particles, to determine what chemical elements were found in a substance.

Dr. Lindsley aided a great museum in New York in determining whether paintings were really the works of Old Masters by checking on pigments used.

But why interest by Russians who had more utilitarian concerns that antique paintings?

The method taught could do in minutes with small amounts of equipment what chemists in huge laboratories required weeks to do in determining what minerals were found in ore deposits and in what percent.

The Russians could decide quickly where to mine for much needed minerals to make tanks or sputniks.

Another advantage was that material did not have to be destroyed to analyze it as a chemist would have had to do. This made it valuable in determining what elements were used to make old coins or to find the tree with the longest fiber that would make the best paper.

His microscopy also allowed a person to determine how much of what materials were used to make an object. This the Russians may have also found useful since our patents were not honored there.

Two of Dr. Lindsley's students at GSCW learned to use so well what the book taught that they were called to Oak Ridge, Tenn., where they worked on the A-Bomb until Hiroshima and Nagasaki were leveled.

Two years before these explosions, Dr. Lindsley wrote an unbelievable article for *The Macon Telegraph* telling of the powerful energy contained in the atom and how it would be released.

His book *Industrial Microscopy* was first published in 1929, the year the distinguished chemist left Columbia University to come here (to Milledgeville). It was not the first on the subject, but the first that contained actual photographs instead of drawings.

The book covered a wide variety of fields in basic research including narcotics which the Chinese found interesting, and structure of trees in detail which was very useful to Dr. Lindsley in his research for Dr. Charles Herty.

Because the tree fiber did not have to be destroyed to be analyzed, Dr. Lindsley was also able to help find a fast-growing poplar with a long fiber which was grafted to other trees to develop a new specie that now grows in abundance in the frigid northland.

Dr. Lindsley had been head of the chemistry department at William and Mary College before coming here and also a member of the staff of the chemical engineering department in summer school at Columbia University. The summer term was attended mostly by graduates returning for courses. His last class included 16 Ph.D.s

He retired from GSCW in 1948 and now lives on his northwest Baldwin County farm where he is restoring his ante-bellum home which burned a number of years ago.

"The trouble with people today is they think everything is new," Dr. Lindsley said. "In 1907, every physics student at William and Mary knew how to put an earth satellite into operation and at what speed it would have to travel to begin an orbit," he stated.

"The difference now is that people have the money and are willing to spend it to do these things," he added.

"In 1927 (sic), while I was studying for my Ph.D., a chemist from England delivered a lecture to a small group of us. He had already, on limited funds, isolated isotopes, the essential elements for producing atomic energy.

"I shall never forget his closing statement, he said that if the heavy hydrogen atoms could be separated from the half of a glass of water which he held that they might produce enough energy to drive the machines of the world, or if applied in one stop as an explosive, might send our world into space as a shooting star.

"But, you see, these things have all come from people other than Americans, isotopes from an Englishman, satellites with their

German background.

"The trouble with today's education in America, except in the medical schools, is that parents want everyone to graduate. They want to rubber stamp the students' foreheads with AB and the year.

"Our colleges and universities are not demanding enough to develop thinkers who can produce creative thought. They require only about one-fourth of the work that students are capable of doing.

"The Russians are demanding and know where they are going; their students have definite goals," the retired Professor said.

Jere Moore, author of this article and owner and editor of *The Union-Recorder*, the local newspaper, is the one who sold land to the family, and gave a warranty deed that was not valid. See the land purchases given below.

LUTHER & LILLAS THE INVESTORS

Real Estate Purchases by Lillas and Luther Lindsley

Luther had survived the Great Depression because his education and his book on microscopy put his skills in demand nationwide. He saw others lose "cash on hand," and money put into "paper" investments; he realized that property was the only investment that would be secure—if it were paid for and never put back in danger.

Never mortgage, never put up as property bond, and never sell.

When he came to Milledgeville, he and Patty Love still owned the Nicholson House. He soon purchased Westover, and then began to expand the landholdings.

These records were taken from the files in the office of the Clerk of Court in Baldwin County, Georgia, and cover the years 1929 through 1950-plus. All purchases made by either one of our parents are given here, together with the deed book and page for anyone who wants details of the purchase.

The names used over time to refer to different tracts of land are given as an aid in identifying all areas.

The records involving Westover itself show that the "dealing" was extensive and continued for several years. His salary for the 1931 school year was $3,200. In 1933, the salary had increased to $3,400.

1930, June 2. From Ophelia Wall to L. C. Lindsley. Deed Book 14, page 295. (DB14/295). 800 acres known as the Jordan Place. Payments to be:

$1250.00 September 15, 1930
$2750.00 November 1, 1930
$1500.00 September 1, 1931
$1500.00 September 1, 1932
$1500.00 September 1, 1933

Interest, 8%

1934, May 22. From Ophelia Wall to L. C. Lindsley. DB 17/597→. 795 acres ($8,500.00).

1934, June 9. From Milledgeville Banking Co. DB 18/120. Security deed on 795 acres (Westover) signed by L. C. Lindsley for $3,100.00 due December 8, 1934.

1934, October 23. From Milledgeville Banking Co to Lillas M. Lindsley. DB 19/249.

She purchased/paid off the security deed debt of $3,100.00 owed on Westover's 795 acres

1935, December 14. From L.C. Lindsley to Lillas M. Lindsley. DB 19/546→.

"For love and affection all real and personal property to the mother of my daughter Thulia Katherine Lindsley."

1935. From Bessie Chandler to Lillas M. Lindsley. DB 22/30

Warranty Deed, 269 acres, for $1,350.00
Known as the White House and the Phil Folsom Place.

The entrance to the Phil Folsom home is now the "yellow gate" that enters Lil James's lands she calls "Jamestown."

1936, March 7. From Susan Myrick to Lillas M. Lindsley. DB 19/596.

1/2 of 135 acres (Dovedale; "Jim's Place" now owned by Susan Lindsley)

That portion of the Myrick estate previously purchased from the E. S. Myrick estate by Susan Myrick and Lillas Myrick.

For $10.00 and other valuable considerations

1941, February. From Exchange Bank to Lillas M. Lindsley.
DB 26/316
Warranty Deed 135 acres $600.00
This tract is the Brown Place, as noted in a letter from Otto Conn, the president of the Exchange Bank: **We have your letter of January 12th, 1938, in which you enclose your demand note for $600.00 as purchase money note for the Brown Place of 135 acres.** This note was paid off at $50.00 per month at a rate of 5%. It lies on the west side of Highway 212; Dad always referred to the creek that flows across the Harper Place as "Miller Branch" and the Miller lands were given as the west boundary of this tract. This refers to the acreage from near the junction of Hwy 212 and Meriwether Road northward and west to the Small Power Line.

When Luther retired, his monthly payment was $50.00, the same as the payments for this land.

1941. From Richard Binion to Lillas M. Lindsley DB 22/332
Warranty Deed for 100 acres, paid $802.50 (transfer tax, $1.10)
Known as the Supple Place and also as the Dave Waller Place.
Our generation called it "Uncle Dave's."

1941, June. T. A. Myrick. DB 25/86
Security Deed, 1/6 interest in 100 acres
John Myrick Place

1941, July. T. A. Myrick, DB 25/91
Security Deed, 5/6 interest in 100 acres
John Myrick Place

1941. Unknown land, DB22/363
Warranty Deed, 108 acres, 319th GA Military District
Sold to Mrs. Lillas M. Lindsley by Jere N. Moore
$500.00

Thulia and Susan remember going with our father to a tract of land on the south side of Georgia Highway 22, on what is perhaps Horace Veal Road today. We believe this is the land. There is no record of the land being sold. Personnel in the tax assessor's office in the courthouse said they could not identify the location of the land from the description in the deed. Thulia remembers some problem about a deed, and believes this may have been the land and that the deed was no good. The warranty deed was signed by Jere N. Moore, at one time owner of the local (then weekly) paper *The Union-Recorder.*

1942, December. From Exchange Bank to Lillas M. Lindsley. DB 28/330
190 acres, 318rh Military District. Called "Comp's" as well as "Manuel's."

1942, December. From Roy L. Nelson, December 1942 DB 22/487
70 acres for $1200.00
Called variously in our lifetimes, the Nelson Place, the Jarrett Place, and lastly, "Missy's" and the TV Tower tract.

1943, February. From T. A. Myrick DB 22/509
Warranty Deed, 100 acres, the John Myrick Place
$425.00

1943, November. From First National Bank, Milledgeville DB 30/27
Warranty Deed, 75 acres $125.00 The Vinson Place

1945, August 2, From W. B Williams, Jones County (Georgia) DB33/448
Warranty Deed, 25 1/3 acres. Blount House
$4,000. (Tax paid $4.40)
Deed description: Begins at a stake in a rock pile in center of an abandoned road that is 119 feet north of the center of a public road leading to Haddock, Georgia ... to a stake, to a rock pile, to a stake in a rock pile and to the beginning.

1948. April. From Paul Farr DB 35/259
Warranty Deed, 46.25 acres $1200.00
Plat in DB 7, page 408

Unknown to LCL, the timber had been sold before he bought the land, and was cut after he bought the land.

1948. May. From J. C. Wilkinson DB 35/304
Quit Claim Deed 58 acres $300.00
319th GA Military District.
Area at the church on Old Monticello Road, left to Lil James, and she deeded it to the deacons of the church located on the land.

1948, August. From Sue Myrick to Lillas M. Lindsley DB 35/452
One-half interest in the Liberty Street House $3,000.00

1948, August. From Charles Griner to Lillas M. Lindsley DB 35/452
Warranty Deed 202.5 acres
$10.00 and other valuable considerations
Now known as The Harper Place

1950, March. From Emily S. Collins to L. C. Lindsley DB 39/5
"Deed" 67 acres 319th GMD, $800.00
Five years later, Luther transferred title to Lillas.

1955, January. L. C. Lindsley to Lillas M. Lindsley. DB 46/502
Deed. 75 acres, known as the Lane Place, in 318th and 319th Georgia Military District. The deed was to replace one destroyed by fire before it was recorded. Same witnesses to this one as to the previous one. We do not know why the discrepancy in the acreage from 67 to 75 acres.

The Lane Place included a house, very rundown. The house had a straight-up staircase in the front hall. All the paneling was wide (12-18 inch boards).

Lillas sold one-half of the land on the east side of the Old Monticello Road, including the house. The buyer immediately sold it, and the new owners tore down the old house and used the wide boards for roof decking.

1952, September. Sue Myrick to Lillas M. Lindsley DB 42/ 74
1/3 interest in part of the Myrick Estate (Home Place)
Share # 5 as shown in DB7/66-67
$10.00 and other valuable considerations.

1952, November 11. Virginia Myrick Stacy to Lillas M. Lindsley
DB 44/ 9
Warranty Deed 22.5 acres of Myrick Estate (Home Place)
Plat Book 7, pages 66-67
$450.00

1952, November 11. Elizabeth Myrick Nichols 1952 DB 44/ 10
22.5 acres, part of the Myrick Estate (Home Place)
$450.00

The map in Appendix X shows the location of the country lands that the Lindsleys purchased before and after their marriage. Lillas had inherited one section of the Dovedale plantation and she purchased these two more, so that she had one for each of her children.

*   *   *

Dad invested in property inside Milledgeville city limits. All titles were in Lillas's name.

1941, December. From Marion Ennis to Lillas M. Lindsley   DB 28/35
Part of Lot 1, City SQ 47

He bought one acre on Screven Street, Lot 4 of City Square 47. Screven Street crosses South Wayne. DB 28/1

Near the corner of Screven and S. Wayne, he bought "a brick constructed combination building" for $5,500. We knew it as the "McMillan Building." It had been the residence and home of Robert W. McMillan, Sr.

1948. Agnes O'B. McMillan to Lillas M. Lindsley DB 41/ 600
Quit Claim Deed dated 1948, filed 1952
Wayne Street, McMillan Building/land
Security Deed, DB 27/121 signed October 22, 1941, and due October 22, 1942 shows second mortgage to be $2,850.00
Warranty deed: DB 26/599

1948. December, he filled in the purchase with the South one-half of Lot 1, City Square 47, known as the "Finney Lot," a clapboard house that he rented as a residence. It stood between the north side of McMillan Building and the corner of S. Wayne and Screven Streets. Price, $1,100. DB 28/35

THE FURNITURE STORE

The McMillan Building had been home to the Moreland Furniture Store, and Luther kept the name. Whether the furniture truck came with the building or not, we don't know, but he used the truck for numerous "haulings"—furniture, cattle and hay, as well as to take the children to school. (They got to sit inside the cab.)

Sketch of the family truck, by Patricia Blanks.

The store had previously been owned by W. B. R. Moreland.

Luther had to obtain the license to operate the store; Hines and Carpenter, Attorneys, handled the legal matters. Their bill shows their fee at $30.00, fees for the local Clerk of Court J. C. Cooper, $8.50, and fees for the Secretary of State, $5.00.

The upper floor was on street level. The building sat on a slope, so the basement door, on the south side of the building, opened on ground level. It was rented out as an apartment for a number of years.

Luther recorded rents received on a Moreland Furniture Company statement as $20.00 per month for three months, then dropped to

$16.00 per month plus utilities of $10.00 per month.

Luther not only sold furniture from the McMillan building, he also repaired and refinished furniture there as well.

He sold spreads ($1.00), table cloths ($1.00), quilts ($2.00), mattresses ($5.00), towels (2/25¢, less in volume), pillow cases (25¢, less in volume), bed ($37.00), wardrobe ($14.00), breakfast suite ($10.00), Range ($34.00), iron bed ($5.00), #355898 Admiral Radio ($22.55, with $3.06 discount if paid in 30 days), icebox ($8.00).

Spread from Moreland Furniture Company, in possession of Thulia L. Bramlett.

He sold items on time. A receipt dated February 3, 1942, shows a sale of two blankets, one for $9.00 and one for $5.00, with a down payment of $1.00 and a balance of $13.00.

The McMillan Building also served another purpose. While the children were in GMC Grammar School, only two blocks away, they could walk to the furniture store and ride home with Luther at the end of his day.

The youngest daughter, Lil, stepped into a box of window panes one afternoon and cut a deep gash in the side of her leg. Luther immediately took her to the Richard Binion Clinic, but the doctor was not available. He then drove to the nearest pharmacy, obtained gauze and wrapped the leg to staunch the bleeding until the doctor was available to stitch up the cut.

Lillas sold the property in 1967, expecting to enjoy a monthly income for several years. She died in March 1968.

THE BLOUNT HOUSE

AN ECHO OF WILLIAMSBURG'S NICHOLSON HOUSE

One summer morning, Dad drove to Haddock for a bushel of peaches, but he came home without the peaches—and with the deed to a two-story clapboard house gone gray with some fifty years of neglect. Empty windows eyed the world with suspicion. Inside, dust and debris from the cracked plaster spread across the floors and showed the tracks of uninvited tourists.

Painting by Frank Herring of Milledgeville, about 1925.

The Blount House stood when Sherman marched his armies down the Clinton/Macon Road on his way from Milledgeville to Macon. Although the Union Army burned some houses, the Blount House, like Westover, survived. To Dad's delight.

Dad called the purchase "fire insurance" since such insurance was impossibly high for an antebellum house (Westover) with no fire department in the county, and no telephone to call one if it had existed.

Daniel Pratt brought Italian artisans to decorate the Blount House, Westover and other houses he designed. Like all houses of the time, it had no closets. And like Westover, the Blount House made a home for a variety of insects: Dirt daubers decorated everything, even the plaster molding, with their red-mud birthing chambers; wasps adorned the outside with gray nests that blended into the weatherboards; bees swarmed into the outside front, right-hand corner, just about eye level.

Luther spent his spare time on weekends at the Blount House, doing all the restoration himself. He built a scaffold so he could replace the plastering on the ceiling at the top of the stairs. Whatever needed doing, he just did, usually with no help. His only company would be one of his daughters, at times.

The house had been empty for several years, and one day when Luther arrived, he discovered a high school history class roaming through the house. The school bus driver had taken a knife to the woodwork to see if it were painted wood or really marble. Luther sent them packing. (*See Blue Jeans and Pantaloons in Yesterplace* for details of the teacher's break in and the furniture theft.)

For Luther, restoring the Blount House was in a way returning to his days as a teacher in Williamsburg, when he purchased the Nicholson House and restored it. His restoration pre-dated that begun by Rockefeller and others that put Williamsburg on the national map.

Dad talked about the difficulty he faced when Pattie Love died intestate. Under Virginia law, her widowed mother was her heir-at-law, not her husband. He had to re-purchase her half of the house. Luther left Virginia in 1928, and probably rented out the house. He sold it in 1940, and did not return to Williamsburg until the mid-1940s, when he toured his family around Williamsburg and the College. (See Appendix XX for information on the sale of the property.)

The Nicholson House in the 1980s. Photo by Lindsley S. Bramlett.

Outside Milledgeville, he restored Westover in the late 1920s. In 1945, he began restoring the Blount House. In the winter of 1954-55, he began rebuilding Westover after the fire. He used only what was available, such as lumber cut from trees on Westover; he did not cash in his "fire insurance," but retained the Blount house.

The "insurance policy" Blount House after restoration, as it looked when Lil and John James lived there.

When their youngest daughter Lil began her internship in Macon, Lillas deeded the house to her, and Lil and her husband John James lived there for several years. Eventually, however, her medical practice and John's law practice demanded they be less distant from Macon. They sold the house to Bill Banks, who took it apart in sections and moved it to Newnan, Georgia. There, Banks had it reassembled exactly as it was in Haddock, Georgia.

The Blount House in Newnan, Georgia.

The Blount House has been the subject of numerous articles in architectural magazines over the years, and one such article was by Luther's sister-in-law, Susan Myrick.

The Macon News, Nov 16, 1945

Beautiful 'Blount Place' Near Haddock Purchased

By SUSAN MYRICK

Front entrance of the Blount House

Parlor, front room to right of entrance hall

Known for many years as The Blount Place, the handsome, century-old house one mile from Haddock, was recently acquired by Dr. L. C. Lindsley, Professor of Chemistry at GSCW, and owner of Westover, six miles from Milledgeville. It is a coincidence that Dr. Lindsley owns both the old homes, for they were built by the same man, Daniel Pratt, architect, from New England, who constructed a number of Georgia residences. The home of Dr. and

Mrs. Frank Jones, Lowther Hall, at Clinton, which burned several years ago, was another of the Daniel Pratt houses.

Similar in type, Westover and the old Blount house are unmistakably New England in many respects and both houses are decorated after the fashion of the French elegances of that period.

The Blount house was built about 1828-30, according to Mrs. Frank Jones, authority on most of the Central Georgia houses of a century ago. John William Gordon first occupied the house and nobody knows much about Mr. Gordon, except that he was a wealthy plantation owner and a general in the Mexican War. From Gordon, the house passed into the hands of Thomas Bowen, who had married Mary Blount, sister of Congressman James H. Blount. That was about 1848, according to Mrs. W. D. Lamar, daughter of Congressman Blount. It was some time in the 1880s that Congressman Blount purchased the house from his brother-in-law, and the home belonged to the Blounts until a few years ago, when it was sold to Walter Williams, who sold it recently to Dr. Lindsley.

Two round, fluted columns, Doric in type, support the roof over the front stoop, and fluted pilasters provide a nice finish as well as a frame for the exquisite doorway. The balcony has wooden banisters of simple design. Doorways on first and second floors are paneled and massive and are finished with fan lights and side lights, graceful in design. Door and window trims, outside and inside the house, are fluted and finished with rosettes.

The gable frieze is plain with an ornamented molding just under the eaves. Pilasters at the end of the house, both front and back, match those of the stoop. The chimneys are inside.

Framed in an archway, the curving stairway leads to the attic. Top of the stairway was finished with a medallion, similar in design to that in the parlor at the right of the hall; the medallion in the parlor is in perfect state of preservation but that over the stairwell, like much of the plastering in the old house, had broken and fallen away.

The archway that frames the stairs is elaborately decorated in gold leaf and in three colors of paint, green, gold and brown; the wainscoting in the hallway is in the same color combination.

More gold leaf is used to decorate the parlor; the mantel is "marbleized" after the fashion of that era, with gold decoration on the reeded posts and the elaborate flower basket design in the mantle frieze.

The most unusual feature of the room is the two arched recesses, one on each side of the mantel; the pilasters are finished in gold, and a decoration of gold follows the curve of the arch. The baseboard of the room is "marbleized" to match the mantel.

As at Westover, Pratt used gold decor extensively; but at the Blount house he was lavish with the gold. All the rosettes at the door and window trims in the hall and parlor are done in gold and the mantel and rosettes in the opposite room are also gold.

There are large, high ceiling rooms on the first floor, and the second floor is the same plan--large, square hall with two rooms on each side.

The doors throughout the house have six panels and each door is painted to represent different woods, gum and walnut and mahogany. Elaborate acorn-like decorations surround the panels.

Like the hallway, the room on the left has a handsome wainscoting and like the parlor, that room has the marbleized-and-gold mantel. The ceiling medallion in the parlor has an acanthus leaf motif, encircled with grape cluster and leaf design. The medallion in the room opposite is of the same acanthus leaf design but with a fluted circle.

Nothing remains of the old kitchen, which once stood in the side yard. But in the front yard stand many crepe myrtles and a number of oaks that were planted many years ago.

If there was ever any plan for a garden, there is no evidence of plantings now. Boxwood and red cedars, which are so abundant at Westover, are conspicuously absent at the Blount place.

Dr. Lindsley is at work on restoration of the house and is planning to begin gardens there, also.

*   *   *

DOUGLAS HILL ESTATE FUNDS

Interesting how life-long beliefs can fall before facts in later life.

For many years, Dad kept a checking account in the Haddock Bank, and he signed each check with L. C. Lindsley on the signature line, and beneath that, "Douglas Hill Estate."

All of the children thought he had sold the family farm in Virginia, called "Douglas Hill," and banked the money in Haddock, Georgia. We all thought that Douglas Hill had funded his purchase of the Blount House.

In searching for deeds, we were unable to discover any in Prince William County that showed he owned land there. Manassas, where he was reared, is in Prince William County. A thorough search by an attorney's staff, plus a personal search by a volunteer at the Office of the Clerk of Circuit Court for Prince William County, showed NO Lindsley as a grantor or grantee after the 1921 deed signed by Luther, Pattie Love, and Luther's sister Virginia. (See Appendix XXI.)

In his letter to his grandmother on February 12, 1904, he asks if the purchaser of Douglas Hill has ponied up. Perhaps his step-grandfather did sell the home place and those funds eventually went to Luther. We just don't know. It remains a family mystery.

*   *   *

LUTHER, THE FATHER

Games We Played

Experience teaching children in primary grades helped Luther to be a participating father of three girls whose early lives were limited to home and yard. He enjoyed playing games, and even knew how to answer questions that began "why" and "how." For example, when asked how he could slide his belt through the loops in his trousers without looking, he said, "But I do look. I have eyes in the ends of my fingers."

At the upper end of the front walk, where the walk and boxwood border ended, sat two old farm bells. They had no clapper and no post, but perched on the ground, as if they were the foundation of the walkway. Their tops were just the perfect size for a small child to perch on. Two of us would sit on the bells while he counted (as Thulia remembered) in German and then in German said, "GO!" We went, all three of us, dashing for the bells, trying to beat the others to a seat. The winners sat, the sole loser had to take a position several feet away and wait for the next count to "go" for one of the bells. We'd push and shove and laugh, always feared to be one who did not get to sit.

One year, Santa brought a bike to Thulia, and Dad declared it was for us all to ride. He took time from his busy teaching and farm schedules to teach us how to ride a bicycle. In the front yard, beneath the cedars, magnolia and elms, he held onto the seat as one by one we learned to pedal and balance the handle bars. In spite of being in his fifties, he kept us upright until we could manage the bike on our own.

One spring, we decided we wanted a kite. Dad made one for us. The paper wrapping from our laundry became part of the kite. We don't know what wood he used. The tail was scrap cotton cloth torn into a long thin strip. Dad got it airborne and left us kids to keep it up. We couldn't. We ran with the wind, not against it, and of course it fell. Our pulling it across the ground finally tore it to shreds.

When we outgrew sitting on the floor in competition with Mother playing quadruple solitaire, he taught us how to play a card game called "five hundred." Invented about 1904, it is similar to bridge in that it is usually played with two pairs of partners, but with variations of bidding rules and cards dealt. (Details can be found on the internet.)

Having played baseball in his youth, Dad taught us about softball the spring after I received both a ball and bat from Santa. I remember him pitching the ball for me to swing the bat. Left-handed, I learned to bat right-handed under his coaching.

Our most nostalgic moments were singing as a family. Only Dad and Thulia could carry a tune, and Thulia was the piano player in the family. We'd gather around the piano some evenings and lift our discordant voices in songs of the Old South such as "Carry Me Back to Old Virginny" and "Tenting Tonight" or of World War I such as "White Cliffs of Dover." The old wars were very relevant to us during the war we were living though.

Lil says she remembers seeing Dad's eyes tear up when we sang of Virginia.

Grading papers

After supper, Dad would sit by the fire in the dining room, a box on the floor on either side of the chair. He'd lift a paper from one box, study and grade it, and drop it into the box on the other side. It never failed that one of the cats would come (as cats always go to the lap of the person who doesn't want the cat!) up to him and jump into his lap, into the middle of whatever paper he was grading. He'd grasp it by the nap of the neck and drop it onto the floor. If it returned to his feet, which were always down to his socks, he'd slip a toe under its belly and lift it away, but the cat always landed on its feet and would persist until one of us rescued both Dad and the cat.

I wonder how he could concentrate with the commotion of three children and the cats, but he could close off his surroundings and put all of his attention on the project at hand.

Conversations at Mealtimes

Every morning at breakfast, Dad brought the news from the barn about the milk cows or the other cattle that fed at that barn. Every evening, we got an update on the livestock at the other barns in the winter feeding months. He kept us posted on which mare had a foal, and we'd immediately begin thinking up a name for the newest addition to the farm.

The breakfast table always held a pitcher of milk, and we were expected to drink more than a glassful. Our glasses at that time would be considered "tea glasses" in size today. When any one of us passed a glass to Dad for a refill, he'd ask "How much" and if we answered a "half-glass," he would fill it up. No use to argue: We failed to say top half or bottom half, so we got the top half.

His Dreams about the Livestock

Air Boy had his own stall at the barn. He had to step over a threshold, and the window was so high that even as adults we couldn't look through it. He was a purebred American Saddle Horse, son of Kings Genius who was son of Bourbon King, the greatest American Saddle Horse stallion.

Door stops of Kings Genius, made of cast iron or of bronze, were sold in the late 1930s.

Offspring of Air Boy carried names to show their heritage: Air Male, Bomber, Lady Air, for example. Even the next generations reflected the names, such as Doll Boy, Doll Air and Dais Air.

We have no picture of Air Boy, but here are two of his grandchildren:

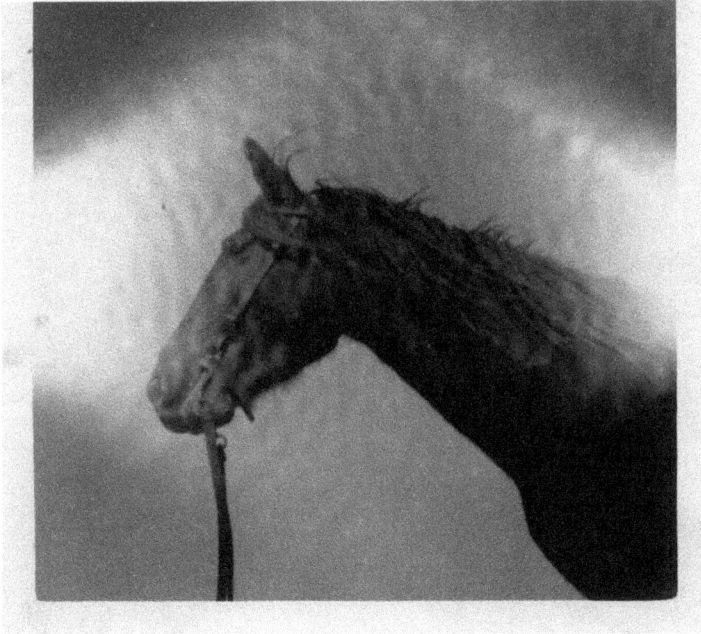

Prince Dan

Lady Air

Lady Air

Air Boy's sire, King's Genius

Bourbon King, Air Boy's grandfather

Dad had a menagerie of mares, mostly plow horses. Bred to either of these stallions, they produced fine mixed foals. But when Air Boy was put with a mare that wasn't receptive, she kicked him to death.

Thulia has the insurance policy on Air Boy. I don't know if Dad collected this money when the stallion was killed.

Before Dad purchased him, the stallion was at stud, at the Cline farm, now known as Andalusia, as shown in this ad that ran in the *Union-Recorder* on May 16, 1935.

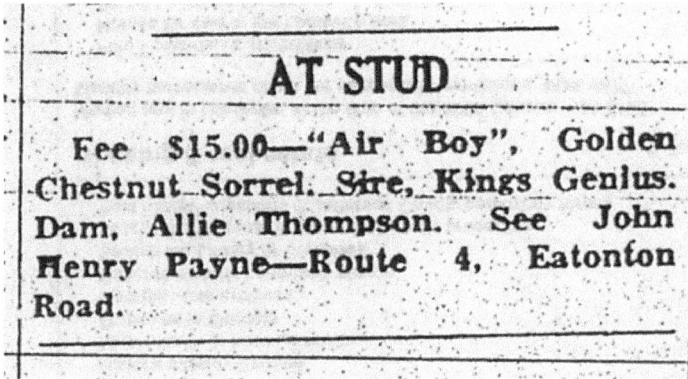

AT STUD

Fee $15.00—"Air Boy", Golden Chestnut Sorrel. Sire, Kings Genius. Dam, Allie Thompson. See John Henry Payne—Route 4, Eatonton Road.

What name Dad gave to his Arabian stallion I never knew. Thulia remembers, however, that he sired many foals, of all colors. One foal I remember was named Doll-Ab, to reflect the names of both parents.

Whittle whittle away from yourself

Dad often told of how he went to the fair and wasted a nickel because of the lure of the barker outside a tent. Come on in, the barker shouted, and learn how to never cut yourself with your knife. Your pocket knife, little boy. Or your kitchen knife, young ladies.

The boy spent his nickel and entered the tent.

A man sat on a stool and whittled. When the tent flap closed, the man didn't look up, but said, "Whittle, whittle away from yourself and never, never cut yourself."

Because of the barker's spiel, Luther wasted his money to learn something he already knew.

Games become work, or vise-versa

Summers were time for gathering hay. One of the Avery boys would drive the horse-drawn mower, with Daisy or Maud pulling it. Our fun then was to crawl up on the machine to ride with the employee and watch the hay as it was slashed and lay back behind us. Then we're argue over who got to ride on the rake, to watch the grasshoppers and mice flee as the rake rolled the hay into fluffy lines (windrows). The smell drifted around us and has stayed inside our heads for more than seventy years.

With the hay in windrows, we would take a sheet and flashlight out during the meteor showers, and Mother would point the flashlight to the stars, to Orion or the Seven Sisters, while we waited for another star to shoot across the sky.

The next day, Dad and his helpers would throw the hay into shocks, a job too heavy for us until our teens. But when they loaded up the truck, we'd be there, barefooted and laughing, packing the hay as the men pitchforked it up, over the tall sides, into the truck. The tighter we packed, the more hay they could add. For us, it was like jumping up and down on a mattress, a joy we were strictly forbidden. Fun, that is, until we stepped, barefooted, on a blackberry or Cherokee rose briar.

LUTHER AND LILLAS: THE FARMER AND THE HOMEMAKER

Dad never asked a hired men to do something he himself would not do. He slopped the hogs. He mended fences. He doctored the horses. He built two barns, with hay lofts. He milked. He fed the livestock in winter rain and snow, in the mire and muck of a wet barnyard. He took part in butchering hogs and cattle.

Mother stuffed the sausages after cleaning out the intestines for casing and grinding up and seasoning the meat. She also made soap from hog fat and lye, and when the daughters were old enough, they got to stir up the pot. She poured out the liquid soap into a large pan, let it solidify, and then cut it into cakes.

Luther was reared on a farm, loved animals, and taught agriculture. When he purchased Westover, he had a plantation-sized farm.

In less than 15 years, he had expanded his holdings from about 800 acres to almost 2,500. Livestock numbered more than fifty horses and more than one hundred cattle, plus hogs, chickens, turkeys, and at times, the children's ducks.

His crops included watermelons (about fifteen acres) and other melons. The family garden grew tomatoes, corn, okra, sugar cane, butter beans, string beans, turnip greens, and probably other veggies that the children no longer remember.

Fruit trees provided apples, peaches and pears. The woods provided blackberries, strawberries and plums.

Lillas, sometimes with the help of her elder sister Tippie, canned for winter food, and in later years, when the family purchased a freezer, she froze both fruits and vegetables.

Chickens provided eggs for daily breakfast, and Lillas pickled them for winter use when the hens failed to lay enough for breakfast and other dishes.

Everyone became involved with the butchering. The children remember black neighbors who were not tenants but were professional-level butchers who came to Westover to help at hog-killing time. These men also handled the butchering of cattle hit by the trains.

These men were paid in kind: They received the cow hide, head, lights, and liver. For help with the hog, they received the head, lights, liver and feet. (Lights were the lungs.)

They would slice the hog's throat, swing it up by the Achilles tendons, and shave the hair off with the aid of hot water and a razor-sharp knife.

When the children grew old enough they helped make sausage, turning the handle of the meat grinder. Lillas became adept at stuffing the sausage; They used a water hose to help clean out the intestines so they could be used as casings.

A story was that you poured water through the intestines, slapped them up against a tree, and then ran the gut between your toes, to clean them out. I never saw that procedure used, however!

During war years and perhaps before, the family sold eggs to Milledgeville merchants. The eggs were gathered daily, washed, and candled to ensure they were fresh. Candling involved holding the egg up to a hole in a cardboard against a light; if a shadow showed an embryo, the egg was not fresh and couldn't be sold.

Although there was a fenced chicken house off the west side of the yard and a hen house down the hill behind the house (both with nests built in), the chickens never seemed to stay in the pens. Hens made nests under the boxwood hedges and other shrubs; their favorite nesting sites, however, were under the spikes of Spanish bayonet. Predators would not enter that jungle of spikes.

Snakes could slip under a hen and eat eggs without her budging off the nest. They also ate the biddies.

Hawks were a constant threat to free-roaming chickens. At one time, Luther killed a hawk and dangled it from the edge of the wash house to deter other hawks from hunting in the yard.

One spring, a fox put an end to the turkey flock; the family thought the fox might have been rabid, for it did not drag off a turkey, but killed them all and left the carcasses.

Luther raised cattle to sell, and periodically sent some to the auction barns in Macon. The children became the herders by the time they entered their teens, and on horseback would round up and drive the cattle to the pasture gate, onto the road and down to the barn. About twenty acres were fenced for a barnyard.

Before the truck came to haul the cattle, the children drove them into the smaller pen and into the barn. Once the truck backed up to the chute, the gate was opened. Cattle bawled and balked, but the girls learned to whoop just the right way to move them into the truck.

Luther had a way of calling "woook-woook" when he wanted to get cattle to the feeding barn in the fall. Somehow they seemed to know the difference in "come get food" and "get on the truck."

He could not bear to see one of his horses die. When a horse "got down" he would build a rack (a narrow stall, with boards beneath the animal) to hold it while he tried to nurse it back to good health. A board at the animal's head held a bucket of water, hand-carried from the spring to the barn, and a bucket of sweetfeed.

In spite of his efforts, few sick horses survived.

PART VII

AFTER THE CHILDREN LEFT HOME

AUTUMN, 1954

When the last of the children left home for college, Luther and Lillas kept up a constant correspondence with the girls, thereby providing a picture of events in their lives and on the plantation. Susan saved many of her letters, and they are given here.

Many of Luther's letters were on a sheet of typing paper he had torn in half; he used only one-half, probably as a result of his poverty as a child and his life during the depression. He usually wrote in ink and in his elaborate script. Lillas usually typed her letters—her children insisted that her handwriting was illegible.

These letters began in 1954, just before Westover burned, and continued throughout the life of both Luther and Lillas. They include not only letters to and from the children but also correspondence with cousins from the Marshall line. They are grouped here together rather than merged into the segment about rebuilding Westover.

This first letter refers to two of the horses. "Compts" (or "Comps") was the name we used to refer to the section of land and house where Sol, Manuel, their wives, and Willie Mae's children lived (called "Manuel's") where Thulia built a tractor shed in 2012.

* * *

Postmark: Oct 27, 1954
Grady and William were gelded riding horses.
From Luther

Dear Sue,

Happy birthday to you! Am sending you $5 worth of eats, etc. Do not get drunk, or in jail.

Grady and William have found the "good life" in Compts, I guess. Have not been to barn. Mom is sending you something. Am on my way to Harpers to try to find the cows. Have not yet seen them.

> **Love to you both**
> **Dad**

* * *

THE HOUSE FIRE

The next letter came after Westover burned.

Thulia was in Colorado (in the U. S. Army, stationed at Fitzsimons Hospital) and did not learn of the fire until she received a letter from our parents. Lil and I were at North Georgia College, where Lil read the *Atlanta Constitution* daily between classes, at the Student Union. She read that Westover had burned. There was no way to directly reach our parents, and we called Eva Sloan, a close friend. Mother's use of my nickname in the "to" line below shows how upset she was—she well knew that I had abandoned it for Susan some months before.

Postmark: November 4, 1954
From Mother

Dear Sis and Miss Lil:

Tip came out this P.M. and brought my glasses, so I can write tonight. As you can see the typewriter was saved.

That night Mr. Blizzard came out to talk pulpwood with Dad. Some time around nine we heard the loud clap of thunder and commented on it. About ten minutes, no longer, we heard a noise, thinking someone was breaking in the house, jumped up and went to the front hall. The whole front of the house was all lit up it was burning so. It hit all across the side of our room. Dad started up stairs and Blizzard, after looking from the front porch, told him it was too far gone to go up.

We all rushed to the ball room and started putting china in the drawers of the china cabinets. In a few minutes, Tip, J. C. Green, his wife and Barbara came up. That was all the help we had until we were forced to come out. We went from the ball room to the parlor then to the hall and then we took things from the other two rooms out the side porch when the stairs were gone and that ceiling falling. By that time the Lowes had come and soon lots of people so with the help we brought things all down here. Right then.

We saved Dad's most valuable pieces of china, all the silver goblets and that type of silver that was in drawers in the ball room.

(We did not get the flat silver, so all of yours is gone, Sis), but we can (get) more of that and are not letting that bother us. We got the one cabinet from in there, the top being a Myrick piece. We got the portrait of my grandparents, all three big mirrors, four little sofas, the big one that used to be in the hall. A number of straight chairs, the TV and the chest that it stood on. The big silver candle stick and the Myrick candle sticks. I guess that is about all.

We are trying not to take it too hard for we realize that we have so much to be thankful for. If Dad had gone to bed early that night, oh, we have so much to be thankful for.

That night Blanche brought us down a couple of cots and mattresses for us to have, with cover, for the night. She also brought a hot plate and food for breakfast. Betty Sloan and George came early and helped move things down here then went home and came back bringing Bob and Mrs. Sloan. The Lowes in fact so many people have done so much for us. The Lowes brought breakfast things including silver also. But I'll write another letter about that.

I've gotten the kitchen cleaned a little but am not trying to hurry about getting the house straight. May wait till you are here for the holidays.

There was nothing wrong with the wiring. It was simply that it was so dry the lightning was not grounded.

I was upset that you saw the paper before you got my letter. I know you were terribly upset and I am glad you called the Sloans. You had said you seldom saw a paper. I thought of asking Sue to call you but knew you would be at class and thought this way you would be less upset.

The fact that Dad has Blount's makes it easier for him I think. He was the most wonderful thing that night, directing every body and not saying a word. In an hour's time after the lightning struck, the house was gone.

I'll write again soon. I'm keeping busy to keep from thinking. You do the same.

Much love from us both. Dad is writing Thulia tonight and will write you tomorrow night and I'll write her.

Mother

* * *

Westover – 1944

A snapshot provided by Allie Myrick Bowden after Westover burned.

From: *Blue Jeans and Pantaloons in Yesterplace* by Susan Lindsley
This section duplicates Mother's letter, but contains much insight into
how our parents managed the dramatic change in their lives.

**Other than the loss of a human life, the greatest loss of my
lifetime occurred in October 1954, when fire took Westover
plantation house.**

**The two youngest children, Lil and I, were away at college, and
Thulia had gone to work in Colorado when lightning blasted
against the westernmost chimney and spread its 10,000 degrees of
heat across the entire roof.**

**The heart pine erupted in flame, and within an hour the house
was gone.**

**Mother and Dad were downstairs in the dining room, where
Dad sat with his shoes off while he talked to a neighbor about
timber. They heard the thunder and crack of lightning, commented
that it was close, and then they continued their conversation.**

**Meanwhile, Tippie had been visiting some neighbors who were
driving her back to her town home when they saw the fire from
three miles away. They knew it was Westover.**

Tippie was running for the front door when she heard the visitor yell, "Your house is on fire, Doc!" She had traveled three miles between the time the fire began and the time Mother and Dad realized their home was going up in smoke.

No one could get up the stairs——by the time they realized the house was burning, the entire upper story was engulfed in flame. We lost the four-posters, the trundle bed, the wardrobes, the cedar chests, the cradle made by a Lamb family ancestor Dad referred to as "Major Lamb," the family portraits, the letters from General Lee to Mother's grandmother, Mother's wedding and engagement rings.

Barefooted, Dad toted out the tall mirrors, the matching Myrick mirrors that stood nine feet tall and the one Lindsley mirror that was ten feet tall. He saved some of the Napoleon goblets and the William and Mary chairs. Some people in the area saw the flames and came to help.

Someone pulled the leaves from the long Myrick dining table, but the base of the table that sat the ten members of Lillas Myrick's family, plus guests, never got out.

The visitor dragged out the small walnut chest from the dining room that contained my scrapbook and the family articles from newspapers, and on top of that chest out came Dad's shoes, the last things to be pulled from the house.

When my parents had to flee the burning building, the family silver was gone, silver that had been saved when the Yankees searched for it during The War. Dad's books were gone, not just his book based on his research of microscopy and copies of his dissertation, but also his books of poems, short stories and essays from his college days.

One thing that came out of the burning house and remained for many years was bad dreams about the house burning; the fear of fire coming again, for it came twice to Mother. She lost not only Westover but earlier had also lost the family home at Dovedale to fire.

Home from school for Thanksgiving, Lil and I spent our holiday sifting through the ashes, looking for our coin collection, for Mother's diamonds (never found), for Indian artifacts, and for any other item that might have survived. Our coins were either melted together or were so scorched we couldn't read the faces.

The bank refused to take the scorched coins, so just washed them up and used the nickels, dimes, quarters and pennies in the parking meters.

We rescued many arrowheads, but the fire had turned the flint and quartz into fragile, glass-like material that cracked and broke with the slightest thump.

When Dad couldn't find some of his porcelains that he knew survived, ones he himself had taken to the door and handed to someone, he asked the black neighborhood people to find those items. They did, and the word came back that these items were in the homes of certain white people who had shown up to help rescue items. Dad never approached them for his property, figuring these people must have considered it small pay for what they had helped to save.

Of course, the day after the fire, word spread, and the tourists started coming by. Mother and Dad had slept in the cottage next door after taking everything to either the overseer's office or the cottage. They had no clothes, no bedding, no cooking utensils. Friends, however, supplied them with what they needed to get started in the next few days.

Emanuel, a tenant and farm hand, walked down to the house the next morning, and when Mother told him to just turn the cows out, that she didn't even have a straining rag, he did, and then he walked the two miles home and came back with a jar and a straining rag. Mother said those gifts were the most precious and thoughtful given to them after the fire.

When the tourists started strolling into the yard to see what they could find, Mother sat in one of the yard chairs, with Tippie for company, and turned the people away. Dad put three strands of barbed wire across the front gate, but still people came into the yard. One lady was halfway through the fence when a cow walked up to her and looked her in the eye——the woman left.

In 1954, Dad was 66 years old. In spite of the work load of managing the plantation lands and livestock, he began the slow task of rebuilding. No architect. No power tools. No blueprints. Just Dad and Manuel. Dad's eyes were so bad he marked the boards with a nail because he couldn't see a pencil mark. Then he guided his handsaw with his fingers to follow that mark as he cut.

Dad didn't buy lumber to rebuild. He had lumber cut on the

plantation: eighteen-inch-wide pine boards lined one room; eighteen-inch cottonwood and gum lined other rooms. Cedar from the trees cut when the road was widened became panels for the front hall.

Someone told him he had a big job ahead, and he said, no, "not a big job, just a lot of little jobs."

REBUILDING WESTOVER

Dad began to rebuild as soon as the ashes had been sifted, raked up and scattered over the daffodils and the debris had been removed. He had no floor plans or blueprints, no electrical tools, and only one helper. Dad was half-blind and sixty-six years old. Although he had retired from teaching, he still ran a 2,500-acre plantation with miles of fences to maintain, more than one hundred fifty cattle and about seventy horses. Hay still had to be cut and moved into the barn in the heat of summer; cows had to be milked, young bulls had to be herded to the barn and hauled off to the sales; winter demanded hay and feed be put out at every barn for the livestock.

He determined to reconstruct his dream.

Eventually he discovered the blueprints made under Roosevelt's Historic American Building Survey in the library at the University of Georgia. He studied them, but did not lay out his house in the same floor plan.

He began by repairing the foundation—replacing broken brick and adding mortar to reinforce some of the joints.

Dad takes a break in rebuilding. The chimney behind him stood at the southeast end of the house. The room behind him would be the new kitchen.

His greatest resource was the land. It provided hardwood for paneling and pines for studs. Old tenant houses, on the verge of collapse, provided floor joists and beams. Large trees were cut into boards as wide as eighteen inches to use for wainscoting and paneling. All boards to be used for walls and flooring were tongue-and-groove; the underfloor was rough cut, as were the studs.

When a Macon businessman heard about Dad's project, he came to see for himself what was going on. He was impressed with Dad's dream and persistence and two days later sent a flatbed full of trim to the site as a gift in admiration of Dad's positive attitude. When Dad said he couldn't accept such a gift, the driver said he'd be fired if he didn't leave the lumber. So Dad saved the driver's job and thanked the family whose gift trimmed the entire inside of the house.

As he framed the house, the throw-away dog "Danny-Might" slept in the shade of the cedars in the back yard. When flooring went down, the dog came up to sleep on the boards. But when doors went up, the dog went back to the yard, for he was not allowed in the house. Here he is on the back porch with them after Dad and Mother moved into the house.

Luther, Lillas and Danny-Might

Dad takes a break on the back porch.

Each room was paneled with wood cut on the place by local mills, who cut the boards the width he wanted, planed them, and put in tongue-and grove edges. These pictures show paneling in the living room, as well as Mother with her favorite hobby, knitting, and her dog Hilda (Princess Brunhilda of the House of Westover).

The door behind Lillas led to the front sitting room. The doors in both pictures were double-cross doors.

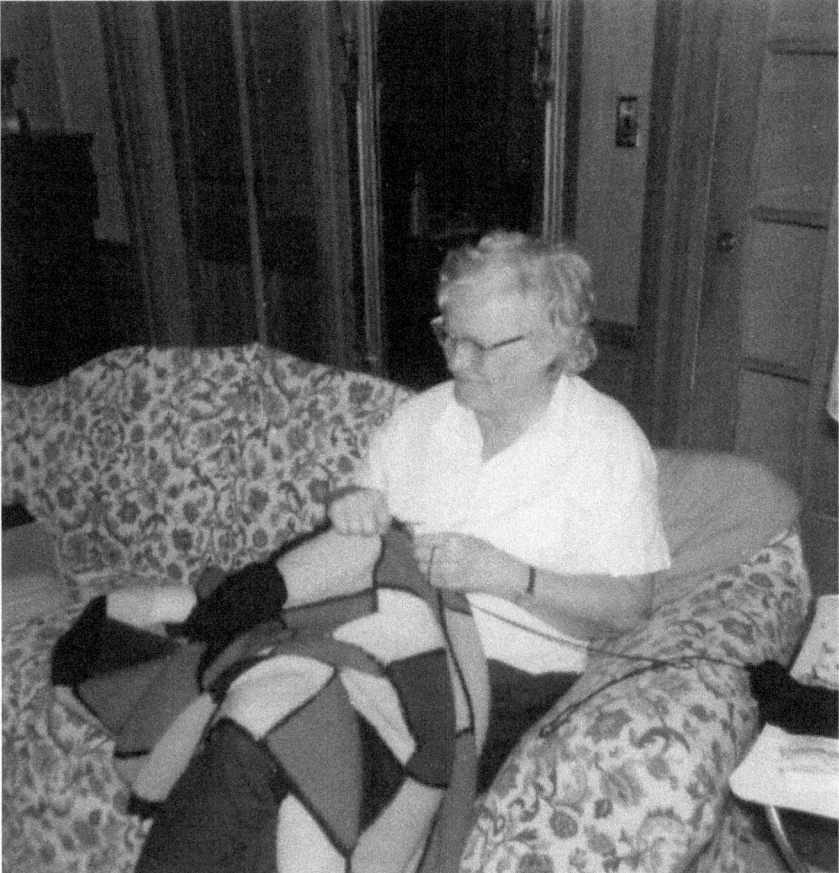

The wooden door behind her leads to the kitchen; the glass panel door leads to the back porch where firewood was stacked in the winter. Lillas made the cover for the sofa where she sits.

The sketches on the next two pages, by Susan's school friend Pat Blanks, provide the layout of the house that Dad built.

Where the ballroom and back porch stood, he built two bedrooms; the south room was paneled with sheetrock and painted blue; the one behind it was all pine, with vertical boards, twelve-to-fourteen-inches wide. The wainscot was eighteen inches wide and topped with some of the trim sent over by the Macon visitor.

And closets! Yes, Mother, who had never had closets in her home, was most pleased that a closet ran the length of these two rooms, each room having one end of it. And the blue room, their room, had an extra closet at the end toward the front hall, a large square walk-in, with a shelf, a perfect storage area.

The entrance hall ran from front to back, with a door in the middle. From the back hall the stairs went up a half-flight and then cut sharply to the left to reach the second floor. The front hall was paneled with walnut; the back hall, with cedar.

The front hall walls reached up to the second floor. Plans were to put in a winding staircase, but it was never installed.

LOWER FLOOR

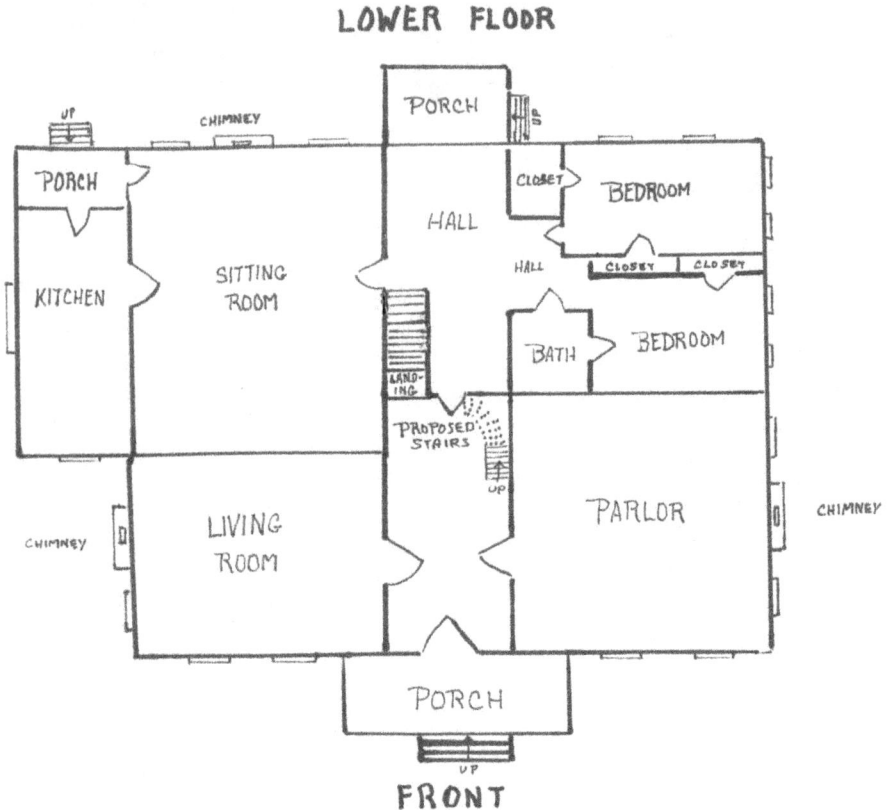

FRONT

UPPER FLOOR

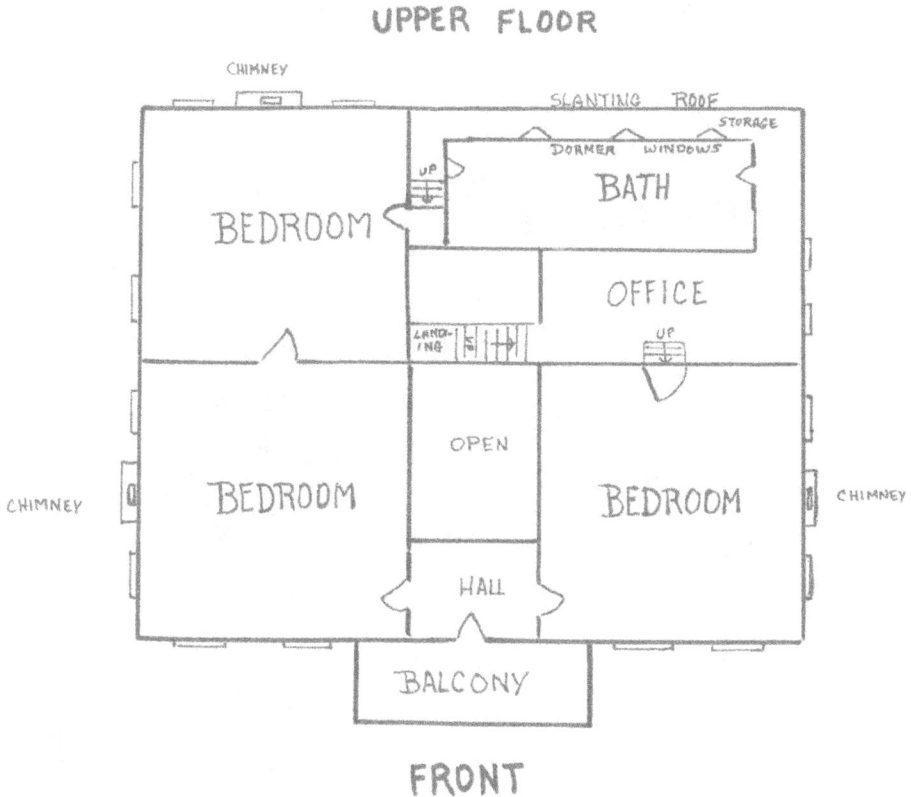

CHIMNEY

SLANTING ROOF

STORAGE

DORMER WINDOWS

UP

BATH

BEDROOM

OFFICE

LAND-ING

UP

CHIMNEY

OPEN

BEDROOM

BEDROOM

CHIMNEY

HALL

BALCONY

FRONT

The upstairs front hall was only half the width front to back as the downstairs hall, so it opened over the downstairs. Dad did not install a safety railing, expecting to complete the stairway and winding the banister over the edge of the opening.

On the south side of Milledgeville, not far from the Rockwell Mansion that once belonged to Lillas's father and grandfather, was an architectural salvage facility. The owner had columns; he had old doors; he had mantels and windows and hardware from old houses and from the recently dismantled Darien Hotel.

A recycled house on Montgomery Street and the Darien Hotel supplied doors, windows, hinges, mantels and other material.

Dad mixed the "fashion" of ante-bellum Georgia with that of his home in Williamsburg by adding dormer windows.

The large windows shown here contained old "wavy" glass that showed imperfections, as did most hand-made panes in the early 1800s.

Note the pyracantha bush on right. It survived the fire and flourished.

Dad found magazines that carried ads for many small items he wanted. The old commissary (which we called the milk house) became a tool house and storage house. He smoothed edges with a hand plane. He had a variety of screwdrivers (no, not power driven); he had the old hand saws, and small artistic saws for the fine work.

All rooms except one were paneled with wood: Oak, cedar, walnut, cottonwood, gum, poplar.

Lillas and Luther take a visitor on tour. They had not yet moved in. Note vertical cedar paneling.

He trimmed the ceiling in different rooms with designs shown here. It's hard to imagine the time it took to cut all these small bits out by hand and assemble them onto boards to trim out fifteen-foot-long walls.

He imitated the Ionic capital in the trim for one room.

He also copied the triglyph of colonial architecture.

Dentil crown molding, popular in early American architecture.

When I came home for vacation one summer, I strongly encouraged my parents to move into the house, although it was unfinished. The columns were not up; siding was up on only a portion of it; but doors and windows were in—a fanlight over the front door, and even a fanlight over the window on the north side of the kitchen. Propane heaters were ready in each room, and the house would be warmer than the cottage they were living in.

Dad was aging. He needed to be in his house. So they moved in and made it home.

Myrick cousins who were downsizing wrote Mother they would sell some of the Myrick family furniture, and since ours had burned, did she want to buy it? Mother did, and the four-poster bed purchased by her grandfather for her uncle Goodwin came to the new Westover. It was lifted by ropes from the front of the house to the upstairs front porch, taken to the southeast room, where it was re-assembled. Other pieces, washstand and dresser, sofa and chair, also came from that line of the Myrick family to the new Westover.

Family portraits were again hanging; both Myrick and the new copy of Dad's Confederate soldier grandfather. The map Lt. Lindsley carried during the War Between the States found a home on the wall when it came from his Aunt Minnie to the new Westover. The picture of Beatrice, who guided Dante through Inferno, which had hung at

Dovedale and later at the Liberty Street house, found a new home over the living room fireplace.

The new living room with the painting of Beatrice over the fireplace. The painting is now in possession of Susan Lindsley. Photo by Luther's cousin Edgar Marshall.

The house in October 1963, after Luther's death. It is hard to imagine Luther, at his age, building this large house, much less roofing it himself or even building the framing of the front porches.

Westover after Mother had it finished. Dad retained all of the chimneys, including the one on the right, here, where lightning struck the original house. Note height of boxwood.

Because the fire killed the boxwood close to the house, treebox was
planted in its stead. Treebox is a "tree" type of boxwood and now lines
the driveway.

Dad hand-made the fanlights over the doors. The columns were too short,
so when Mother had the front finished, she built up the brick base. The
crepe myrtle was killed back by the fire, but rose again from its roots.
Bees returned to make a home in one of the columns.

Here the new kitchen is visible to the left; note the fanlight, also hand-made.

Inside view of the north windows of the kitchen. Note the "H" hinges.

This snapshot shows a portion of the original fence that remained into the 1960s. This gate was on the east side of the house and separated the front and back yards. The wooden panel fencing was added after Luther's death, to confine Lillas's German shepherd, Princess Brunhilda of the House of Westover (Hilda).

Front gate in 2013, as restored by Thulia Lindsley Bramlett. The original fencing had fallen to rot, as shown in the upper snapshot.

Dad continued to work on the house when not tending to the farm chores. The cattle and horse herds were slowly being downsized. The pig sty had been empty for many years. So most of Dad's day could be spent on his carpentry work. When he tired, he would stretch out on the sofa in the living room to rest and if William and Mary were playing football on TV he would watch the game—until he dozed off. He had begun the work in the winter of 1955 and worked on the house until he died eight years later. But he and Mother had made it home.

Rebuilt Westover, August 1964, back of house.

A former tenant came by Westover several years after it burned, and expressed his thoughts about Luther's efforts to improve the world around him in a Letter to the Editor, *Macon Telegraph*, Monday, March 7, 1960.

WORLD WOULD BE LOVELIER WITH MORE DR. LINDSLEYS

Editor, The Telegraph:

Recently while on a business trip trough Baldwin County I stopped by to see some old friends. When I first met these friends some 16 years ago I was only 24 years old. At the age of 24 most of us haven't learned to appreciate the simple yet finer things of life. In fact, there are some who never learn to appreciate life's beauties.

My friends, Dr. and Mrs. L. C. Lindsley, not only appreciate these things which most of us take for granted, but do much to improve them. Fifteen years ago I lived in a cottage near the large old colonial house that was the home of the Lindsleys.

I do not know Dr. Lindsley's age at that time, but he was of an age when a majority of men who are not financially able are forced to retire. In spite of a foot condition which was very painful to my friend, he continued with his teaching and upon returning home each day worked at hard physical labor until well after dark.

Fifteen years ago I could not understand why a man of his financial standings should push himself so very hard and do so much physical labor on things that mattered so little. Or so it seemed to me.

At the time I lived in the cottage there was a red hill that ran behind the cottage and continued on behind the large house. This hill was hopelessly eroded. The gullies were spaced so close together that only a ridgeback was between them. They were 6-to-10 feet deep and up to 1,000 yards in length.

The situation was such that it looked impossible to correct even with bulldozers and other modern equipment at great expense. This did not stop my friend. He picked up stones, put them into buckets and carried them to be placed in these red gullies.

Recently, I was shown this red hill. I couldn't believe it. There was no red to be seen. Grass and beautiful shrubs were everywhere. As I observed the just pride with which Dr. Lindsley showed me this reclaimed land, I knew that he did not mind all the falls that he must have taken while stumbling along those gullies with buckets of rocks, the backaches he must have had, or the torn and bruised hands he must have received quite often. To him these things were expected but were not excuses to drop so large a project.

This project was by no means his only undertaking. There are too many more to mention and all would seem impossible even to a young man. Some are complete and some he is just starting. When he reaches one hundred years of age if he thinks a pecan orchard is needed on his plantation, then he will put one there. And he won't hire it done but will do it himself. The possibility that he wouldn't live to see the trees bear pecans would never enter into his mind. It would be something he wanted done and so he would do it.

We need many more Dr. Lindsleys in this world. It would be so much more useful and beautiful

GEORGE WOODALL

MORE FAMILY LETTERS

Postmark: November 18, 1954
From Dad

Horses: Dolly was Susan's riding horse; Prince Dan was Thulia's. Grady and Prince William each of the girls rode at different times.

Wednesday Night

Dear Miss Lil and Sue,

The rains have come, the oats are up, good stand, the house has a few leaks and Mom has begun knitting again so I guess all's right with the world! Today we scattered rye grass in the back of the big field in front of the yard and will be steadily putting it out for a few days.

Have been busy painting rooms, cleaning up furniture and shopping for Frigidaires, mattresses etc. Things are still piled up in the house but we are getting on with things pretty well considering. Have gotten up one of the mirrors—quite an accomplishment!

When I get in from the fields about five I lie down for a little rest before supper and am ready to start over again on the walls, floors or furniture.

Most of the horses are holding their own. Grady and Prince William are still back in Compts, Dan is in excellent shape. Dolly a little thin. Clover is coming up all over the big front pasture, better than I hoped.

I am sending each of you $5.00 which I suspect you can use. Do not worry about finances. We still have considerable cash from timber and pulpwood is growing good, bad trees, never would be good.

Let us know if we must meet you in Milledgeville or if Mrs. Jones is coming through by Harper's Store, only two miles farther.

Love,
Dad

* * *

Post mark: December 2, 1954
From Dad

Wednesday Noon

Dear Susan and Miss Lil,

Here are your checks for winter quarter. If I have made any errors have the office write me.

Am carrying them to town with me now to mail.

Found my William and Mary Flat Hat Medal, the Hittite clay coin, Alex the Great and one other. Hoping to find the (illegible) etc.

Love to you both.

Dad

* * *

Postmark: January 19, 1955
Return address: L C Lindsley, Milledgeville Ga
Addressed: Virginia Sue Lindsley
North Ga. College

**Sunday night
8:30 o'clock**

Dear Sue,

How it has rained today! Fed stock tonight on fields covered with 4 inches of water. Guess the lake is roaring over the spillway. It has stopped now and is getting colder!

One jonquil is open and a few more are showing yellow. One new calf at the barn Sunday, a whiteface. Dolly is better, still a little thin.

The Dodge is in shop for a new starter and clutch. Am still repairing base of columns. Set out a wheelbarrow load of jonquils on gullies and have 3 more to put out plus bridal wreath, naked jasmine, crepe myrtle. Think we will lose another pine on path to lake.

Sue is back in Macon but Nan has not been able to get over yet. Tell Miss Lil I'm giving her for birthday a holster and 1/2 interest in a .22 revolver like she used to have, and <u>one</u> buck to blow (illegible). The enclosed check is $5 for you and 6 for Miss Lil, extra for birthday.

Mom has not been well. Yesterday went to Dr. Bailey and got some medicine and feels much better.

The land case against the government is coming up June 29th. I've got to do another sample before then.

Love to you both.

Dad
Wed. Morning; Mom went to Macon today to see Sue.

Naked jasmine is also known as winter jasmine.
The land case was for a local man whose land in South Carolina was seized and became the site of the H-bomb plant. Luther was going to collect more sand and water samples for testing.

* * *

From Dad
Postmark: Mar 9, 1955

Wednesday

Dear Sue,

It has occurred to me that you and Miss Lil might be in need of a little "wampum." Enclosed is $5.00 for each of you.

Allie and Mom have gone to town. Edwin and I have just come in from selecting trees for the sawmill man.

Had a wonderful time out west. Will tell you all about it when you come. Thulia was a beautiful bride. Thought only about a dozen would be to the wedding. *The church was packed.* All ranks!

She got many nice presents. Mr. and Mrs. Bramlett drove us everywhere! To the snowcapped top of the world, and to the great desert.

**Love,
Dad**

They flew to Denver, to Thulia's wedding to Terry S. Bramlett. I think it was the first airline flight for each of them. Mother said later that Dad knew the geography so well he could tell where they were by the view below.

* * *

From Dad
Postmark: Mar 30, 1955

Dear Susan,

I am sending you another $5 on your books. Am glad you got some fine ones. Ask Miss Lil if she needs more. Write us again confirming your plans to come with other girls so I can clean up yard a little.

We have had coldest weather of the year since last Friday. Flowers killed, new leaves on trees <u>black</u>, grass killed or damaged. Am feeding again like in January. It's hard on bugs, too, thank the Lord.

Got a fine young colt. I think "Flag of Arabia" or one like her.

> Love,
> Dad

*   *   *

From Mother
Postmark: April 5, 1955
No date information on letter inside

Dear Susan,

Only a note. I have an infected eye and shouldn't be using it. This is my 3rd day for shots. But I'm feeling fine.

Caught a <u>4</u> lb bass yesterday, so you know what I'm doing every afternoon. Couldn't see any way.

Had an invitation to Honors Day saying you would be honored because of your high record! They have it here on 7th too, so we'll go here (They did not put in it the *Recorder* this time.)

Sue hasn't been back to see us. Guess she'll come when Katie is here.

Let me know when you are bringing guests.

> Love,
> Mother

*   *   *

From Dad
Postmark: May 12, 1955

Dear girls,

I do not know if Mom has written you about the stolen

Napoleon goblets and Frankenthal jewel box. Afternoon of Saturday John Parker's boys reached through the windows (of the brick house) and stole them.

Police, sheriff and I searched frantically for three days and kept quiet. Then announced it on radio. The boys brought them back. They had also stolen your best snake skins and fox furs. They returned them.

They had shown their treasures to many people and when it was carried on radio their parents had to return them, but only them (the items mentioned on radio). Big church people. About 15 Chelsea (porcelains) were stolen same night. About half of them have been returned. Different thieves.

Love,
Dad

* * *

From Dad
To Virginia Susan Lindsley at North Georgia College; Lil was also a student there.
Postmark: December 3, 1955

Saturday

Dear Susan

Enclosed is the necessary Wampum to keep the Dahlonega Medicine Men in venison and heap much fire water for the holidays, also keep their wigwams warm and much "whoopee."

Not much news! They've found the drowned person and buried him and we have fixed a good deal of fence. Also got paid for the big fine bull killed by railroad.

Write us a line between now and homecoming time to verify time to come get you.

Love to you both,
Dad

* * *

Postmark: Mar 7, 1956: Envelope contained two letters, one from each parent.

Dear Susan,

This is my third attempt. First time some hay came and they wanted to know where to put it. Then next the mail came and then some one came to see about renting an apartment.

Thulia writes that she will not come down this summer, that just as soon as she is feeling like work after the baby arrives they want her to come back, have given her a better job and more pay. Mrs. Bramlett will take over the baby. I am disappointed of course, but hope to go there for a few days anyway.

The Mark Hodges asked us to come over and see their flowers at their lake place. They have about 4 acres of bulbs planted in the pines and all were in bloom, simply beautiful. They showed us their house too, which is grand, water on three sides.

Our spirea hedge is gorgeous now. As I write, it is so pretty through my window.

No special news. Will enclose checks with this, soon as Dad comes.

> **Much love,**
> **Mother**

> **Tuesday night**

Dear Girls,

Tonight we are mailing in your checks dated March 15th as per your letter and I'm sending in a bit of farm news.

Mom and I are putting a new roof on Liberty Street porch, about half through. Am marking trees for Smith's loggers on East end of Harper Place—the only place trucks can get in on account of rains. Trees marked at other two places could not be cut on account of mud.

Counted twenty-two young calves yesterday. Most of them are

good looking. Cattle are still eating hay but sometimes do not come up. Dogwoods at College are showing white so winter will soon be over. Thanks to the Lord.

The last big wind blew down a tree across Cline fence and I've just gotten in 6 cows from Cline's bottom after a three mile walk.

The house is making slow progress due to time spent in politics, county commissioners, cow chasing, fence repairs, bulb planting, etc.

Saturday, Sue, Mom and I went over to Mrs. Mark Hodges lake place. She has a beautiful ranch house on a point of the lake in lovely pines and thousands of bulbs growing and blooming like mad under the pines.

Our jonquils and bulbs have been better than ever before. The ashes we put out contained much potash and there was plenty of rain and not too much cold.

Mom says she is writing so I guess this is about all the news.

Love,
Dad

* * *

From Dad
Postmark: April 20, 1956

Friday

Dear Susan

You have an 8 1/2 lb. nephew. All things come to him who waits, including $5 from each of us. Champaign and Cigars are costly. No startling news. Mom is going to town and waiting to mail this.

Love,
Dad

* * *

Postmark: Sept 22, 1956
Excerpts only; letter is from Lil the daughter, sister of Thulia and Susan

Dear Susan,

... . Tennessee was wonderful! And Lindy was cute as pie. I fell in love with Terry, so I guess it's a good thing Thulia met him before I did—I couldn't have caught him—this way he is in the family.

> **Lil**

*   *   *

Postmark: October 2, 1956
Two notes, each of a half sheet of paper

Dear Susan-

Your letter just came telling about your job. Why not just come on Sunday and get a Sat off when Miss Lil comes. There would be nothing to do about the horses on Sat, anyway.
Have cooking to do, will write more later, when time.

> **Love,**
> **Mother**

Monday night
Dear Sue,

I'm sending you five "bucks" to help finance your trip home this weekend and pay your helpers. You certainly do not have to look after laundry!
Lots of things are happening. Will tell you when you come. The Wall boy wants horses to train to tricks, not particularly a saddle show horse, more like a "quarter" horse. Be thinking it over.
> **Dad**

*   *   *

From Mother
Postmark: January 12, 1957

Dear Susan

Thought you'd enjoy see these clippings from this weeks *Recorder*. Had you heard Von Pippin was married? I am also sending Pat's letter. The money she sent back we'll put on her account and send her a receipt with her next payment. Maybe you'd better keep the phone number.

(Note: No idea re Pat's letter or money. Flora Lee Von Pippin was first cousin to Lucille Humbert, a classmate of mine, who lived on Liberty Street. Through her mother we were distant Lindsley cousins.)

I saw Regina in town yesterday and said how proud she must be of Flannery. She told me that Flannery would have only one of the lessons and have the entire time at that meeting. So they didn't have to make but one trip.

Some one knocked all the slats off the Dovedale barn so cows could get to our hay. We got all the hay moved yesterday. The man never did come to rent the house. Sol said he had gone North. And I think I told you last week they stole the farm bell that was on top of the store. I'm sure that was some one at the lake that could use it to call the family in off the lake, etc.

My cold is much better after a week of no ice cream or sweets. I got 1/2 gal. last Monday and Dad finished it up today. Imagine it lasting that long.

      Much love,
        Mother

*　*　*

Excerpts only. Elizabeth Storm was one of Luther's high-school students in Virginia, and they stayed in touch.

Postmark: February 24, 1957, Baltimore, Md.

Dear Folks,

I imagine Georgia is just a fairy-land now as your first flowers come out.

Thank you so very much for the box of pecans you sent me at Christmas. I was surprised and delighted for myself and for you when I received the package. I know that your crop has been so poor in recent years. It was good to know that you had a supply again. How kind you are to share them with me.

How is Thulia's little boy? I know how you must enjoy him.

Most sincerely,
Elizabeth (Storm)

*   *   *

Postmark: Mar 9, 1957

Saturday morning
Dear Susan,

Mother is going over town to mail this check. In regard to the jewels our greatest problem will be source of materials. Have written "Marine Minerals" near Aiken, but have not heard anything.

Hope the feast will not give you the stomach ache! After big periods of starvation it is dangerous to eat much. I do not think of $12 worth of Bible or religion will be an overdose for you. I could use a little myself.

I'll be glad to buy Lil's Anatomy. It is part of my job.

Dad

The comment about the jewels referred to those he made from the sand on the South Carolina land the government seized from the friend he testified for in federal court. The Woodmen of the World wanted him to make hundreds of them. But Luther decided not to undertake the project for several reasons, one being the time involved. His interests lay elsewhere. His daughter Susan had some of the experimental glass cut into jewels and mounted for the "girls" in the family.

Postmark: July 18, 1957
From Mother

Dear Susan,

Terry came on Saturday and they left Sunday P.M. soon after dinner. Tippie, Terrell and his family spent the afternoon with me, on till 7 o'clock. I am certainly missing Lindy, not to mention Thulia. It is just like when you and Lil leave for school.

I went fishing one P.M. and caught 5 bass. The biggest weighed about 2 lbs. But all nice size.

We have a politician a day visiting us. The reports say that Roy put Dr. Woods up and is paying all his expenses. Others say that the Allens and Bells and someone else gave $800 for the campaign, so on and on the rumors go. I told Mrs. Green that I would be glad to help hold the election so if they came for Mr. Green to help to tell them.

Is this something from Mercer that you sent yourself?

Hope the snake skin was the one you wanted; it was the only one in the house. And that it reached you on time. I got it off on the next mail.

The TV is working fine.

Much love, Mother

*   *   *

From Dad
Postmark: July 31, 1957

Dear Susan,

Enclosed is $10.00. You will probably need more for books, etc the second quarter. Also college dues, board, etc., amounts I know not, and have no way here to find out. The $10 is cost of one big load of pulpwood. (A 1959 statement from Georgia Timberlands dated January 30, 1959 shows pulpwood at $6.50 per cord.)

A good formula for getting rich is to make a list of all the things you wish to have, and the cost thereof, sit back for an hour or two and think of all the pleasure you would be getting out of them. Then put aside the list after counting up the cost and congratulate yourself on how much you have saved.

Come when you can.

Dad

*   *   *

From Mother
Postmark: August 5, 1957
The envelope contained a receipt from Mercer University, dated August 7, 1957, for $88.00 "for Matric." Bo in the letter was the son of Paul Farr, from whom Dad bought the land we call the "Farr Place."

Dear Susan:

I will not be by to see you tomorrow for Miss Lil came home on the bus yesterday. They decided not to go on the 30-mile hike. I had planned to make some cookies today to bring you, since I'm not coming here is a $ to get something to eat—or a show.

Did Dad send anything for books? Let me know if you are needing anything.

Regina's brother died last week and I went over to see them. Flannery asked if you had heard from Iowa. I told her they had asked for a story to be sent and you had sent it in but had not had time to hear anything from them. She said for you to let her know when you heard. So many other people came in that I only talked to her a minute or so.

You never did send that list of books you wanted me to get. They close next week so you'd better hurry with it.

Bo Farr brought the new Methodist minister out to see us yesterday. I like him.

The work Dad is doing on the house is certainly showing up now. I am anxious for you to see what he has done this week.

Do you want me to send this dress by Sue next Sunday?

I'll be so glad when you get home to help me on the house.

Hope all is fine and that the new work is going fine.

Much love, Mother

* * *

From sister Lil
Postmark: Aug 10, 1957

Friday Night

Dear Susan,

Just got back from Augusta and looking for a place to live.

Have been helping Dad with the hall of the house which he is boarding with cedar. It looks beautiful. Have been haying all week, too. Went out and raked some. I really enjoyed it.

Must go out early in the morning to bring in cows with screw worms.

Dad told me that Thulia was expecting another baby in March! They'll operate and take it out just before it is due so that she won't have any trouble. I'm not supposed to know about it as far as Mother is concerned though. For some reason she hasn't mentioned it. She may be worried about Thulia. Dad told me to wait for her to mention it to me. So I don't guess you are supposed to know until somebody else tells you.

Can't think of any more news.

Much love,

Miss Lil

* * *

From Dad
Postmark: September 23, 1957

Monday

Dear Sue

Sorry you were gone when I came back. Here is a small check. Try to get you some "Blue jeans" and etc.

Mom says if you come home Saturday or Friday drop a card and she will come for you.

Love,
Dad

*   *   *

Postmark: Sept 23, 1957, Augusta, Ga
Excerpts only, from sister Lil, at Medical School

Dear Susan,

Hooked a big shot in Northwestern Insurance who is really great. He's 24 but made it (his money) all himself. Will buy me a plane ticket to Atlanta to see Tech ballgame at Thanksgiving if I will come. Don't know yet whether can get away.

Am having time of life at school but do have to study oodles. All the more fun.

Love,
Lil

*   *   *

From Dad
Postmark: November 14, 1957

Thursday
Dear Susan,

Mom got back safely and reported your interest in the business school.

We are cashing in the three insurance policies. They were originally carried for education purposes in case something unfortunate happened. In spite of the fire I've managed to carry on without them.

Sign the application enclosed and have it dated and witnessed by someone there and get it back to us before the end of the month.

Best of luck,
Dad

Dad had taken out a life insurance policy on each of us at birth. Value, $1,000.

From Dad
Postmark: November 18, 1957

Saturday
Dear Sue,

A Mr. Hodges came by looking for horses for the young boys. Will probably come by again during Thanksgiving. He really means business.
Love,
Dad
Thanks for your good grades.

* * *

From Susan to Mom

February 10, 1959

Dear Mom,

I got your letter and it literally brought tears to my eyes. I too remember the feeling that filled our home last winter, the willingness of everyone to do for the others—Lil getting up to help you when you got sick, Dad going so hard Saturday to be sure you were both comfortable, Sue there Sunday ready and willing to do any task, however menial, for us all, and you too sick to sit up, getting out of bed to take most of the load off my back, for with you on your feet and Doctor Bailey looking after Dad, I knew I did not need to worry.

The events referred to here include Lil's being home, sick, from medical school for several weeks. She was bedridden. I came home to find Mother also ill. January 1959 was COLD. We were in the "cottage," which had no insulation, no heat other than fireplace in Mom's and Dad's room, where Lil stayed. Dad was sleeping in the "front" bedroom, with only a porch door for access and a small gas heater that didn't take the chill off. He came inside the main house (by way of the porch) to ask me to handle the feeding of the livestock. He was sick. Pneumonia. He went back to bed. I packed the windows with whatever I could find to cut down the draft, piled more blankets on his bed and turned the heater on full blast.

I slept on the floor in the room with Mother and Lil, and when the cold woke me up, I stoked the fire.

Manuel was there to help me cut and bring in firewood and to help with the feedings. We lost numerous livestock that week—my horse Dolly, for one. We found someone's beagles eating a cow that was down, and had to put her down permanently.

Mostly I remember the cold. And Dr. Bailey, who came out daily to tend to Dad. Penicillin saved him, but he was a long time coming back to full strength.

Lil made up her missed courses at medical school with a summer session at the University of Minnesota.

* * *

From Lil
Postmark: Apr 29, 1959, Augusta, GA.

Excerpts only:

Dear Susan,

...went by Emory and then home.
 The electrician had come and the plumbers were on the way! The upstairs and the kitchen look out of this world.
 Wedding plans are still for June 12. Can you make it home then? No plans so far save time and place.
 Dad is selling another colt. The population is getting unbelievably low!

Much love,

Lil

* * *

From Mother
Postmark: May 5, 1959

Dear Susan:

 There is no news but thought you'd like to have a letter from home and know that all is fine.
 I got up early this morning and worked cleaning up the little porch that Dad had so much trash on, including that broken up marble he will not throw away. I moved it back of the milk house and suggested that he mark the Negro graves in the slave cemetery with it.
 I worked while it was cool, then after dinner I'll read and when

it is cool again I'll fish. Still having good luck and am sick of eating them.

I have enjoyed "Fairoaks" that you sent Dad. Did you read it? I am now reading one of Al's—"Anatomy of Murder."

Miss Lil gets out on Friday the 19th. I'll go for her since John will be in Tenn. Not Memphis.

I guess then she'll say whether she really wants any one to come or not. I don't think she does. With John and Lil present, I asked Miriam if she had been invited to the wedding and she said, "Not yet." I told her I guess she'd have to drive her mother and father down so she'd be here, and I rec'n in that case she could come invited or not. It is all right if she doesn't invite Tip but I think she should ask Sue. But, I am willing for her to run her own affair and so far she has.

What do you think about getting a safety deposit box at the bank for your things? However, as they are government things they can easily be replaced, so I guess there is no need. But, when here, check on them and see that they are together.

Much love, and hope all is fine,

Mother

Why don't you send me a Kodak showing your new haircut? I have a new permanent.

*　　*　　*

From Mom
Postmark: May 9, 1959

Dear Susan:

I'm writing twice this week for I will not have time to write at all next week. I am tiling the bathroom floor. The tiles will not be here till Monday but everything is ready for them to go. Then the plumber comes back and finishes up.

John was here Wednesday night, getting here in the early

afternoon so we had time to get in some fishing. John got two big ones, I just got one. When he left the next morning he expected to go on to Atlanta after finishing up his work in Milledgeville, so we were surprised when he walked in late in the afternoon. Said he didn't finish his work here. He left early this morning after an early breakfast. Mr. Avery came just as we finished to use his truck for hauling things for Dad for the house from 3 places. Dad went over to help him load something and came in and said he had hurt his shoulder and would I go along and drive him.

So, I did, getting back at noon. His arm is feeling better; anyway he is over working now. I'm going over to help soon as I finish up in my kitchen.

I couldn't decide what I wanted to do about the fan until I talked with several people about it. Then decided to exchange it and get two plain fans for it. I figured that way it would help more people, in more places. I just turned it in this week and haven't gotten the others yet. If this weather keeps up, I'll need one soon.

John said he thought both of his sisters would come for the wedding. They will come the day of the wedding and stay that night with us. If Thulia does come, we'll have plenty of room for we are getting a mattress for the four-poster.

Are some of these things that come for you, checks that should be deposited? I've put them all with the bonds in the safe.

Mr. and Mrs. Hammock made us a long visit the night John was here. She asked all about you. You seemed to have made a hit with all of them.

John got an enormous turtle on his hook. I came up the hill and got the rake to help pull him in and the wrecking bar to kill him. I couldn't find any bullets for the pistol (I did later). We pinned him down with the bar and went and got Sol. He brought his gun to kill him, put it in a sack and went joyfully home.

      Lots of love,
      Mother

The Hammock's daughter Faith was Thulia's classmate in high school and kept up with us for the rest of her life. When she would visit, if I could get her to the lake, I'd invite her to go out in the boat and then turn it over. Much fun for me. When I sent her a package in later years, she swore she put it in her freezer overnight, before opening it, just in case it was a snake.

* * *

From Mother
Postmark: May 17, 1959

Dear Susan:

Had a note from Thulia saying she is coming, but doesn't yet know about Terry. I have just written her and sent $20 to pay part of her plane fare in case he does not come. Suggesting that they come that way and that you meet her in Atlanta. Why don't you send her $10 and that with mine would be over half, I think for the 1 1/2 fares. If you come home on Monday would you want to meet her on Tues or would it be better to wait till Wed? When you write say what day suits you and if that doesn't suit her what day will. Get it all arranged without so many letters.

I am glad Thulia has decided to come and I hope that Miss Lil is pleased and that she will not be upset by the boys. I am going to try to do everything she (Lil) wants for this time, it is her day.

Got lots done in the yard today and both feeling fine. I think you'll be surprised at how pretty the house looks when you get here.

Much love, Mother

* * *

From Mother
Postmark: May 21, 1959

Dear Susan:

Congratulations. I wish I could have seen the parade and especially you and your girls. I am sure they know that anything you are given to do is done as it should be.

I'm anxious to see the pictures.

I have started getting Miss Lil's room ready for her next week end. I cannot realize that the time is so near. She wrote that John would come back from Tenn. to bring her home. Then he has to go back for another week. I thought I'd better get the baby bed out of her room. So, I'm leaving it in mine ready for Thulia. I'll give Thulia my room while Miss Lil is home and I'll sleep in the new house. We have gotten a mattress on the bed. I am trying not to be pushed at the last minute.

Who is going to climb the magnolia tree to get some flowers for decorations?

I have found a home for all the kittens but one and have to keep it another week anyway. We have a new colt.

Much love from a proud Mother.

Lil and John married in the living room of Dad's new Westover.

* * *

From daughter Susan
Excerpts only

July 26, 1959

Dear Mom and Dad,

Got your note yesterday, Mom, and am glad to know you are "enjoying" court. Give my regards to all the lawyers. (See: "Going Courting at 54" in *Myrick Memories*.)

-—I'm going to write a letter to the two sisters. (See August 26, 1959, letter.)

When you see Flannery and Regina, give them my regards. I got a note from Flannery.

Much love,
Susan

*   *   *

From daughter Susan
Excerpts only

August 13, 1959

Dear Folks,

——I'm glad to hear Lil and John are journeying to Westover frequently. I know you both greatly enjoy seeing them and I'll bet you had fun watching the stars.

——How are things on the farm? Selling any cows or horses or trees? Got hay in for the winter yet? Now, Dad, this is not pressure to sell cows, but in Chicago canners and cutters are above 20¢ and I'm just wondering what they are there, and also, what is hay per pound?

                    Much love

                      Susan

*   *   *

From daughter Susan
                  Wednesday
                26 August 1959
Dear Folks,

Well, I finally have something to write home about, and this news will please you greatly, Dad. I went with Georgia, Morris and Edna (his wife) last night down to see Aunt Minnie. To be 89, she is certainly spry. She sends you her love and greatly desires you to come to see her. I certainly wish you could, for the whole family would like to see you.

On the way down, they took me by Clover Hill and your Grandmother Johnson's home. The latter, they said, has been altered somewhat since you saw it last, but it is in good condition yet.

Jimmy, Aunt Minnie's grandson, and I hate to admit it but I'm not sure whose son he is, lives with her. He's about 20 or so and he's going to college and working at the same time. He plays a guitar some and I talked him into giving us a demonstration last night.

Speaking of musical instruments brings me to the whole point of the letter. Dad, remember the harp you played when you were selling them when going to school? Well, Aunt Minnie had yours and she gave it to me to give back to you when I come home again. Unfortunately, some strings are missing and some are broken, but I'm sure that it can be fixed as good as new. I played it some myself last night—she had some of your music there, too.

Aunt Minnie is having her house re-done on the outside with a sheetrock-like stuff that gives the impression of a brick house. I think it's a beautiful job; the men began work yesterday and will probably finish today, tomorrow at the latest.

Dad, I want you to know that I was much impressed with your side of my relatives. They are charming people and all of them genuinely interested in you and your family. I am looking forward to visiting with them again.

Must stop. Let me hear from you on the rest of the family since they're bad as I am at writing.

Love,
Susan

* * *

From Georgia H. Embry
Postmark: September 4, 1959
She was a cousin and was Aunt Minnie's daughter. This check shows that Luther lived in Portsmouth in 1913. "Virginia" in the letter is Virginia Susan Lindsley. They called me Virginia because that name came to me from Dad's sister.

September 3, 1959
Dear Luther,

—Have seen Virginia several times since I wrote you. In fact, I talked to her on the phone a few minutes tonight. She is counting the days until she can get home to see you all.

Maurice, his wife, Virginia and I all went down to see Mother one night last week. She was so sorry that Virginia couldn't stay longer but maybe she will have a chance to go back later.

Am enclosing a check that Mother found the other day in some old papers that were in a chest that Aunt Maud had. She thought perhaps you would like to have it.

PORTSMOUTH, VA., *June 2f* 1913 No.

THE FIRST NATIONAL BANK 68-68
OF PORTSMOUTH.

PAY TO THE ORDER OF *G. W. Johnson* $10.⁰⁰

L. C. Lindsley

Your house sounds wonderful. I know you have really been putting in the work on it to get so much finished. Has your wife finished the new bedspread to go in the new house? She said she wanted to try a new pattern that I sent her. —

Write when you can. Am always glad to hear. Also, you all should come up and pay us a visit. Would be so glad to have you.

As ever,
    Georgia

*   *   *

Edgar Marshall was a first cousin and close childhood "buddy." He and Luther reunited in the late 1950s and they began a lengthy correspondence. Excerpts from Edgar's replies to Luther's letters provide an insight into Luther's activities during those years.

He did "straighten out" much of the genealogy of the Marshall and Douglas lines of our family.

We have only a few of the letters, and much of the material in the letters dealt with matters other than Luther's activities or their joint interests and is not included here.

But included here is all the material we have that he wrote about the family lines. His letters are intermingled with those of Luther and Lillas to Susan, for a chronological view of activities.

April 16, 1961

Dear Luther,

We were happy to hear of the progress you are making on your place, and wish you luck in getting the four columns for the front. How you are able to accomplish as much as you do, singlehanded, is truly phenomenal, and you need not worry about the age of 74 years because there will be, for you, many more "another day."

We have been looking around the various stores for artificial wreaths for the cemetery but so far nothing has appealed to us. We are going to look again Wednesday and in any event you may be assured that we will find something nice which we will place on the graves Saturday.

Love to you and Lillas from all of us,

Your devoted cousin

Edgar.

Left to right: "Sister," Luther, Lillas, Edgar

From Luther
To Virginia Susan Lindsley, Boston
Postmark: October. 24, 1961

Tuesday
Dear Susan,

Enclosed is a little check in remembrance of that day in October when you entered this world without assistance from anyone, thus establishing the fact that you were of an independent nature.

Our cousins, the Marshalls of Maryland, who are now living in Virginia, stopped by for a few days last week and brought the Marshall family tree. It seems that my children are entitled to join several organizations, including the "Daughters of the Barons of Runnymede," a most select group, who meet once a year in

Washington in evening dress and I suppose dig up their ancestors for a few minutes then bury them for another year.

It costs $6.00 per year, mostly for the big banquet at the meeting. I believe it will be a good thing for you to join <u>now,</u> Thulia and Miss Lil can later. You can pay the $6.00 out of this check.

Write me or phone us if you wish to join this group and I'll have Cousin William Marshall fill out your lineage blank.

> Love,
> Dad

*   *   *

From Mother
> **Friday Morning**

Dear Susan,

We both thoroughly enjoyed our weekend guests who drove all the way from Alexandria just to see us. Mrs. Fitton ("Sister"), her brother, Edgar Marshall and his wife. Their father was brother to Dad's mother, and they had been together quite a bit in their younger days.

Sister and Gertrude both helped in the kitchen fixing meals and washing dishes. (Lillian came one day but she and Flossie are both so busy in the cotton patch.) On Sunday we went to the Sanford House for dinner. One afternoon when Miss Lil was home we went over to see them. Dad enjoyed showing the house off. (The Blount House)

You never heard such bragging on children and grandchildren, but Sister had 6 children and 2 grandchildren (though not as old as I) so she had the advantage to start with. They brought pictures of all the family for us to see.

I have finished Thulia's sweater and it is so big I can wear it myself, but like you I do not want a white one, so I am not making you one. All that work and then the size all off.

I got up when Dad did this morning and went with him to get Manuel and drove them to the Lane Place. It is all bailed and ready to move. Trucks are to come today and they'll have it all in by night. The weather has been terribly dry, but this cutting made more than last.

The people who were buying my furniture moved out last week and I am now renting it furnished. Some one moved in immediately. I had to buy a refrigerator and moved table and chairs from here. She had own cook things.

Allie wrote and asked for Thulia's address. Said they would be in Memphis one night on their way to Martin, Tenn. and on to Ga. in Nov. Thulia is moving again this week and says she is looking forward to it for she has not liked this house, too little.

I'm mailing a birthday present on Monday. I will insure it, but will I need to for all packages to you? Is it left outside as at your last apt?

Happy birthday and love, Mother

*   *   *

From "Sister"
Excerpts only

**Alexandria, Va.
October 21, 1961**

Dear Susan:

I want to let you know I got down to Ga. My brother Edgar and his wife Gertrude took me. He has been wanting me to go every since he moved back from Maine. We enjoyed every minute that we were there. You have a wonderful and intelligent father and a very sweet mother. I have heard my mother and father talk so much about him, they loved him very much.

I was a long time finding out where he was, and it was by accident that I did, and it was such a thrill to see him. I loved his sister; she lived with us for a long time.

She was just like a big sister.

I have never seen so much beautiful antique furniture and such beautiful dishes. I met your sister and her husband; she looks like a school girl instead of a doctor.

Love,

Sister

*   *   *

From Edgar Marshall
Only the first page survived

October 30, 1961
Hyattsville, Md.

Dear Luther and Lillas:

Again permit me the privilege of expressing on behalf of Sister, Gertrude and myself our sincere appreciation for the most cordial reception extended to us on our recent visit with you and your charming wife. To us it was one of the happiest experiences of our lives. It seems that everything was in our favor.

The weather was perfect, the roads excellent and traffic light, and to cap it all your hospitality so home-like and genuine that it was only by a supreme effort were we able to convince ourselves that we should not stay longer.

We visited the Marshall lot in Glenwood Cemetery Friday the 27th and found it in excellent condition. They recently removed the iron pipe fence, which they stated made it difficult for mowing and which accounted for high grass and weeds growing around the fringe of the railing and supporting posts. I might add that the cemetery as a whole was as well kept as any that I have seen.

In the circumstances there is nothing that can be presently done that would add to its appearance. We mentioned flowers (spray or the like) to be placed on the grave and she suggested it would be more appropriate to wait for a holiday, namely Christmas, Memorial Day, Independence days, etc. In this connection we walked around the cemetery, to be convinced, and none of the graves had flowers.

Evidently they prefer holidays for decorations because of the scarcity of help which she stated was a major problem in cleaning up the debris later. After discussing this matter we decided that it may be best if we returned this check and when Christmas arrived we would purchase a spray or wreath for the plot, send you the bill and we would split the amount three ways. You will remember that Grandfather and Grandmother Marshall are in the same lot and we want to do our share by splitting the amount spent for flowers.

We also discussed the matter of "Perpetual Care" and enclosed you will find the statement they furnished me regarding the rates. It is my candid opinion that perpetual care is not warranted. As I have stated all of the graves are in excellent condition and they are mowed regularly. The ground is level and there is little likelihood that there will be any further sinking. ... Also enclosed you will find a chart showing the location of the graves and those buried therein. You will be shocked to know that the records in the office list your mother and Virgie's mother as "Lindsey." However, on the gravestone of Virgie who is buried in the same grave with her mother, the name is spelled "Lindsley." I would have suggested that the records be changed to show the correct name but hesitate without having your consent.

See Appendix XXII for information on Virginia's burial site and the cemetery.

*   *   *

From Edgar
Excerpts only

W. E. Marshall
Hyattsville, Maryland
Nov 9, 1961

Dear Luther:

To begin with I wish to express the pleasure it gives me to receive your letters. The first arrived November the 3rd and the second November 6th. It was very kind of you to send me some of grandmother's letters together with the will of John Provost Marshall, our second cousin thrice removed. He incidentally was a brother to George Robert Wilfred Marshall, the father of cousin Gertie.

Some years ago while visiting Alton she turned over to me many of her father's letters received from his parents, brothers and sisters. I just went through them and was surprised to learn they were so bad off around the year 1888, which must have been shortly after the loss of their place in Maryland.

They were living in Virginia at the time and your father must have been living close by. I am enclosing a few mainly because reference is made to you, Virgie and your mother.

I will take good care of Uncle Sam's note in favor of your father. ———

Some years ago I talked to Edna Shaw, cousin Gertie's daughter (about Vivian). For some unknown reason Vivian has never appeared to show any aloofness towards me. Even her mother, whom no one in the family seemed to like, made a lot over me when I paid them a visit. However, this was not true of Uncle Sam. We could never agree on anything which usually resulted in an argument. I have been called down on many an occasion by my mother and father for arguing with him. While he never borrowed any money from me, he, on several occasions, has asked me to do personal favors for him, which I never refused.

(He discussed his attempts to learn the admission policies for the Daughters of the Barons of Runnymede.)

I have a vague recollection of the trials, tribulations and hardships you endured to get through school. I remember very well Virgie telling me about you getting up long before dawn to clean out the school and to build the fire in order to earn money for your college education.

She never knew how envious I was of you. I suppose I did not have, at that time, what may be referred to, as the "intestinal fortitude" to take it, as you did. I was just a gadabout whose only interest in life was entertaining and the fairer sex. However, through her encouragement and perseverance I did finally weaken and finished high school, at night. Later, I took college subjects which were of interest to me and after the war finished law school with an LLB degree. When I was asked by the Editor of the Year Book to write a sentence as an introduction to the write up on me, I remembered Virgie's encouragement and wrote "Whoever Perseveres Will be Crowned." Guess I was pretty sentimental in those days.

You have reached the top in your chosen profession by your resolute determination to succeed. With your fighting spirit how could it have been otherwise? Considering our two lives in retrospect, I feel ashamed that I lacked in my younger days those attributes, which you came by so naturally. Yes, Luther, you are the only member of the Marshall Clan, that I know of, who has gone as far as you have and I can assure you that we admire, respect and love you for it. Nothing would please me more than to have my children meet you and I certainly hope it can be arranged sometime. It would be nice if you and your lovely wife could visit with us, spending some time with Sister and then with us, or vice versa. There have been so many changes in Washington you would not recognize the place. We could have such a fine time sight-seeing together.

I am afraid we have lost contact with most of our relatives. I called Sister this morning to see if she knew their whereabouts and she could not recall when she last saw them or where they are living. Am sending under separate cover a paper bound book of the First Census of Maryland, compiled in 1790, which may be of interest to you. The enlargement of the picture I took of you and Lillas is due today and will mail that also.

The law books I promised your son-in-law were shipped by freight and addressed to you. Enclosed is a copy of Bill of Lading, dated Nov. 2nd. I'm looking upon this as a wedding gift to them although it is a very poor one.

I do not belong to the "Sons of the Barons" but feel tempted to join when I get things settled. Maybe we could join together. And in this connection I am going to keep after things until they are settled which I hope will be very soon. Will keep you currently advised as to the progress.

Your devoted Cousin,

Wm. (Edgar) Marshall

From Edgar
Postmark: Undated.   Hyattsville, Maryland

Dear Luther:

In my last letter to you I neglected to cover several questions which required an answer.

First there was the matter concerning the cemetery lots. The answer is there are six lots. At that time the cemetery permitted three persons to be buried in each lot. The rules at the present time permit not more than two to a grave. In grave (4) Bettie (Virgie's Mother), Virgie's son Frances, and Virgie; in grave (5) your mother and infant brother; in grave (6) Lulu and an infant daughter of Sister; in grave (10) Uncle Sam and Aunt Rena; in grave (11) grandmother Marshall; Papa was in same grave until we moved him to another lot; in grave (12) grandfather Marshall and Uncle John.

Second there was the matter re the Boxwood. The next time I go to the cemetery I intend to inquire as to permissibility and further take a picture of the plot and tomb stones and send them to you.

Third whether you should send some old letters or keep them until we come down. In this connection I would suggest that you keep them as it will give us an excellent reason for coming down in the spring.

Fourth should there be something missing between the emigrant Marshall and the Earl of Pembroke perhaps we could get someone in England to fill it in. It is on this question that I have been working. If you will refer to page 39 of my compilation you will notice at the top of page the caption, "Lineage to Generation 22 accepted by Daughters of Barons of Runnymede." Accepting this on its face it would appear that everything is in proper order. Cousin Edna had this line compiled by a Mrs. Mary Turpin Layton, who wrote under the name Mrs. O. L. Layton. Mrs. Layton, like the majority of genealogists, can't be trusted for accuracy. They take short cuts accepting what other have reported without verification of the facts. I am not sure whether this is, or is not, an authentic piece of work. Recently I was told Mrs. Layton (now deceased) was not too reliable. And I might add Edna paid a pretty price for it too.

Most of the material in the D. A. R. library has been compiled by these so called professional genealogists who never quote the citation of the source material. To illustrate, I found in a leather bound volume, entitled *American Monthly Magazine*, Vol. 7, page

410; July–Dec, 1893; compilations by the so called experts, as follows:

> "Mansion 'meaning Marshall,' built by Joshua Marshall in 1700. This Joshua, whose grandfather, William Marshall came from England, between 1640 and 1650 and settled in St. Marys. Bought the land from the Indians at Piscataway about 1690. The home was built of brick imported from England."

> *Note: Joshua was the son and not the grandson of William. In the last paragraph, page (16) of my compilation it is shown that the records indicate that John Fendall, and Randall Hanson and Joshua Marshall were jointly associated in many land transactions, one of the most interesting being the acquisition of a large tract of land from Accatamacca, the Indian Emperor of Piscattaway. Liber A—4.3, 414; 11 day September, 1700; and Liber "A" 1921, November 24, 1696, Charles County, Maryland.*

> "The Marshalls (meaning the Maryland Marshalls) have the coat of arms of the two branches of their family emblazoned on the old Marshall Hall silver and other heirlooms of the place. One of the coats of arms was used by Thomas Marshall of Farmington, County Devon, England, A. D. 1525, consist of a shield, whose upper part contains three antelopes' heads, erased or torn off, the ground of the upper part is in gold with a red stripe under the antelopes' heads.

> The lower half is of silver color and contains a millbrand, shaped like a Roman Cross, in the center. The millbrand is in silver and black."

(Susan's Note: See The American Monthly Magazine, Volume 7. It can be seen on-line)

(Edgar's letter continues)

When I talked to the Marshall in Maryland who had what

remained of the engraved silverware he informed me that he was familiar with the coat of arms used by the Virginia Marshalls and assured me that the coat of arms they claimed was not on any of the Marshall Hall silverware.

The other escutcheon, mentioned in the book as being used by the Marshalls of Maryland, is the one claimed by the Virginia Marshalls, and is quoted as follows:

> "The coat of arms used by John Marshall of Headingly et al, County York, England, member of Parliament for that Shire, A. D. 1550, consists of a shield divided in alternate Bars; three red and three silver, with a place in upper left hand corner, in which are 5 plumes and on top a man in armor."

I only had time to go through six books on the Douglas family and the only information I found on the Maryland Douglas family was the following:

> "DOUGLAS, Ancestral Record and Portrait, Maryland, Grafton Press. 1910.
> One of the leading military figures of Colonial Maryland, John Douglas, arrived in Maryland in 1659 and in that year he demanded land for transporting himself into the colony. In his will he bequeath Cold Spring Manor in Charles County, a tract of over a thousand acres also Blithwood,
> etc.
> Col. Douglas has not been identified with earlier and distinguishing families of Virginia, or with any branch of Douglas in Great Britain, but his record, both civil and military are recorded."

I hope what I am saying makes sense. But I would hazard a guess that eighty per cent of the members of these exclusive organizations are not members by right of entitlement but contrarily by false pretences by these so called Genealogists.

This has been a trying week for me. (running errands with family) Tomorrow (Thursday) we are having Thanksgiving dinner with Gertrude's daughter Jean. With this week shot to pieces I won't be able to visit the Library of Congress until Monday.

While at the D. A. R. Library, I did manage to get the name

and address of the President of the Daughters of the Society of Runnymede. I am enclosing a copy of the letter I wrote her which is self-explanatory. If Madam President is not away I should get an answer sometime next week.

We were pleased of course by your kind words attributing our visit to your good luck, monetarily. We certainly hope it continues that way.

Sister, Gertrude and I had dinner with our sister Aldine (Deanie) the baby of our family last Sunday. I hadn't seen her for three years. She was very interested in hearing us expound on our visit with you.

I must reiterate, that I just can't remember when I have enjoyed myself so much as seeing and visiting you and meeting your family. This applies equally so to Sister and Gertrude.

Sister and I do wish it was possible for you and Lillas to visit us. We feel certain both of you would enjoy it.

Guess this about wraps things up for the present at least, so with love to the family, I am,

Your devoted cousin,

Edgar

* * *

W. E. Marshall
1912 Erie Street, Apt. 102
Hyattsville, Maryland

November 18, 1961

Mrs. John B. O'Brien, President
Daughters of the Society of
Runnymede.
25 Parkview Avenue
Bronxville, N.Y.

Dear Madam President:

The purpose of this letter is to inquire what procedure is required under the charter and bylaws of your organization in making application for membership, assuming of course that the applicant's qualifications are acceptable.

My interest in writing you is in behalf of my first cousin, once removed, Virginia Susan Lindsley, who is presently employed as an Editorial Assistant, with the Electronics Division, Massachusetts Institute of Technology in Boston where she is now residing. She is in her mid-twenties.

Our lineage dates back (9) nine generations in this country to Col. John Douglas of Charles County, Maryland, who emigrated to Maryland in 1667, and from this John Douglas, (18) eighteen generations to Richard De Clair, Magna Charta Survey, Earl of Hertford, 1218; and others.

In conclusion I might add that Virginia Susan, if found eligible, would like to be associated with a society in Boston.

Thanking you so much for any information you may be privileged to advance me, I am

Most respectfully,

William E. Marshall

* * *

From Edgar

December 4, 1961

Dear Luther,

Herewith is the letter I received from the President of the National Society, Daughters of the Barons of Runnemede, which needs no explanation. In one of my letters I believe I referred to a conversation I had with a member whose husband belonged to the S.A.R., at the time I was Secretary. She inferred that branches of this organization were located in several states, but that she did not know whether they had an organization in Boston. From Madam President's letter it appears there are only two select cities, which should indicate that it is only for the elite. On this point I am in full accord.

We were very happy to hear of the excellent progress you are making on the rooms upstairs. Personally I wish I were there to help. But I must freely admit that I am not the man you are by any means.

I have not heard from my son in Maine re the Daughters of Runnemede.

Edna called while we were at Sister's. She was just back from Florida. She told me for the first time that she paid $75.00 for the Douglas compilation. It seems that the woman who compiled it was a Douglas and the only thing she had to do was work on the Maryland line.

If and when I get our genealogy straightened out I am going to join the following organizations:

Get reinstated in the
>> S.A.R.
>> Founders & Patriots
>> Sons of American Colonists
>> Sons of the Barons of Runnemede
>> et al.

Oh yes. Sons of the War of 1812
If I were eligible Sons of the Confederacy

>> Your devoted cousin,

>> Edgar

P.S. While I wanted the book *Early Architecture of Georgia* very much, I am somewhat embarrassed having you buy it for me. I don't know how I can ever repay you for it.

* * *

From Edgar and Gertrude Marshall

December 5, 1961

Dear Lillas,

It was so nice of you to write, but please believe me when we say that the blanket was as nothing compared to the pleasure and excitement we derived from our visit with you and our long lost cousin. You may be assured that the three of us never had a more enjoyable time. We get together with Sister as frequently as we can and the subject always turns to our visit with you. Our royal reception and your genuine and graceful hospitality will always be remembered.

The pecans and Luther's book arrived yesterday while we were visiting Sister. We will enjoy the pecans, I can assure you. It is embarrassing to receive such an expensive gift as this book, and I just can't find words to express our appreciation. I fully intended buying the book as I think it is a beautiful piece of work. I mentioned it to my daughter Jane over the phone this morning and she can hardly wait to see it. I treasure it more than anything I ever received.

Even more will I treasure the remarks of Luther on the fly leaf.

P.S. Ed should have mentioned that we will have a couple of good pecan pies during the holidays. Wish you two could be here to enjoy them with us.

Gertrude and Edgar

*   *   *

Addressed to Susan in Boston
From Dad
Postmark: December 12, 1961

Tuesday
Dear Susan,

It is a rainy day and it will make our grass grow. It's the second rain this fall, and the first thunder for many months.

I am enclosing a letter to my cousin Edgar Marshall from a Mrs.--- concerning the Daughters of the Barons of Runnymede. I suggest that you write her for a list of those members living in the environs of Boston and if it's necessary to submit lineage records on special forms and if any one of the Daughters is available for assistance in preparation of such.

I have about finished the bedroom and framing yours. The cornice is somewhat like that in the front room downstairs, the parlor.

On the general election, Williams went in by over a hundred votes and I suppose everyone is having to settle up bets!

Mom is having some pulpwood cut along the highway above the lake. The trees have not grown any there in a long time. It will help the others to grow.

A few thousand young pines are due in this week for us to plant behind the old Flagg place near Antioch Church. The recent survey shows we own quite an area (several acres _____) there.

We have built back the hay house in the field at the road junction toward Milledgeville and it helps a lot.

I'll probably get a chance to write again before Christmas. If you get lonesome during the holidays, call us up collect for a pow-wow, and remember you can always   (illegible).

> Love,
>   Your Dad

The Antioch Church is on the Old Monticello Road. It is on land that went to Lil, but she donated it to the Elders of the Church. The only deed Dad had was a quit-claim deed.

*   *   *

From Edgar

February 8, 1962 (Thursday)

Dear Luther,

Your letter of the 6th arrived today.

During the luncheon the conversation naturally turned to you, and Sister couldn't get it out of her mind that you might be ill. Edna, who is quite a gadabout and would-be club woman, was very happy to hear from you.

It is too bad that there is not some way of apprehending these cattle thieves and prosecuting them by legal means. Possibly there is collusion between the thieves and the law enforcement officers. Such things exist you know, but it's hard to believe that we are reverting to the trickery of the Old West, with the sheriff and the cattle thieves in league with one another.

Gertrude, the flower devotee of this family, was thrilled to hear about the jonquils, jasmine and red flowering quince coming into bloom. She would be in her glory there. — My father was exceptionally good and our Grandmother Marshall had one of the prettiest flower gardens I've ever seen in the back yard of Uncle Sam's house on Emerson Street. I recently saw a picture of it with Grandmother and Virgie posing beside an arbor of roses. I don't recall where I saw it and will ask Sis if she has it.

I was more than pleased with your determination and fortitude to live 15 more years to see your objective to defeat any of Uncle Sam's confiscatory plans fully realized. I fully believe you will do just that thing and even better.

Hoping this finds you both well and with love to all,

Your devoted cousin

Edgar

*   *   *

From Edgar
No date
Only page 2 of this letter remains.

As Easter is forty days away I am going to deposit your check in the amount of ten dollars. As to the flowers the question is do you wish me to buy fresh flowers or an artificial wreath. The custom at present is artificial wreaths as they last for months and the fresh flowers at best wither in two days. The artificial wreath I bought at Christmas time cost around five dollars and it was beautiful. I will get whatever you desire. If it's a wreath the amount

of your check will take care of both Easter and Memorial Day.

Love to you both

Edgar

On back of page, handwritten, probably by Gertrude:

I just wanted to wish you and Lillas the best of luck on the upholstering of the Victorian chair in the bed room we occupied. It is a beautiful chair and I am certain that under the direction and guidance of your good wife Lillas it will exceed in beauty the product of the master artisans who created it.

Luther's wife Lillas upholstered chairs, refinished furniture, caned chairs and wove corn shuck bottoms in chairs, and knitted sweaters for the children and herself, as well as knitted bedspreads. After Westover burned, she set about to make new bedspreads for each of her children.

*　　*　　*

From Edgar
May 1, 1962

Dear Luther,

The Colonel and Mrs. (Allie Myrick) **Bowden paid us a call a week or so ago and we were thrilled to meet them. They are two very charming persons and we enjoyed every minute of their visit.**
We were all so very glad to hear of Doctor Lil's good fortune in receiving a foundation grant to do research at Milledgeville State Hospital. She is a very smart girl and you may feel assured that she will go places in her profession. It's nice too knowing she will be close to home.
Saturday, the day before Easter, we placed wreathes on our Mothers' and Virgie's graves. We showed them to the Bowden's when they were here and they liked them very much. They were very nice but inexpensive, each costing $2.65. Monday after Easter we again visited the cemetery and they still looked just as nice as

they did the day we placed them. The flowers on a few of the graves close by had withered and died.

It is not possible to tell the artificial wreaths from the fresh flowers unless you touch them. Gertrude strolled over to a grave to look at what appeared to be fresh lilies only to find they were artificial.

As we may not be here the 30th of May I am enclosing a check for the $4.70 the difference between the cost of the two wreaths and the amount you sent me. If I am here I will place a wreath on your Mother's grave and advise you of the cost.

Again let me say how disappointed we three are in not being able to come down as planned.

Your devoted cousin,

Edgar

Edgar had a lengthy illness, involving surgery, and did not write for weeks.

August 8, 1962

Dear Luther,

I can't begin to tell you how pleased we were to hear from you and particularly that your daughters and grandchildren were home for a visit. It is so nice to have them around if only for a short period.

We were pleased too about Doctor Lillas's good fortune in being selected for such a responsible research job with the State Hospital. She is a very smart girl and I can well appreciate how proud you must be with her success.

We are so anxious to see your accomplishments since we were last there. Also your recent antique acquisitions. How you can keep so many irons in the fire is a mystery to me, especially with so many varied activities such as cattle, horses, pulpwood and lumber which require so much attention to say nothing of the time you are devoting to the re-modeling of the mansion.

We would like so much to spend a few days with you and

Lillas. Hope this finds you all well and with love to you both,

Your devoted cousin,

Edgar

Family gathering at the Blount House. Left to right, back row: Lillas, Luther, Susan Lindsley. Front row: Thor (John & Lil's dog), Lil Lindsley James, Russell Myrick Bramlett, Thulia Lindsley Bramlett, Lindsley Bramlett. Our last picture of Luther. (Photo by John E. James)

Luther died March 2, 1963. Emanuel Bryson slept on the back porch that night. He wanted to be available if the family needed him for any reason.

The daffodils in Wordsworth's Acre were in full bloom, and the children picked enough flowers to completely cover the casket with their gold.

Dad was carried from the east front room of Westover to the cemetery. The *Baldwin Bulletin* ran this obituary on March 5, 1963:

Services for Dr. Lindsley Are Conducted Sunday

Graveside services for Dr. L. C. Lindsley, retired Professor of the Woman's College of Georgia, were held Sunday afternoon in Westview Cemetery with Dr. William Littleton officiating.

Dr. Lindsley was Professor of Chemistry at the Women's College from 1929-1949.

A native of Virginia, Dr. Lindsley was a graduate of William and Mary College in Williamsburg, and took his doctorate from Cornell University.

He had taught at William and Mary before coming to Milledgeville and was one of the early promoters of the proposal to restore Williamsburg.

His interest in Colonial and ante-bellum homes led him to the restoration of several old houses in Georgia and others in Virginia, the most notable of which was "Westover," near Meriwether. This house burned about 10 years ago, and for the last several years Dr. Lindsley had spent much of his time in rebuilding it in replica. He had virtually completed the work when illness prevented further work on the structure.

Dr. Lindsley's death occurred Saturday at a local hospital where he had been ill for several days. He was 75.

He is survived by his wife, the former Miss Lillas Myrick; three daughters, Mrs. Terry Bramlett of Memphis, Tenn., Miss Susan Lindsley of Boston, Mass., and Dr. Lillas James of Haddock.

The cemetery was packed with people—colleagues from the college, the children's school friends, local business people and neighbors, including Regina and Flannery O'Connor, when Flannery had medical orders to stay out of the sun. She stood on her crutches in the sun for the funeral.

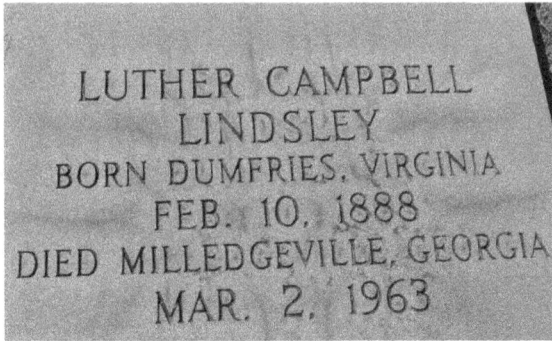

LUTHER CAMPBELL
LINDSLEY
BORN DUMFRIES, VIRGINIA
FEB. 10, 1888
DIED MILLEDGEVILLE, GEORGIA
MAR. 2, 1963

LILLAS M. LINDSLEY, WIDOW

Lillas remained at Westover and worked at closing down the farm operations. She depended heavily on Emanuel Bryson, who lived on the place with his family. Even after the last of the cattle were gone, she continued to live in Luther's Westover and continued the work to finish the outside.

She expanded her knitting hobby into a social event, hosting (and attending) "sewing circles," at which the hostess would provide dessert for the group.

Her daughter Lil gave her a German shepherd, which became very protective, and Lillas would keep Hilda in the bedroom until all her guests had arrived, and then the dog would enter the living room, lie beside her chair, and watch the ladies knit and sew.

Lillas never forgot the Great Depression, and when she purchased a new car, her first since her marriage, she did not spend the extra dollars for air conditioning.

With the new car, she began to attend some of the theatrical events at the college and to accept other social invitations.

Her days were filled, but she said that her most lonesome hours were after dark in winter, when she would be alone in the house with only the dog and the TV for company. Hours were more empty when the power went off and her only light would be the kerosene lamp.

She said that when spring thunderstorms rattled the house, she was ready to crawl under the bed with the dog. She remembered the tornado that ran by when they lived in the cottage and they had thought the sound was the train until it went by without whistling.

Her sister Sue Myrick visited almost every Sunday, arriving in the late morning. They would fix dinner (noon meal) together, and when the weather was bad, would knit. In good weather, they often fished at the family pond, or sometimes would work together in the yard.

She told her children what her mother had told her children: "I love you most because you're the fartherest away."

From Mother
Postmark: May 24, 1963

Dear Susan,

Do you have one of Dad's books with you? I found 2 upstairs. He said there was a 3rd one.

I had planned to start spraying boxwood again today but showers prevented it.

Mr. Wooten signed a 5 yrs lease with the privilege of breaking it if given in writing with in 30 days. He said he might not stay more than 4 years.

Wednesday
The Wooten's moved in today.
So Hilda and I are alone here. Thulia comes Friday night.

Thursday
No mail today and I missed hearing from you.
Yesterday was too much for me. The man came to put a top on the well of cement, the plumber came back to fix the leak in the bath room, and Kilgore came to do work on my porch. I am having the back porch screened in. He also worked on several doors that would not shut as they should. I had to stop and go see if the men were cutting the wood the right length for pulpwood and have them cut any hard wood into fire place lengths. Then I went over to see about getting my hay cut. I thought he was going to do it today but he did not show up. It has been too wet.

It was "too wet to plow" so Manuel and Sol finished the loading chute.

Today Manuel is hauling the fire wood in the Dodge and I went with him on the 1st trip in my car to look it over and brought back a

load. I'm getting it hauled before some lie teller steals it. Manuel says they are too lazy to bother about it before cold weather.

The porch is coming along fine. He will come back next week to paint and then put the screen on.

Flossie comes to clean in the morning. I'll have the extra bed brought in and get things ready for them. I think Miss Lil and John will meet them. If not——

I have read one group of your stories. I think one good for *Good Housekeeping*, or *McCalls*. It's their kind and they pay fine, I've heard.

Let me know what Mrs. T said.

Love, Mother

* * *

From Sister

May 24, 1963

Dear Lillas,

Received your letter this morning and was so glad to hear from you, but I have bad news for you, Edgar passed away at two a.m. this morning, so I thought I would just write you these few lines to let you know.

Will write you a long letter next week.

Much love,

Sister
(Bernice Marshall Fitton; Mrs. Nelson Fitton)

* * *

From Mother

The envelope and second page are missing, but there is no doubt that the letter is from Mother. Her handwriting and her typewriter were both distinctive.

Her reference to the Timber Place is probably the Harper Place. For the rest of her life, she faced down poachers. By leasing the lands to hunters, she was able to stop most of the poaching on the land; road shooters, however, continued to be a problem for many years. The local ranger, Jack Benford, seemed to be nearby when he was needed.

Oct. 24, 1963

Dear Susan:

One day this week a man from Atlanta, who is with the Chamber of Commerce, came by. He said he had been here a number of times before to see Dad. He got lost coming out and when he asked the way he was told that Dad was dead. He said each time he came he took pictures to show the progress made. That originally he was writing a story of Ben Jordan and now wanted to put the house in and a story of Dad. Could you write a short one giving him facts like Dad's work with Herty and the fact that he taught at Columbia and Emory summer school. He asked me where Dad went to school and I did not even know when he graduated from William and Mary. I remember that Dad and I used to laugh at the fact that he entered college the year I started first grade.

This Mr. Wiliford asked me if I objected to his writing the story and I told him I did not want any publicity about the house for I would be flooded with visitors. But, if he wrote anything about Dad, I would want something good and not just bare facts that he asked me. I will hear from him soon since he is sending me some of the pictures he took. WOULD YOU LET HIM?

And another question. I had asked Guy, who used to live at Dovedale, if he would like to have me buy some fertilizer for the nut trees at Dovedale, let him put it out and then for him to gather the nuts on half. He was not interested. The only other people I know in that neighborhood are Dan Lumpkin and the man who married one of the older Napier girls. Don't think you ever knew her. Do you think either of them could be depended on to give me my share of the nuts after they gathered them? They'd have to shoot crows too.

I am beginning to think I'll not be able to hold the place together. Yesterday I caught the Peavey boy who used to live out here hunting just beyond the forks going toward the Farr Place. I balled him out and told him if I ever heard of him on the place again I'd get out a warrant for this time. I was afraid if I did get one out that he'd burn the place up. I later heard a shot gun in the same pasture but no car up or down the road. I went to all the gates on that side and checked. This morning, Manuel and I put locks on all the openings and found that they had cut the wire we put up going into the Farr Place.

While Manuel fixed it I followed the tracks to see how far they had gone and found where they had killed a deer. Some of the hide left. After I went home I sent Manuel to nail the gate at the Harper Place. He reported a tree house on the Timber Place near our gate and a deer hide stretched up there to dry. I asked him why he didn't get it down and he said it was too high.

* * *

From Mother
Postmark: Nov 26, 1963

She typed the letter below with a copy to each of us. This letter is so unlike the mother I remember. She was always decisive and showed confidence. I can only imagine that the indecision was a result of her pain and loneliness and her wanting to settle the land as her three children wanted, and her concern over money. In this letter she indicates that she is asking Susan and Thulia for advice because she planned to will the house jointly to her two elder daughters. Dad's pension was only about $50 monthly and I don't know what kind of benefits she had from that; she did have widow's benefits from Social Security, but that was very little. The farm's income had always been from timber sales, not from the livestock. Cattle and horses kept the farm in the red. She planned to sell the land to the three of us, which would leave her with the house to keep up and to pay taxes on, and she would have the routine expenses of everyday life. Her other income came from rents on the cottage, the apartments in the Myrick house on Liberty Street, and later the sale of the property on South Wayne Street.

Monday night

Dear Thulia and Susan:

Today I have been lonelier than in a long time. I am sure it is in

part because on TV I attended the Kennedy funeral.

But in part it was because this morning as I was having Manuel put a new cover on the cistern I saw that the scaffolding on the front was falling and the part of the up stairs balcony that had been built was getting in such bad shape that it would soon fall. And I began wondering how long the other part that had no weather boarding and paint would last. It is something we must talk about when you come Christmas, so be thinking about it. I am sure I could not afford to finish the house though I have no idea what it would cost. I don't know what to do and you'll have to help me decide.

John has been so good to me in giving advice but this is something that I haven't mentioned to him, for eventually the house will be yours. And I think you'll sell it, for it isn't practical for either of you to live here. After a few years, it will not seem so hard.

Mr. Sirmans came out one day and went with me to look at the clover. He suggested that I do nothing now and fertilize it heavy in the spring. I'll do that and try to keep the one pasture and sell 30 cows again this year. He also went with me to Farr's. I asked him if I should plant the vacant spots in the lespedeza fields and make it enough to cut another year.

He suggested that I plant it in coastal Bermuda and keep if for a hay field, even if I sell all of the cows. I went by the agricultural office and they will pay 70% of the cost. I can get it planted and the Bermuda plants for $15 per acre. But, do not know what getting the field in shape and fertilizer will cost. It is more than 10 acres. I'll try to get more information before you come.

Mr. Paton is coming Wednesday to go with me to Dovedale and appraise the land. Another thing to settle while you are here is what part you want to buy. Or do you want me just to settle that.

Miss Lil and John are doing lots of work on their house. I think John is getting it in good shape so that if they move to Macon and sell it they will get a big price for it. They were here yesterday. John always does some work around the house for me when he comes over. He brought his electric saw and cut the door in two, so it would be easier to open and close. And he put a new lock on the front door.

We did get rain, slow and soaking in. I picked up the last nuts this afternoon. Bob and Grady finally came up. I'm hoping to sell some horses soon.

Much love, Mother

*   *   *

Postmark: May 6, 1964
From Mother to Susan
Nanette was daughter of Lillas's Aunt Josey (Josephine Whitehurst Rozar). Her health was very bad at the time, and she had to rest after any exertion, which included such simple tasks as getting up in the morning, getting dressed and having breakfast—she then had to rest again before she was able to socialize.

Tuesday night

Dearest Susan

Thank you for my bird book. I just glanced at it and it looks so interesting. I'm saving it for a night when I need something to pep me up, and can't get interested in anything.

When I wrote last I did not intend to sound so disappointed about your being home next year. But I was worn out after a lot of company. Nanette had been with me most a week and I had done too much and I wrote too soon after talking with the girl.

Your card today said no news 'cept you were making plans for hitting the trail. The card earlier said you'd be here when the weather got hot. I'm beginning to think it may not be. I had Manuel come and cut some kindling for me yesterday.

I finally got my last cow up and sold. I got for the 12 cows (some with calf) more than half as much as I got for 30 last summer. But, I'm sure when I start selling again I will not get as much for them. They will sell by weight.

Mrs. H. N. Fitton (address). We all called her Sister. She is sister to Edgar Marshall (Edgar died soon after Dad died.) Dad was their first cousin. Dad's mother Lillian Marshall was sister to their father. I'll enclose a slip about their children. Any questions?

Miss Lil calls every night. She just called and said no news and when will the work on the house start. Soon, I hope.

Nothing going on but the regular work, cleaning, sewing, T. V.

and the extra is the work on Liberty St. They'll probably finish it tomorrow. I am hoping any day to hear from the man in Macon with the real estate company about renting the property on Wayne St. He said he was interested and would be over this week.

I enjoyed Herty Day. It simply poured all day and the crowd was good considering the weather. Mrs. Guy was there but few from the old days.

I've let my fire go out so I must go crawl under my electric blanket.

Much love,
Mother

The last Herty Day at GSCW was in the late 1960s. It moved to Atlanta and then to Savannah.

*   *   *

From Mother
Postmark: January 5, 1965

Dear Susan,

I went to Liberty Street this morning and Mrs. What's her name was as nice as ever and as talkative. She said she intended to pay rent for the two apts. for the time she had moved out, and would pay me as soon as her soc. sec. check came. She had cleaned up the apt quite a bit and will pay $1.00 per day till all her things are out. The paint is peeling and the room walls are terrible. I'm having wall boards put over plastering and the ceiling lowered. That will be less wall to paint in future and less gas for tenants to pay for.

I do not know about paint that I have stored, which is inside and which outside. Some have a label on them and some do not, but that with the label does not say if it is inside or out. Do you know about the paint you got for me? I need inside for Liberty St. and outside for the cottage. Let me know if you remember anything about it.

Miss Lil called and asked me to meet them at Haddock on

Wed. P.M. for supper. She did not know whether Thulia was still here or not. Said her patient was doing fine, the one she rushed back to that night.

It was grand having you home for two long weekends.

Manuel opened the gate and left food on the outside while he fed at the barn. When he came back both of the cows were out eating. Tomorrow he'll take them a little farther away and maybe eventually he'll get them moved.

Hope all is going fine.

Much love from Mother

*   *   *

The first half of Mother's next letter dealt with possible customers for Allie's book, *The Story of the Myricks*, which Allie had given me to sell. Rice was a surveyor; Bonner Jones, a pulp wood buyer; James Ritchie, a forester with the State; Mrs. Hammock, the mother of Faith and siblings who were good friends from Thulia's high school days; Jessie Trawick, a chemistry professor at the college; Virginia Satterfield, a librarian at the college.

Postmark: August 30, 1965

Sunday night

Dear Susan:

Sue, Tip, Lil and John came by for the day. Sue will go to the mountains next week end instead of here.

Was feeling blue and lonesome yesterday morning so went to town. I got lots of work done, talked with many people and came home feeling fine. Saw Rice, Jones, Ritchie, Mrs. Hammock's neighbor, Jessie and Virginia. Then got something to read.

Hope you had a good day today and all is fine.

Much love, Mother

*   *   *

From Mother
Postcard
Postmark: September 1965

Dear Susan

Letter from Georgia telling about Aunt Minnie's death. Busy trying to get things in shape at the White House.
  Love,
    Mother

The "white house" stood on the Chandler Place. It was rented a number of years. Mother was preparing it for another tenant. It went to Lil L. James, who eventually donated it to the local volunteer fire department; they burned it for training a couple of years after the 9/11 attack, so we were careful about saying we were going to burn the white house.

The picture below was in the "WC Thirty," a newsletter of "Activities at the Woman's College of Georgia," Vol. XII, No. 24, May 9, 1966. Mother's initials probably reflect her maiden name: Lillas Stanley Myrick.

MISS SUSAN MYRICK (right), Associate Editor, Macon Telegraph-News, presented a painting by her sister Kate Myrick Lowerre, Rome, N. Y., to the Mamie Padgett Art Collection at The Woman's College. The presentation was made at Alumnae Day. Two other sisters attending the presentation were (left) Mrs. E. M. Hubert and (2nd from right) Mrs. L. S. Lindsley. George Gaines, (2nd from left), chairman of the WC art department, accepted the painting for the college.

Lillas died February 6, 1968, while on vacation in Hawaii. Although her death came a month earlier in the year than Luther's, the daffodils in Wordsworth's Acre were again in full bloom. Once more, the daughters picked the flowers for the coffin blanket, which draped over the ends and sides of the casket.

Lindsley Rites Held Saturday

Graveside services for Mrs. L. C. Lindsley were held at 3:30 p.m. Saturday in Westview Cemetery with the Rev. Rembert Sisson officiating.

Mrs. Lindsley, the former Miss Lillas Myrick, died last Tuesday in Hawaii where she and one of her sisters, Mrs. William Lowerre of Rome, NY were visiting.

Mrs. Lindsley had said to her sister Tuesday evening she would rest rather than go to dinner because she was not feeling well. Mrs. Lowerre found her sister dead when she returned to their hotel room.

Mrs. Lindsley was the widow of Dr. Lindsley who was for many years a professor of chemistry at Georgia College. Daughter of the late Mr. and Mrs. James D. Myrick of Milledgeville, she was a graduate and former faculty member at Georgia College. She held a master's degree from Columbia University.

Survivors include three daughters, Mrs. Terry S. Bramlett of Memphis, Tenn., Miss Susan Lindsley of Atlanta and Dr. Lil James of Macon; two grandchildren; four sisters, Mrs. E. M. Hubert of Milledgeville, Miss Susan Myrick of Macon, Mrs. Edwin T. Bowden of Washington, D. C., and Mrs. Lowerre.

Luther and Lillas are buried in Westview Cemetery, just two blocks off Highway 22 on the west side of Milledgeville. Since Lillas died in Hilo, Hawaii, while on vacation, her place of death is not given on her stone to avoid any possible confusion in the future about her place of residence.

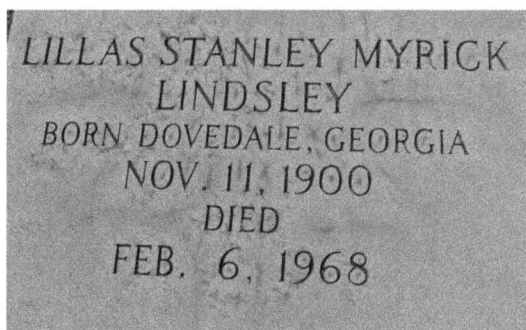

LILLAS STANLEY MYRICK
LINDSLEY
BORN DOVEDALE, GEORGIA
NOV. 11, 1900
DIED
FEB. 6, 1968

PART VIII

REMEMBRANCE OF OUR FATHER

LIL LINDSLEY JAMES REMEMBERS DAD

Luther, daughter Lil, Lillas, daughter Susan, at North Georgia College for Lil's graduation.

Dad was an unusual man. He was a Virginian—a Tidewater Virginian. Also he was a chemist, a philosopher, a writer, a historian, a lover of nature and of justice, a seeker of knowledge and an educator.

If ever the child was father of the man it was so in his life. His very early life is a story of extreme hardship. His grandfather was killed at the Battle of Cedar Creek in the beautiful Shenandoah Valley of Virginia in 1864. (See Appendix III.)

As a young boy he lost his younger brother, his parents and later an elder sister. He was preoccupied with death and loneliness. Left to the loving care of his grandmother and his step-grandfather, and his Aunt Minnie, he thrived. It was his grandmother and her family whose love and support enabled him to endure the despair and loneliness of his early years and fortified him for life's future adversities. With their support he was able to enter as a student at William and Mary College in the fall of 1903. His record there was astounding. His writings were well recognized. He described the emotions of despair amongst the beloved of the dying in a manner that superseded Hemingway. These stories reveal the compassion he developed for others.

As might be expected, he reveled in the classics. He read extensively and deeply into philosophy, history and religion. He was a friend of all he met there. He was deeply impressed by the great teacher Socrates who drank the hemlock rather than betray his beliefs.

After Dad's amazing career at William and Mary he went on to receive his Ph.D. in chemistry at Cornell University and came back to be Professor of Chemistry at William and Mary.

He merged with the socially elite wherever he was: In Williamsburg, Cornell and Columbia, and particularly at William and Mary. He developed an understanding and appreciation for the fine manners of his social level. He would have fit in at Versailles.

His first wife Pattie Love also fit into this group. She supplied the love he so desperately needed and for a few years relieved the loneliness which he had endured since childhood. His colleagues and friends in Milledgeville said that when she died he was so crushed that they thought he would not survive. They had no children.

Dad was never defeated. He was well integrated and self-sufficient to a large degree. He came through childhood without complaint. He set to work and excelled. He overcame the loss of his wife with dignity and resolve.

Shortly after Pattie Love's death he found himself a new wife, one of his colleagues. He married my mother, a Southern intellectual whose family had more than a century earlier migrated to Georgia and suffered severely financially because of the War Between the States.

As a Tidewater Virginian my father landed in depression-era Georgia where the average education was third-grade level and the educated were as a rule very provincial. He was as much a displaced person as a Connecticut Yankee in King Arthur's court.

After his home, Westover, burned, he set out to rebuild it.

He responded to disaster with constructive energy.

His life is an example of how one can endure hardship but with love and understanding be molded into a truly just, objective and compassionate individual—one who truly understood his gifts and the obligations they placed upon him. He was a true Southern Gentleman in the old sense of the word but lived in a time when that genteelness was rapidly fading.

Dad's great passion was to create beauty—Wordsworth's Acre is a prime example. After he retired, he turned gullies on the hill behind the house into a garden of azaleas, daffodils, crocus and other plants. These gardens remain today.

Dad's heart, like Wordsworth's, leaped up when he saw the waves of daffodils in bloom, a newborn foal, a whitetail deer, a frolicking calf, the fields of crimson clover, or a beautiful vase. To him, a Greek coin embedded the whole of an idea—Greek philosophy, the Pantheon, the Battle of Marathon, and the foundation of the American republic. When he told us of these things his enthusiasm flowed with his words.

Dad was a deeply religious man who prayed his own prayers and developed his own character of God. But he also had respect for organized religion and great love for his wife and children. He worked to make things better and more beautiful for them and all mankind not only during his lifetime but for all time.

I'm sure that when he died he was proud of his children. One child was happily married and rearing two of his grandchildren, one was working for MIT editing research papers, and one had an MD degree from Emory University and was married to a law student whom he also loved.

Lil spoke about her memories of Dad's fun and repeated stories that he told on himself, as well as conversations she overheard. Her husband John would sit up late into the night to hear his stories.

When Dad came to Georgia to teach at the local college, he soon learned that Westover Plantation house and some 800 acres were for sale. When he wrapped up his purchase at the local bank, the banker said, "Doc, you know you're paying $10.00 an acre for land, and you can get land anywhere around here for just $5.00 an acre."

Dad replied, "The boxwood alone is worth what I'm paying for all of it."

"Box wood? What kind of boxes are you gong to make?"

Dad told his family that when he heard that question, he knew he had come to the Promised Land.

Someone asked Dad why he had scrub cattle instead of full-blood Herefords. Dad replied that if these got through the fence and into the swamps or got onto the railroad and killed, he wouldn't be losing a lot.

When he bought the Blount House, a visitor noticed that it had no indoor plumbing. He asked Dad where he was going to put the bathroom. Without cracking a smile, he said he just might put it on the front porch so it would be handy for visitors as well as whoever was living inside.

He told Lil that he had been considering going to China and becoming a missionary back when he was in Virginia. He decided to drive down to Florida to meditate over the idea, but when he got to Georgia, he thought he was needed more here than in China.

John, Lil's husband, came in beat up from horseback riding, and Dad asked him if he had gotten any windmills.

Some of our pigs got out of the sty and headed off toward a neighbor's, where they feasted in the corn field. When the landowner sued Dad in court to get paid for the destruction, the judge asked Dad "how big are the pigs?"

Dad replied, "About your size, Judge."

The county road crews were bulldozing our land when Dad happened to drive up and catch them. He immediately ordered them off our land. The black men said they'd be in trouble if they quit their work. Dad told them they'd be in more trouble if they didn't quit.

In court, he told the jury how history changed the value of everything—a coin was just a coin, but if it were one of the coins given to Judas to betray Jesus, it wasn't just a coin. And since Sherman's army had camped on that land and marched down that road, the land wasn't just "land," it was history.

At a time that land was valued at $10.00 an acre, the jury found for Dad, valuing the land at $50.00 per acre, and included the original road bed because the county did not have any title to it.

Having been reared in Virginia and unaccustomed to the language of the rural Negro of the 1930s, he had communication problems with many of his hired men. When Dad told one helper that "the bovine have pierced the ferrous strips and entered the apian way," the employee turned to my mother and asked, "What does he mean?"

She replied, "The cows are out and up on the road."

Someone asked him what he was doing when he was rebuilding Westover after it burned, and he said: "Building a temple. A delegate is here from Ethiopia to help."

Dad was rebuilding the house when he told the hired man to nail a board up horizontally. Fortunately, Mother was again there to translate: "Put it up criss-cross."

When Dad went to Atlanta, he couldn't find DeSoto Street, and he asked a number of pedestrians for directions. No one could help him. He finally asked a policeman who was directing traffic, and fortunately the officer was a student of history. "Oh, sir, you probably mean Ponce de Leon Avenue," and he gave directions.

On the one trip he took the children on, to Virginia where they toured the College of William and Mary and saw his desk in one of the classrooms, he asked the family if they would like to move to Virginia. Lil said his tears showed when he asked. All the children said no they wanted to go home to Westover.

Some quotes Lil remembers:

To his future son-in-law John James, he said: "John, it's fine if you want to marry Lil, but remember, she won't ever be able to put on a proper tea."

He told his wife Lillas Myrick, granddaughter of Stith Parham Myrick: "You know Virginia lost The War because it couldn't get supplies from Georgia. My dear wife, your grandfather was Quartermaster. If Georgia had sent food and shoes to Virginia, Virginia would have won The War."

The quote we all remember: "It's rude to ask someone where he is from. If he's from Virginia he'll tell you in the first five minutes; if he's not, it doesn't matter."

THULIA LINDSLEY BRAMLETT REMEMBERS DAD

When I think about Dad, and I do often since I've moved

back to Westover, I've found myself doing many of the same things he used to do when I was growing up.

Dad was 47 years old when I was born, so I never knew him as a young man, only as a middle-aged and older man. He was loving, but always serious, and not inclined to play with us much.

He worked hard all the time. He was the first one up in the morning and went to bed early, worn out from the day's work. In wintertime, he got up and built a fire in the downstairs dining room, where we all would get dressed and have breakfast. Then, while Mother fixed breakfast, he walked down the hill to the barn and milked.

When we were old enough to go to school, we rode with him in an old furniture truck. He stopped at least three times along the roadside to feed the cattle. While we waited in the truck, he went to the dilapidated shed and pitchforked hay out to the cows. Then back in the truck, he drove to the next shed and repeated the feeding. In the afternoons, he fed at these same sheds, dropped us off, and feed the cattle and horses at other barns.

After cutting firewood for the fireplaces and eating supper, he graded papers, and finally, would go to bed.

I remember how hard he worked to save the life of a sick cow or horse, and how he worked in summertime to cut and get the hay in for the winter. We had several miles of fencing that he was constantly repairing. He used to laugh and say his PHD stood for post-hole digger.

He loved Westover, both the house and the gardens, and was proud to show off the house and the boxwoods to visitors. I still have some of the original guest books that lay on a table just inside the front door.

It was terribly sad for him when Westover burned, but he immediately began plans to rebuild. He spent the rest of his life building it back. In his sixties at the time, with a bad shoulder and bad knees, he would work for several hours, then come inside and lie on the sofa for a while. But he would soon be up again and back to work. He still loved visitors and showing them the progress he was making on the house.

I remember his pulling honey suckle from the boxwood and how hard he worked to stop erosion on the gulleys behind the house. He built rock steps and planted azaleas, iris, daffodils and wildflowers to stop the erosion. These steps and many of the plants are still there.

Steps Luther built to block erosion. He moved the rocks in a wheelbarrow. This 1957 photo also shows one of the remaining slave houses in the background. He halted his work after Westover burned, to devote his time to the house.

He sowed different kinds of clover and planted forage in the pastures for the livestock, and planted pines in the worn out cotton fields.

Herty Days, when chemists from all over the Southeast came to Milledgeville for Herty Day weekend, were memorable. Dad made wine from scuppernongs, and served it with the punch. He and Mother planned far ahead for the weekend, and enjoyed the camaraderie with the other chemists and the medalist who stayed over night with us at Westover.

In late afternoons, he drove slowly down the road (now Highway 212, but a country dirt road then) to look at the cattle and horses visible from the road, to check fences that needed repair, and to see how much grass there was for the cattle or if they had eaten it too far down.

In remembering life with Dad when I was growing up, I

know that he needed sons and must have wanted them, but he had three daughters instead. We still helped him in the hayfields and with the cattle and horses and with the fences as much as we could.

He taught me to read in a little French book when I was probably five years old, and he counted in German for a game we played. We didn't have much money to spend on clothes, etc., when we were growing up because every penny he could spare was spent on buying land so that his wife and daughters would have some security when he died.

When my first child was born, a boy, he and Mother came to Memphis to see him. Having no sons, Dad was proud to have a grandson.

Now that I have aged and am again living at Westover, I find that I am doing many of the same things he did. I don't have cattle and horses, but I am repairing buildings, planting trees and flowers and clover, and building ponds. I, too, love to read history.

He instilled in me many of his loves and values, and I will always remember him and be thankful for all that he taught me.

SUSAN LINDSLEY REMEMBERS DAD

I have entered personal comments about my father throughout this book, so I will be brief here.

Dad loved to tell his two favorite stories about the boxwood. One was about the banker who thought he was going to make wooden boxes. The other story dealt with Henry Ford. Dad was slopping the hogs and dressed in his usual workman's attire when Ford rode up in his chauffeured limousine and began to inquire about Westover. Ford thought Dad was the hired man.

Dad did not say anything to change Ford's mistaken belief. Turned out, Ford wanted to buy some of the old boxwood plants. Since "Mrs. Lindsley" the owner was not home, he asked "the hired man" to dig them up. "She won't miss them."

Dad said, "I couldn't do that to my wife."

Ford left.

In going through old papers, I found an almost rotted away

letter dated January 13, 1937, from Miller Bell, then president of the Milledgeville Banking Company which stated:

I hasten to offer hearty congratulations on the splendid success you are meeting with on your farm. It seems to me that you make an unusually find showing. However, I should not be surprised, since I realize how beautifully you bought out the old Jordan home at such small cost.

One childhood experience shared with my father that still influences my day-to-day activities is photography. I had a small "box camera" and Dad taught me how to make contact prints using the porch (at night) as a darkroom and the lamplight in the living room to expose the paper. Eventually I had my on darkroom equipment and held photography shows. More than sixty years later, I still love taking pictures.

Another aspect of Dad that influenced my life was his writings. My earliest memories are of sneaking bound copies of the *William and Mary Literary Magazine* from the secretary in the living room and reading. And reading. And memorizing.

After we published the collection of his writings, I discovered a new poem, apparently written about 1943-44. In pencil, it is on the back of a letter advertising *Children's Activities Magazine* dated November 15, 1943.

When I first scanned the poem (his handwriting is difficult to read), I glanced over the first and last lines and thought it was in honor of our mother. but no, it was in honor of an oak tree. To me, my mother was the oak tree, strong and unbending as she faced the winds of life.

The location of Watson's Glen is unknown. Monticello Road runs through the land we call the "Lane Place," which was once owned by the Lane family whose daughter married a Watson. The Watson family farm is near the Monticello Road.

There is a Monticello Road in Charlottesville, Virginia, but I have found no reference to Watson's Glen there, and DeSoto himself did not enter Virginia.

UNTITLED

I am the aged oak that stands
At Watson's Glen on Monticello Road.
Hallowed by Time I still defy
The tempest and the lightning of the sky,
I *was* before the white man came. I made
For Indian Prince and Maiden grateful shade
And red skin children climbed among my boughs.

I was a signal oak, and from afar
Could see the signal smokes of peace and war
Or council calls to near and distant ones.

I heard the echoes of DeSoto's march
And distant rumble of Cornwallis' guns,
Beneath me passed the Legions of the Blue,
Beneath me lingered wearily the Gray,
Below me stand the children of my seed
Strong and rigorous through the coming years
For *YOU* have saved them for yourself and me
  ---is it only love can save a tree!

Dad's great respect for Charles Herty led him to originate the Herty awards, and their deep friendship led him to write of this admiration when Herty died. I don't remember seeing Dad's pain at the time—he tended to be private in such matters, but I know that he worked it out with this poem, as do many writers.

The first version of the poem (below) is given in *The Literary Works of L. C. Lindsley.* I found the second version after that book was printed, and decided to include it here.

Herty

1

God stood upon Stone Mountain at the Dawn.
Around Him stretched the Seas of Miocene
To the far horizon, where lines of wild fowl
Winged home their flight to salt marshes

They had left at light.

The southern pines were creeping up the hills
And laughing streams flowed crystal to the sea.
The valleys were carpeted in green,
God said, "All this is good.
Let there be man."

2

God stood upon Stone Mountain at the noon,
Around him stretched the Seas of Desolation.
Gone were the forests and hills of green.
The Rivers ran with Life Blood to the sea,
Man had made a desert of a Garden.
God said, "Georgia, create a man."

3

The granite gave its feldspar for a dauntless courage
The pine its stateliness; the Dawn its youth,
The mountain peaks their vision,
The sun its friendliness, the Southern Seas
Their salts to form his blood.

And lo! At Milledgeville,
Herty was born.

Below is the other version, not in the *Literary Works*.

HERTY

God stood upon the summit of a shell-capped peak;
Seas of Miocene surged to the far horizon,
Where lines of sea fowl winged home their flight
To salt marshes they had left at dawn.
Millions of pine were creeping up the hills,

Sweet waters ran through forest to the sea;
"All this is Good, let Man here reign supreme."

God wept upon Stone Mountain in the dusk;
About Him desolation and erosion stretched
To the horizon, where the rivers ran
Red with Georgia's life blood to the sea.
The flaming forests dimmed the sunset's glow!
Man had made a desert of a Garden
The desert had made savages of men.
He said, "Georgia, can thou create a man?"

The granite gave its feldspar for a dauntless courage
The mountain peak its vision, and the pine
Its stateliness; the Dawn its youth,
The oak its strength. Sunlight gave its friendliness,
The Southern Seas their salts to form his blood,
Dahlonega, a heart of gold,

And lo! At Milledgeville,
Herty was born.

Pictures in the *Literary Works of L. C. Lindsley* are those used in the *William and Mary Literary Magazine* alongside his poetry. On a visit to Williamsburg, I was able to take pictures of the Powder Magazine and Old Bruton Parish Church, which I'm including here.

The Powder Magazine

Bruton Parish Church

JIM WILLLIAMS SPOKE OF LUTHER

In his book *Midnight in the Garden of Good and Evil* (Random

House), John Berendt quotes Jim Williams' remarks about Luther, on pages 299-300.

Jim Williams was an antique dealer in Savannah and lived in Mercer House (once home to Johnny Mercer). He was in jail, awaiting his third trial for the murder of Danny Hansford. The transcript of the second trial ran to fifteen hundred pages, and Jim and his attorney had a massive amount of work to prepare for the third trial.

"How do you plan to do all that it will take to be prepared?" I (John Berendt) asked.

The same way I restore houses. Step by step. Inch by inch. I learned an invaluable lesson from my old mentor, Dr. L. C. Lindsley. Did I ever tell you about him? Dr. Lindsley was a college professor who restored and lived in one of Georgia's great houses, Westover. It was built in Milledgeville in 1822 in the grand style. It had spiral stairs and a pair of white double-height columns on each side of the front entrance.

Dr. Lindsley told me than an old house will defeat you if you try to restore it all at once—from roof to windows, weatherboarding , jacking it up, central heating, wiring. You must think of doing one thing at a time. First you say to yourself: Today I am going to think about leveling off the sills. And you get all the sills leveled. Then you turn your mind to the weatherboarding, and gradually you do all the weatherboarding. Then you consider the windows. Just one window at a time. That window right there. You ask yourself, 'What's wrong with that part of that window?' You must do it in sections, because that's the way it was built. And then suddenly you find the whole thing completed. Otherwise it will defeat you.

It may seem impossible to you, but let me point out something else—something else I learned from Dr. Lindsley. One day he said, 'You know, robins move houses. Little birds with orange tummies can move a house. In fact, they tried to move Westover.' I said, 'All right, I give up. How do they do it?' And he said, 'They eat chinaberries, and then they drop the chinaberry seeds near the foundation of a house. A chinaberry tree grows there and uproots the house.' And he was right. I've seen it happen. Chinaberry trees grow very rapidly, and they will tear up the

foundations of a house.

Jim was found guilty at this third trial, but appealed again. At his fourth trial, he was found not guilty and returned to his beloved Mercer House.

On page 31, Dr. Dorothy Williams Kingery, ***Savannah's Jim Williams & His Southern Houses***, The Sheldon Group, L.L. C., Publisher, Savannah, Georgia, his sister quotes Jim's essay on the Butler House:

Dr. L. C. Lindsley was one of my first mentors. (He mentioned Dad's backgrounds and continued.) **Dr. Lindsley told me the roof of Westover was to have been covered with beaten silver dollars but the governor of Georgia stopped the builder, saying it would take too much money out of circulation. Both Westover and the Gordon house** (the Blount house to us) **were examples of a final flowering of what was to become known as the southern plantation mansion.**

PART IX

REMEMBRANCE OF OUR MOTHER

THULIA LINDSLEY BRAMLETT
REMEMBERS MOTHER

I have few if any preschool memories of Mother. But I do remember a few things.

Living six miles out in the country on a red clay dirt road and with one vehicle, we did not go to town very often. A trip to town was a big event. Especially for Mother since she had to get three little preschool girls ready to go. I remember her taking the three of us little girls to the Binion Clinic on Greene Street across from GMC to get our annual shots. I remember her taking us to visit Aunt Josie (Rozar) on the corner of Columbia and Hancock and to use her phone. She had one attached to the wall. You held the receiver and talked into the wall unit. She also took us occasionally to visit Cousin Ella Green who lived on Columbia Street next door to Mrs. Beeson. She also took us to see Mrs. Beeson and sometimes to the College Library to see Betty Ferguson and Virginia Satterfield. The entire faculty used to ooh and aah over us since Mother had taught there and Dad was still teaching there.

I remember not wanting to go to school. Mother would take me to the first grade at GMC and have to stay for a while every day or I would cry. I would cry if she left me without staying awhile. Sometimes she took me out of class and spanked me and then would take me back to the class.

As we got a little older, I remember her spending a lot of time with us in the summer. She took the three of us girls on long walks in the fields and woods. We picked blackberries and plums and she made lots of jelly. I remember helping her wash jars and peel and cut up peaches to can.

Every afternoon we spent some time on the shady side porch. She played school with us, using math and English workbooks that she had purchased. We also played a nutrition game every day. We had to review what we had eaten and could move tokens on colored cards for the different vitamins, calcium, protein, etc. In the late summer, my Aunt Tippie would come and she and Mother would alter old dresses and make new dresses for the next school year. Our dresses were nothing like the ones I loved to look at that were stored in a closet—the big puffy-sleeved and the low-waisted, pleated ones she wore in the 1920s before her marriage.

She taught us to swim, first playing in a big creek on her family's Dovedale Plantation, then the old country club across the Oconee River in Milledgeville, the farm pond behind our house, Lake Jonesco and at Lake Burton one summer.

I remember her doing what today we might call crafts. She refinished a lot of furniture. Store-bought paint strippers were maybe not available or not affordable. She used a lot of glass, broken window panes I think, and did a lot of scraping off layers of old paint. She wove cane bottoms in chairs. And in the winter time she did a lot of knitting of sweaters and also bedspreads and afghans. She crocheted rag rugs from some of Dad's old suit pants and from any material she could acquire. I still have items she knitted and still use her rugs in my house forty-five years later.

After Dad died, she renewed friendships with many of her old friends from Milledgeville. One group was a sewing club and another group a bird watching club. They frequently met here at Westover. Lil and John gave her a German shepherd puppy which she named Hilda. Hilda remained with her the rest of Mother's life and was a wonderful companion. Hilda loved to ride in the car with Mother. The old car Mother drove around the farm became known as Hilda's car. Mother chauffeured and Hilda sat upright in the back seat. After Mother died, Hilda moved to Memphis and became part of my family.

After I married and was living in Memphis, Mother and Dad both came for a week when my first child (Lindy) was born and then Mother came and stayed a couple of weeks after the second (Rusty) was born. My fondest and best memories of Mother are when Lindy and Rusty and I would come to Westover and spend several weeks with her in the summer. We did many of the same things she had done with us as children. We went for long walks, picked berries and plums, and played in creeks—this time with Hilda along.

Mother loved to fish and she was patient with the little boys with their fishing poles and the wooden fishing boat at the lake behind the house. We still had horses and she helped them ride.

One night we slept (camped out) at the lake with the horses grazing nearby.

Mother always loved to read. We had no telephone, no television and she had no car when Dad was using it to drive to town to teach. But we did get mail! For years she subscribed to *Ladies Home Journal, Life, Colliers,* and *Readers Digest.* Of course it followed that she not only read to the three of us girls as children, but she read to her grandchildren. She made them a wonderful poem book, cutting pictures from magazines and using lines not from children's poems, but from authors such as Shakespeare, Coleridge, Wordsworth, etc.

Almost every summer morning Mother, Lindy, Rusty and I would have "feshments" on the front porch of the house. Something to drink and some of the teacakes she made. They became known as Lindy cookies.

I remember good times with Mother. One of the funniest memories I have of her is the time that my sister Lil, the physician, wanted Mother to lose weight. Lil purchased some diet drink for Mother and suggested she have it for her lunch. A week later, Lil asked Mother how she was doing with the diet drink. "Oh, I like it. It's real good poured over vanilla ice cream."

I know that my life has been easier than hers. The house was huge, no air conditioning in the summer time and only wood-burning fireplaces in the winter time. No washer or dryer. She cooked on a kerosene stove for years before REA ran electricity to our part of the county. A family on the place washed our clothes and even my children's diapers in wash pots with a fire underneath. I don't think we ever had a new car. Money was always scarce. She often said we were "land poor."

I was married when they got a telephone and a TV. She and Dad found time to love us, to teach us the importance of education and hard work and to instill in us a love of our family history and of our heritage. I only hope that I have done at least half as good a job with my own children as she did with us.

LIL MYRICK LINDSLEY JAMES
REMEMBERS MOTHER

Mother was influenced greatly by the historical time and place into which she was born—the South only thirty-five years after the end of The War and the inversion of society. From aristocratic, slaveholding grandparents of great wealth, she inherited great genes. Some of the finer virtues of that small element of Southern Society were also passed along. Neither her grandfather nor her great-uncle (by marriage) U. S. Senator Benjamin Harvey Hill were secessionists and both were active in forging a regenerating South.

The family survived The War intact, and by example left a legacy of respect for equal justice under the law, for education, for work and for reconciliation. The economic conditions which Mother encountered were prevalent all over the South where cash was almost non-existent.

But she had great advantages in her early years on Dovedale Plantation: A good library, a live-in school teacher, loving and generous parents and life in the country with its home-grown foods and diverse neighbors. Her personality was shaped by a father who reached manhood after The War and had a futuristic attitude. His family thrived.

Mother was the youngest of eight children. Her personality contrasted with the somber and serious but deeply religious and scientific attitude of my father who was surrounded by death and calamity throughout his early life and whose adult companions had personally endured severe non-pecuniary losses during The War.

Mother was very attached to her home place, Dovedale, and her keen knowledge of country life and austerity can be traced back to those years when clothes were made at home and corn was carried by horses and mules to the mill to be ground. She met and understood Southern country people, black and white.

With the death of her father when Mother was only ten years old, the family moved to Milledgeville and a few months later to the Liberty Street house near the Georgia Normal and Industrial

College, where she obtained her education.

In Milledgeville, life changed. Social life expanded, and Mother took up activates such as tennis. But with the gaiety came hours of studying. During these years Mother would return to Dovedale, the country she loved.

There were few cars then. Mother's older sister (Elizabeth "Tippie") had married a physician at an early age and lived in between Dovedale and town. The other older children gradually left home, and Mother remained living with her mother at the Liberty Street House. After graduation from GSCW, Mother taught during regular school sessions but spent summers at various graduate schools working on her master's degree and later her doctorate.

She attended Columbia University at one time, as did her sister Allie and her cousin Nan Whitehurst. She also studied at the University of Colorado, Columbia University, Cornell, and the University of Minnesota. Although education seemed to have been great fun for the Myrick siblings, Mother did not limit her summers to study. One summer, she waited tables at the "Lodge" in Yellowstone Park.

A family story goes that the Myricks would sit on the front porch at Liberty Street to cool off in the hot summer evenings. There was always a lot of laughter. The neighbors across the street sneaked over once to find out what was so funny. One person after another would speak, but the comment wasn't a bit funny—but everybody laughed.

Mother and her siblings continued this laughter for all of their lives, swapping stories of childhood and family.

The early years of marriage must have been rough for Mother. Cash was in short supply since she no longer received an income, and Luther had debts for his Virginia property and for Westover and other investments. Not only did she have three pregnancies in far too rapid succession, but she had acquired the task of managing a prominent social event (Herty Day) with renowned visitors at her home annually, and she was the only one of the eight Myrick siblings left in Milledgeville to tend to the Milledgeville residence and Dovedale Plantation.

Shortly after her third child was born, she sustained a

severe back injury from a fall from a horse, which kept her bedridden for weeks.

Growing up, I realized that although we lived at Westover and were isolated by bad roads, no telephone, and poor cars, Mother continued to have a lot of downtown friends. Most were well educated and taught at the college or had government jobs. In a way, Mother was an early feminist. She was anxious for her daughters to be well educated and independent. She was instrumental in getting Peabody High School to include Latin and advanced mathematics courses. She saw to it that we registered to vote. And she was thrilled when her pressure on the Clerk of Court finally resulted with her getting called for jury duty—probably the first woman in our county to serve. She also helped with voting and vote counting at the Meriwether Precinct. She stayed current with local, state and national news.

When she inherited one-eighth of Dovedale Plantation, she constructed a camp house of two rooms, with a central chimney and double fireplace, and with a screened porch. She named her section "the Camp Place." Mother rode horseback the twelve miles to camp, and after a day or so would ride back to Milledgeville. Some of her lady friends who rode horseback would ride up with her to camp.

Mother always loved birds. Early on, she obtained recordings from Columbia University and played bird songs to attract birds. She was always excited to see a new species. Long after we had no chickens, she continued to purchase scratch grain to scatter for the cardinals that practically ate from her hand.

My earliest memories are of the period during World War II and shortly thereafter. We kept a one-acre garden across the road in front of the house. Mother picked and canned tomatoes; gathered, husked and put up corn; picked and canned beans. She picked blackberries for jelly, made pear preserves, canned peaches, made muscadine wine and picked apples to make apple pie and apple sauce. She strained the milk Dad brought in, skimmed it, reclaimed the cream, churned butter, made ice cream. She gathered and candled eggs and fed the chickens. She wrung the necks of those chosen for dinner, steamed, plucked and fried them.

I remember family and friends coming to get eggs and milk

which could not be bought at stores without ration stamps. Mother was so happy when chocolate was available for us.

But most of all, she was pleased when shoe rationing ended and she could get shoes for us.

She never complained. And she met our needs.

As we grew into our teens, we had hundreds of acres to roam over and wild horses, rattlesnakes and rabid foxes to contend with. But we also had riding horses, a German shepherd dog, a collie that produced countless puppies, and cats to play with. We had cows and horses and chickens to tend to and learn from. We learned from our chores how to drive cows in to be milked, where to find the hen nests, when to cut hay, where to plant the clover, how to tell what the weather might do, and where to find blackberries without getting bitten by the rattlesnakes. We tamed horses and broke them to ride. We explored and found liquor stills. We did many dangerous things. Most modern-day mothers would have gone crazy, but Mother had the wisdom and the guts to keep the leash loose and let us take some chances and learn our limitations.

Early on, she taught us what to do in an emergency: One stays with the patient and the other goes for help.

Mother's interests varied. She knew the constellations and would take us out into the pasture at night, to tell us about the stars and the myths. She grew excited when there was confluence of planets or when a storm of "falling stars" was predicted, or when an eclipse was coming. The first launch into space thrilled her, and she would go out at night to watch our satellites go by.

Fishing became her favorite outdoor sport. When Dad retired and built a pond behind the house, she spent free hours fishing. We children would go frog gigging and Mother would fry the legs and watch them jumping in the frying pan. Once we went gigging and got no frogs, but our cat arrived with a frog in her mouth shortly after we reached the house. We all laughed, and cleaned the frog for Mother. She really enjoyed those frog legs.

Knitting kept her busy in all of my remembered years. She not only knitted many sweaters for us, but she also knitted fancy bedspreads. Whenever she sat down, she picked up her knitting. I can still see her in her mother's rocking chair at night, settled down to knit while we did our homework on the dining room table in a room warmed by a blazing fire.

Mother was a good nurse. Although Dad usually picked out the splinters, Mother was the one who got the carbolic acid to soak our feet in when we stepped on nails. She simply put us to bed for concussions and when we had the breath knocked out in a fall from a tree or a horse. However, she carried me to the physician when I drank gasoline from the Coke bottle and to the dentist when I was thrown from a horse and had teeth knocked out. She got an ambulance when a sister coughed up blood after an "accident" with a horse and after a friend broke her back and had a closed-head injury from another horse "accident."

One Halloween, when I was about second grade, my sisters and I went to a neighbor's house to "scare" them, and in the darkness I fell, stabbing my hand on a pitchfork. Mother had me soaking the hand in carbolic acid for a long time, but because I was in such pain, she slept in the bed with me that night. A mother's arms and love do decrease pain.

Mother taught us in various ways. When I was very young, she borrowed $5.00 from my hard-earned dollars, from chores. Then, when I asked her to return it, she told me that I wouldn't get it back because I hadn't gotten an IOU. For a moment, I believed it.

Once when I was bored, she told me to memorize the "Vision of Sir Launfal." This project led me, at the age of 14, to follow her other advice: Read some good books. I read John Calvin. Afterwards I debated myself as to whether or not I was free to read the book.

Mother encouraged me to raise chickens for sale. I did, but Mother had to help me sell to some of the neighbors. I got a good lesson in economics: Gainesville, Georgia, was rapidly becoming the chicken capital of the world. The competition was tough.

Susan and I left for college in the fall of 1954. I will never forget the first weekend home from college, to a fire in the fireplace, wonderful parents and a reunion with Nature. I have never been so deeply happy. Only a few weeks later while reading the Atlanta newspaper, I learned that "Westover Plantation, the historic home of Dr. and Mrs. L. C. Lindsley" had burned to the ground. I located Susan and we mourned together. There was no way we could immediately contact our parents.

Mother and Dad moved into the overseer's house next door. A few family heirlooms survived, but the house they had to move into was not ready for living. Running water had to be connected; the kitchen stove was an old wood-burner; only too-small fireplaces provided heat; the bath was as antiquated as the kitchen.

Mother rose to the occasion. By the time we arrived from college in a few weeks, there was a new stove, running water, beds for everybody, and my great-grandfather's gold-plated mirrors were hanging.

But there was still a little leak in the roof. Mother had adapted well. She helped erase some of the gloom. We sifted the ashes for endeared artifacts, and plans were underway to rebuild.

A few months later, Mother's sister Susan Myrick had a heart attack. Sue did well, and Mother pulled through that too with flying colors.

The next few years had to be difficult for Mother. The children were gone, but she was engrossed by the task of rebuilding. I finished college in 1957 and returned to live at home in between times that I attended medical school in Augusta. During these and the next years I began to understand more fully my parents values. Mother was not ever visibly depressed although she was often tired. She had successfully reared her children and money was not one of her proudest possessions.

I married in 1959 and Mother set about to have the new house ready for my wedding. With a lot of help from my sister Susan she had bedrooms and baths put into functional shape. I was happily married in the new house. Two years later, when I finished medical school, my Mother and Dad were there for my graduation. I was surprised but pleased.

When my husband, John, entered law school in Macon and I was beginning an internship at the Macon Hospital, Mother and Dad gave us the old Gordon Bowen Blount house to live in. She was greatly pleased to have the support of both of us as she grew older.

In 1963, my father died after a brief illness. Mother was distraught. "Your father was so strong," she said, "that I just depended on him for support. I never thought he would die in my lifetime."

After my father's death, I was busy with a residency and John was busy in law school and starting a law practice. Dismantling the plantation would be the work of several men, but with the help of Susan she managed. I visited her at every opportunity and saw that the stress was getting to her. Her blood pressure rose and she developed angina. She set about to manage her estate for the benefit of her children, and did so very well.

Mother eagerly looked forward to a vacation, a trip to Hawaii with her sister Katie. Their trip had been delayed once because of the death of Katie's husband. The last time I saw Mother was at my Aunt Sue's just before her departure.

When the call came from Hawaii in the middle of the night the next week, I felt the loss severely. I still cherish all she did to make my life productive and happy, and cherish her memory and the values she transmitted.

SUE MYRICK'S COMMENTS ON OUR MOTHER

This letter to Mother from her sister Susan Myrick gives us insight into Mother's strength when faced with her own mother's death and reflects the same thought that Mother wrote in her notes on an envelope: "I never talked my troubles."

Dearest Lil,

I first thought to send some flowers for Mama's grave to-day, but I thought about it and decided she would probably not want it, so I am not. I am writing instead, a note to you, for I know that to-day you will probably be thinking of her often and I know how the greatest of all our griefs has been yours to bear. Because none of us seem to have the habit of talking about things much and also because I have hoped to help you more by keeping your mind on other things, I have said little, but I have known all along that you have suffered much and I have loved you and wanted to help. I want to tell you that I think you have been swell and brave and that all of us have admired the fight you have made. Of course, you have made it because you know Mama was like that, herself, always brave and facing with courage anything which came.

    With all my love, Sue

Sue often wrote of family events in her newspaper columns.

I'm No Doctor
Sue Myrick

"NOW, YOU'LL HAVE something to write about," the doctor said.

He wasn't kidding.

I have seldom been scairder.

My sister and I were fishing. She had a new lure which somebody had recommended as the best thing for fishing at that particular time of the moon or the fishing calendar. She was real excited as she fastened the lure on the leader of her fly rod.

She is accustomed to casting flies, light ones, and she's hung plenty of bream and a few bass on flies and she gets as excited over catching a fish as most women would get over a new mink coat.

She flung out the lure on short throws, sort of feeling it out, and when it seemed to work pretty well, she grew bolder with it and whipped it far out.

"Gosh," she said, "the thing caught in my sleeve."

We got it out of the sleeve without tearing the cloth and she kept whipping out the line, while I cast out a Lucky Thirteen and hoped for a bass.

"Un-uh," she said in a quiet voice. "I caught the thing in my back, this time."

The lure had stuck through the back of her dress and hooked deep into the flesh. I pulled the dress away from her back and took a look at the lure and I turned sort of green around the mouth and white around the eyes and tried to say casually that I reckoned we'd better take her in for the doctor to cut the thing out.

*   *   *

SHE VOWED it didn't hurt and she sat still while I went to the house and got a knife to cut the line off the lure. That would be the only time, I think, I ever fished without taking along my tackle box which has a knife in it.

I got the car and brought the knife down to the pond and cut loose the lure from the line and we got into the car and I drove her some six miles to town and the doctor's office.

There was nothing to it, after all, he said. He teased her about catching "a big one" and told her to change the dressing next morning and she didn't even know when he cut the hook out of her back.

"More trouble to get the hook out of the dress without tearing it than to cut the hook out of her back," the Doc said in that quiet, pleasant voice which always makes a patient feel better.

But I'm telling you, I was glad to find that doctor in his office, with a needle full of something to keep it from hurting when he took that hook out. I've had to get a hook out of a bass' mouth when the poor thing had swallowed it and that made me sick enough. Taking a hook out of somebody's back—well, I never could be a doctor—that's all there is to it.

DAUGHTER SUSAN REMEMBERS MOTHER

In my mother's days, when a woman married, she gave up her life for her husband's dreams. My mother did so, following the ways of her elder married sisters. She gave up her teaching position at GSCW. Her tennis games. Her horseback rides with other town ladies. Her gatherings with her social friends—although she has been quoted as saying she never went anywhere that she had to wear white gloves.

She left the comforts of home in town for the country. And for life not in the "big house," because children would ruin walls, but in the "cottage," with no gas heat, just a fireplace, which she had to keep going with wood when she was home alone. A wood-burning stove that eventually gave way to a kerosene stove and then to an electric one. No running water when the pipes froze. No grocery just a few of blocks away. No telephone. No electricity when strong winds blew.

Her children were all out of the family nest before Mother and

Dad had a telephone, and then it was an eight-party line.

As the family grew, she became a chef—no goose-liver sandwiches for supper any more. She became a professional canner of vegetables and a rapid picker of both fruits and veggies. She learned how to kill, pluck and cut up a chicken, as well as fry it correctly.

She sought eggs to feed the family breakfast. Sometimes, the hens laid under Spanish bayonet, a "sticker bush" that kept foxes and coons away from the nest, and often punctured the human hand reaching for eggs. Sometimes, she faced snakes in the hen house or under the hen, or even in the living room. Doors stood open to catch the summer breeze.

She became adept at straining trash from the milk each morning when Dad brought it by the bucketful from the barn where he milked two cows by hand. After the cream rose, she would skim the milk. Cream went on the breakfast table for coffee; some she used to make ice cream, which she churned by hand until the children were old enough to turn the crank.

During the days of rationing in WWII, ice cream was a rare treat. Cream and whole milk were needed for butter. Again, she churned it by hand until the girls were old enough to help out. Some eggs went to town to be sold. Some were "pickled" in wide-mouth gallon jars for winter cooking.

One egg hatched in the refrigerator. (See *Blue Jeans and Pantaloons in YESTERPLACE* for details and for a picture of Thulia with the rooster.)

In my very young days, I asked how she seemed to always know what we children were doing. She said, "I have eyes in the back of my head." I often studied the back of her head to try to find those eyes.

Her research in nutrition which was taking her to a Ph. D. led her instead to teach her girls about vitamins and the daily needed vitamin intake. Those lessons became after-supper games.

She wasted nothing. The colorful cotton sacks from the livestock feed store became dresses for all of us. Her feet would whip the sewing machine pedal faster than the cat could run through the house.

When our linens went to the college laundry instead of to the wash pot, the paper used to wrap the laundry found another use: It served to drain the fat from the bacon. No such thing as paper towels then.

When she took the children picking blackberries or to the garden to pick beans or peas, she would go behind the girls with words that echoed the days of the Great Depression: "Don't leave so many ripe ones. Fill up your bucket."

She put up with the children's pets—cats in the house, kittens that appeared in a dresser drawer, newborn puppies that were slipped into pockets when the girls went to town with her, and were pulled out to show the relative being visited.

She worried when the girls went out on the horses because she herself had taken a terrible fall after her children were born; she cracked a vertebrae and was bedridden for a time.

She doctored bruises from falls; feet stabbed by nails and thorns; knees scraped on the raw gullies where the girls played; sliced legs and toes from broken glass. She learned from her older sister, wife of a physician, the value of turpentine on injuries. Her chemistry background taught her that carbolic acid could prevent infection.

She read to us and instilled in each of us our love of reading, of poetry and of learning. *The Weekly Reader* came with stories and exercises. She ordered workbooks and had us study all summer long.

Robert Francis Weatherbee would not go to school so he could not read. She read that book to me so many times, I could quote it as she turned the pages long before I could read. There is no greater tragedy than being unable to read.

She would let me check out *Make Way for Ducklings* over and over when the Book Mobile came by. Years later, I lived in Boston and followed the ducks' path from Boston Common to the Charles River.

One of her stories taught us social behavior. I can't remember the title, but the lesson remains: "Children should be seen, not heard."

Dad had a lake built about the time WWII ended, and we swam and fished there. Mother soon became an avid fisherwoman, and I loved to join her, especially in later years when I would come home from college or from wherever I was living at the time.

Mother waits for the fish to bite.

She was not a silent fisherwoman. From the lake to the house, she could be heard when she hooked something. Women who squeal at a mouse had nothing over her—her squeals of delight were louder than any whoop of victory by a baseball player making a walk-off hit and winning the World Series.

She would clean the fish herself and then cook them for us. She could do something with seasoning on a large bass that made it taste better than ambrosia.

She made many of our clothes until we left home for college. And college was never considered an option. College was a fact. The only options were our major and our selection of schools.

From our early years, she also knitted our sweaters. You want blue or brown? We had our choice of colors and style. Long sleeve? Pullover? Cardigan?

And bedspreads. When Westover burned, she lost all of her bedspreads, but began again, to knit one for each of us, just as her mother had for her children.

This "square pattern" is made up of two sizes of squares. One shows 16 squares knitted in one block. The other, I cannot even count the tiny squares in one block. The border was knitted separately also.

Here she knitted one row at a time and sewed them together.

I remember only one disagreement about how to use the land. Dad wanted to use the then-abandoned cotton fields at Dovedale for hay fields. Plant lespedeza, even though it was several miles from the cattle barns and hay sheds. Mother wanted to plant pines. She won that argument. That was *her* land, and she wanted a long-term crop that would take little attention. That Christmas, when I came home from college, I joined the two of them and a couple of hired men and learned how to plant pines by hand, with a dibble.

It was during the years that the government paid a landowner not to plant cotton. It also paid for pine seedlings and paid the landowner to plant them. Those "government" pines have now long been harvested.

After Westover burned, she said she would be happy with a small modern house, but Dad wanted his Westover back. Mother did not try to keep him from his dream, although she must have been terribly worried over his hours on ladders and the hard physical labor he put upon himself.

When deer season began, we chased poachers together. Up before light and ride the roads. Catch the culprits when they came out of the woods and challenge them. Arrest for trespassing or join others and pay a fee to hunt? And thus we met the men who initially leased our land for hunting rights. Today, timber sales and hunting fees provide the income from the land for all three of us.

Dad helped establish the pulpwood business in Georgia with his work with Charles Herty, but Mother was the one who insisted on planting the pines in the open fields. And after his death, she was the parent who began leasing for hunting rights.

In our young years, even before all of us were in school, she taught us to play cards. Rainy days, and cold winter days, we would sit on the floor in front of the fireplace and Mother dealt the cards for us to play quadruple solitaire. We were all fiercely competitive, and I remember the squeals and laughter as all of us would vie to play our card on the same stack.

Mother taught me a lot about living, but the most important lessons were to understand the differences in people and to laugh.

I try to live those lessons today by sharing at least one smile daily with a stranger and hope to perk up that person's day. The returned smile also perks me up, even if my day feels bleak.

PART X

SUSAN MYRICK

AND

THE THREE LITTLE GIRLS

BACKGROUND

When Sue Myrick, Lillas's sister, was editor of the Sunday supplement for the *Macon Telegraph*, she began to feature Lillas's three daughters (The Three Little Girls) in her articles.

The earliest we have is the picture used in an article on December 21, 1941, in conjunction with an article by Harry Hervey and titled *A Christmas Carol*. He "mused on the present world situation and upon the capture of Savannah in 1864." The article did not deal with the "three little girls."

"St. Nichols soon would be there." These three little girls are the daughters of Dr. and Mrs. L. C. Lindsley of Westover near Milledgeville. Standing is Lillas; the one with pigtails is Susan; the Alice-in-Wonderland hair belongs to Thulia. (Myrick photo)

The girls are in the parlor at the front, west corner of the house.

Xmas With Princess

Sue Myrick

NOT MANY PERSONS had the privilege of spending the Christmas holidays with a princess. But I did.

She is a white princess, who always wears a fur coat, a soft and silky one which she keeps very clean, and she is queen of the household. Though she looks big enough to be called a cat, her mistress insists that she is not a cat; that she is, in addition to being a princess, a kitten.

The Princess occupies the most comfortable chair, the one closest to the fireplace, and when you start to put her out of the chair so you may sit there and warm your feet, there is a yelp of disapproval from her mistress, who insists that your warmth or comfort is of small consequence compared to that of the princess.

She is a good hot water bottle, though, and she takes the place of an extra blanket on a cold night, for she is sneaked into the room of her mistress at bed time and sleeps at her feet until about day light, when she climbs on the mistress' chest, meows softly, and starts to scratch at the covers to wake up the mistress, who sleepily crawls out of bed to open the door so her majesty may go outside

THE PRINCESS received more Christmas presents on the family tree than anybody. The gift she did NOT care for was a bell on a red ribbon which was tied about her royal neck to her intense disgust. She didn't seem to be too eager about the cans of cat food, either, preferring the bones from the chicken and the scraps from the Christmas dinner. Needless to say, she got what she wanted.

I must admit that the Princess behaved in a bounteous fashion, though. She gave gifts to all the household. In exchange for a rubber mouse that I gave her, she gave me a chocolate candy bar wrapped in beautiful Christmassy paper and tied with a red ribbon. One of her gifts was addressed to "The One Who Smothers Me but Does Not Feed Me"; another to "The One Who Fights For Me"; while a third went to "The One Who Feeds Me."

THOUGH I AM a great lover of kittens, I hold a little resentment against the Princess. She insisted that we should go for a boat ride and a little fishing on the farm pond and I stuck a splinter under my thumb nail. The doctor used nova cain to get the splinter out and it didn't hurt, but I look like such a horrible thing with the red stuff he used to paint my thumb.

It's all the fault of the Princess.

A Real Christmas
Sue Myrick

CHRISTMAS WITH your folks in the country is the only really happy Christmas there is!

I spent the night before and Christmas Day with my sister and her family, and the chores of the farm went on just as they do 365 days in the year. On Christmas Eve there was much talk on how to get everything done as early as possible next morning so we could have the Christmas tree and the opening of presents.

As every farmer in Georgia knows, there is a chore that takes considerable time these days---the putting out of hay for the cattle.

"Who's gonna feed up?" was the question.

So we arranged it that I would go with one of the girls up to "Missy's" and to the "white house" and up to the "other place," while another girl went with Dad to feed the critters at the barn, and the other girl helped get breakfast ready.

It was raining and dark when we crept out of bed to start on the "feed-up" routine. I put on slacks and my oldest shoes and a sweater. I borrowed a heavy coat from one niece, a scarf for my head from another, and a cowboy hat from a third, thinking thus to keep the rain off and the cold out. We got into the car and the niece drove off at a good clip, wondering if she would stick in that mud-hole, but negotiating the car as only today's youth can.

SUCH A RACE to see how fast you could get the wire-tie off the bale of hay, break the bale open and scatter it about for the patient kine that followed you trustingly as you walked off with an armful of feed. Such scurrying to get back down the hill, crawl through the barbed wire fence into the car and off to the next feeding place!

Such giggling and stamping of muddy, wet feet, and such fine fun and such a building up of appetite.

Breakfast was ready when we got home and we beat the other feeders by a couple of seconds. Then we raced to see who could get out of wet shoes and into dry ones, wash up a bit and get down to breakfast.

You've never tasted good coffee nor truly enjoyed five or six slices of bacon nor reveled in the flavor of fresh eggs, scrambled, until you've gotten up at first light, "fed-up" in the cold rain, and then got warm and dry again before eating your breakfast.

Three Little Girls—and Rural Life

By SUSAN MYRICK

THE DAY was chilly but the Three Little Girls had gone out into the yard to shoot marbles and Mom and I settled down to cut out three little dresses. We cut bias folds and ruffles and skirts and blouses and sashes, and then Mom stitched seams while I pressed down the edges of bias folds with a hot iron.

Came five o'clock and we carefully arranged the sewing so that we could do the finger work after supper, and I went out for a breath of air and a game of marbles with the Three Little Girls.

The day had grown colder as dusk came on, and when Mom called us to come wash up for supper, we were glad to go in to the big log fire to pull our skirts up in back and rub our hands across our hindsides and indulge in little shivery wrapping of our shoulders about our necks.

Mom had the sausage cooked and the waffle batter all ready and she told the biggest of the Three Little Girls to lay the table and attach the waffle iron.

As the Biggest Little Girl turned on a light in the closet to look for the waffle iron, the lights blinked:

"Mom, did I pull that light cord too hard?" asked the Biggest Little Girl.

The lights blinked again and Mom came to look. But she didn't see anything, for the house was plunged all at once, into total blackness. All the lights had gone off.

So had the electric stove, and Dad's look at the fuse box indicated it wasn't a local trouble. The REA, probably the finest thing to come out of the Roosevelt administration, had flunked out.

Somewhere along the line, Dad guessed, a tree had fallen across the wires, making a short.

While he avowed that the shortage might be this or that, the Three Little Girls hovered together, giggling with the excitement and half fright that darkness brings when one is light-accustomed. Mom found some candles and lighted them and the Littlest Little Girl said she thought candles were nice and she was glad the electricity had gone off.

Not so Mom! What to do about feeding six hungry people with no electricity for cooking was presenting a problem to her.

Well, the sausage was done, thank goodness. There was of course no chance to make waffles. But there was bread and butter and she would make toast before the fire. And a few coals raked out on the hearth would set the coffee to perking---and maybe one could scramble a few eggs over the coals, too.

The comic section of the *Telegraph and News* was handy, so Mom folded it against a big stick of wood and propped the toast, all nicely buttered with home churned butter, against Terry and the Pirates.

A yelp went up from the Three Little Girls:

"Mom! I haven't read the funny paper, yet."

So, we moved the ten pieces of toast, rescued Orphan Annie, Dagwood and the rest of the favorite characters, found a page of day-before-yesterday's *Telegraph*, and replaced the toast.

Mom set the coffee on the coals and placed the skillet of sausages at one side of the hearth to keep them warm.

The house, which is more than a century old, has as lovely mantels as may be found in the country; the fireplace is huge, the hearth broad, but no hearth was ever made big enough to hold ten pieces of toast, a coffee percolator, and a skillet of sausage and Three Little Girls, all at the same time. And the Three, who had been playing marbles barefoot, suddenly decided their feet were cold and told Mom so in very decided tones when she urged them to stand back or to sit down or do anything but stand on the hearth over the supper.

BUT MOM suddenly had a thought that was highly satisfactory from two angles:

"You two better go get a bath, right quickly. Supper won't be ready for a while and you'd better hurry and get clean before all the hot water is cold," she said. And to the Biggest Little Girl:

"Honey, you take the candle for them and help them find their things."

A candle was more alluring than the hearth, so the Three went giggling upstairs, dripping candle grease over themselves, the stairs and the bathroom but leaving an unhampered hearth for the eggs and toast.

The Three were back by the time the meal was ready and we ate by the light of six candles in silver candelabra:

"Just like Christmas" the Three said, and burst into Silent Night, Little Town of Bethlehem and Noel, Noel.

When the argument about who's time is it to sleep with Sue was settled and the two smaller of the Three Little Girls had gone off the bed, leaving the Biggest to sit up an additional half hour, we felt a quiet that was almost lonely. And while Abraham Lincoln could study by the light of a lightwood knot, our eyes were not strong enough to sew on the Three Little Girls' dresses by candlelight; so, we had to go early to bed.

Anyway, everybody had to be up at 6:30 a.m. The school bus picks up the Three Little Girls at quarter to eight, each morning, and one always had to figure the clock may be a little slow or the bus driver a few minutes early.

Life in the rural section is never dull.

* * *

SUSAN MYRICK:
Decorates A Few 'Heroines' of Camp

STANDING STIFFLY at attention, the three answered as the "captain" called the roll.

"Private Thulia."

"Here, sir."

"Private Lillas."

"Here, sir."

"Corporal Sue."

"Here, sir."

Thulia was tall for her age, 10; she wore a soiled sweat shirt and very short shorts, which showed how suntanned were her sturdy legs. Private Lil was short and plump and very blond and her violet eyes sparkled behind her dark lashes but she maintained the proper solemnity for the occasion though she was only 7. Corporal Sue was solemn, too, and her brown eyes showed that she recognized her superior rating. Her sweat shirt of blue and white was none too clean and her bare feet, like those of her sisters, gave evidence of the day's play over the plantation.

*   *   *

The "captain" made a sharp about face and saluted the "general."

"ALL PRESENT and accounted for, sir." The "general," scared stiff that her behavior was not quite all the military would demand, returned the salute and just stood there. If the "captain" had not been the wife of an army officer, the "general" would have been sunk.

It was an occasion of vast import. No Congressional Medal, bestowed upon a gallant soldier for bravery far beyond the call of duty, could compare with the situation the "general" faced. For, presenting good conduct badges to three small girls who had spent two weeks on a camping trip with their mother and aunt was a matter not lightly to be considered. Making your bed, picking up your clothes, acting as KP, coming promptly when your swimming time is over and your mother calls, going to bed when bed time is announced, and not whining when you can't do exactly as you wish—all those are mighty important to the adults on the trip and they require gallantry and courage on the part of small girls even as knocking out a pill box takes courage and gallantry on the part of soldiers.

So, the "general's" responsibility lay heavy on her shoulders and she leaned upon the "captain" for support [once again proving the occasion was not unlike that of the real military, where higher officers lean upon those of lower rank, even on down through Pfc].

The "captain" was equal to the occasion:

"Sir, does the general wish to make a few remarks to the candidates before delivering the medals?"

"The general will dispense with remarks" she answered, and the "captain" executed another about face and called out:

"Private Lil to the front."

PRIVATE LIL'S eyes grew to the size of saucers but she marched smartly forward and planked her fat, suntanned, brier-scratched little feet squarely in front of the general's, about two paces from her, and gave her a salute that would have shamed many an air forces man. The "general" returned the salute, not so smartly, it is sad to relate, and cleared her throat nervously:

"Private Lillas," she began. And that was too much for the risibility of the young private; she snickered! The "general" chose to ignore the snicker and went on gravely to say she found pleasure in conferring this badge of honor which signified that Private Lillas had carried out her duties in the manner of a good soldier. She pinned the bit of red ribbon on the grimy blouse of the blue-eyed soldier, offered her hand and said "I congratulate you, Private Lillas."

Private Lil stuck out her left hand, first, then switched to her right; quickly, but not so quickly that the other privates did not see it and burst into a storm of giggles. Again the officers chose to ignore the non-military behavior, and when Private Lil had returned to the ranks, the presentation of good conduct medals continued. Private Tulia's manner was above reproach, as befitted the eldest.

Corporal Sue, chosen for the high rank because her bed was better made at each morning's inspection and because she didn't cry that time she stumped her toe and for other reasons of like nature, stood so straight she almost fell over backwards—didn't she have to prove she was worthy of those two stripes? And her about-face was well done, as she returned to ranks, after shaking hands gravely with the "general" and saying "Thank you, sir."

ONCE MORE the "captain" took over to save face for the poor, stupid "general," who didn't know what on earth to do next:

"The platoon will stand at attention until the general has withdrawn," she said.

With a smart about-face, the "general" turned and walked away in a military fashion that many a brass hat might envy. Maybe another general has been more relieved to finish up a difficult task, but it is doubtful that even Eisenhower was more grateful for the cessation of welcome ceremonies than "General Myrick" was to be through with the conferring of good conduct badges.

But it was worth the struggle. The enlisted "men" came rushing over to the "general" and hugged her and giggled explosively, after the fashion of youngsters who are delighted beyond words, and they told her:

"I'm going to change my badge to another shirt every time I take a bath and put on clean clothes."

The "captain," who devised the plan for good conduct medals, is a wizard at child psychology!

Pets In Your Home
Sue Myrick

EVERY TIME you went to their home you found yourself with a puppy or a kitten in your lap---except such times as those when you had three puppies and a couple of kittens in your lap.

"Look at the puppy. Ain't he the cutest thing," the littlest of the three girls would say and she'd put him in your lap.

"Look at THIS one; he's the cutest" the next-sized one would say and she'd put HER puppy in your lap.

A big pure bred collie, a mongrel whose ancestry was so mixed as to make recognition of any breed impossible, a dog which country people call a Shepherd [I don't know what dog fanciers call it] and a regular hound comprised the dog family, plus the puppies which were always on hand.

That was when the children were quite small. There were always baby kittens, too, plus an assortment of mamma cats and an occasional Tom.

The children grew older and, little by little, Mamma managed to get rid of dogs and cats, until only the big hound was left in the dog family. Then he strayed off ---or was stolen, and there were no pets.

That was too awful, so the youngest, now junior high age, brought home two white kittens. One of them got stolen or strayed off. But there was only a brief time until there were some new kittens, which Mamma managed to give away.

For a while, peace reigned. No fretting about whether the cat was in the dining room waiting to jump onto the table and poke her pretty nose into anything that smelled good; no worry lest the hound stray into the kitchen when somebody left the back door open and devour tomorrow's roast; no tearing one's hair when the mongrel howled all night at the moon.

THEN ONE DAY the family came in from a trip to town and what could that be, there on the front porch? Yep, two puppies. Somebody had wanted to get rid of two puppies, had driven to the country and found a house with nobody home, had left the puppies for somebody else to worry with.

What some people do about kittens and puppies certainly should not happen to a dog.

Youth and Springtime

By SUSAN MYRICK

IT WAS a beautiful Sunday afternoon; there was just enough coolness in the air to make the sunshine feel good on your arms and legs as you sat in an easy chair on the lawn trying to get an early suntan. And the Spring was not yet advanced far enough for bugs and mosquitoes to annoy you.

Oldest of the Three Little Girls lay on the grass near me, her overalled legs kicked up behind her as she sprawled face downward, her chin propped on her elbows. The two younger of the Three had gone bicycling; one rode the bike down the road to the barn and back, while the other waited beside the gate for her turn.

The oldest was singing a "new" song. She had learned it just the week before at school and she was greatly intrigued with it, even as I had been when I learned it about 1920 or so.

"I'll be down to get you in a taxi, honey.

"You better be ready 'bout ha'f past eight."

She sang it through from beginning to end, a little off key; in fact, a little off the tune, and when she had finished singing it through, she started again.

The fact that her chin was propped upon her hands interfered to some extent with her pronunciation of the words but that was nothing compared to the fact that she was chewing a huge piece of bubble gum, which she popped now and then as a sort of orchestral accompaniment to the song.

SHE FLOPPED over on her back and started over: "I'll be down to get you—"

It was a fine lazy feel I had acquired, my mind a complete void, and a sense of vegetating pervading my whole self. Through my euphoria there crept a faint sense of "dancing out both of my shoes when they played the jelly-roll blues."

So, as the song went through its fifth rendition, I endeavored to provide a diversion:

"Did you ever try singing a song, using the initials of the words instead of saying the words, themselves?" I asked.

"What do you mean?"

"Like this: Instead of singing 'I wish I was in the land of cotton,' sing it. 'I W. I W. in the L. of C.,' or you can vary it to suit yourself. You might sing it. 'I wish I W. in the L.O. C.'"

I warmed to the idea and went on:

"O. T. T. am N. for G., L. away, L. away, L. away, D. L."

"I can't do that," the oldest of the Little Girls said. Then she began to try:

"I'll B. D. to G. you in a Tee, H., You better be R. about H. P. E., Gosh! That sounds funny. I'll B. D. to G. you in a T. I., Honey. No that's wrong, I didn't mean T. I. I meant T. I'll be down to---No, I mean I'll be D. T. G. you in a T-ee, Honey—I mean T-ee, H."

I closed my eyes. The idea had been a mistake. I could see that, now. I tried to listen to the mocking bird that was singing (on the key, too) in the tree above me and I tried not to hear anymore about being down to get you in a taxi. But my effort was not a success.

Again I sought to divert: "Bet you can't sing Dixie Land

with the initials. The easiest way to do it is to write the words down and look at the initial letters and sing them. Pretty soon, it will be easy."

THAT, my pretty, was a keen idea, I thought. She'd go into the house, find paper and pencil, write out all the words to all the verses of Dixie and I'd have a half hour of peace and quiet while she wrote.

Again I was not smart enough for the eldest of the T. L. G. She didn't want to do things the easy way. She lay on the grass and practiced on singing initial letters for Dixie Land until I wished I was up Nawth instead of in the land of cotton and I wanted to go away---not look away.

However, I had to acknowledge an admiration for her persistence and the appearance of the younger two of the T. L. G. compensated for everything. I was delighted to be in the land of cotton and particularly glad to be a guest in the house in Dixie where I was.

For the younger two bore a gift. And what a gift! Red-ripe, wild strawberries!

I ate a few of the largest and ripest and reddest; then, the middle one of the T. L. G. took the bowl of berries into the house where she washed them and removed the stems and crushed them in a wee bit of sugar and combined them with some rich, yellow cream, which she had whipped, and into the refrigerator tray went the delicious combination.

When we ate that ice cream, a few hours later, I was in such a mood that I urged the eldest to please sing for me, once more, while I joined in, all the verses of Dixie. And when we finished with those initials we sang:

"I'll B. D. to G. you in a T-ee, H.

"You better B. R. about H. P. E.

"Now, H., D. B. L.

"You better B. T.---at the D. T. strutter's ba-ll."

*   *   *

Ten years after the first Christmas picture appeared of the three little girls, Sue featured them in another Christmas page. Once again, the article that accompanied the pictures was not about the girls. This one was titled "The Earth's Christmas Message" and dealt with the first Christmas—the baby, the animals, the star, shepherds and the magi—which she related to the Christmas of 1951.

The headline read:

CHORES ON THE FARM CONTINUE
EVEN DURING CHRISTMAS

The Macon Telegraph and News

FARM PAGE

SUNDAY MORNING, DECEMBER 23, 1951

MILKING TIME: Whether it be Christmas or New Year's, Sunday or Tuesday or Saturday, the cows must be milked. So, Lillas Lindsley rides her horse to bring in Old Horney and Peachblossom from the pasture at her parents' home in Baldwin County. Dr. and Mrs. L. C. Lindsley live some six miles from Milledgeville, with their three daughters. Dr. Lindsley is a retired professor, devotes his farm entirely to timber and pastures, and raises grade Herefords. The milk cows are strictly for home milk production. Lillas raises chickens for her major projects, counts bringing up the cows as more fun than work. The family lives in a house built more than a century ago, and Christmas time brings log fires and laughter and carols, as it did 100 years ago.

THE CHRISTMAS TREE: The Lindsley girls do not like to see a tree cut, so each year at Christmas they dig up a cedar, set it in a container of rich soil, keep it watered, and replant it when Christmas is over. Left to right, the girls are Thulia, Sue and Lillas. They are forestry minded, for their father has most of his land in trees. He is an ardent lover of native shrubs and wild flowers and has spent much time in restoring the eroded areas about his house built in 1822.

CHRISTMAS PARTY: Thulia Lindsley oldest of the three sisters, comes down the century-old stairs at the home of her parents, Dr. and Mrs. L.

C. Lindsley, ready for the Christmas party. She is a student at the Georgia State College for Women at Milledgeville, likes driving the tractor to cut hay as much as she likes dressing up for a party, thinks riding a horse to herd the cattle from one field to another is as much fun as going to a dance.

SHELLING PECANS: Sue Lindsley cracks pecans making ready to pick out nuts for Christmas cookery.

Like most farm homes today, the Lindsley's kitchen is equipped with electricity, but picking out nuts is a job to be done by hand. As in every household in the nation, the Lindsley kitchen is a flurry of preparation as Christmas time draws near, and the white kitten, The Princess, and the dog, Worthless, snatch goodies, now and then, as do the girls who help with the cookery.

THE WITCHING HOUR; The Night Before Christmas is always the witching hour, no matter if you have apparently outgrown Santa Claus.

You still regard that sugar plum tree as a marvel of great renown, a tree that bears fruit so "wondrously sweet, as those who have tasted it say, that good little children have only to eat of that fruit to be happy next day." These three girls take delight in a final chat in front of the open fire before they dash upstairs to bed to dream of those sugar plums and the presents which will be on the Christmas tree tomorrow. Standing is Sue Lindsley; seated are (left) Lillas and Thulia. For these girls, as for all girls on a farm, Christmas day will bring its chores before the tree will give up its presents.

APPENDICES

APPENDIX I

FAMILY LINES

Family lines are given in this order: Lindsley, Marshall, Douglas, Lacy and information on the Campbell and Lamb lines.

Information from Generation I through generation V in the Lindsley line is from the book *The History of the Lindley-Lindsley-Linsley Families of American History* by John Lindly.

The number in brackets after the first five generations in our Lindsley line refer to the number of that name in Lindly's history of the family. The page number of the entry in his book is given in parentheses after the bracketed entry number.

I . Francis Linley   [1   ] (page 19 for list of children)
  b. England. Arrived colonies about 1639
  m. June 24, 1655 Susana Culpepper
  d. 1704

II. Ebenezer Lindsley [5]   (page 63)
  b. 1665
  d. 1743

III. Elihu Lindsley   [29] (page 85)
  m. Kezia
  d. 1762

IV. Elihu Lindsley   [58] (page 112)
  b. 1748/49
  m. Elizabeth (1751/2 - April 22, 1812)
  d. July 22, 1808

Children included:
  Sarah m. Charles Ogden
  Jeptha
  Luther m. Nancy Lacy

V. Luther Lindsley [188] (page 254)
  b. November 5, 1779, in New Jersey
  m. Nancy Lacy (b. July 18, 1783)
    (See Lacy family line.)
  Children included Mahlon Smith Lindsley

Our line in John Lindly's book ended with Luther Lindsley who married "---Lacy" (Generation V). The Lindsley Bible picks up with Luther Lindsley who married Nancy Lacy (Generation V).

VI. Mahlon Smith Lindsley
  b. October 7, 1804
  m. Jan 11, 1829, Mary Louisa Campbell (b. Aug 8, 1810 , daughter of ____ and Keziah Campbell)
  d. March 4, 1887, San Marcos, Texas
    Children (from Lindsley Bible)
      Luther C. Lindsley
      Elizabeth Ann
      Emily Ann
      Mary E. Pierpoint (adopted)

VII. Luther Campbell Lindsley
  b. September 2, 1830 (in New Jersey)
  m. Jan 16, 1856 Hannah M. Lamb (d. about 1921)
  d. October 19, 1864, Battle of Cedar Creek, War Between the States
    Full marriage license is given in at end of this family line.
    Hannah M. L. Lindsley
    m. 2nd: George W. Johnson, Jan 2, 1868. He was 22, she was 28. At Douglas Hill, Prince William County, Virginia
    Children:
      Robert E. Lee
        b. Nov 10, 1868

Minnie Josephene
> b. Oct 27, 1870
> m. Julius Egbert Herrell (sp. as Harrell and Herrell)
> d. Aug 17, 1955

Maud Minton
> b. Dec 16, 1872
> m. Gus Hutchinson
> d. Jul 22, 1959

Willis L.
> b. Jul 29, 1874
> d. Oct 29, 1920

Ralph Valentine
> b. Feb 14, 1879
> m. Musie Harrell (sister of Minnie's husband)
> d. Mar 11, 1959

VIII. Ernest L. (Lamb or Lacy?) Lindsley
- b. January 29, 1859
- d. October 22, 1893, in Brightwood, D C., of typhoid.
- m. 1st: Elizabeth (Bessie) Marshall
  > b. Dec 17, 1861
  > d. Dec 1, 1885

  One child:
  > Fannie (Frances) Virginia (Virgie) Lindsley
  > b. July 7, 1881 at Douglas Hill
  > m. Grover Hoxton, January 26, 1904
  >> One child: Francis (1909-1917)
  > d. 1922

- m. 2nd Lillian F. Marshall of Shelby Co., KY
  - m. Dec 29, 1886 OR Dec 30, 1887
  - b. October 30, 1865
  - d. March 29 (Lindsley Bible; March 28 Marshall Bible), 1892
    > Two children, born at Douglas Hill:
    > Luther Campbell Lindsley
    >> b. Feb. 10, 1888
    > William Marshall Lindsley
    >> b. Feb 14, 1890
    >> d. 1890, buried, Washington, D.C.
    >> Prince Wm County Death Records show William

died 19 June 1890 from cholera, age 4 months;
the family Bible indicates he died at 3 months.

IX. Luther Campbell Lindsley
> b. February 10, 1888, at Douglas Hill, Prince William Co., VA.
> d. March 2, 1963, Milledgeville, GA
> m. 1st August 13, 1913 Pattie Love Jones
>> at Boydton, Mecklenburg County, Virginia
>> d. October 3, 1933
> m. 2nd June 4, 1934 Lillas Stanley Myrick of Dovedale, Georgia
>> at home of Josephine Whitehurst Rozar (her aunt)
>> b. November 11, 1900
>> d. February 6, 1968
>> Children:
>>> Thulia Katherine
>>>> b. February 28, 1935
>>>> m. Terry Shayne Bramlett March 6, 1955
>>>>> d. March 10, 1986
>>> Children:
>>> Lindsley Shayne
>>>> b. April 18, 1956
>>>> m. Sandra Jean Speck Aug 2, 1985
>>>> Divorced. September 2012
>>>> Children:
>>>>> Rebecca Elizabeth
>>>>>> b. Oct. 31, 1990
>>>>> Victoria Lindsley
>>>>>> b. May 20, 1991
>>> Russell Myrick
>>>> b. February 28, 1958
>>>> m. Amy Tyree Gilis March 28, 1981
>>>> Children:
>>>>> James Myrick
>>>>>> b. Oct. 18, 1988
>>>>> Elizabeth Kate
>>>>>> b. Dec. 19, 1991

Virginia Sue
    b. October 27, 1936

Lillas Myrick
    b. January 23, 1938
    m. John Elvis James, June 12, 1959 at Westover
        b. September 7, 1932
        d. April 5, 2015

The information below on the early Lindsleys is taken from *The History of the Lindley-Lindsley-Linsley Families of American History* by John M. Lindly, from family Bibles and from Prince William County records. Some "interesting facts" other than genealogy information are give here also.

I. FRANCIS LINLEY

"Two brothers, John and Francis Linsley, came from England, first locating in Branford, where Francis married Sarah Culpepper. Later, he removed to New Jersey, and present residents of that name in the central part of that State claim to have sprung from this pioneer couple." Commemorative Biographical Record of New Haven County, Conn., J. H. Beers & Co., Chicago, 1902.

Marriage records in Vol. I, of the records of the town of Branford, Connecticut read: "Fransus Linsly the one partie & Susana Culpepper married June 24, 55" (1655).

A deed from Francis to his son Ebenezer is in the Lindsley collection of manuscripts in the NJ Historical Society in Newark, and is probably the only document remaining that was signed by Francis. A facsimile is given in *The History of the Lindley-Lindsley-Linsley Families of American History.*

On spelling of the name: On January 20, 1697/98, Francis received a patent from the "Proprietors of the Province of East New Jersey" for his land. His surname was written 'Lindsley,' the first known instance of this spelling. When he chose to dispose of the land, for legal reasons he had to keep that spelling, or his legal ownership might be in dispute. Some lines of the family (e.g., descendants of his brother John) never used the "s"; some who use the "s" keep it silent. (Page 13, Preface, John Lindly book)

II. EBENEZER LINDSLEY

He is buried in Orange, New Jersey, in the old Orange graveyard. "Here lyes ye body of Ebenezer Lindsley aged about 78 yrs. Died Nov ye 1st 1743"

First reference to him is in quit claim deed made in 1691. Next reference is on p. 111 of Newark Town Records' Town meeting January 1, 1697/98.

In the New Jersey Historical Society records, Lindsley papers include a deed of gift to "my well beloved son Benjamin Lindsley" signed by Ebenezer and dated June 1, 1733.

He is referred to as "Ebernezer" Lindsley of Newark in records of the County of Essex.

III. ELIHU LINDSLEY

Other than the name of his wife (Kezia) and the year of his death, we know only that he moved from Orange, New Jersey to near Morristown, New Jersey.

He signed his will on April 7, 1762 and it was probated April 24, 1762. It is stored in Liber H, folio 135, East New Jersey Wills at the State House in Trenton. (John Lindly, p. 85)

IV. ELIHU LINDSLEY (1748-1808)

His will is dated July 20, 1808, of Morris Township, Morris Co., New Jersey, and probated July 30, 1808. It names his wife Elizabeth, sons Jeptha and Luther, and daughters Sarah Ogden, Phoebe Eddy, and Catherine Green.

John M. Lindly of the Lindsley History visited the old graveyard in Madison NJ on August 23, 1903 and found four brown stones in a row on the hillside in the east part of the yard, to the memory of Elihu Lindsley and wife and two grandchildren. One reads: "In memory of Elihu Lindsley who departed this life July 22, 1808 in the 60th year of his age." Then follows a verse:

> "Ye children if ye learn to run
> The great salvation race,
> Know that the name of Christ alone

Can answer every case."

One of the other stones reads: "In memory of Elizabeth wife of Elihu Lindsley who departed this life April 22, 1812 in the 61st ye of her age."

V. LUTHER LINDSLEY

Morris County records show that Luther dealt in real estate:

Jacob Lacy and wife Mary Lacy of the County of Morris, NY, on Mar 22, 1809, sell to Luther Lindsley of same place 19.14 acres for 160 £.(Apparently British money was still is use.) (Morris County Deeds).

Luther Lindsley and wife Nancy Lindsley of the township of Morris, on October 8, 1809, deed to Joseph King of same place 8 acres for $202.50. (Morris County Deed Book 4, page 173).

Luther had a sister who married Charles Ogden.

*   *   *

Information on these Lindsleys came from the Lindsley family Bible, from family papers, and from Ronald Ray Turner's web site: "Prince William County Virginia," which contains census records, marriage and death records and many other collections of information about residents of Prince William County:

VI. Mahlon Smith Lindsley

b. October 7, 1804

m. Jan 11, 1829, Mary Louisa Campbell (b. Aug 8, 1810 , daughter of _____ and Keziah Campbell)

d. March 4, 1887, San Marcos, Texas

In the papers of L. C. Lindsley of Westover was a summons for "Mr. S. Lindsly" to appear before a justice of the peace in Dumfries on 23 September 1871 to answer a complaint for non-payment of $14.14. He served on the Grand Jury in Prince William County October 12, 1868. No information as to when he went to Texas.

His name is given as Mahalen S. Lindsley and his occupation as farmer in the 1860 census records, which also show that his household consisted of his wife Mary Louisa (age 50), daughter Emma A. (age 21), son Luther C. (age 29) and Luther's wife Hannah M. (teacher, age 24) and son Ernest (age 01), and Mary Pierpont, age 7, who was adopted by Mahlon and Mary.

Other census records spell his name correctly and show city of residence: 1850, Washington, D. C.; 1860 and 1870, Prince William County; and 1860, Dumfries, Virginia.

Emily Ann Lindsley, one of Mahlon's daughters, married John Turner Mann, Oct 22, 1865. Pictures of the Mann family are given with other family photographs in Appendix II. Mahlon also moved to Texas, probably after or when Emily did.

VII. Luther Campbell Lindsley and Hannah Maria Lamb

To The Clerk of Prince William Cty Court.

    This is to Certify that I solemnized a marriage on the 16th January 1856 by authority of a license from our office, between Luther C. Lindsley and Hannah M. Lamb; that that the following is a correct statement of the condition of the parties to the said marriage.

Place of Marriage At Thomas K. Lamb's Prince Wm Cty, Va

Age of the husband: 25 years
Age of the wife: 19 years
Condition of husband: Single
Condition of wife: Single
Place of husband's birth: Morris County, N. J.
Place of wife's birth: Onondaga, N. Y.
Names of Husband's parents: Mahlon S. and Mary L. Lindsley
Names of Wife's parents: Thomas K. and Louisa Lamb
Occupation of Husband: Farmer

    Given under my hand this 19th day of January, one thousand eight hundred and fifty-six.

Marriage records in Prince William County also show the marriage of Hannah Lamb Lindsley (widow) to George William Johnson (farmer) on January 6, 1868.

VIII. Ernest L. Lindsley and Lillie Marshall

Ernest's first wife Bessie (Lillie's sister) died December 1885. Ernest and Lillie apparently consoled each other for they soon married. The marriage year is in doubt, however.

December 29, 1886 is given as the marriage date for Ernest and Lillie by Ronald Ray Turner's web site: "Prince William County Virginia, segment Prince William Marriages from Sources Outside the County." Turner also states that she was from Shelby County, Kentucky, and that they were married in Stafford County, Virginia.

In the Marshall family Bible, the date was clearly December 30, 1887 and was confirmed as the correct date by members of the Marshall family on a visit by Susan Lindsley.

Lillie was born November 30, 1865, and her age in records quoted by Turner is 21, which would make the date 1886.

We must each draw our own conclusion as to which record is correct.

Records in Prince William County show an interesting fact: Ernest served on the juries for two felony cases, one April 3, 1884 and the other on January 1, 1886.

MARSHALL FAMIILY LINE

Luther wrote a memoriam to his Marshall/Douglas ancestors which he based on family tradition and lore. Unfortunately, searches of various records have given information that contradicts some of that available to Dad when he wrote this. The corrections are given below the copy of what he wrote:

In Memory
of
My Mother and her People

(1) The William le Marshall who unhorsed Prince Richard the Lion Hearted, at the Battle of LeMans and who later was rewarded with the hand of the Princess of the Earldom of Pembroke, and

Who ruled England as Regent for many years, under the infant King Henry III, and

Who led King John to Runnymede in 1215 and persuaded him to sign the Magna Charta of English Liberties,

(2) whose other ancestor, Lord James Douglas as Field General of Robert Bruce led the Scottish Army to victory at Bannockburn to establish again the freedom of Scotland and who later was chosen to carry the heart of Bruce to the Holy Land.

(3) whose other Hanson ancestor, husband of Princess Vasa of Sweden fell mortally wounded beside his slain cousin King Gustavus Adolphus of Sweden at the Battle of Lutzen, in the cause of religious freedom.

Facts relating to these praises of our ancestors:

(1) William le Marshall did indeed unhorse Richard the Lionhearted when the future king was in a skirmish against King Henry II, his father. Because Richard was heir to the throne, in spite of the battle at LeMans, Marshall did not kill Richard, but instead killed his horse. King Henry offered Marshall the hand and estates of Isabel de Clare, but died before final arrangements were made. Newly crowned, Richard fulfilled his father's promise. When Richard himself died,

Marshall became regent to the child-king, Henry III.

(2) On his deathbed, Bruce asked his knights to go on a crusade and take his heart with them. Sir James Douglas carried it; he was, however, killed in battle with the Moors in Spain, and the casket was returned to Scotland and buried at Melrose Abbey.

(3) George Adolphus Hanson published the book ***Old Kent: The Eastern Shore of Maryland*** in 1876, and he is given credit for the hoax which has been repeated for more than 130 years. Perhaps he started the story because of his middle name. No one knows. The story of the Hanson fighting beside King Adolphus and the story of the same Hanson marrying a royal princess in Sweden cannot be verified. There is no record of a Hanson in the Swedish army at the time of the Battle of Lutzen (1632).

The story has been recognized as a complete hoax only in recent years.

Allie Myrick Bowden, author of *Story of The Myricks*, said that no genealogical "fact" was indeed a fact unless it was supported by two separate records. No records support George A. Hanson's claims about our ancestors. I'm sure Dad would have been very disappointed.

*   *   *

William Edgar Marshall, Luther's cousin, researched the Marshall family line and provided the lineage from the first Marshall to reach the American Colonies. All the information we have is given here. I have used **boldface** type to indicate our line in the list of children.

1. **William Marshall**
b. 1607 (He stated his age as 50 in 1657.)
m. Katherine Hebden (or Ebden), widow of Thomas Hebden
d. 1673 (Will dated Feb 25, 1673, probated December 1673)
Sailed from Plymouth, England, August 1, 1635. Reached colonies Oct 8, 1635.

> Children: Three named in will:
> **William** (b. Abt. 1653)
> Joshua (d. 1702) (unwed)
> Elizabeth (b. Apr 15, 1667, m. John Hawkins)

2. William Marshall, Jr.
b. About 1653
m. Elizabeth Hanson (date estimated, 1689)
    b. England
    Dau. of Lt. Randolph Hanson and Mrs. Barbara Hatton Johnson
    m. 2nd Col. John Fendall
    d. 1735
d. About 1697 (Will proved January 28, 1698)
Builder of Marshall Hall in Maryland.
Children:
    William Marshall III, b. September 12, 1690, d. 1734
    Barbara 1692-1692
    Thomas (Called "Senior) 1694-1759
    Richard 1696-1750

3. Richard Marshall
b. 1696
m. Mary Douglas, daughter of Joseph Douglas and Penelope Morris
    (see Douglas line for her ancestry)
d. June 13, 1750 Charles County, Maryland (will probated June 13, 1750)
    Children:
        Samuel
        Josiah
        Richard
        Benjamin
        William
        Robert
        Mary
        Videtta

4. Josiah Marshall
m. Mary
d. Will dated May 29, 1775
    Children
        Benjamin Hanson*
        Thomas*

John
Richard*
* Served in Revolutionary Army

5. Richard Marshall
b. About 175?
m. Margaret Wilcoxen Hardy (widow of Thomas Dent Hardy)
March 5, 1782. She died May 2, 1826. She bore 12 children, 7 sons
(including **Richard Hanson Marshall**), 5 daughters.
d. January 18, 1816

SOURCES: Generations 1-6, information from a narrative by
Edgar Marshall. The narrative is in the Marshall Family Files.
Entries below are from the Marshall Family Bible, from a Xerox
copy made by Susan Lindsley on a visit to the Marshall family. This
copy is not notarized. Owner of the Bible at this time is unknown. Last
known owner was Mrs. Nelson Fitton, now deceased.

6. Richard Hanson Marshall
b. March 16, 1786
m. Ann Summers (Sommers) January 8, 1815
d. October 16, 1853
    Two children
        Richard O. Marshall b. August 10, 1823
        William Hanson Marshall
His tombstone reads:
    Sacred to the Memory of Richard H. Marshall, the
    son of Richard and Margaret, was born March 16th
    1786, died October 16, 1853 Aged 67 years and
    7 months.
    "Blessed are the Pure in Heart for they shall see
    God."

7. William Hanson Marshall
b. November 1, 1832
m. February 22, 1856 Fannie Melvina Davis
    b. Feburary 22, 1856
d. November 11, 1895

His children:
    John Davis Marshall
            b. February 1, 1857
            d. August 22, 1897
    Samuel Hanson Marshall
            b. July 7, 1859
            m. September 19, 1895 Lorena L. Wynkoop
            d. April 5, 1939
    Elizabeth (Bessie) A. Marshall
            b. December 17, 1861 ("Bettie" on birth page, in Marshall
            Bible, Bessie elsewhere)
            m. Ernest Lindsley, September 23, 1880
            d. December 1, 1885
                    One child: Frances Virginia (Fannie Virgie) Lindsley
                            b. July 7, 1881
                            m. Grover Frances Hoxton, January 26, 1904
                            d. 1922
                            Son: Francis Hoxton, b. 1907; d. 1917
    Lula Edmonia Marshall
            b. January 11, 1863
            d. February 11, 1891
    Lillian Gertrude (Lillie) Marshall
            b. November 30, 1865
            m. December 30, 1886/87, Ernest L. Lindsley
            d. March 29, 1892
            Two children:
                    Luther C. Lindsley
                            b. February 10, 1888
                            m. Lillas Stanley Myrick
                            d. March 2, 1963
                    William Marshall Lindsley
                            b. February 14, 1890
                            d. June 19, 1890 (the Lindsley Bible shows his
                            death in 1890, age 3 months; Prince William
                            County shows d. June 19, 1890, from cholera,
                            per his mother.)
    William Edward Marshall
            b. February 12, 1867
            m. March 23, 1892

d. September 3, 1928

Since Ernest Lindsley married 1st, Bessie A. Marshall and after her death, he married her sister, Lillie, his two surviving children, Virginia and Luther, were half-siblings and also first cousins.

Information re the marriage date of Lillie Marshall and Ernest Lindsley was provided by Mrs. Fitton, owner of the Marshall family Bible.

The Marshall family Bible shows birth, death and marriage dates, but does not show who married whom. But we can glean more information from it than we have from the Lindsley Bible. Some information here is from other notes as well as personal conversations with Mrs. Fitton.

Some information was verified or obtained from Ronald Ray Turner's web site: "Prince William County Virginia," which contains census records, marriage and death records and many other collections of information about residents of Prince William County.

THE DOUGLAS LINE

Edgar Marshall, Luther's cousin, researched the family lines of Marshall and Douglas and provided enough information to enable us to complete the line from William de Duglas to Elizabeth Douglas who married Richard Marshall.

Many details were gleaned from various web sites, which agreed on the lineage, but unfortunately there seems to be some confusion and disagreement about various dates.

1. William de Duglas, the first known Douglas
   Created Lord De Duglas by King Malcom Canmore in Forfar, Scotland, in A.D. 1057. Canmore used the castle in Forfar to repel Danish invaders. Died after 1100. One child, a son.

2. Knight, second Lord of Duglas John de Duglas.
   d. about 1145

3. Knight, third Lord of Duglas William de Duglas.
   b. Douglasdale, Lanarkshire
   m. Margaret de Kerdal (daughter of Eriskinus de Kerdal)
   d. About 1213, Douglasdale, Lanarkshire
   Ninth child: Archibald de Duglas

4. Archibald de Duglas
   b. 1198
    m. Margaret Crawford, daughter of Sir John Crawford
   d. About 1240
   Two children

5. Knight of Herdmanstern Andrew de Douglas of Morton
   "Of Morton" refers to his being progenitor of the Morton Branch
   of the Douglas Clan.
   Two sons, second was William.

6. Knight of Herdmanstern William de Douglas (living 1277)
   b. About 1245
   m. 1st Eleanor de Lovaine (two children)
   m. 2nd Elizabeth Stewart, daughter of (OF Scotland) Alexander
   Stewart
   Her first child: Knight of Lothian James de Duglas
   d. Aft. August 28, 1296

7. Knight of Lothian James de Duglas
   m. Joan, d. After 1337
   d. Before April 20, 1323
   First child: Knight John de Duglas

8. Knight John de Duglas
   b. Aft. 1300
   m. 1st Agnes Munfode
   m. 2nd Agnes Stewert
   His 7th child (by Agnes Munfode): Nicholas de Duglas
   d. January 25, 1350

9. First Laird of Mains Nicholas de Duglas
   b. Abt. 1348, Scotland

m. 1373 Janet Galbraith, daughter of William of Garconnel
He acquired the lands of Mains, which were in Dunbartonshire, by his marriage to Janet Galbraith in September 1373
    d. About 1406 in Mains of Lanarkshire
        One child: James Douglas

10. Second Laird of Mains James Douglas
    d. About 1430 in Scotland
    One son, James

11. Third Laird of Mains James Douglas
    m. (OF Newark) Catherine Maxwell
        Fourth Son: William Douglas

12. Fourth Laird of Mains William Douglas
    b. ABT 1436
    m. Elizabeth Houston
    d. AFT 1491
    First son, John

13. Fifth Laird of Mains, John Douglas
    b. ABT 1467
    m. 1st: (OF Kincaid) Margaret Kincaid
    One child, Alexander
    m. 2nd Janet Napier
    d. About 1549

14. Knight, Sixth Laird of Mains, Alexander Douglas
    m. Margaret Stewart, daughter of Matthew Stewart, 2nd Earl of Lenox, and Elizabeth Hamilton. Dame Margaret Stewart's first husband was the second Earl of Fleming.
    One child: Matthew

15. Seventh Laird of Mains, Matthew Douglas
    b. ABT 1519
    m. Margaret Buchanan, daughter of James Buchanan
    d. AFT 1571
    One son: Malcolm

16. Eighth Laird of Mains Malcolm Douglas
    b. ABT 1540-1545, Scotland
    m. 1562 Janet Cunningham, daughter of (OF Drumquhassil) John
    Cunningham
    d. Beheaded February 9, 1585
    Fifth son, Alexander
He was involved in a plot to release Mary Queen of Scots from
prison and return her to the throne. In August 1582 he and others
participated in the "Raid of Ruthven." (Named for the castle where the
king was hunting when kidnapped.) They captured King James and
held him prisoner for two years. When the king escaped the "Ruthven
Raiders" were tried for kidnapping and treason. Malcolm Douglas of
Mains and Cunningham of Drumquhassil were found guilty and
beheaded February 9, 1584 (or 1585). He was later proved innocent of
the charges of treason.

17. Ninth Laird of Mains Alexander Douglas
    b. ABT 1584,Scotland
    m. Grizel Henderson, daughter of James Henderson and Jean
    Murry
    d. ABT 1618
    Children: Archibald, Mary, Robert.
    Archibald left his estate to his wife, and Mains was sold to another
    branch of the Douglas family

18. Knight Robert Douglas of Blackerston
    b. About 1602 near Glasgow, Scotland
    m. 1st (OF Iville) Elizabeth Douglas March 6, 1623/24 in
    England (dau of William Douglas and Elizabeth Home)
    m. 2nd February 3, 1634/35 in St. Andrews Church at Holborn,
England, Susanna Douglas, daughter of Sir Robert Douglas, Viscount
of Belhaven, and Miss Whally. Susanna was born out of wedlock about
1617 in London and died 1692 in London. Her birth was legitimized by
Royal Decree on July 30, 1631, when she was thirteen. Susanna was the
mother of his son Gentleman John Douglas, who came to America.
    d. About 1669 in Scotland
    Note: He did indeed marry two ladies nee Douglas.
Sir Robert's older brother Archibald became the Ninth Laird of
Mains. Archibald obtained Blyswood by marriage. Robert's son

Colonel John Douglas named his Maryland plantation Blyswood for his uncle's manor. (See below.)

19. Gentleman/Colonel John Douglas
   b. 1636 near Glasgow, Scotland (He gave the year of his birth.)
   m. Sarah Bonner, about August 17, 1663, Charles County, Maryland. She was born about 1636 in Charles County and died July 1718 in Bowls Plantation, Charles County, Maryland.
   d. December 14, 1678, Picawaxon, Charles County, Maryland
   He rose to colonel and was paid with 10,520 pounds of tobacco for his service in the expedition against the Susquehanna Indians in 1675.
   Because of Colonel John Douglas's military service, any female descendent is eligible for membership in the National Association of Colonial Dames of the Seventeenth Century, the Daughters of Colonial Wars, the National Society of the American Colonists and many more organizations.
   He served in the Burgess of Maryland from Charles County; as Lordships Justice, Colonel of Calvary of Charles and St. Mary's County, Maryland; as Lord of Cool Spring Manor; and he patented Blythewood.
   He fathered six children. The youngest was Gentleman Joseph Douglas.

20. Gentleman Joseph Douglas
   b. About 1674, Charles County, Maryland
   m. 1st Penelope Morris about 1704 in Bowls Plantation. Born, November 13, 1684 in Ceder Point, Charles County, Maryland; she was the daughter of Richard Morris and Penelope Theobald. She died bef. December 17, 1711.
   d. November 20, 1756, in Charles County, Maryland.
   Several children, incl. Mary
   NOTE: One record shows "Elizabeth" as a child of Joseph and Penelope, but in his will Joseph names Mary Marshall as a daughter and heir. Joseph and his third wife Catherine Musgrove named a daughter Elizabeth (b. 1749, d. 1787), who must have been mistaken for Mary at some time.

21. Mary Douglas
    In her father's will, she is named "Mary Marshall."
    b. 1705, Bowls Plantation, Charles County, Maryland.
    m. Richard Marshall, Bowls Plantation
    d. BEF Mar 23, 1782

And thereby our Douglas line became Marshall.

BARONS OF RUNNEMEDE

As descendents of Richard de Clair (given below) the ladies in our family qualify as daughters of the Barons of Runnemede. The line given below was obtained by William Edgar Marshall, first cousin to Luther Campbell Lindsley.

This organization is one of the most prestigious in the United States.

Lineage accepted by the Daughters of the Barons of Runnemede

Founded by Mrs. Robert G. Hogan

MAGNA CHARTA ANCESTOR:
    *Richard de Clair
    Gilbert de Clair
    Hugh Bigod
    Roger Bigod
    Robert de Vere
    Saire de Quincey
    William Lanvalie

*Richard De Clair, Magna Charta Surety, Earl of Hertford, 1218.
    m. Lady Amica

Gilbert de Claire, Magna Charta Surety, 5th Earl of Hertford and Earl of Gloucester, died October 25, 1230. Buried in the choir of Tewsebury

Abby.

    m. Lady Isabell Marshal, daughter of William, Earl of Pembroke, Protector of England

Lady Isabell de Clair

    b. 1226

    m. 1240 Robert de Brus, Earl of Annandale, who d. 1295

Robert de Brus, Sixth Earl of Annandale and Carrick

    b. 1253

    m. 1271, Lady Majory, widow of Adam de Kilconeath and only daughter of Neil, Earl of Carrick. She died 1291

    d. 1304 in the Holy Land; he had gone as companion to Prince Edward, later King Edward I of England

Robert Bruce, First King of Scotland

    b. 1274

    m. 1st. Lady Isabell Mar, daughter of Donald, 10th Earl of Mar. She died 1327

    d. June 7, 1329

Princess Margaret Bruce

    m. 1315. First wife of Walter Lordart, Lord High Stewart of Scotland, Earl of Renfrew, who died in 1326.

    d. 1316

Robert, 2nd King of Scotland

    b. March 2, 1316

    m. 1st Lady Elizabeth Mure, daughter of Sir Adam Mure of Rowallan

    d. 1390

Robert Third

    b. 1337

    m. Annabel Drummond, daughter of Sir John Drummond

    d. 1436

James I, King of Scotland

James II, King of Scotland
    b. 1430
    m. Lady Mary (d. 1465)
    d. 1460

James, Lord Hamilton
    m. 1474 Princess Mary Stewart (her second husband)

Matthew Stewart, 2nd Earl Of Lenox
    m. Elizabeth Hamilton
    d. Killed September 9, 1513 at Battle of Flodden Field

Alexander Douglas Of Mains
    m. Margaret Stewart (her second husband)

The lineage continues down the Douglas line to the Mary Douglas (daughter of Joseph Douglas) who married Richard Marshall of Bowls Plantation. Then down the Marshall line to Lillie Marshall, mother of Luther Campbell Lindsley of Westover.

LACY LINE

This family line comes from a web site, Lacy Family Genealogy Forum, from a posting by Heather Dutcher-Ross, who was asking for family information. Although she did not give her sources, I feel sure her listing is correct.

1. John Lacy
    b. Abt. 1586, Nottingham, England
    d. 1690, Salem, Massachusetts Colony
    m. Mary in England
        b. Abt 1588
    Children:
        Edward
        John
        Mary
2. Edward
    b. 1655
    m. Abt 1675, Sarah Jackson, in Fairfield Connecticut
        b. Abt 1655
    Six children

3. Henry
    b. Abt 1681, Salem, Massachusetts Colony
    d. Abt 1768, Morristown, Morris County, New Jersey
    m. December 11, 1716, Hannah Morehouse, in Stratfield, Connecticut
        b. September 1694
        d. 1741, Morristown, Morris County, New Jersey
        She was daughter of Jonathan Morehouse and Rebecca Knowles.
    Eight children

4. David
    b. 1719
    m. 1735 Martha Parrot in New Jersey
        b. Abt 1717
        d. Elizabethtown, Essex County, New Jersey

5. Jacob Lacy
> b. 1735
> d. 1846 in New Jersey
> m. Abt 1760 Mary Clawson in New Jersey
>> b. Abt 1738
>> d. After 1786
> Children:
>> Nancy Lacy
>>> b. July 10, 1784
>>> m. March 20, 1803 Luther Lindsley, son of Elihu
Lindsley, in Morris County, New Jersey. Luther was born February 15, 1780, in New Jersey and died in Carroll Township, Ottawa County, Ohio.
>>> d. March 25, 1850, in Locust Point, Carroll Township, Ottawa County, Ohio

See the Lindsley Line (above, in this appendix) for descendents of Nancy Lacy and Luther Lindsley.

CAMPBELL LINE

We do not have the genealogy of the Campbell line, but we do have this story told to Susan Lindsley by her father Luther, to explain the long-standing bitterness between the Campbell and MacDonald clans of Scotland.

Highlanders were opposed to the Glorious Revolution, and the government, fearing a French invasion, said everyone had to take an oath to the government by December 31, 1691. Alexander MacDonald of Glencoe went on that day to an official who couldn't legally receive his oath of loyalty. Therefore he didn't take the oath until Jan 6, 1692. The Under Secretary of State, Sir John Dalremple, Master of Stair, took the chance to set an example. He planned to expel the clan from its territory, and disperse its members, but the government made even better plans. Campbell troops were sent to Glencoe and stationed in homes of MacDonald's, living as one of the family, for two weeks. At (or after) midnight of February 12-13, 1692, they struck. Campbell had already placed guards at passes, etc., so the MacDonalds couldn't escape. Plans fell through, however, and most escaped only to die of exposure. But 30-40 were murdered. This murder developed a sympathy for highlanders which is still felt today.

THE LAMB FAMILY

We have two conflicting stories about our Lamb relatives.

1. Hannah Lamb, who married Lt. Luther C. Lindsley and was mother of Ernest L. Lindsley, was **daughter** of Colonel Lamb of the Battle of Quebec and grandmother of our Luther.

2. Hannah's **uncle** commanded artillery of Montgomery and Arnold in 1775 at the Battle of Quebec. They stormed the town. Lamb was shot through the jaw. He was opposed to the attack. This same Lamb commanded part of Washington's artillery at Yorktown and recaptured the guns he lost at Quebec.

Details of the battle can be found in *Washington* by Douglas Southall Freeman and also on-line.

Luther always said a Colonel Lamb, a relative, made the cradle that several generations of Lamb-Lindsley children slept in and that burned in Westover. Logically, it would have been Hannah's direct up-line ancestor. I have not researched the family of the Colonel Lamb who fought at Quebec.

APPENDIX II-A

LINDSLEY FAMILY PHOTO SCRAPBOOK

These are the few family pictures that Luther had. Aunt Minnie sent them after Westover burned. The original photographs are identified on the back, many in Luther's handwriting.

Thulia Bramlett has the original picture of his grandfather, Lt. Luther C. Lindsley. Other originals will be donated to the special collections section of the Georgia College Library, Milledgeville, GA. Copies of all family pictures will be preserved on computer discs to accompany this book.

Mahlon Smith Lindsley

Great, Great-Grandmother,

Mrs. Nancy Converse Lamb, wife of Samuel Lamb, and daughter of Adair Marcy Converse, a soldier of the Revolutionary War who was wounded at the surrender of Cornwallis at Yorktown, Oct. 19th, 1781. Great-great grandmother of L. C. Lindsley of Westover, and grandmother of Hannah M. Lamb, wife of Lt. L. C. Lindsley of the Confederate Army. Great-great-grandmother of L. C. Lindsley of Westover.

Lt. L. C. Lindsley of the Confederate Army, killed at the Battle of Cedar Creek. (See the book *Blue Jeans and Pantaloons in Yesterplace* **for more information. See also Appendix III for information on the Battle of Cedar Creek.)**

Written inside the case holding the picture of Lt. Luther C. Lindsley of the Confederate Army in his own hand

"To My dear Wife H. M. Lindsley
$12.00
Aug `8th 1862
L. C. Lindsley

This Ambrotype was after the first Battles around Richmond"

Luther Campbell Lindsley joined Company G, which was organized and went into barracks at Dumfries, Virginia, on July 1, 1861, and was mustered into service on July 16, 1861. About May 1, 1862, the organization became Company B of the 49th Regiment, Virginia Infantry.

He was promoted to Sergeant on October 1, 1861, elected 2nd lieutenant April 22, 1862.

His grandson, our Luther wrote:

Lt. L. C. Lindsley, Commander of Co. B
49th Va Regt. (Stonewall Brigade).
The last brigade to stop firing at Appomattox, and the last to surrender
Last commander Col. Kye Dougong
and part of Gordon's Division at Appomattox.

Left, a Marshall cousin; right, Frances Virginia Lindsley, Luther's sister. In his letter dated February 8, 1962, Edgar Marshall refers to a photograph of Virgie and his grandmother by a rose arbor. This is probably not the picture he referred to. This cousin could not be the Marshall grandmother, for Edgar's Marshall grandmother was also Virgie's Marshall grandmother.

Frances Virginia Lindsley (Virgie), half-sister of L. C. Lindsley of Westover. Same father, their mothers were sisters, so they were half-siblings and first cousins.

Frances Virginia Lindsley

Frances Virginia (Virgie) Lindsley in back yard at 1344 Emerson St., Washington, DC

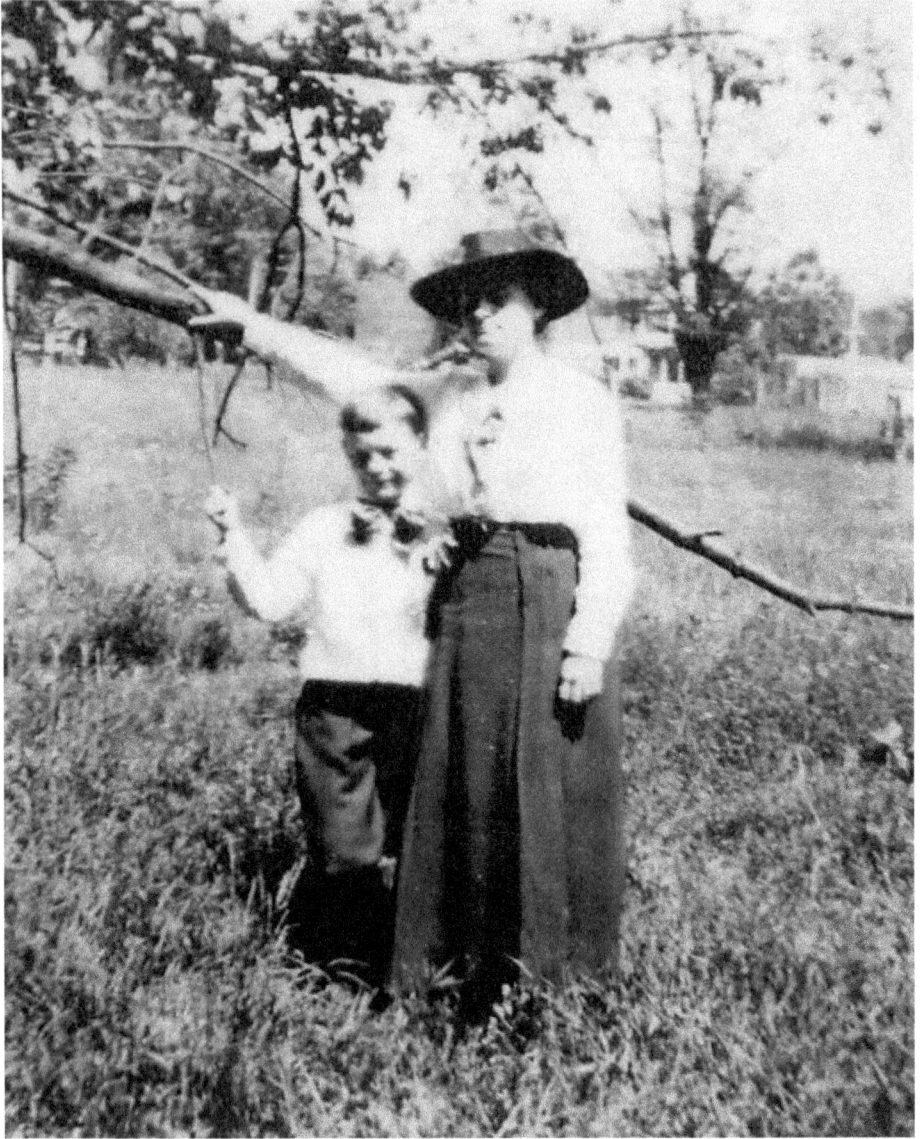

Frances Virginia Lindsley Hoxton and her son Francis.

Luther Campbell Lindsley in uniform of the horse-drawn artillery, with his grandmother ("Gamma"), Hannah Lamb Lindsley Johnson.

Close-up of L. C. Lindsley of Westover and his grandmother (Gamma) Hannah Lamb Lindsley, widow of Lt. L. C. Lindsley of the Confederate Army.

William E. (Edgar) Marshall, age 21 years. E think he is the Marshall cousin whose letters are quoted in the section of "after the children left home."

THE MANN FAMILY COUSINS

Mary Mann (left) and Bettie Mann (right) daughters of Emily Lindsley Mann

Members of the Mann family

Emily Lindsley Mann

APPENDIX II-B

MYRICK FAMILY PORTRAITS AND

BUILDINGS

MYRICK FAMILY PHOTO ALBUM

These pictures begin with the earliest ancestors we have pictures for. Intermingled with these are also pictures of ancestral homes and the family coats of arms.

The pictures begin with the Dowdells and follow generation to generation to James Dowdell Myrick of Dovedale.

James Dowdell, who married Caroline Smith. (Portrait burned with Westover.)

Caroline Smith m. James Dowdell. (Portrait burned in Westover.)

Caroline Smith Dowdell, wife of James Dowdell.

Bodorgan, ancestral home of the Myricks, in Anglesey, Wales. Photo by John E. James.

After their marriage in 2011, Prince William and Kate Middleton rented a four-bedroom farmhouse on the Bodorgan estate while William served in Anglesey, Wales, as an RAF Valley Search and Rescue pilot. Rent was about £750 per month.

BODORGAN CASTLE in Wales HAS BEEN OCCUPIED BY THE SAME FAMILY - THE MEYRICKS - *CONTINUOUSLY FOR 1110 YEARS*

"Ripley's Believe It or Not" ran this item in its syndicated column November 17, 1955

HEB DDUW

DDUW A DIGON

HEB DDIM ;

Merrick

The name has changed over the years from Merrick to Myrick.

Grave of first Myrick in Baldwin County, Georgia.

Elizabeth Stegira Dowdell m. Stith Parham Myrick. (Middle name found in an autograph inside a book, dated 1842. This is the best estimate of the middle name from her handwriting.)

Stith Parham Myrick from an old tintype.

General Stith Parham Myrick

The Rockwell Mansion, home of S. P. Myrick and his family. Located in Midway, suburb of Milledgeville, as it appeared in 2008. One room was removed and relocated into the Winterthur Museum in Delaware.

Elizabeth Dowdell Myrick, wife of Stith Parham Myrick.

James Dowdell Myrick, father of Lillas Stanley Myrick, from a color pastel portrait in possession of Susan Lindsley.

Whitehurst

Wilkinson Mayberry Whitehurst, father of Thulia Katherine Whitehurst who married James Dowdell Myrick.

Nancy Averette Bryan Whitehurst, mother of Thulia K. W. Myrick

THE ATLANTA JOURNAL

Above--- Homestead in Houston county, built in 1832 by James Avrette Bryan, where 175 of his descendants held their annual reunion recently.

To the left--- 175 descendants of James Avrette Bryan at their annual reunion held at his old homestead in Houston county, now owned by Mr. and Mrs. O. M. Heard.

Nancy Averette Bryan's family home.

Thulia Katherine Whitehurst Myrick.

James Dowdell Myrick

Myrick's Mill in Twiggs County as it appeared in 1961, from a water-color painting by Katie Myrick Lowerre, Lillas's sister. James Dowdell and Thulia Katherine lived on the plantation where the mill was located when they first married.

From the December 20, 1873, issue of the *Augusta Chronicle*:

Bankrupt Sale. By virtue of an order of the Honorable the District Court of the United States for the Southern District of Georgia, will be sold, free from all encumbrances whatever, on the first Tuesday in JANUARY next, in front of the Court House door, in Jefferson, to the highest bidder, the following property, to-wit:

*   Three thousand two hundred acres more or less, lying in Twiggs County, known as the Myrick Mill's Place. The above property to be sold in lots of 202½ acres, more or less.*

*   Property sold as assets of Stith P. Myrick, Bankrupt. Terms-Cash.*

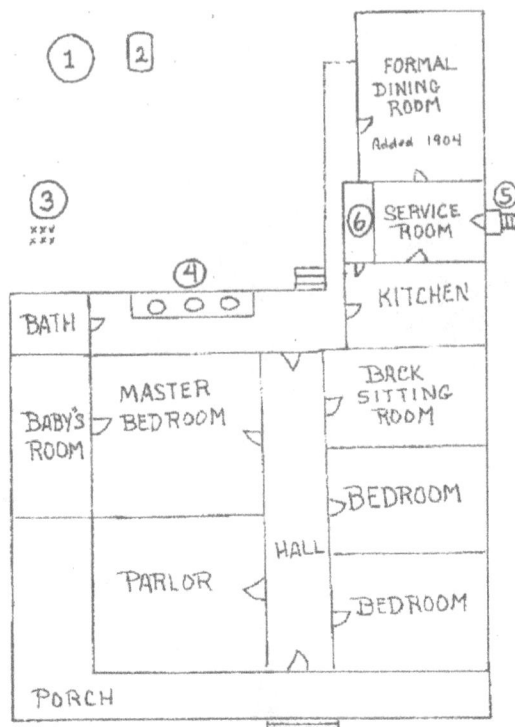

Layout of the Dovedale house, not to scale. The formal dining room held a table that could seat twelve people. From a rough sketch by Allie Myrick Bowden. Legend: 1, the well; 2, the water tank; 3, the woodpile; 4 the bench and wash bowls where the children had to wash up before meals (even in winter); 5, stoop and stairs leading into service room that faced the vegetable garden; 6, the locked food pantry. The house faced north.

Dovedale store and post office. The children could charge items there. Thulia has the records book. This building was east of the house. Beyond this and to the left stood the barn.

JDM

JDM

JDM

James Dowdell Myrick, 1878, from a tintype Allie shared. Note the eyes. Here and in the first two photographs of James D., they are sharp and direct.

OTHER RELATIVES

Goodwin Myrick, brother of James Dowdell, son of Stith Parham Myrick.

The second James Dowdell Myrick, son of James Dowdell Myrick and Thulia K. W. Myrick. Brother of Lillas Stanley Myrick of Westover.

Nannaline Myrick (left), oldest child of James D. and Thulia K. Myrick.

Lila Daniel, granddaughter of S. P. Myrick by his first wife Elizabeth Peebles. She married Dr. L. M. Jones.

Lila Daniel Jones, possibly the namesake of LILLAS (Lilla) Stanley Myrick.

Aunt Willa, 1901. Sister of Thulia Katherine.

Katie Myrick Barron, a cousin.

1896. R. L. Stanley, probably the namesake of Lillas STANLEY Myrick.

APPENDIX III

BATTLE OF CEDAR CREEK

Macon Telegraph, October 15, 2006, p. 2D

BATTLE OF CEDAR CREEK

Surprise at Cedar Creek

By Chuck Myers: McClatchy/Tribune News Service

The Shenandoah Valley in Virginia attracts a wide range of visitors each autumn.

Many people travel to the valley to soak up the rich and colorful fall foliage.

Others head out on apple-picking excursions at one of the valley's many groves.

And some make a final camping foray into the Blue Ridge Mountains before the weather turns frosty.

But on one weekend each October, thousands call on a sweeping field outside Middletown in the northern Shenandoah, dressed in their best Civil War uniforms and period costumes, to participate in a large-scale reenactment of the Battle at Cedar Creek in 1864.

During the American Civil War, the Shenandoah Valley was a hotbed of Confederate activity. Between 1861 and 1863, Union forces attempted to drive the Confederates repeatedly from the valley, but without success.

By the summer of 1864, the South had come under heavy pressure from Northern forces on several fronts. And soon, the Shenandoah became one of the key focal points for Confederate survival.

The Union army under the command of Lt. Gen. Ulysses S. Grant had put a chokehold on Confederate General Robert E. Lee's beleaguered troops around Petersburg, Virginia. In an attempt to alleviate the pressure, Lee dispatched Gen. Jubal Early and a small army north to divert union military attention. Early's force briefly threatened western Maryland and Washington, D. C. in July 1864, but later withdrew to more friendly confines in the Shenandoah Valley.

Grant countered Lee's move by sending Gen. Phillip H. Sheridan and the newly organized Army of the Shenandoah to pursue Early.

Defeating Confederate forces in the Shenandoah, though, was not Sheridan's only goal.

Often called the "Breadbasket of the Confederacy," the Shenandoah provided the South with crucial food supplies during the war, including corn, oats and livestock. And Grant wanted Sheridan to destroy this economic lifeline.

In early August, Sheridan set out to confront Early, and carry out Grant's desire to turn the Shenandoah into "a barren waste," with a scorched-earth campaign that became know as "The Burning."

Self-assured and cocky, Sheridan stood a mere 5- feet-5-inches tall. He rode a black horse named Rienzi, and had earned a reputation as an audacious field commander during battles in Tennessee and Georgia in 1863.

Sheridan bested Early in successive battles. Determining that Early's force did not pose an immediate threat, Sheridan headed to Washington for a scheduled strategy session with Secretary of War Edwin Stanton.

Following the meeting, Sheridan returned to the Shenandoah and stopped off in Winchester for the evening of October 18. Meanwhile, Early prepared for a morning surprise attack at Cedar Creek.

In a thick, pre-dawn fog, Early sent roughly 21,000 troops into action against the approximately 32,000-strong Union Army on October 19, 1864. Three Confederate divisions slammed into Union Camps at different points near Cedar Creek. The attack shocked the Union soldiers. Many still lay asleep when the Confederates hit. Several others simply took off in retreat.

Some Union soldiers, however, made a stand.

Two Union regiments, the 8th Vermont and the 128th New York, organized a hasty resistance, but suffered heavy losses. A monument to the 128th New York sits at a pull-off on Route 11.

Emerging from woods along the creek, the Confederate

onslaught spilled out on to open farmland.

The Confederates halted their attack at mid-morning. Early's troops were tapped out. Hungry, exhausted and low on supplies, the Confederate soldiers had set about plundering the abandoned Union camps for food and weapons.

A road sign on Route 11, about a mile north of Middletown near Lord Fairfax Community College, indicates the Confederates' farthest advance.

Sheridan received words of Early's attack around 6:00 a. m. At first, he dismissed the news as Union reconnaissance fire. But he grew restless, and by 9 a.m. was riding Rienz at breakneck speed down the Valley Pike.

As Sheridan weaved his way through throngs of retreating soldiers on the road during the 14-mile ride, he implored them to turn and fight.

The sight of Sheridan barreling down the road electrified the Union ranks. Cheers went up, and the revitalized troops turned and headed back to Cedar Creek.

When Early finally resumed his attack, the Union force beat it back.

Sheridan then went on the offensive. Under a clear blue sky, a Union division led by General George A. Custer attacked the Confederate left flank at 3:30 p.m., and cracked it. A half-hour later, Sheridan ordered an assault on the Confederate center. After a pitched battle, Early's troops finally withdrew, and retreated back over the ground they had taken earlier in the day. By 5:30 p.m., the battle was over.

Today, the Cedar Creek Battlefield Foundation oversees a significant stretch of this part of the Battlefield.

Established in 1988, the Cedar Creek Battlefield Foundation owns and manages approximately 150 acres of the Cedar Creek battlefield. The annual Cedar Creek reenactment takes place on 135 acres of rolling landscape adjacent to the foundation's Cedar Creek Battlefield Visitor Center on Route 11.

Unlike most Civil War reenactments, the Cedar Creek event allows participants to commemorate a major battle on the place it occurred. The annual reenactment takes place on a weekend close to the battle's October 19th anniversary date, and has become one of the largest in the country.

Attendance had grown from a few hundred re-enactors at the first event in 1990 to about 6,000 in recent years.

The Battle of Cedar Creek at a Glance

Location: Cedar Creek and Middletown, Virginia
Campaign: Sheridan's Shenandoah Valley Campaign (August - December 1864)
Battle Date: October 19, 1864
Commanders: Union General Phillip Sheridan and Confederate General Jubal Early
Forces engaged: 52,945 total (Union, 31,945; Confederate, 21,000)
Estimated casualties: 8,575 total
(Union, 5,665; Confederate, 2,910, including Lt. Luther C. Lindsley, grandfather of Dr. Luther C. Lindsley of Westover)
Result: Union Victory.

APPENDIX IV

LETTERS FROM OREGON AND THE

PHILIPPINES

These letters are not of special significance for the Lindsley family, but are of interest because of their insight into the settlement of Oregon and into the aftermath of the Spanish-American War. And the writers are obviously friends of Fances Virginia Lindsley, sister of our Luther.

We do not know who these men are, but perhaps as the "Web" advances, some reader may find more information about them.

Salem P. O. Ore
April 6, 1899

Dear Bro. Gard,

Yours of the 1st and 11th of Feb. arrived yesterday in answer to mine of Dec. last and you can feel sure that we were glad to hear from you. Perhaps before this was written you have received Mothers and my last.

The place we are on at present is railroad land. I am waiting in the balance—as it were—for the tide to turn one way or another. The balance happens to be in this case whether I will have mother file on a piece of government land here for me or begin payments on a piece costing $500. The payments are $100 down and the rest in yearly installments of $50 at 5% interest. I have written father for the necessary money to file on the government land and if he will advance that much on Eleanor's board money I think I will take the government land of which I speak is one of four like claims lying across the mouth of a large valley that reaches away up into the Cascade Range. The other three are taken and if I should or rather if mother should take this piece of land the four different families would form a blockade across the mouth of this valley and keep the immense cattle range thus formed for ourselves. If the tide turns in favor of the latter, i.e. should I decide to buy the piece (160 acres) I spoke of I must content myself with the road as a range as many others do. This piece has about 5 acres in meadow with a house, barn and small garden plot.

Enclosed please find a small aluminum pocket comb that I feel will be very handy. I also send by this mail but in a separate parcel a small pocket mirror. As you will readily see these have seen considerable use already but are none the worse for it and I think that you will prize them more because they have been used when you learn their history. The comb I bought in Austin, Tex while I was stopping at the Capitol Hotel. I carried it in my pocket and used it every day from there south to San Antonio, Tex, thence west to El Paso Tex then west across New Mexico to the western border of Ariz. where I was "pinched" at Yuma, and from there to Los Angeles then to S. F. and finally by boat to Portland and then by wagon to here. So you see it is no common comb even now if you judge quality by the distance a thing has travelled. The mirror was also given to me in "Frisco" and has travelled from there here.

I send the above things not because of their actual worth but because of the benefit they will be in aiding you to "primp up" when you are about to sally forth like a gallant knight to see your dusky "Filipino-Lady-Love." And there it will aid you to see that "Mustn't Touch-it" of which you speak.

But to tell the truth the reason I send these is because they are the best that I can get at present as I am some forty miles from no-where, i.e., Portland. I hope to be able soon to remember you along with mother with some thing more substantial.

These will probably reach you on your birthday the others a little later.

When I came through Portland a year ago last month I saw Maude from a distance. I was standing on the corner in front of your old house when she came home. From what I saw I would say that she has got to be very pretty.

You say you like to receive letters—then remember that "There are Others" and I'll do the same.

Do not fear about my enlisting as I have no such intention.

Last Christmas I received my release from Father made out and signed before a justice and two witnesses by father so you see I became my own boss before you and am older than you are you might say in the eyes of the law.

The other day I sat thinking of the past and I began to follow my life over again as you might say. The panoramic scene began in Fairview, that is where the detail became important. Do you remember the time father and mother had a fuss and you and I started to leave home and had started towards Benhams when father sent us back. At that time we built air castles about how we would leave home when we were sixteen and fourteen respectively. When I think of those vows I begin to see how they have become true. Before we reached that age we were on either side of the U. S. Before another 4 yrs. had elapsed one of us was in a foreign land the other on the summit of the Cascades. As I think of these numerous and quick changes I realize the truth of the saying "we know not what a day or an hour may bring forth." Who knows what will happen in the next four years to us

It is true we may liken it unto a man on the plains with a spirited team. If we hold a tight rein and guide them our course will be pretty near what we wish although we may hit a few rocks that we could have missed and perhaps the wheels may sink into a prairie dog hole that it seems impossible to get out of, but by careful driving we reach our destination at last. But if we drop our reins and fix our gaze too steadfastly on our surroundings and the lost or past beauties of the rear, the team will wander recklessly along keeping no particular row, going slow, now at break neck speed while we gaze on, entranced at the beauties surrounding us or look back behind with sad eyes and wonder why we prized those forever lost scenes so little and why we did not take advantage of the many opportunities that opened up but are now closed forever by old father time who will not let us turn back but is hurrying the unguided horses on and on—to what? All the time we dream thus of present beauties and past mistakes the team wander on until we are suddenly awakened by their stopping at a place marked "Premature Grave" or we suddenly go over the precipice to die without an awakening or are rescued by loving hands but branded "A wreck of a Misspent Life" or we may only take occasional naps and awake each time in time to start in the right direction again. I wonder what is our course. So far it has been the latter general one or the "Dreaming Way." Have we awakened? I think I have not!

But enough of this. Hoping that I will get as long a letter in return, I remain,

Your Loving Bro.

R. V. Sefton

Salem P.O. Ore.
Clackamas Co.

Salem is not in Clackamas County, but apparently this letter writer went to Salem for his mail.

*   *   *

Note: The Spanish-American War lasted from February to December 1898.

On Envelope: **Thomas G. Sefton**
Troop A 3rd US Cav.
Savoy Luzon
P. I.

My address is on the outside of the envelope in the lower left hand corner and on the last page of this letter. Gard.
Dingras, Iloco Nortre
Feb. 22, 1900
Dear Friend Virgie,

I agreed to write you a letter upon leaving Washington but although we were joking at the time I take this opportunity to write hoping that you will do me the favor of answering it. At the time I made the above promise I was thinking of entering upon a mercantile career but instead I enlisted in the Army and a more disgusted boy you never saw with Army life and surroundings but will stick to it for my three years and then go on and maybe fulfill the little skeme that we were talking about.

As some of my church "Friends" (two of them) have no doubt told you I left Washington on August 7 without anyone of them being on hand to see me off. The only ones who were present were my Father and two sisters, the "kids" (my nephews) Ada Briggs, and Orla Knowles the latter two more on Paul Knowles account than mine.

You laughed at me when I said that I would see foreign lands well I guess the laugh is the other way now as I have seen and landed on Alaska, Japan and the Philippines besides sighting Russia in Asia.

Maybe you don't believe that on New Years eve I didn't think what the difference was in my surroundings this year and last New Years a year ago I was (at) "Flossies" party (although I wasn't wanted as I afterward found out) where I spend a very pleasant evening and this year I was sleeping on the floor of an old shack that the wind blew through and rats ran over your body and we were short of rations and supposed to be surrounded by Insurrectos. Which do you think the best situation?

I have succeeded in saving $60 over here and the government owes me two more months pay which is $30.95 clear of expenses.

Give my regards to my friends. We have very fair quarters here and the town is quite a large one. Meals cost a Indian Peso or 25 cents American and you get all the chicken eggs and other such stuff that you can eat. Bananas and cocoa-nuts are about as expensive here as they are in Washington. Oranges and lemons are very scarce and consequently very dear. Every thing is made out of rice and bamboo here even the houses are of bamboo and rice straw. The natives have chicken fights every Sunday and so (there is) some very high betting.

Cigars cost 1.2 cent a piece, cigarettes about 1 dozen for a cent while leaf tobacco costs almost nothing & liquor is about 5 cents a quart. It is called "Bino" and the boys say it makes a horrible drunk of the fighting class and leaves you sick to the stomach besides a severe headache but I don't know as I have not tasted either liquor or tobacco since leaving the States.

Card playing and "crap" shooting for money and cigars is very plentiful one seargeant winning $1000.00 last pay day. That also is a dead letter with me.

There was a fair in Savoy (pronounced Sawog) in which they had chicken fighting, pony racing, and parades galore The church and bell tower which by the way are separate building over here, were lighted up at night by paper lanterns. There were about 20 bands in the parade they were all carrying an American flag (which is the prettiest flag that floats) and all playing a different tune. The bands are just getting such pieces as Rag Time Jimmy and there's a like nature over here some of them even know the Star Spangled Banner and a few other National Airs. During the parade whenever an American flag passed we all took off our hats and now the natives do the same. There were floats carried by the niggers, all kinds of church scenes, the Virgin and lots of other saints, besides a large figure of Christ and all were made of tin. One kind of race they had here was where they tied chickens up by the legs and the nigger who pulled the most heads off while his pony was galloping won the race. Then they had pacing races and running races besides buggy races all of which attracted equal attention from the boys.

The natives here are dark toned and remind me of our American Niggers except they are not so lazy and will work when their grub gives out. They nearly all have the Doby Itch a scaly skin disease which leaves red blotches where ever it attacks you. He works all day for about 2 1/2 to 4 cents and his principal food is rice of which there is much grown here; you can pass along the road and see thousands of acres planted to rice and all of this land must be flooded most of the year. The natives all smoke cigars even the women and children, the latter begin when they cant walk and it is a common sight to see a pickaninny (a modification of *pequenino* "very little"), as they are called with a cigar in his mouth as big as him self and which he seems to be enjoying hugely.

If a native owns a caribou which is a kind of cow which must be put in water about every 15 minutes when you are working him and which is slower than sin, he is considered a rich man and it is the same with a few dollars. The native has no bed but 2 or 3 familys bunch up together like so many sheep and sleep on mats in one house. He is quite honest as far as his neighbors are concerned but he will cheat an American out of his (the American grandmother's) false teeth. They even go so far as to carry rocks that weight a pound or two a couple of miles in the grass that they only get 7 cents for 50 pounds so as to beat us.

We feed our horses grass and rice over here and some of them don't like oats anymore. The heads of the rice cost us 5 cents a bunch, which weights about 25 pounds.

The native shacks are handier than the houses in the States in that the floor is all cracks and not so much trouble to sweep, the cracks being about 1 inch wide while the bamboo slats are only about 3.4 in wide it makes a better bed than the ground for I have tried both.

Well I will close now hoping to hear from you by the return mail.

My reason for not putting a stamp on this letter is that there is no post office where I can get a stamp any where within two days march.

Remember me to friends and oblige
Your Friend
Thos. G. Sefton
don't forget to write soon.
Yours, etc.
Gard

* * *

Postmark: Provincia de Ilocos Norte Presidenoia

Pidig, Ilocos Norte
June 5, 1900
Dear Friend Virgie:

I received yours of April 8th on the 31st of May but have been unable to answer before owing to being moved about so much. First the troop was moved back to Dringras and then a detachment of 30 were sent off to this place for ten days and possibly 3 months we are enjoying ourselves more than we would with the troop as we have hardly any duty. Guard duty every four days and mounted patrol through the mountains every other day and then of course we have to feed and groom twice a day but most of the time we are doing bunk fatigue, that is, laying on our bunks. We haven't had a fight for about a month now but the last was a warm affair although we lost no men either killed or wounded. The "googoos" had us surrounded but we made a six shooter charge through them, and then back after which we vamoosed leaving about 40 dead niggers to mark the place. There was about 250 riflemen among them and only 15 of us, counting Lieut. Thayer our troop commander.

I am certain that I killed one here. I was in three fights that week, killing five that I know of.

As I write this I am surrounded by about a dozen Filipinos (all of them clerks). They are asking for paper, envelopes and anything else that happened to catch their eye and always "para amigo" (for a Friend) and any one of them would stick you in the back if they got a chance.

The letter that I got from you was the most interesting that I got among a batch of seven and you now know how surprised and pleased I was as I was not expecting any for a couple of weeks any way.

I am going to write to Roy and will ask the favor that you asked but I will ask that he and my mother have theirs taken together as that would be least likely to arouse suspicion. Enclosed you will find Roy's last letter. The Maude he speaks of used to be an old flame of mine. Now Virgie if you are willing I am going to engineer a science in regards to you and Roy but I will wait until I find out if you are willing and I will wait until you write to me before I begin. Don't get insulted as you see I am using that blessed thing distance some 11500 miles to talk plain. I am subject to the intermittent fever over here and a couple of weeks back I thought I was going to croak and if I had it would not have made such a difference as I have very few friends to mourn my loss. A few young men and possibly my relation. Since I enlisted I have learned to value life very lightly.

The moustache that Roy speaks of has vamoosed under the ravages of the razor. The above about going to croak is only a joke as I have about as many friends as the average mortal but I did get scared when my fever went up to 107 degrees. I go on guard to-night. Am learning to speak a little Spanish and can understand a good deal more than I can speak.

Will send you cigarettes as soon as we get paid which will be about the 1st of next month and you don't want to get surprised if I write another letter at that time as I am a great hand for liking to receive letters and I know that if I don't write I wont receive any.

The stamp at the head of this letter is the local stamp of this city or pueblo.

I promised to get you a heart for you to keep in remembrance of me and as soon as possible I will mail you one probably before I get an answer to this.

Government food is dammed poor and if we didn't buy sweet potatoes eggs and chickens we would go hungry. Mangoes cost 6 for 5 cts Pineapple 2 for 5 cts finer than you can get for 20 cts in the States bananas 5 cents for about 3 doz but it is a common occurrence for a soldier to eat 3 dozen at one sitting. Chickens from 2 and a half to 10 cents, eggs 10 cents a dozen and other things in proportion.

Write by the return mail as letters are interesting reading, especially such as you write. You and Roy ought to write each other as you can both write such interesting letters.

Give all my friends my regard Give Gamma my love.

Will close now hoping to hear from you in about 5 months.

I remain ever Your Friend
Thomas G. Sefton
Troop A 3rd U.S. Cav
Savoy, Luzon, P. I.

P. S. There is a rumor afloat over here that we will be in the States by xmas but I don't believe it. I think we are billed for 2 years foreign service.

I won't send your letter to Roy. I got yours two days after my 21st birthday so you see you un intentionally gave me a birthday gift.

Good Bye
Gard-

The boys have nicknamed me Doc.
Gard

* * *

Savoy, Luzon, P. I.
November 1, 1900

Dear Virgie,

Although I wrote some weeks ago I will write again as I am feeling rather lonely for letters are scarce and time hangs heavy on any hands.

We are now stationed in the above named place which is called Fort Savoy. The town is situated above six miles from the Ocean on a very sallow river of the same name. It is surrounded by a number of other cities the smallest of which contains 6,000 inhabitants and each of them contains a company of infantry while there is at present two companies of infantry and one Troop of Cavalry stationed here. So you see we are well protected here and besides that the town is surrounded by a strong bamboo fence about 10 feet high.

The commanding officer of this town had a native working for him who thought that he would take the adjutant's carbine and "vam" to the jungle, but he was caught in just the nick of time and brought back and put in jail.

We will get paid in a few days and then I hope to send you the heart that I spoke of and believe that it will get there in time for Christmas.

I don't know whether I shall come back to Washington to finish my schooling when I get out or not but expect to try farming. Do you think that I would make a successful farmer? Or would Dentistry suit me better?

I am going to commence now picking up souvenirs of this Island and hope to get a very good collection before I leave.

I am enjoying the best of health at present and hope to continue doing do. I hope you are enjoying yourself now that the winter festivities are in full blast. I hope that you are in good health. Are you? Give Gamma my love and tell her to write.

Does Eleanor tell any more of her infernal stories about me or rather did she as I now suppose she is with Royal. You probably know that I hear very little of her as she has lost no love for me and as long as I can help it I won't go near her.

Give my regards to any one who knows me, or rather asks about me. Write soon.

How are the Naybors? The Gregorys? The Iveys? Does Walter still hang on?

Now, Virgie, what did you do to make Royal think that you were deceitful for he says that is the only defect in an otherwise perfect character. Now I on my part never thought you deceitful but then neither do I think you perfect as we are none of us perfect.

Give my regards to "Flossie."

There are very few amusements here except bathing and listening to the poor music of a poorer band.

Guess I will close now as it is raining hard and consequently a good cool night to sleep.

Write soon and oblige
 ever your Friend
 Thos. G. Sefton

P. S. don't forget to give Gamma regards. Tell her to write. My address is the same as this letter is headed.
 Gard

APPENDIX V

LUTHER'S CORNELL RECORDS

This first letter was the recommendation from William and Mary for Luther's admission to the special classes in agricultural chemistry under the Smith-Hughes Act. He attended the summer of 1918, with strong recommendations from William and Mary:

COLLEGE OF WILLIAM AND MARY
WILLIAMSBURG, VIRGINIA

HERBERT L. BRIDGES, A. B.
REGISTRAR

July 10, 1918.

Dean of the Department of Agriculture,

Cornell University,

Ithaca, New York.

Dear Sir:

Mr. L. C. Lindsley, who is making application for admission to your University, graduated at the College of William and Mary with the degree of Bachelor of Arts in June 1907. Mr. Lindsley completed the regular prescribed course of study for this degree which requires one hundred and twenty (120) credit hours, covering a period of four (4) college years.

Mr. Lindsley proved himself a very capable young man, and I do not hesitate to recommend him for admission to your University.

Very truly yours,

H. L. Bridges

Registrar.

B/M.

That summer saw the beginning of his love affair with chemistry, and the next summer Luther began his application for admission into the post-graduate school at Cornell.

Charlotte C. H. Va.,
6/12/1919.

Pres. Cornell Univ.
Ithaca, N.Y.

Dear Sir,

Last summer I attended the college of Agriculture at Cornell, taking the emergency course for teachers of Agriculture under the Smith Hughes act. While at Cornell I became very much interested in Chemistry, and desire very much an opportunity to secure a Ph.D in chemistry from Cornell.

I have had almost five years of college work at William & Mary College. I hold the degree of B. S., and lack one unit for my Master's degree. For eleven years I have taught in the High Schools of Virginia, and am now thirty one years old, and should like to climb up a little as I have reached the very pinnacle in rural educational work in Virginia. As principal here of the Charlotte County Agricultural School, my salary is larger than any rural Principal's in Virginia, at the time, and so far as I can see there is no future for me in this field.

I am married but have no children. Should I come to Cornell I could bring with me only about a thousand dollars. This means that I must secure outside employment of some kind. If I could secure a position that would bring me in as much as $600 a year I could manage to make out very nicely.

I am hoping that you can put me in touch with something no matter how humble, from an assistantship on down to day laborer, that will enable me to finish my chemistry course under Dr. Dennis.

Dr. Dennis had me slated for an assistantship last session, but the war broke up my plans. It may be I could win certain fellowships. I would appreciate your sending me any possible information.

Yours very truly,
L. C. Lindsley (signature)

June 18, 1919.

Mr. L.C. Lindsley,
Charlotte C.H. Va.

Dear Sir :

Your letter of June 13th, 1919, addressed to the
President of the University has been referred to this office
for reply. I am glad to inform you that your degree from
William and Mary College, together with your subsequent
teaching experience, is sufficient to render you eligible
for admission to the Graduate School of Cornell University.
You are also eligible to become a candidate for an advanced
degree provided that you have had adequate preparation for
graduate study in the subjects which you expect to choose
as majors and minors for your degree of Doctor of Philosophy.

I am enclosing herewith an application form which
should be filled out and returned to this office at your
convenience.

Our appointments to Fellowships and Graduate Scholarships
for next year have already been made. It is possible however,
that Professor Dennis could give you information regarding
any vacancies there may be in the department for assistants
and instructors.

If I can answer any further inquiries regarding graduate
work I shall be glad if you will write me.

Very truly yours,

CORNELL UNIVERSITY
THE GRADUATE SCHOOL
ADMISSION

Graduates of Cornell University, and graduates of other institutions who have pursued a course of study substantially equivalent to that required for a first degree at Cornell, are eligible for admission to the Graduate School without further question. In determining eligibility for admission in other cases, studies pursued after graduation and experience gained by professional work, or otherwise, are taken into consideration.

A distinction is made between admission to the Graduate School and admission to candidacy for an advanced degree. A student holding a first degree may be admitted to the Graduate School (but *not* to candidacy) if his training is regarded as less than one year short of that required for the first degree at Cornell University. After a student has duly registered in the Graduate School, he should consult with the Dean regarding the terms of his admission to candidacy for an advanced degree, and obtain a blank for the formal statement of his candidacy.

At some time before admission to the Graduate School it will be necessary to present evidence of the degree already received i.e., either the diploma or a statement from the Registrar or from some other official of the college granting the degree.

APPLICATION FOR ADMISSION TO THE GRADUATE SCHOOL
[To be sent to the Dean of the Graduate School, Cornell University, Ithaca, N. Y.]

The undersigned applies for admission to the Graduate School of Cornell University, and submits the following statement regarding his previous work:

Graduated from *William & Mary* .... Degree received *B A* ✓

Date of Graduation *'08* .... Number of years spent in study at the above institution *4½*

Outline of course of study pursued. [If more space is needed use the back of this sheet. If more convenient, send a catalogue with the courses of study marked.] ....

See List attached ....

....

....

Outline of work since graduation, so far as it has had any bearing upon advanced study ....

....

....

....

Do you wish to apply for admission as a candidate for an advanced degree ? *Yes* ...... For what degree ? *PhD*

Statement of studies to be undertaken after admission to the Graduate School ....

Inorganic Chemistry

Organic   "

Agricultural   "

Name in full *Lester Campbell Lindsley*

Home address *Manassas Va*

Ithaca address *104 Maple Ave*

Date ....

CORNELL UNIVERSITY
THE GRADUATE SCHOOL

CANDIDACY FOR AN ADVANCED DEGREE

The following advanced degrees are conferred by Cornell University: Doctor of Philosophy, Master of Arts, Master of Science, Master of Architecture, Master of Civil Engineering, Master in Forestry, Master in Landscape Design, Master of Mechanical Engineering, and Master of Science in Agriculture. The requirements for these degrees are stated in the Announcement of the Graduate School. A student who has been admitted to the Graduate School may become a candidate for one of these degrees under the following conditions:

(a) The candidate must have had general preliminary training substantially equivalent to that required for the first degree in one of the four year courses in Cornell University. In the case of any of the advanced technical degrees [M.C.E., M.M.E., M.Arch., M.S. in Agr., M.L.D. or M.F.] the candidate must have had training equivalent to that required for the *corresponding* first degree at Cornell University.

(b) The candidate must have had such training in each of the major and minor subjects, and in essentially related fields,' as will prepare him to undertake graduate work in these subjects.

The candidate should first present evidence to the Dean of the Graduate School that requirement (a) has been met.

After consultation with those in charge of the work which he desires to undertake, he should then select his major and minor subjects and obtain the endorsement of the professors concerned.

Candidacy for the degree will date from the time when this application, duly endorsed, has been filed in the office of the Dean of the Graduate School.

M r. Luther Campbell Lindsley has met the general requirements for admission to candidacy for the degree of Master of Arts, Doctor of Philosophy or Doctor of Philosophy

Date October 1919   *J. E. Creighton* Dean.

The undersigned hereby makes application for admission to candidacy for the degree of

Doctor of Philosophy with the following major and minor subjects:

Major subject Inorganic Chemistry

First Minor Subject Organic Chemistry

Second Minor Subject (For the Master's degree only one minor is required) Agricultural Chemistry

Date 10/1/19   Name *Luther Campbell Lindsley*

Approved by* *M. D. Ennis* Representing the major.

W. R. Orndorff Representing the first minor.

Geo. W. Cavanaugh Representing the second minor.

For the purpose of general supervision, the work of each candidate for an advanced degree is in charge of a committee constituted by members of the Faculty representing the major and minor subjects of study. The member of the committee who represents the major subject is chairman.

Endorsement of this application indicates: (1) that the endorser approves of the proposed selection of major and minor subjects; (2) that the candidate is qualified by previous study or experience to undertake such advanced work in the subject represented by the endorser as is demanded by the requirements of the degree.

8329

CORNELL UNIVERSITY
THE GRADUATE SCHOOL

TO THE DEAN OF THE GRADUATE SCHOOL:

The undersigned, constituting the special committee in charge of the

work of MR. *Luther C. Lindsley*

a candidate for the degree of Doctor of Philosophy, recommend that he

be allowed residence credit to the extent of...*1*...terms because of his work

as a graduate student, candidate for the degree of *Ph. D. M. A.*

Sept. 1907–Feb. 1908 at *College of William + Mary*

Signed *M. Ennis* ....Chairman

June 1, 1921

E. M. Ernest } Representing
Geo. W. Cavanaugh } the minor
subjects

The Faculty rules regarding the granting of residence credit are as
follows:

Time spent in study for the Master's degree may be counted as residence for the
Doctor's degree, provided the special committee approves, certifying the work done as
suitable for such doctor's degree.

Resident graduate work elsewhere may be accepted in place of residence here upon
recommendation of those members of the student's special committee who would naturally have charge of the same work here. Provided, however, that graduate work elsewhere, in order to be accepted toward residence here, must have been done after the
student was prepared to meet our requirements for admission to candidacy.

Work done elsewhere will not be accepted toward our residence requirement unless
done while the candidate was a registered graduate student in residence at a college of
satisfactory standing. In other words, work done *in absentia*, however satisfactory it
may be in character, is not allowed to reduce the minimum amount of residence work
required for an advanced degree.

Residence for work carried on here by a candidate who is at the same time an instructor or an assistant is estimated on the basis of a four years' minimum residence
for the Doctor's degree; in other words, one academic year counts one term and a half
toward meeting the residence requirement.

CORNELL UNIVERSITY
THE GRADUATE SCHOOL

Report Regarding Language Requirement
for the
Degree of Doctor of Philosophy

This statement is to be filed at the office of the Dean of the Graduate School not later than the beginning of the second year of residence.

M . *L. C. Lindsley* .... has demonstrated to the satisfaction of his Special Committee that he has a reading knowledge of French and German.

.... *Chairman*

Fred H. Rhodes

Geo. W Cavanaugh } Representing the minor subjects

Date **Nov. 26, 1921**

    The Faculty rule in regard to the modern language requirement for the degree of Doctor of Philosophy is as follows:

    ''Candidates for the doctor's degree will ordinarily be expected to have a working knowledge of French and German before beginning graduate work; and in all cases they must, before beginning their second year of residence, show to the satisfaction of their special committees that they possess a reading knowledge of those languages. If the subjects chosen by the candidate are of such character as to make it desirable that he should be familiar with some foreign language other than French or German, the special committee may, with the consent of the Dean, permit the substitution of that language for one of the two required.''

CORNELL UNIVERSITY

DEPARTMENT OF CHEMISTRY

F. H. RHODES
PROFESSOR OF
INDUSTRIAL CHEMISTRY
ITHACA, N.Y.

Dec 6, 1921

Prof. J. E. Creighton,
Dean of Graduate School,
Cornell University.

Dear Sir:

Enclosed please find the "Report Regarding Language Requirement for the Degree of Doctor of Philosophy" of Mr. L.C. Lindsley, a graduate student in the Department of Chemistry. The special committee of Mr. Lindsley is composed of Professor Dennis, representing the major subject, and Professors Cavanaugh and Chamot, representing the minor subjects. It so happens that both Professor Cavanaugh and Professor Chamot are now absent on leave and are therefore unable to sign this report. Mr. Lindsley requests that Professor Rhodes be appointed temporarily as the Professor in charge of his first minor, thus taking the place of Professor Chamot while Professor Chamot is absent.

This arrangement has been suggested by the Office of the Graduate School and Mr. Lindsley has been informed by that Office that in view of the fact that the absences of both Professor Chamot and Professor Cavanaugh are merely temporary, it will be satisfactory for Professor Rhodes to sign this report and that a third signature will not now be required. This third signature can be placed on this report when the absent members of the committee return to the University.

Very truly yours,

FHR: P   L.C. Lindsley (signature)

P. S.

I was fortunate to locate Prof. Cavanaugh and secure his signature.
(handwritten)

THE GRADUATE SCHOOL
CORNELL UNIVERSITY
ITHACA, NEW YORK

OFFICE OF THE DEAN

December 10, 1921

Mr. L.C.Lindsley
Cornell University.

My dear Mr. Lindsley:

      I notice from your letter of December 6, 1921,
that you have mentioned Professor Chamot as being a member of
your Special Committee. According to the records in our office
your first minor subject of Organic Chemistry with Professor
Orndorff has never been changed. If you wish such a change
made, please notify us, and ask Professor Rhodes to approve
this change in Professor Chamot's absence.

                Yours very truly,

                       Secretary.

Office of Graduate School
Ithaca N.Y.

According to your letter the change on Committee
from Prof Orndorff to Prof Chamot, made two years
ago, has not been recorded on your books.
This is to officially notify you in writing
that this change was made and is approved
by Prof Rhodes, acting for Prof Chamot
              Yours truly,
                L C Lindsley

Approved
F. H. Rhodes-

"Some New Double Selenates"

The above is the title of the thesis to be offered by L C Lindsley to the faculty of Graduate School of Cornell Univ. for degree of Dr of Philosophy.

Approved
[signature]

February 6, 1922.

Mr. L.C. Lindsley
104 Maple Street
Ithaca, N.Y.

Dear Sir:

In reply to your inquiry of February 2nd, 1922, I can report to you that the minimum residence requirement for the Ph.D. degree has now been met by you, as well as all of the other requirements set down in our legislation as precedent to the candidate's appearance for examination.

As soon as your thesis is accepted by the Committee and presented at this office, a date can be set for your examination at any time that is convenient for the members of the Committee and yourself.

Congratulating you on the completion of these requirements, I am, with regards,

Very truly yours,

JEC/DEO

CORNELL UNIVERSITY
THE GRADUATE SCHOOL

EXAMINATION REPORT
Send to the office of the Dean of the Graduate School

TO THE DEAN OF THE GRADUATE SCHOOL :

On June 5 1922 Mr. Luther Campbell Lindsley was examined on his major and minor subjects and the subject matter of his thesis and is recommended by the undersigned members of the examining committee for the degree of Doctor of Philosophy.

Chairman.

E. M. Chamot

Geo. W. Cavanaugh
Representing the Minor Subjects.

Williamsburg, Virginia.
November 5,1925.

Registrar of Cornell University
Ithaca, New York.

Dear Sir,

   Kindly mail me another certificate stating that
I hold the Ph.D degree. Also please mail me a record of the
courses I took in Chemistry.

    Yours truly,

     R. C. Lindsley

   * * *

In a handwritten letter to the dean of the graduate school of

Cornell, Luther gave his mailing address as only "Williamsburg, Virginia," and asked that his degree be mailed to him there.

To the Faculty of the Graduate School:

Having completed all requirements for the degree of Doctor of Philosophy except the publication of my thesis, I request that the degree be conferred upon me before the thesis appears in its published form. I hereby promise and undertake to publish my thesis as soon as possible and in any case within two years of this date, and to furnish a hundred printed copies in due form to the Dean of the Graduate School.

(Signed)

L. C. Lindsley

(Date)

June 5th, 1922

Williamsburg, Virginia.
November 5, 1925.

Registrar of Cornell University
Ithaca, New York.

Dear Sir,

Kindly mail me andther certificate stating that I hold the Ph.D degree. Also please mail me a record of the courses I took in Chemistry.

Yours truly,

L. C. Lindsley

November 12th, 1925

    THIS IS TO CERTIFY THAT Mr. Luther Campbell Lindsley received the degree of Doctor of Philosophy in Cornell University in June, 1922.

Secretary of the Graduate School
Cornell University

November 12th, 1925

    THIS IS TO CERTIFY THAT Mr. Luther Campbell Lindsley, B.A.(William and Mary) 1908, Ph.D.(Cornell) 1922, has the following record in the office of the Registrar:

	1919-1920	First Term		Second Term	
Chemistry	46	2 hrs.	G		
"	65			2 hrs.	B
	1920-1921				
"	66	2 hrs.	G		
"	51	3 hrs.	D	3 hrs.	78
"	72			2 hrs.	A
	1921-1922				
"	Research		G		
Geology	12		G		
"	11		G		

Secretary of the Graduate School
Cornell University

APPENDIX VI

TECHNICAL PUBLICATIONS AT CORNELL

This technical article was published in the *Journal of the American Chemical Society*, Volume 47, 1925, pages 377-379.

It was also summarized in *Chemical Abstracts*, Volume 19, 1925, page 941.

[CONTRIBUTION FROM THE DEPARTMENT OF CHEMISTRY, CORNELL UNIVERSITY]

SOME DOUBLE SELENATES OF THALLOUS SELENATE AND THE SELENATES OF BIVALENT METALS

BY L. C. LINDSLEY AND L. M. DENNIS

RECEIVED NOVEMBER 28, 1924   PUBLISHED FEBRUARY 5, 1925

An exhaustive study of the double sulfates and double selenates of the type $R_2M(SO_4)_2.6H_2O$ and $R_2M(SeO_4)_2.6H_2O$, where R is potassium, rubidium or cesium and M is magnesium, zinc, iron, cobalt, nickel, copper, manganese or cadmium, has been made by Tutton.[1] Of the series $Tl_2SeO_4.R''SeO_4.6H_2O$, Tutton studied only one—$Tl_2SeO_4.ZnSeO_4.6H_2O$. Five new compounds of this type are described below.

The conditions most favorable to the formation of each double salt were first studied under the microscope and the relative amounts of the two salts, the concentration and the temperature thus indicated were then followed on a larger scale.

Thallous Copper Selenate, $Tl_2SeO_4.CuSeO_4.6H_2O$.—This compound crystallizes best from a solution containing an excess of copper selenate in the proportion of 8 g. of the copper salt to 3 g. of thallous selenate. The light blue crystals were finely ground and then air-dried between filter papers.

ANALYSIS.—Water of crystallization was determined by heating a weighed sample to constant weight at 105°. Copper, thallium and selenium were determined in a single sample by dissolving the substance in water, adding a few drops of acetic acid,

---

[1] Tutton, *J. Chem. Soc.*, **69**, 344, 495, 507 (1896).

and then an excess of a solution of potassium iodide, which precipitates thallous iodide and cuprous iodide. The precipitate was collected on a filter and the amount of copper in the salt was ascertained by titration of the free iodine in the filtrate with sodium thiosulfate solution. This solution, which contained most of the selenium, was preserved. The mixture of thallous iodide and cuprous iodide was treated with ammonium hydroxide which dissolved the copper salt. The filtrate and washings were added to the first filtrate and the selenium was precipitated by hydrazine hydrate.[2] The thallous iodide was collected in a Gooch crucible, dried at 120° and weighed. The method was first tested with solutions containing known amounts of thallous selenate and cupric selenate and was found to give results that were sufficiently accurate for the purpose in view.

Anal. Calcd. for $Tl_2SeO_4 \cdot CuSeO_4 \cdot 6H_2O$: Tl, 47.11; Se, 18.28; Cu, 7.34; H_2O, 12.48. Found: Cu, 47.10, 47.20; Se, 18.26, 18.20; Cu, 7.30, 7.285; H_2O, 12.80, 12.82.

Thallous Cobalt Selenate, $Tl_2SeO_4 \cdot CoSeO_4 \cdot 6H_2O$.—The method of preparation was essentially the same as that for the copper salt.

In the analysis, two slightly different methods were used. With one sample, the thallium was first precipitated with potassium iodide, the cobalt in the filtrate with sodium carbonate and the selenium in the final filtrate with hydrazine hydrate. With the second sample, the cobalt was first precipitated with sodium carbonate, the precipitate was washed with hot water until free from thallium, the thallium then precipitated as the iodide, and the selenium as before with hydrazine hydrate.

Anal. Calcd. for $TlSeO_4 \cdot CoSeO_4 \cdot 6H_2O$; Tl, 47.36; Se, 18.38; CO, 6.84; H_2O, 12.54. Found: Tl, 47.497, 47.305; Se, 18.30, 18.33; CO, 6.93, 6.96; H_2O, 12.66, 12.58.

Thallous Nickel Selenate, $Tl_2SeO_4 \cdot NiSeO_4 \cdot 6H_2O$.—This compound required a higher temperature, 120°, for its dehydration than either of the preceding salts. The anhydrous compound is yellow.

The analysis was made by the first method described under the cobalt salt.

Anal. Calcd. for $TlSeO_4 \cdot NiSeO_4 \cdot 6H_2O$; Tl, 47.37; Se, 18.39; Ni, 6.81; H_2O, 12.55. Found: Tl, 47.47, 47.30; Se, 18.34, 18.30; Ni 6.72, 6.76; H_2O, 12.51, 12.60.

Thallous Magnesium Selenate, $Tl_2SeO_4 \cdot MgSeO_4 \cdot 6H_2O$.—The salt was heated at 125° to expel water of crystallization.

Magnesium was determined as the pyrophosphate, the thallium and selenium as with the nickel salt.

Anal. Calcd. for $TlSeO_4 \cdot MgSeO_4 \cdot 6H_2O$; Tl, 49.34; Se, 19.15; Mg, 2.94; H_2O, 13.07. Found: Tl, 49.40, 49.21; Se, 19.20, 19.22; Mg, 2.90, 2.86; H_2O, 13.05, 13.07.

Thallous Manganese Selenate, $TlSeO_4 \cdot MnSeO_4 \cdot 6H_2O$.—In the analysis, manganese was precipitated as ammonium manganous phosphate and was weighed as manganese pyrophosphate.

Anal. Calcd. for $TlSeO_4 \cdot MnSeO_4 \cdot 6H_2O$: Tl, 47.58; Se, 18.47; Mn, 6.41; H_2O, 12.60. Found: Tl, 47.51, 47.30; Se, 18.38, 18.58; Mn, 6.54, 6.34; H_2O, 12.80, 12.70.

Crystal Forms and Angles of the Thallous Double Selenates

The crystal system of the salts above described is uniformly monoclinic, and the crystal class is prismatic. The crystals are highly refractive.

Tutton states that the differences in the angles of isomorphous com-

---

[2] Dennis and Koller, THIS JOURNAL, **41**, 951 (1919).

pounds should not be over two degrees. Two angles of each of the new salts were measured and the results, together with those of Werther[3] on the double sulfates, and of Tutton on the thallous zinc selenate, follow:

DOUBLE SULFATES $R'SO_4.TlSO_4.6H_2O$			DOUBLE SELENATES $R'SeO_4.TlSeO_4.6H_2O$		
	Angles			Angles	
R'	70°+	109°+	R'	71°+	108°+
Fe	38'	24'	Zn	32'	28'
Zn	48'	12'	Mn	17'	48'
Ni	54'	6'	Cu	50'	54'
Mg	54'	6'	Mg	35'	25'
			Co	28'	26'
			Ni	34'	26'

The substitution of selenium for sulfur in these double salts causes an increase of about 40' in the acute angles and a corresponding decrease in the obtuse angles.

Summary

New double selenates of thallous selenate and the selenates of copper, cobalt, nickel, magnesium and manganese are described, together with confirmatory analyses. Composition and crystal measurements show that the compounds are directly analogous to the corresponding double sulfates.

ITHACA, NEW YORK

APPENDIX VII

DOCTORAL DISSERTATION

The dissertation turned in for his degree was different somewhat from the one he eventually published as a pamphlet. This is the dissertation he submitted to the committee:

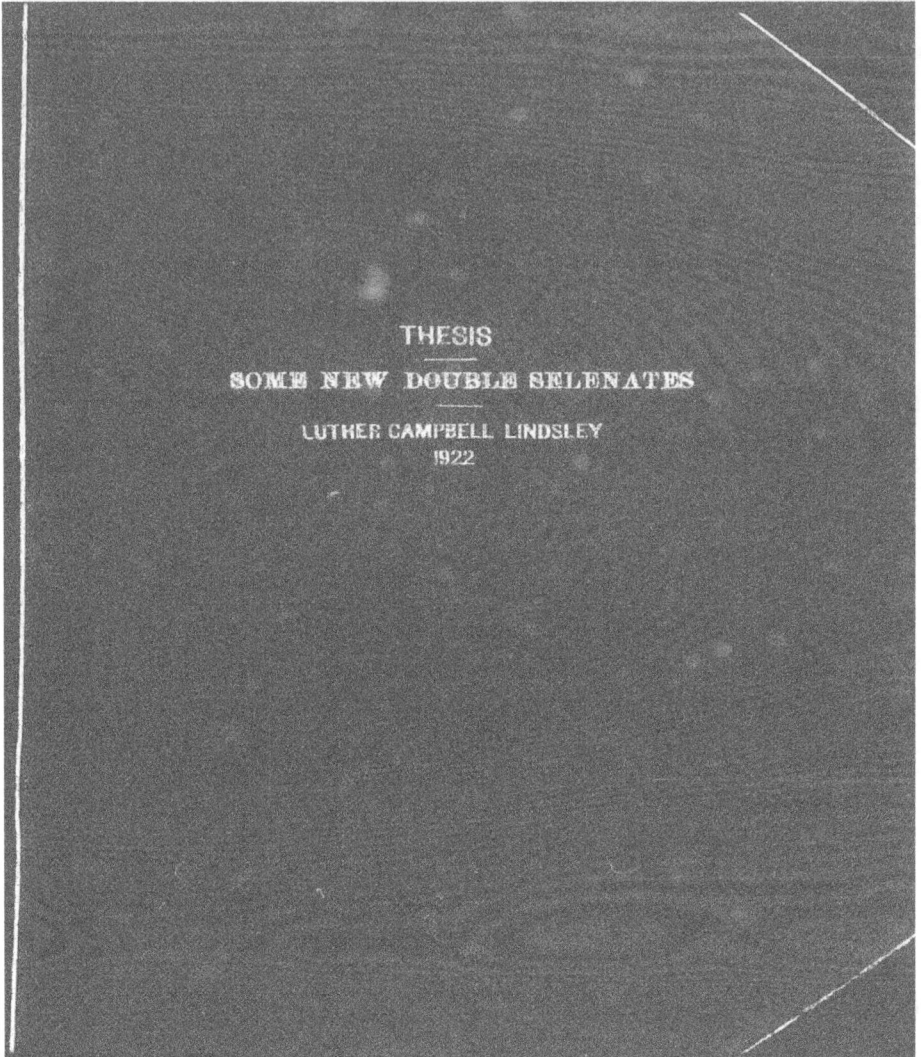

THESIS

SOME NEW DOUBLE SELENATES

LUTHER CAMPBELL LINDSLEY
1922

SOME NEW DOUBLE SELENATES

A THESIS

Presented to the Faculty of the Graduate
School of Cornell University for the degree of

DOCTOR OF PHILOSOPHY

by

LUTHER CAMPBELL LINDSLEY

March, 1922.

H

ACKNOWLEDGMENT
_____

This investigation was suggested by Professor L.M.Dennis, and the work was carried out under his supervision. The writer desires here to express his appreciation of the kindly criticisms and helpful suggestions offered by him from time to time as the work progressed. For these, for the deep interest he has shown and the inspiration he has been, the author is indeed grateful.

The writer also wishes to express his appreciation to Professor A.C.Gill, who has given many helpful suggestions and much of his time.

INDEX

HISTORICAL

In 1832, fifteen years after the discovery by Berzelius of selenium, Mitscherlich clearly established
the fact that selenates were isomorphous with the sulphates. In 1858 some measurements were made by Murmann
and Rotter on two double salts, potassium magnesium sulphate, and ammonium magnesium sulphate. Two years later
Emil Wohlwill[1] prepared and studied some mixed sulphates
and selenates but made no measurements. He gave these
salts the following formulas:-

$$3MgSO_4.CuSeO_4.28H_2O$$
$$3FeSO_4.CuSeO_4.35H_2O$$
$$2FeSO_4.NiSeO_4.21H_2O$$
$$3ZnSO_4.CuSeO_4.28H_2O$$

He also prepared the chromium, potassium, sodium, and
ammonium alums of selenic acid. From his results it appeared probable that selenic acid could be substituted
for sulphuric acid in the entire series of the alums.

In 1861 William Crookes discovered the new element,
thallium, in the residues left in the purification of
crude selenium obtained from ten pounds of seleniferous
deposit from the sulphuric acid factory at Tilkerode, in
the Hartz mountains.[2] His discovery was followed in a few

1. Ann.der Chemie und Pharmacy, 114, p.180, (1860)
2. Chem.News, 3 , p.193, (1861)

months by the independent discovery of the same element by M.Lamy, a Belgian chemist,who officially announced his discovery to the Imperial Society of Lille on the sixteenth of May,1862. On the tenth of June he placed an ingot of thallium on exhibit in the International Exhibition, and received a medal for the discovery of new and large sources of thallium. The judges also awarded Crookes a medal for the discovery of the element.

A number of compounds were made in the laboratories of Mr.Crookes and of M.Lamy. From the reactions of thallium with hydrochloric acid, potassium iodide, potassium dichromate, and ammonium sulphide, Crookes believed the new element should be placed with silver and lead. M.Lamy believed from certain experiments made in his labratory that it should be placed among the alkalies.

The differences of opinion regarding the position of thallium caused H.Werther[1] to prepare the double sulphates of thallium with iron, magnesium, nickel and zinc. He showed by drawings of the crystals obtained, and by measurements of some of the angles, that these four double sulphates with six molecules of water of crystallization were isomorphous with those of ammonium and po-

---

1. Journal für praktische Chemie,92, p. 128, (1864)

tassium. He found the crystals of thallous ferrous
selenate very hard to prepare, and when prepared they
were not very satisfactory. In all of the salts mentioned, he found that the substitution of thallium
for potassium caused the crystals to appear cloudy.

A large amount of work has been done upon the
double sulphates and also the double selenates by
A.E.H.Tutton. The work has covered a period of over
twenty years, and was begun in the year 1890.

In 1893 appeared his first memoir.This included the results of three years work done upon the
goniometrical investigations of twenty-two salts of
the series, $R_2M(SeO_4)_2.6H_2O$, where R is potassium,
rubidium or caesium, and M is magnesium, zinc, iron,
nickel, cobalt, copper,manganese or cadmium. This
work was completed in 1896. The number of salts described would have been twenty-four had he been able
to prepare potassium cadmium sulphate and potassium
manganese sulphate.

Tutton later considered it advisable to bring
the double selenates into the scope of his investigation. The six corresponding double selenates containing the same three alkali metals, with zinc and
magnesium respectively as the dyad M metal, were

1.Journal Chem.Soc., _69_ ,495, (1896)

4

studied goniometrically and physically.[1] Four years
later he completed the investigation of the two ammonium salts, ammonium magnesium sulphate and ammonium zinc sulphate. The two selenates corresponding to these were also completely studied.[2] Since
then, two typical thallium salts of the series, thallous zinc sulphate and selenate were investigated in
detail by Tutton[3] and he found that the ammonium and
thallous double salts crystallize in habits closely
resembling the rubidium salts. The optic axial angles
of the ammonium salts are almost equal to those of the
caesium salts, and the optic axial angle of the thallium double sulphate lies between the optic axial angles of the corresponding potassium and rubidium compounds. The axial ratios of the thallous salts entitle them to be placed in the same isomorphous series
with the analogous salts of the alkali metals, potassium, rubidium and caesium. The molecular distance
ratios of the thallous selenate and sulphate are almost identical with those of the rubidium salts, which
gives further evidence of isomorphism. However, the
thallous salts show very high refractive indices compared with the potassium and rubidium, and the double
refraction is not only greater in the thallous double
salts but is opposite in sign, being negative.

1. Proc.Roy.Soc., 66, p.248 (1900) & 67, p.58, (1900)
2. Journal Chem.Soc., 87, p. 1123, (1905)
3. Proc.Royal Soc., 83A, p. 216, (1910)

The substitution of thallium for potassium causes the
optical ellipsoid to rotate backwards, and its substitution in the double selenate $(ZnSeO_4.Tl_2SeO_4.6H_2O)$
causes almost complete opacity.

Since only one double selenate of thallium and
a divalent metal, namely the thallous zinc selenate,
hexahydrate, has been prepared and described in the
literature, it occurred to us that by preparing others,
the isomorphism of these compounds would be more clearly
established.

6

The Preparation of Thallous Copper Selenate

$$(Tl_2SeO_4.CuSeO_4.6H_2O)$$

For preliminary work on a problem of this kind a polarizing microscope is very valuable. With this instrument it is possible to see and study many phases which would ordinarily escape observation. With practice one can often determine what compounds are crystallizing from solution.

Fortunately a supply of both copper and thallous selenate was available in the labratory at the time this investigation was begun. A fragment of copper selenate was dissolved in a drop of water on a glass slide and warmed gently. The crystals separating on the outer edge of the drop were crushed toward the center, and the preparation was then placed under the microscope. The crystallization was observed under a sixteen millimeter objective. A similar study was made of thallous selenate, and then a mixture of the two selenates. From this last solution three kinds of crystals appeared. The rhombic, bipyramidal thallous selenate precipitated first, followed by crystals light blue in color and different from those of the single salts previously studied. As the drop approached dryness the copper selenate crystallized. The light crystals were monoclinic, were very

cloudy in appearance, and resembled the crystals of
nickel thallous selenate described by Werther in 1864.
If these crystals were those of the double salt, then
the microscope had shown the possibility of preparing
the new compound, and had pointed out one difficulty
in the way of its preparation would be the low solubility of thallous selenate. At 12^0 this is 2.4 grams in
100 of water.

After several attempts to prepare the double salt
in quantity, it was found that it crystallizes best from
a solution in which the concentration of the copper selenate is from .11 to .12 grams per cubic centimeter, and
the thallium selenate .0422 grams. At higher concentrations larger yields can be obtained but the crystals
will not be so perfectly developed.

Four grams of copper selenate was dissolved in 36cc.
of water. Then 1.52 grams of thallous selenate was added
and the solution was warmed to 85^0. After slow cooling in
a Dewar flask until a temperature of 20^0 was reached, a
crop of very good crystals was obtained. The yield was
1.1250 grams. The volume of the solution had been reduced
to 30cc. by evaporation, and, although .409 grams of the
copper selenate had been removed from the solution in

the formation of the double salt, the concentration
was slightly higher than at the beginning by .0086
grams per cc. By adding just enough thallous selenate
to this mother liquor to make the concentration of the
thallous salt equal to its original concentration of
.0422 grams in every cubic centimeter, a second crop of
crystals was obtained. By careful control this process
can be repeated until only a small amount of mother liquor remains.

One can determine what is the best concentration
to use by making an analysis of the mother liquor at the
time the best crystals begin to appear.

The Determination of Thallium

The ease with which thallium passes from one degree of oxidation to another gives the means of determining the metal volumetrically by potassium permanganate. This method was used by E.Willm. The same
property of thallium is the basis of a method employed
by Hugh Marshall.[1] He heated a weighed quantity of a
thallous salt with hydrochloric acid and a measured volume of standard solution of potassium bromate or sodium bromate, more than sufficient to convert all of
the thallium into thallic salt. He distilled off the residual bromine into potassium iodide solution and titrated the liberated iodine with standard sodium thiosulphate. A third method in which bromine is used for
the oxidation of thallium and the excess of bromine is
titrated with potassium iodide, is described by Sponholz.[2]
A simpler method was employed by R.Nietzki.[3] He titrated
the thallium with a standard potassium iodide solution,
and found that very accurate determinations could be made,
provided the thallium present was in excess of 0.5 percent,
and was in the thallous condition.

1. Journal Soc.Chem.Ind., 19, p.994, (1900)
2. Z. Anal.Chem.,   31 , p. 519 , (1892)
3. Z. Anal.Chem.,   16 , p. 472,   (1877)

10

Carstanjen found the gravimetric determination
of thallium[1] as a sulphate most practicable. The sulphate is very stable, and can be heated for a long time
in a platinum crucible until constant weight is reached.
He also found that under certain conditions accurate results could be obtained by weighing it as a chromate.

A method for the quantitive estimation of thallium
has been developed by V.Thomas[2]. The thallium is converted to thallous chloride, and auric bromide is added to
the hot solution as long as metallic gold is precipitated. The gold is collected on a filter and weighed. Two
atoms of gold correspond to three atoms of thallium.

Thallium can be determined gravimetrically as the
chlorplatinate, which is soluble one part in 15,585 parts
of water at 15°. It can also be determined as the sulphostannate. This method was developed by Hawley[3], at
Cornell University, and is very accurate. The electrolytic
process described by Neuman is too tedious to use when
many determinations are to be made. Werther[4] found that
weighing it as an iodide is very satisfactory.

---

1. Journal für praktische Chemie, 102 , p.88 (1867)
2. Comptes Rend. 130 , p. 1316
3. Journal Am.Chem.Soc., 29 , p.1011,(1907)
4. Journal für praktische Chemie, 92, p137,(1864)

A sample of thallous selenate weighing .5213 grams
was dissolved in warm water, and the thallium was precipitated by the addition of an excess of potassium iodide. A few cubic centimeters of acetic acid had been
added to make the precipitated thallous iodide less soluble. It was then filtered into a weighed Gooch crucible,
dried in the oven at a temperature of 105° to constant
weight, and the weight recorded. The amount of thallium
calculated as the iodide from the original sample was
.6255 grams. The weight of thallium iodide obtained was
.6251 grams.

The selenium in the filtrate from the precipitation
of the thallium as thallous iodide was determined by hydrazine hydrate. Gutbier[1] and Meyer[2] prefer this method.
Jannasch and Muller[3] use hydrazine sulphate to reduce selenious acid to selenium and obtain very good results.
Gooch and Scoville boil selenic acid with hydrobromic, pass
the liberated bromine into potassium iodide solution and
titrate the liberated iodine. When hydrazine hydrate is
used as a reducing agent no preliminary reduction of the
selenic acid to selenious acid is necessary.

1. Z. anorg. Chem., 41 , p.291, (1904)
2. Z. anal. Chem., 53 ,p.145, (1914)
3. Ber., 31 , p. 2393, (1898)

12

The calculated amount of selenium in .5213 grams of
thallous selenate is .07487 grams. The selenium found
by experiment was .0748 grams. In the determination of
selenium by hydrazine compounds no ions of metals
should be present, for these also may be reduced to the
metallic state and will interfere in the weighing of
selenium.

The Determination of Copper in the Presence
of Thallium and Selenium.

1

A solution containing known weights of copper and
thallous selenates was prepared. The copper was precipitated by hydrogen sulphide. The precipitation of the
thallous sulphide was prevented by the addition of 15cc.
of sulphuric acid. The copper sulphide formed was dissolved in nitric acid, and evaporated to dryness. The
residue was redissolved in water and diluted to 100cc.
This was slightly acidified with nitric acid and the
copper determined electrolytically. A rotating copper
gauze cathode was employed and a platinum flag anode.
A current of 1.5 amperes was used for an hour, and at
the end of that time a slight yellow coating appeared
on the anode, and the solution gave no test for copper.
The results showed too large an amount of copper, and a
later determination of the thallium from the filtrate
after the removal of the copper sulphide, showed a loss
in the thallium. Evidently a part of the thallium was
precipitated with the copper sulphide, was deposited on
the cathode with the copper, and on the anode as thallium
peroxide.　　The results follow:

14

$CuSeO_4.5H_2O$	Copper found	Calculated
1. .4135 grams	.0980 grams	.0875 grams
2. .4611 "	.1189 "	.0974 "

Tl_2SeO_4	Thallium found as iodide	Calculated
1. .5625 grams	.6610 grams	.6705 grams
2. .3119 "	.3400 "	.3743 "

	Selenium found	Calculated
1.	.1920	.1913
2.	.1668	.1679

2.

The low solubility of thallous iodide in ammonium hydroxide offers a means for the quantitive separation of copper from thallium, for the cuprous iodide is readily soluble. Potassium iodide precipitates thallium as thallous iodide, and the copper as cuprous iodide according to the following equations:

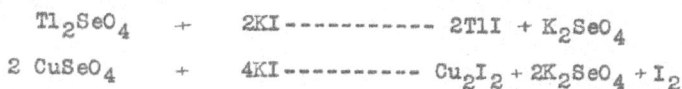

$$Tl_2SeO_4 \quad + \quad 2KI \text{----------} 2TlI + K_2SeO_4$$
$$2\,CuSeO_4 \quad + \quad 4KI \text{----------} Cu_2I_2 + 2K_2SeO_4 + I_2$$

The amount of free iodine can be titrated with sodium thiosulphate, and from this the copper can be calculated. To find how accurately thallium can be determined from an ammoniacal solution .6251 grams of thallous iodide was washed with 200cc. of fifty percent ammonium hydroxide. The loss in weight of the thallous iodide was only .0008 grams.

A determination of both copper and thallium was then
made in a solution containing .2956 grams of copper
selenate and .4130 grams of thallium selenate.

The two salts were dissolved in 50cc. of warm water,
a few drops of acetic acid was added and then both the
copper and thallium were precipitated with an excess of
potassium iodide. The liberated iodine was titrated with
standard thiosulphate solution, using starch as an indicator. Both iodides were filtered into a weighed Gooch
crucible and the cuprous iodide removed with ammonia until no trace of copper remained. The thallium iodide was
dried at 104° to constant weight.

	Found	Calculated
Copper	.0629	.0617
Thallium Iodide	.4959	.4969

The thiosulphate must be added very slowly, and the
flask shaken after each addition. The starch as andi-
cator gives an adequately sharp end point if care is
used. After the blue color has disappeared it is best
to allow the solution to stand for a few minutes to be
sure the reaction is complete; and to be certain of accurate results the concentration of the thiosulphate
solution used in the titration must be small, so that
the last drop added will not give too great an error in
the calculation of the copper.

16

This method has the following advantages:

1. It removes any free iodine from the solution so that later it will not interfere with the weighing of the selenium.

2. The ammoniacal copper solution can be worked back for the redetermination of the copper.

3. The thallium, after the dissolving of the cuprous iodide,can be immediately weighed,when dried, as thallous iodide.

4. The thallous iodide in ammonium hydroxide is almost completely insoluble.

The Analysis of Copper Thallous Selenate

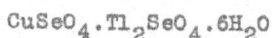

$$CuSeO_4 . Tl_2SeO_4 . 6H_2O$$

Using the methods previously described, and whose
accuracy had been tested on known quantities of material,
a complete analysis was made of the light blue salt believed to be the double selenate.

The Determination of Water of Crystallization

A small quantity of the salt was first finely ground
in a mortar and was then dried between filter papers to
remove any adhering moisture. Two samples were taken.
After heating for seven hours at a temperature of 100°
constant weight had not been reached . The temperature
was then raised to 105° for about one hour longer, and
the weight became constant. The loss was .586 grams. The
smaller sample was heated for five hours at 100° and for
one hour at 105° before reaching constant weight. Its
loss was .138 grams.

	Weight of sample	loss	% loss	Av.% H_2O
1.	4.5740 grams	.586	12.84	
2.	1.0750 "	.138	12.80	12.82

18

The Determination of Copper & Thallium

A sample of the salt was dissolved in warm water.
A few drops of acetic acid was added, and then an excess
of potassium iodide. The precipitate contained both thall-
lous and cuprous iodides. The iodine which had been oxidized in the reduction of the copper to the cuprous condition was titrated with standard thiosulphate solution,
each cubic centimeter of which contained .01275 grams.
Starch was used as an indicator. In the titration, 11.5cc
of the standard solution of thiosulphate was used, which
corresponds to .0594 grams of copper. This was equivalent
to 7.3 % of the original sample.

The copper and thallium iodides were then filtered
together into a weighed Gooch crucible, and the filtrate
containing the potassium selenate was set aside for the
later determination of selenium. The mixture of iodides
in the Gooch crucible was washed with ammonium hydroxide
until the filtrate gave no reaction for copper with
ammonium mercuric sulphocyanate. The thallous iodide remaining was washed with water, dried to constant weight
at a temperature of 120° and a weight of .6204 grams recorded.

The selenium was determined as before with hy-

drazine hydrate. The method as developed by Dennis
and Koller[1] is essentially as follows:

The solution containing selenium is diluted to about
125 cc. Then about 10cc of a 90% solution of hydrazine
hydrate is added and the solution warmed to 60°. Concentrated hydrochloric acid is added carefully until
there is a slight excess of acid. If the liquid is kept
just below the boiling point for two hours the selenium coagulates, and on cooling will settle to the bottom.
It is then collected into a weighed Gooch crucible, dried
at 105° and weighed.

The following are the results of the complete analysis of two samples of the double salt.

	Calculated	(1)	(2)	Av.
Copper	7.341	7.27	7.30	7.285
Thallium	47.105	47.30	47.00	47.150
SeO_4	33.084	32.80	33.03	32.915
H_2O	12.470	12.84	12.80	12.820
Total	100.0000	100.21	100.13	100.170

The formula for the salt calculated on the basis of
the above figures is:

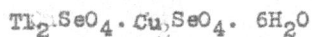

$$Tl_2SeO_4 . Cu_2SeO_4 . 6H_2O$$

---

1. Journal of American Chem.Soc., **41**, p.951 (1919)

20

The Preparation of Thallous Cobalt Selenate
$$(Tl_2SeO_4.CoSeO_4.6\ H_2O)$$

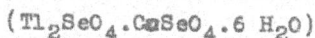

Thirty cubic centimeters of selenic acid was
placed in a porcelain evaporating dish and diluted
to 200cc. Cobalt carbonate was added in small amounts
until there was an excess of the cobalt carbonate
after the mixture had stood over night. The solution
was then filtered, and evaporated on a water-bath until
very concentrated. When the solution cooled to room
temperature a large crop of crystals of cobalt selenate
separated. These were dissolved in water and recrystallized.

A fragment of cobalt selenate and a smaller one
of the thallous selenate were dissolved in a drop of
water on a glass slide and warmed gently. As the solution became more concentrated numerous crystals appeared. These were examined under the microscope in
the same manner as the copper had previously been.
Some seemed to be isomorphous with the thallous nickel
sulphate prepared by Werther. Some crystals of thallous
selenate were also present and had crystallized first,
indicating that a high concentration of the thallous
selenate must be avoided in the preparation of the new
salt.

21

The method used for the preparation of thallous cobalt selenate hexahydrate in quantity was essentially the same as that used for the preparation of the corresponding copper salt previously described, and with a few modifications it was used in the preparation of all of the other salts of the series.

The analysis of a sample of the mother liquor, taken at the time that the best crystals were forming, showed that the cobalt double salt crystallizes best from a solution, each cubic centimeter of which contains .09 grams of the cobalt selenate and .045 grams of the thallous selenate.

22

The Analysis of Cobalt Thallous Selenate

The   Determination of Water

A small quantity of crystals of the double salt
was finely powdered in a porcelain mortar and then
pressed between filter papers. From this powder two
samples were taken, were placed in weighed porcelain
crucibles and heated at a temperature of 110° for five
hours until there was no further loss in weight. The
larger sample had lost .1108 grams and the smaller .0983
grams. The percentage of water of crystallization calculated from these losses in weight amounts to 12.49% for
the larger sample and 12.66% for the smaller.

The   Determination of Cobalt

The ease with which cobalt iodide dissolves and
the very low solubility of thallous iodide, give a means
for the quantitive separation of each metal in the presence of the other. The solubility of thallous carbonate,
which at 100° is 27.2 grams in 100 of water also makes
possible their separation by means of fixed alkali carbonates, the cobalt being precipitated in the form of a
peach red, basic carbonate,$Co_8O_5(CO_3)_3$.

A sample of the anhydrous thallous cobalt selenate was dissolved in about 50cc of water. The thallium
was precipitated with potassium iodide, filtered into a
tared Gooch crucible, and dried to constant weight. To
the filtrate containing the cobalt iodide and potassium
selenate an excess of sodium carbonate was added to precipitate the cobalt as the basic carbonate. This was filtered into a weighed Gooch crucible which had previously
been ignited, was dried in the oven, and then ignited.
The Co_3O_4 thus formed was weighed as such, and from this
the percentage of cobalt in the original sample was calculated.

The filtrate from which the cobalt had been removed contained the selenium. This was determined as before with hydrazine hydrate, and from the weight of selenium found the percentage of selenium in the sample
was calculated.

A second sample was treated first with an excess of sodium carbonate which precipitated the cobalt,
and was then heated to 100° to be sure that all of the
thallous carbonate was dissolved. The solution was then
filtered into a tared Gooch crucible which had previously
been heated to redness, and the precipitate was washed
with hot water until the spectroscope showed no green
line of thallium in the wash water.

The precipitate was then dried, ignited and weighed. The percentage of cobalt was found to be 6.96% as compared with 6.93% in the previous determination.

The filtrate contained both thallium and selenium after the removal of the cobalt. This was warmed to keep all of the thallous carbonate in solution, and then the thallium was precipitated with potassium iodide. The precipitate was filtered into a tared Gooch crucible and dried to constant weight. The percentage of thallium found was 47.3 as compared with 47.50 in the first determination.

The selenium found in this sample was determined as before with hydrazine hydrate. The results of the analysis given below show that it makes little difference whether the thallium or cobalt is removed first.

	(1)	(2)	Average	Calculated
Weight	.8870	.7762		
	%	%	%	%
Cobalt	6.930	6.960	6.955	6.850
Thallium	47.497	47.305	47.401	47.360
SeO_4	33.100	33.150	33.125	33.250
H_2O	12.500	12.660	12.580	12.540
	100.027	100.075	100.061	100.000

The formula for the compound when calculated from the average percentage composition is the following:

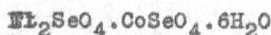

$$Tl_2SeO_4 \cdot CoSeO_4 \cdot 6H_2O$$

25

The Preparation of Thallous Nickel Selenate
$Tl_2SeO_4 \cdot NiSeO_4 \cdot 6H_2O$

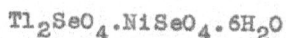

The same kind of preliminary investigation was made with the microscope in the study of this salt as was made in the study of those salts previously prepared. This difference however was noticed and made of use later, namely, that the thallous nickel selenate seemed less soluble, and crystallized out more readily than either the corresponding copper or cobalt salt.

The same general method used in preparing the copper and cobalt double salt was used in preparing thallous nickel selenate. It crystallized best from a solution containing .09--- .11 grams of the nickel selenate and .0465 grams of thallous selenate per cc. This double salt crystallized quite readily, was monoclinic, and except for color, which was light green, could be distinguished from the thallous cobalt selenate only by careful measurements.

The Analysis of Thallous Nickel Selenate

The Determination of Water

The material was finely ground in a mortar
and the powder pressed between filters to remove
adhering moisture. From this material two samples
were weighed. It had been noticed that the cobalt
held its water of crystallization more tenaciously
than did the copper. This tendency is greatest with
the nickel. The two samples were kept in a water
jacketted drying oven for eight hours at a temperature of 100° and there was no appreciable loss in
weight. In an air oven at a temperature of 110° the
loss in weight was very slight, but when the temperature rose to 120° for about an hour the salt
lost its water of crystallization very rapidly. The
larger sample lost .0926 grams and the smaller .0781
grams before constant weight was reached. The anhydrous salt is yellow.

The Determination of Thallium

The anhydrous thallous nickel selenate was dissolved in 50cc. of water. A few drops of acetic acid
was added and the thallium was precipitated with potassium iodide, dried and weighed as thallous iodide.

27

The Determination of Nickel

After the removal of the thallium the nickel
which was in the filtrate was precipitated with sodium carbonate. This was filtered into a tared Gooch
crucible which had been previously ignited, was dried
and then heated to redness to convert the carbonate to
nickel oxide. From this the percentage of nickel in
the original sample was calculated.

The Determination of Selenium

The solution after the removal of the nickel
contains the selenium. This was determined in the
usual way with hydrazine hydrate and hydrochloric acid.

The results of a complete analysis made on two
samples of thallous nickel selenate are as follows:

Weight	(1) .7400 grams	(2) .6195 grams	Average	Calc.
	%	%	%	%
H_2O	12.51	12.60	12.55	12.547
Thallium	47.47	47.30	47.38	47.381
SeO_4	33.20	33.10	33.15	33.267
Nickel	6.72	6.76	6.74	6.805
	99.90	99.76	99.82	100.000

The formula of the new compound was determined
from the average percentage composition and found to be

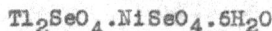

$$Tl_2SeO_4.NiSeO_4.6H_2O$$

28

The Preparation of Thallous Magnesium Selenate
$$Tl_2SeO_4 \cdot MgSeO_4 \cdot 6H_2O$$

The preliminary investigation of the crystallization of this double salt was conducted in the usual
manner with the polarizing microscope. Some thallous
selenate soon crystallized . After the drop became
quite small the double salt appeared. The crystals although slow in forming were the most satisfactory yet
obtained even under the microscope. The higher the solubility of the single salts the slower the double salts
seem to crystallize, but more perfect crystals are obtained.

The study of the double salt with the microscope
had shown that the new double selenate would crystallize
from a more concentrated solution than either the copper or the cobalt. Numerous experiments made in preparing
this salt in quantity showed that it crystallizes best
from a solution containing .160 grams of the magnesium
selenate and .046 grams of the thallous selenate in every cc.

The Analysis of Thallous Magnesium Selenate

The Determination of Water

Some crystals of the new compound were finely
ground in a mortar and dried between filters in the usual way. Two weighed samples of this powder were placed
in porcelain crucibles and subjected to a temperature
of 100° for five hours. The loss in weight was slight.
The temperature was then kept at 115° for two hours
without the weight becoming constant, although the loss
was appreciable. At 120° it lost its water of crystallization very rapidly, and in an hour the weight had
become constant, and an increase of temperature to 138
for thirty minutes failed to decrease the weight further.

The Determination of Thallium

Two samples of the anhydrous salt were each dissolved in about 50cc of water, and the thallium was
precipitated as thallous iodide. The magnesium iodide
formed at the same time is quite soluble, and is found
with the selenium in the filtrate, in the form of magnesium iodide and potassium selenate.

30

The Determination of Magnesium

The magnesium was precipitated from the solution as ammonium magnesium phosphate, by the addition of sodium phosphate and ammonium hydroxide,in the presence of ammonium chloride. The precipitate which formed on standing over night was filtered into a tared Gooch crucible which had been previously ignited, was dried and then heated to redness to convert the ammonium magnesium orthophosphate to $Mg_2P_2O_7$, and it was weighed as such.

The Determination of Selenium

The selenium in the filtrate after the removal of the magnesium was reduced by hydrazine hydrate and hydrochloric acid. After standing over night it was filtered into a tared Gooch crucible, dried to constant weight and weighed. The results of the complete analysis follow:

Weight	(1) .8290	(2) .2295	Average	Calculated
	%	%	%	%
Magnesium	2.900	2.860	2.880	2.950
H_2O	13.050	13.072	13.061	13.060
Tl	49.400	49.300	49.300	49.350
SeO_4	34.720	34.760	34.740	34.640
	100.070	99.892	99.981	100.00

The formula for the unknown salt, calculated from the above percentage composition, is $Tl_2SeO_4 \cdot MgSeO_4 \cdot 6H_2O$

31

The Preparation of Thallous Manganese Selenate
$Tl_2SeO_4 \cdot MnSeO_4 \cdot 6H_2O$

A small fragment of one of the most perfect
crystals of the manganese selenate was dissolved in a
drop of water on a glass slide. A much smaller fragment
of the thallous selenate was then added and the solution slightly warmed. The preparation was then placed
under the microscope and the formation of the crystals
studied. A new salt, white, opaque, and monoclinic in
appearance could be distinguished, mixed with the crystals
of thallous selenate, which had evidently been in excess.
If these crystals were those of the desired compound, there
remained only to find at what concentration of the two
components the double salt would crystallize out. Since
Tutton had found the potassium manganese sulphate incapable of preparation, unusual care was used not only in the
preliminary work with the microscope but also in the preparation of the thallous and manganese salts which were
to be used.

It was found that the new salt crystallizes best
from a solution containing .250 grams of the manganese
selenate and .048 grams of the thallous selenate.

32

The Analysis of Thallous Manganese Selenate

The Determination of Water

A small quantity of the salt was very finely powdered in the porcelain mortar and then pressed between filter papers. From this two samples were taken, placed in porcelain crucibles, weighed, and then kept in a drying oven at a temperature of 100° for three hours. The loss in weight was slight. The temperature was raised gradually to 120° and the salt lost weight rapidly. When constant weight had been reached the smaller had lost 12.8% and the larger one 12.7%.

The Determination of Thallium

The two samples of the anhydrous salts were dissolved in water. The thallium was precipitated with potassium iodide, was filtered into a weighed Gooch crucible, dried to constant weight, and weighed as thallous iodide. From this the percentage of thallium in the two samples was calculated.

The Determination of Manganese

The filtrate from the determination of the thallium contained the manganese and selenium. The manganese was precipitated from this solution as manganese ammonium phosphate. After standing over night it was filtered into a weighed Gooch crucible, ignited to $Mn_2P_2O_7$, and weighed as such. From this the percentage of manganese in the original sample was calculated.

The Determination of Selenium

The selenium was reduced with hydrazine hydrate and hydrochloric acid in the usual manner. It was allowed to stand over night so that the selenium might better coagulate. After being filtered into a weighed Gooch crucible, it was dried to constant weight, and weighed as gray selenium. The results of the complete analysis follow:

	(1)	(2)	Average	Calculated
Weight	.2132	.3110		
	%	%	%	%
Thallium	47.51	47.30	47.405	47.59
Manganese	6.54	6.34	6.440	6.41
H_2O	12.80	12.70	12.750	12.60
SeO_4	33.25	33.60	33.420	33.40
	100.10	99.94	100.015	100.00

The formula of the new salt based on the average percentage composition is $Tl_2SeO_4 \cdot MnSeO_4 \cdot 6H_2O$

34

The Crystal Form of the New Selenates

The crystal system of the five double selenates of
the formula $Tl_2SeO_4 \cdot R''SeO_4 \cdot 6H_2O$ is monoclinic, and the
crystal class is monoclinic-prismatic. The crystals are
highly refractive, and invariably lighter in color than
the salt of the divalent metal used.

Those angles of the five double salts which have
been measured show a difference of less than two degrees when compared to the corresponding angles of the
double sulphates prepared and described by Werther[1], and
even less when compared to the angles of the only double
salt of this general formula so far described in the
literature, namely the thallous zinc selenate described
by Tutton[2].

A more thorough study of the angles is being undertaken, although a sufficient number have already been
measured to establish the fact that these five new double selenates are isomorphous with the thallous zinc selenate and the corresponding double sulphates described by
Tutton and Werther.

1.Journal für praktische Chemie,92, p. 128, (1864)
2.Proceedings of Royal Soc.,   83A, p. 216,(1910)

35

The Solubility of the New Selenates

An effort was made to determine the solubility of these five salts but without success. They have a tendency to dissociate into the difficultly soluble thallous selenate, and the more easily soluble selenate of the divalent metal. The results of such a determination would be merely the solubility of thallous selenate in a solution of the divalent metallic selenate, and would be of little interest.

36.

SUMMARY

1.

The following five new double selenates have been prepared:

$$Tl_2SeO_4.CuSeO_4.6H_2O$$

$$Tl_2SeO_4.CoSeO_4.6H_2O$$

$$Tl_2SeO_4.NiSeO_4.6H_2O$$

$$Tl_2SeO_4.MgSeO_4.6H_2O$$

$$Tl_2SeO_4.MnSeO_4.6H_2O$$

2.

The concentration at which each double salt will best crystallize from solution has been determined.

3.

A method for the quantitive determination of copper in the presence of thallium and selenium has been worked out.

4.

The isomorphism of these salts with those of the corresponding double sulphates is established.

PUBLISHED PAMPHLET BASED ON THE
DISSERTATION AND OTHER RESERCH

COVER:

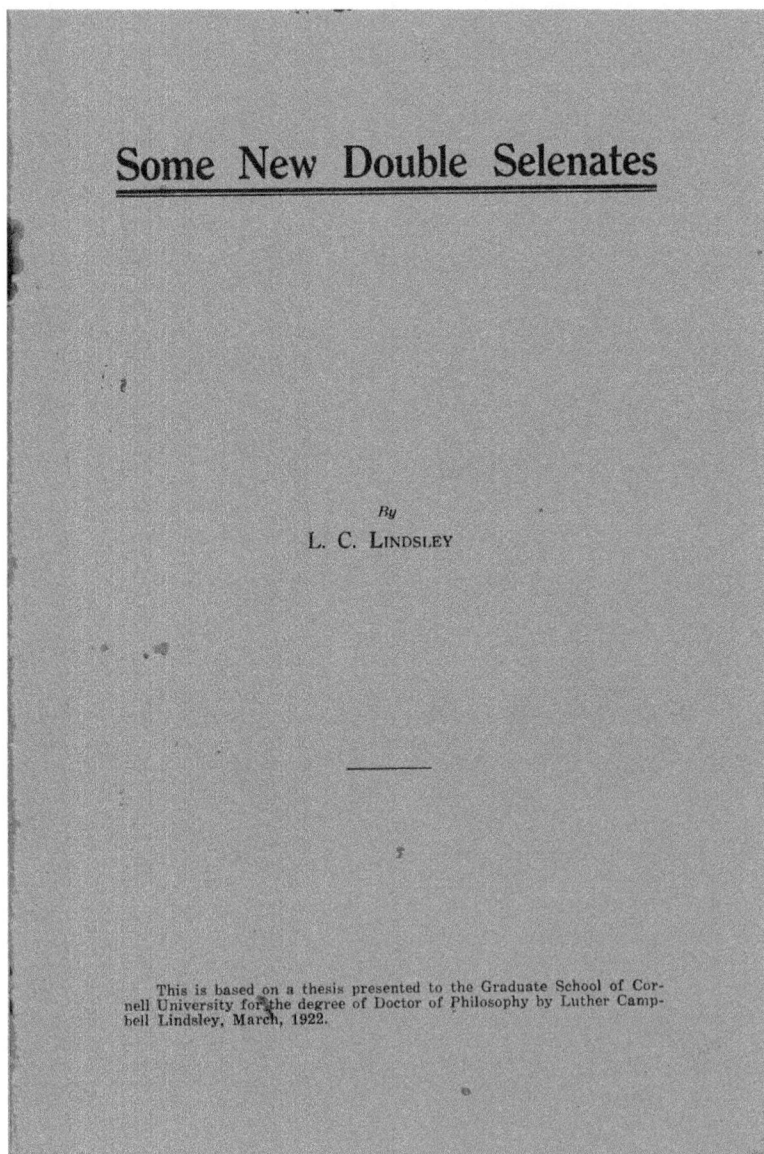

Some New Double Selenates

By

L. C. LINDSLEY

This is based on a thesis presented to the Graduate School of Cornell University for the degree of Doctor of Philosophy by Luther Campbell Lindsley, March, 1922.

TITLE PAGE:

Some New Double Selenates

By

L. C. LINDSLEY

This is based on a thesis presented to the Graduate School of Cornell University for the degree of Doctor of Philosophy by Luther Campbell Lindsley, March, 1922.

ACKNOWLEDGMENT

This investigation was suggested by Professor L. M. Dennis, and the work was carried out under his supervision. The writer desires here to express his appreciation of the kindly criticisms and helpful suggestions offered by him from time to time as the work progressed. For these, for the deep interest he has shown, and the inspiration he has been the author is indeed grateful.

He also wishes to express his appreciation to Professor A. C. Gill, who has given many helpful suggestions and much of his time.

HISTORICAL

In 1832, fifteen years after the discovery of selenium by Berzelius, some selenates were found by Mitscherlich to be isomorphous with the sulphates. In 1858 some measurements were made by Murmann and Rotter on two double salts, potassium magnesium sulphate and ammonium magnesium sulphate. Two years later Emil Wohlwill[1] prepared and studied some mixed sulphates and selenates but made no measurements. He gave to these salts the following formulas:

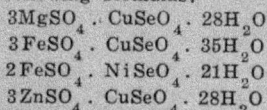

$$3MgSO_4 . CuSeO_4 . 28H_2O$$
$$3FeSO_4 . CuSeO_4 . 35H_2O$$
$$2FeSO_4 . NiSeO_4 . 21H_2O$$
$$3ZnSO_4 . CuSeO_4 . 28H_2O$$

He also prepared the chromium, potassium, sodium and ammonium alums of selenic acid. From his results it appeared probable that selenic acid could be substituted for sulphuric acid in the entire series of the alums.

In 1861 William Crookes discovered the new element, thallium, in the residues left in the purification of crude selenium obtained from ten pounds of seleniferous deposit taken from the sulphuric acid factory at Tilkerode, in the Hartz mountains.[2] His discovery was followed in a few months by the independent discovery of the same element by M. Lamy, a Belgian chemist, who officially announced his discovery to the Imperial Society of Lille on the sixteenth of May, 1862. On the tenth of June he placed an ingot of thallium on exhibit in the International Exhibition, and received a medal for the discovery of the element.

A number of compounds were made in the laboratories of Mr. Crookes and of M. Lamy. From the reactions of thallium with hydrochloric acid, potassium iodide, potassium dichromate and ammonium sulphide, Crookes believed that the new element should be placed with silver and lead. M. Lamy believed from certain experiments made in his laboratory that it should be placed among the alkalies.

The differences of opinion regarding the position of thallium caused H. Werther[3] to prepare the double sulphates of thallium with iron, magnesium, nickel and zinc. He showed by drawings of the crystals obtained and by the measurements of some of the angles, that these four double sulphates with six molecules of water of crystallization were isomorphous with those of ammonia

1 Ann. der Chemie und Pharmacy, 114 p. 180 (1860).
2 Chem. News, 3, p. 193 (1861).
3 Journal für praktische Chemie, 92, (1864).

—3—

and potassium. He found the crystals of thallium ferrous selenate very hard to prepare, and when prepared they were not very satisfactory. In all of the salts mentioned he found that the substitution of thallium for potassium caused the crystals to appear cloudy.

A large amount of work has been done upon the double sulphates and also the double selenates by A. E. H. Tutton. The work, begun in the year 1890, has covered a period of over twenty years.

In 1893 appeared his first memoir. This included the results of three years work done upon the goniometrical investigations of twenty-two salts of the series, $R_2M (SeO_4)_2 6H_2O$, where R is potassium, rubidium or caesium, and M is magnesium, zinc, iron, nickel, cobalt, copper, manganese or cadmium. This work was completed in 1896.[1] The number of salts described would have been twenty-four had he been able to prepare potassium cadmium sulphate and potassium manganese sulphate.

Tutton later considered it advisable to bring the double selenates into the scope of his investigation. The six corresponding double selenates, containing the same three alkali metals, with zinc and magnesium respectively as the dyad M metal were studied goniometrically and physically.[2] Four years later he completed the investigations of the two ammonium salts, ammonium magnesium sulphate and ammonium zinc sulphate. The two selenates corresponding to these were also completely studied.[3]

Since then two typical thallium salts of the series, thallous zinc sulphate, and also the selenate were investigated in detail by Tutton. He also found that the ammonium and thallium double salts crystallize in habits closely resembling the rubidium salts. The optic axial angles of the ammonium salts are almost equal to those of the caesium salts, and the axial angle of the thallous double sulphate lies between the optic axial angle of the corresponding potassium and rubidium compounds. The axial ratios of the thallous salts entitle them to be placed in the same isomorphous series with the analogous salts of the alkali metals, potassium, rubidium and caesium. The molecular distance ratios of the thallous selenate and sulphate are almost identical with those of the rubidium salts, which gives further evidence of isomorphism. However, the thallous salts show very high refractive indices compared with the potassium and rubidium, and the double refraction is not only greater in the thallium double salts but is opposite in sign, being negative. The substitution of thallium

1. Jour. Chem. Soc., 69, p. 495, (1896).
2. Proc. Roy. Soc., 66, p. 248 & 67, p. 58.
3. Jour. Chem. Soc., 87, p. 1123, (1905).

for potassium causes the optical ellipsoid to rotate backwards, and its substitution in the double selenate ($ZnSeO_4 \cdot Tl_2SeO_4 \cdot 6H_2O$) causes almost complete opacity.

Since only one double selenate of thallium and a divalent metal, namely the thallous zinc selenate, hexahydrate, has been prepared and described in the literature, it occurred to us that by preparing others, the isomorphism of these compounds would be more closely established.

THE PREPARATION OF THALLOUS COPPER SELENATE
$$Tl_2SeO_4 \cdot CuSeO_4 \cdot 6H_2O$$

For preliminary work on a problem of this kind a polarizing microscope is very useful. With practice one can often tell with considerable accuracy what compounds are crystallizing from solution.

Fortunately a supply of both copper and thallous selenate was available in the laboratory at the time this investigation was begun. A fragment of copper selenate was dissolved in a drop of water on a glass slide and warmed gently. The crystals separating on the outer edge of the drop were crushed in toward the center, and the preparation was then placed under the microscope. The crystallization was observed under a sixteen millimeter objective. A similar study was made of thallous selenate, and then a mixture of the two selenates. From this last solution three kinds of crystals appeared. The thallous selenate which is rhombic, bipyramidal precipitated first, followed by crystals light blue in color and different from those of the single salts previously studied. As the drop approached dryness the copper selenate crystallized. The light blue crystals were monoclinic, were cloudy in appearance, and in shape resembled the crystals described by Werther in 1864. If these crystals were those of the double salt, then the microscope had shown the possibility of preparing the new compound. It had also pointed out that one difficulty would be the low solubility of thallous selenate. At 12 degrees this is 2.4 grams in 100 cubic centimeters of water.

After several attempts to prepare the double salt in quantity it was found that the copper selenate should be in excess. It crystallizes best from a solution in which the concentration of the copper selenate is from .11 to .12 grams per cubic centimeter, and the thallous selenate .0422 grams. At higher concentrations larger yields can be obtained but the crystals will not be so perfectly developed.

Four grams of copper selenate was dissolved in 36cc of water. Then 1:52 grams of thallous selenate was added and the solution was warmed to 85 degrees. After slow cooling in a Dewar flask until a temperature of 20 degrees was reached, a crop of very good crystals was obtained. The yield was 1.125 grams. The volume of the solution had been reduced to 30cc by evaporation, and, although .409 grams of the copper selenate had been removed from the solution in the formation of the double salt, the concentration was slightly higher than at the beginning by .0086 grams per cubic centimeter. By adding just enough thallous selenate to this mother liquor to make the concentration of the thallous salt equal to its original concentration, a second crop of crystals was obtained. By careful control this process can be repeated until only a small amount of mother liquor remains.

One can determine what is the best concentration to use by making an analysis of the mother liquor at the time the best crystals begin to appear.

THE QUANTITIVE DETERMINATION OF THALLIUM

The ease with which thallium passes from one degree of oxidation to another gives the means of determining the metal volumetrically by potassium permanganate. This method was used by E. Willm. The same property of thallium is the basis of a method employed by Hugh Marshall.[1] He heated a weighed quantity of a thallous salt with hydrochloric acid and a measured volume of standard potassium bromate or sodium bromate more than sufficient to convert all the thallium into thallic salt. He distilled off the residual bromine into potassium iodide solution and titrated the liberated iodine with standard sodium thiosulphate. A third method in which bromine is used for the oxidation of the thallium, and the excess bromine is titrated with potassium iodide, is described by Sponholz.[2] A simpler method was employed by R. Neitzki.[3] He titrated the thallium with standard potassium iodide solution, and found that very accurate determinations could be made, provided the thallium present was in excess of .5 percent, and was in the thallous condition.

Carstanjan found the gravimetric determination of thallium[4] as a sulphate most practicable. The sulphate is very stable, and can be heated for a long time in a platinum crucible until constant weight is reached. He also found that under certain conditions accurate results could be obtained by weighing it as a chromate.

A method for the quantitive estimation of thallium has been

1. Journal Soc. Chem. Ind., 19 p. 994.
2. Z. Anal. Chem., 31, p. 519.
3. Z. Anal. Chem., 16, p. 472.
4. Journal fur praktiche Cheme, 102, p. 88, (1867).

developed by V. Thomas.[1] The thallium is converted to a chloride in the thallous condition, and auric bromide is added to the hot solution as long as metallic gold is precipitated. The gold is collected on a filter and weighed. Two atoms of gold correspond to three atoms of thallium.

Thallium can be determined gravimetrically as the chlorplatinate, which is soluble one part in 15,585 parts of water at fifteen degrees. It can also be determined as the sulphostannate. This method was developed by Hawley,[2] at Cornell University, and is very accurate. The electrolytic process described by Newman is too tedious to use when many determinations are to be made. Werther[3] found that weighing it as an iodide was very satisfactory.

In order to find how accurately thallium could be determined in the presence of selenium a sample of thallous selenate was dissolved in warm water, and the thallium was precipitated by the addition of an excess of potassium iodide. A few cubic centimeters of acetic acid had been added to make the precipitated thallous iodide less soluble. It was then filtered into a weighed Gooch crucible and dried in the oven at a temperature of 105 degrees to constant weight. The amount of thallium calculated as the iodide from the original sample was .6255 grams. The weight of thallium iodide obtained was .6251 grams.

The selenium in the filtrate was determined by hydrazine hydrate. Gutbier[4] and Meyer[5] prefer this method. Jannasch and Muller[6] use hydrazine sulphate to reduce selenious acid to selenium and obtain very good results. Gooch and Scoville boil selenic acid with hydrobromic, pass the liberated bromine into potassium iodide solution and titrate the liberated iodine. When hydrazine hydrate is used as a reducing agent no preliminary reduction of the selenic acid to selenious is necessary.

The calculated amount of selenium in .5213 grams of thallous selenate is .07487 grams. The selenium found by experiment was .0748 grams. In the determination of selenium by hydrazine compounds no ions of metals should be present, for these also may be reduced to the metallic state and will interfere in the weighing of selenium.

1. Comptes Rend.., 130, p. 1316.
2. Journal Am. Chem. Soc., 29, p. 1011, (1907).
3. Journal für praktische Chemie, 92, p. 137, (1864).
4. Z. anorg. Chem., 41, p. 291, (1904).
5. Z. anal. Chem., 53, p. 145, (1914).
6. Ber., 31, p. 2393, (1898).

THE DETERMINATION OF COPPER IN THE PRESENCE OF THALLIUM AND SELENIUM

1

A solution containing known weights of copper and thallous selenate was prepared. The copper was precipitated by hydrogen sulphide. The precipitation of the thallous sulphide was prevented by the addition of 15cc of sulphuric acid. The copper sulphide formed was dissolved in nitric acid, and evaporated to dryness. The residue was redissolved in water and diluted to 100cc. This was very slightly acidified with nitric acid and the copper determined electrolytically. A rotating copper gauze cathode was employed and a platinum flag anode. A current of 1.5 amperes was used for an hour, and at the end of that time a slight yellow coating appeared on the anode, and the solution gave no test for copper. The results showed too large an amount of copper, and a later determination of the thallium from the filtrate after the removal of the copper sulphide, showed a loss in the thallium. Evidently a part of the thallium had precipitated with the copper sulphide, and had deposited on the cathode with the copper, and on the anode as thallium peroxide. The results follow:

$CuSeO_4 \cdot 5H_2O$	Copper found	Calculated
1. .4135 grams	.0980 grams	.0875 grams
2. .4611 grams	.1189 grams	.0974 grams

Tl_2SeO_4	Thallium iodide found	Calculated
1. .5625 grams	.6610 grams	.6705 grams
2. .3119 grams	.3400 grams	.3743 grams

	Selenium found	Calculated
1.	.1920	.1913
2.	.1668	.1679

The low solubility of thallous iodide in ammonium hydroxide offers a means for the quantitive separation of copper from thallium, for the cuprous iodide is readily soluble in ammonia. Potassium iodide precipitates thallium as thallous iodide and the copper as cuprous iodide according to the following equations:

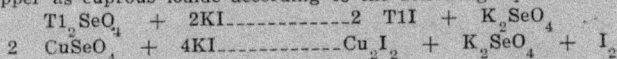

$$Tl_2SeO_4 + 2KI _____2\ TlI + K_2SeO_4$$
$$2\ CuSeO_4 + 4KI _____Cu_2I_2 + K_2SeO_4 + I_2$$

The amount of free iodine can be titrated with sodium thiosulphate, and from this the copper can be calculated. To find how accurately thallium can be determined from an ammoniacal solution .6251 grams of thallous iodide was washed with 200cc of ammonium hydroxide. The loss in weight of the thallous iodide was only .0003 grams. A determination of both copper and thallium was then made in a solution containing .2956 grams of copper selenate and .4130 grams of thallium selenate.

The two salts were dissolved in 50cc of warm water, a few drops of acetic acid was added and then both the copper and thallium were precipitated with an excess of potassium iodide. The liberated iodine was titrated with standard thiosulphate solution, using starch as an indicator. Ammonium hydroxide was added to dissolve the cuprous iodide, and the thallous iodide was filtered into a weighed Gooch crucible, washed with ammonium hydroxide until there was no trace of copper in the washings. The thallium iodide was dried at 105 degrees to constant weight.

	Found	Calculated
Copper	.0629 grams	.0617 grams
Thallium Iodide	.4958 grams	.4969 grams

The thiosulphate must be added very slowly, and the flask shaken after each addition. The starch as indicator gives an adequately sharp endpoint if care is used. After the blue color has disappeared it is best to allow the solution to stand for a few minutes to be sure the reaction is complete; and to be certain of accurate results the concentration of the thiosulphate solution must be small, so that the last drop added will not give too great an error in the calculation of the copper.

This method has the following advantages:

1. It removes any free iodine from the solution so that later it will not interfere with the weighing of the selenium.
2. The ammoniacal copper solution can be worked back for the redetermination of the copper.
3. The thallium, after the dissolving of the cuprous iodide, can be immediately weighed, when dried, as thallous iodide.
4. The thallous iodide in ammonium hydroxide is almost completely insoluble.

THE ANALYSIS OF THALLOUS COPPER SELENATE
($Tl_2SeO_4 . CuSeO_4 . 6H_2O$)

Using the methods previously described, and whose accuracy had been tested on known quantities of material, a complete analysis was made of the light blue salt believed to be the double selenate.

THE DETERMINATION OF WATER OF CRYSTALLIZATION

A small quantity of the salt was first finely ground in a mortar and was then dried between filter papers to remove any adhering moisture. Two samples were taken. After heating for seven hours at a temperature of 100 degrees constant weight had not been reached. The temperature was then raised to 105 degrees for about one hour longer and the weight became constant. The loss was .586 grams. The smaller sample was heated for five hours at 100 degrees and at 105 degrees for one hour before reaching constant weight. Its loss was .138 grams.

	Weight of sample	loss	% loss	Av. % loss
1.	4.5740 grams	.586 grams	12.84	
				12.82
2.	1.0750 grams	.138 grams	12.80	

THE DETERMINATION OF COPPER AND THALLIUM

A sample of the salt was dissolved in warm water. A few drops of acetic acid was added, and then an excess of potassium iodide. The precipitate contained both thallous and cuprous iodides. The iodine which had been oxidized in the reduction of the copper to the cuprous condition was titrated with standard thiosulphate solution, each cubic centimeter of which contained .01257 grams. Starch was used as an indicator. In the titration, 11.15cc of the standard solution of thiosulphate was used, which corresponds to .0594 grams of copper. This was equivalent to 7.3% of the original sample.

The mixture of copper and thallous iodides was then treated with ammonia to dissolve the cuprous iodide, and the thallous iodide was filtered into a weighed Gooch crucible, and the filtrate containing the selenate radical was set aside for the later determination of selenium. The mixture of iodides in the Gooch crucible was washed with ammoium hydroxide to remove the last traces of copper and this too was added to the beaker containing selenates. The thallous iodide was washed with water, dried to constant weight at a temperature of 120 degrees and a weight of .6204 grams recorded.

The selenium was determined as before with hydrazine hydrate. The method as developed by Dennis and Koller[1] is essentially as follows:

The solution containing selenium is diluted to about 125cc. Then about 10cc of a 90% solution of hydrazine hydrate is added and the solution warmed to 60 degrees. Concentrated hydrochloric acid is added carefully until there is a slight excess of acid. If the liquid is kept just below the boiling point for two hours the selenium coagulates, and on cooling will settle to the bottle. It is then collected into a weighed Gooch crucible, dried at 105 degrees and weighed.

The following are the results of the complete analysis of two samples of the double salt:

Copper	7.341	7.27	7.30	7.285
Thallium	47.105	47.30	47.10	47.200

1. Journal of American Chem. Soc., 41, p. 951, (1919).

Selenium as				
SeO$_4$	33.084	32.80	33.03	32.915
H$_2$O	12.470	12.84	12.80	12.820
Total	100.000	100.21	100.23	100.220

The formula for the salt calculated on the basis of the above figures is:

$$Tl_2SeO_4 . CuSeO_4 . 6H_2O.$$

THE PREPARATION OF THALLOUS COBALT SELENATE
(Tl$_2$SeO$_4$. CoSeO$_4$. 6H$_2$O)

Thirty cubic centimeters of selenic acid was placed in a porcelain evaporating dish and diluted to 200cc. Cobalt carbonate was added in small amounts until there was an excess of the cobalt carbonate after the mixture had stood over night. The solution was then filtered, and evaporated on a water bath until very concentrated. When the solution cooled to room temperature a large crop of crystals of cobalt selenate separated. These were dissolved in water and recrystallized.

A fragment of cobalt selenate and a smaller one of the thallous selenate were dissolved in a drop of water on a glass slide by warming gently. As the solution became more concentrated, numerous crystals appeared, and were examined under the microscope. Some seemed to be isomorphous with the thallous nickel sulphate prepared by Werther. Some crystals of thallous selenate were also present, and had crystallized first, indicating that a high concentration of the thallous selenate must be avoided in the preparation of the new salt.

The method used for the preparation of thallous cobalt selenate hexahydrate in quantity was essentially the same as that used for the preparation of the corresponding copper salt previously described, and was also used in the preparation of the other salts of the series.

The analysis of a sample of the mother liquor, taken at the time that the best crystals were forming, showed that the cobalt double salt crystallizes best from a solution, each cubic centimeter of which contains .09 grams of the cobalt selenate, and .045 grams of the thallous selenate.

THE ANALYSIS OF THALLOUS COBALT SELENATE
THE DETERMINATION OF WATER

A small quantity of crystals of the double salt was finely powdered and pressed between filter papers. From this powder

two samples were taken, were placed in weighed porcelain crucibles and heated at a temperature of 110 degrees for five hours
until there was no further loss in weight. The larger sample had
lost .1108 grams and the smaller .0983 grams. The percentage
of water of crystallization calculated from these losses was 12.49%
for the larger and 12.66% for the smaller sample.

THE DETERMINATION OF COBALT

I.

The ease with which cobalt iodide dissolves and the very low
solubility of thallous iodide, give a means for the quantitive separation of each metal in the presence of the other. The solubility
of thallous carbonate, which at 100 degrees is 27.2 grams in 100
of water also makes possible their separation by means of fixed
alkali carbonates, the cobalt being precipitated in the form of a
peach red, basic carbonate.

A sample of the anhydrous thallous cobalt selenate was dissolved in about 50cc of water. The thallium was precipitated
with potassium iodide, filtered into a tared Gooch crucible, and
dried to constant weight. To the filtrate containing the cobalt
iodide and the potassium selenate sodium carbonate was added to
precipitate the cobalt as the basic carbonate. This was filtered
into a weighed Gooch crucible, which had previously been ignited,
was dried in the oven, and then again ignited. The Co_3O_4 thus
formed was weighed as such, and from this the percentage of cobalt in the original sample was calculated.

The filtrate from which the cobalt had been removed contained the selenium. This was determined as before with hydrazine hydrate, and from the weight of selenium found the percentage in the original sample was calculated.

2.

A second sample was treated first with an excess of sodium
carbonate which precipitated the cobalt, and was then filtered into
a tared Gooch crucible which had been previously heated to redness. The filtering was done at 100 degrees to be sure that all of
the thallous carbonate was dissolved. The precipitate was washed
with hot water until the filtrate showed no trace of thallium on
being examined with the spectroscope. The precipitate was then
dried, ignited and weighed. The percentage of cobalt was found
to be 6.96% as compared with 6.93% in the previous determination.

The filtrate containing, after the removal of the cobalt, both
the thallium and the selenium as warmed to keep the thallous
carbonate in solution, and then the thallium was precipitated with
potassium iodide. The precipitate was filtered into a tared Gooch
crucible, and dried to constant weight. The percentage of thallium

found was 47.3 as compared with 47.5% in the first determination. Thus, analysis shows that it makes little difference if the thallium or the cobalt is removed first. The selenium was determined as before with hydrazine hydrate. The results of the complete analysis follow:

	1	2	Average	Calculated
Weight	.8870	.7762		
	%	%	%	%
Cobalt	6.930	6.960	6.955	6.850
Thallium	47.497	47.305	47.401	47.360
SeO_4	33.100	33.150	33.125	33.250
H_2O	12.660	12.580	12.620	12.540
	100.187	99.995	100.101	100.000

The formula for the above compound, when calculated from the average composition is $Tl_2SeO_4 . CoSeO_4 . 6H_2O$.

THE PREPARATION OF THALLOUS NICKEL SELENATE
$Tl_2SeO_4 . NiSeO_4 . 6H_2O$

The same kind of preliminary investigation was made with the microscope in the study of this salt as was made in the study of those salts previously prepared. The thallous nickel selenate crystals crystalized out more readily than either the corresponding copper or cobalt salt.

The same method used in preparing the copper and the cobalt double salts was used in preparing thallous nickel selenate. It crystallized best from a solution containing .09-----.11 grams of the nickel selenate per cubic centimeter. The double salt was monoclinic, was a light green in color, and very similar in shape to the crystals of thallous cobalt selenate.

THE ANALYSIS OF THALLOUS NICKEL SELENATE
THE DETERMINATION OF WATER

It was found to be more difficult to remove the water of crystallization from the thallous nickel selenate than from the corresponding copper and cobalt salts. Two samples were kept in a water jacketted oven for eight hours at a temperature of 100 degrees without an appreciable loss in weight. In an air oven at a temperature of 110 degrees the loss in weight was slight. When the temperature was raised to 120 degrees the salt lost its water of crystallization rapidly. The anhydrous salt is yellow.

THE DETERMINATION OF THALLIUM

A weighed amount of anhydrous thallous nickel selenate was dissolved in 50cc of water. A few drops of acetic acid was

—13—

added and the thallium was precipitated with potassium iodide, dried and weighed as thallous iodide.

THE DETERMINATION OF NICKEL

After the removal of the thallium, the nickel which was in the filtrate was precipitated with sodium carbonate, filtered into a tared Gooch which had been previously ignited, was dried and then heated to redness to convert the carbonate to nickel oxide.

THE DETERMINATION OF SELENIUM

The solution, after the removal of the nickel, contained the selenium. This was determined in the usual way with hydrazine hydrate and hydrochloric acid.

A complete analysis was made on another sample of the new salt, the results of which are tabulated.

	1	2	Average	Calculated
	%	%	%	%
H_2O	12.51	12.60	12.55	12.547
Thallium	47.47	47.30	47.38	47.381
SeO_4	33.20	33.10	33.15	33.267
Nickel	6.72	6.76	6.74	6.805
	99.90	99.76	99.82	100.00

Sample no. 1 contained .7400 grams and no. 2 contained .6195 grams. From the average composition the formula for the new compound was determined and found to be $Tl_2SeO_4 \cdot NiSeO_4 \cdot 6H_2O$.

THE PREPARATION OF THALLOUS MAGNESIUM SELENATE

Before this salt could be prepared it was necessary to make in the labratory some magnesium selenate. This was done by treating pure magnesium carbonate with selenic acid and then recrystallizing the magnesium selenate. The usual preliminary investigation was made with the microscope, and it was noticed that the crystals of what was apparently the double salt were slower in forming than had been the crystals of the double salts previously studied. It was evident that the thallous magnesium selenate was more soluble than the salts previously studied. Numerous experiments, made in preparing this salt in quantity, showed that it crystallized best from a solution, each cubic centimeter of which contained .160 grams of the magnesium selenate and .046 grams of the thallous selenate. The higher the solubility of the salt of the divalent metal, the slower is the crystallization of the double salt.

—14—

THE ANALYSIS OF THALLOUS MAGNESIUM SELENATE
THE DETERMINATION OF WATER

Two samples were placed in porcelain crucibles and subjected to a temperature of 100 degrees for five hours. The loss in weight was very slight. The temperature was then kept at 115 degrees for two hours without the weight becoming constant. At 125 degrees it lost its water of crystallization very rapidly, and in an hour the weight had become constant.

THE DETERMINATION OF THALLIUM

Samples of the anhydrous salt were analyzed for thallium. The usual iodide method was used, as magnesium iodide is very soluble, and the separation of magnesium and thallium therefore quite complete.

THE DETERMINATION OF MAGNESIUM

The magnesium was precipitated from the solution as ammonium magnesium phosphate. The precipitate was allowed to stand over night. It was filtered into a tared Gooch crucible and ignited, then weighed as $Mg_2P_2O_7$.

THE DETERMINATIOF OF SELENIUM

The selenium in the filtrate, after the removal of the magnesium was reduced by hydrazine hydrate and hydrochloric acid, dried and weighed as before.

The results of the complete analysis follow:

	1	2	Average	Calculated
Weight	.8290	.2295		
	%	%	%	%
Mg.	2.900	2.860	2.880	2.950
H_2O	13.050	13.072	13.061	13.060
Tl	49.401	49.210	49.305	49.350
SeO_4	34.720	34.760	34.740	34.640
	100.071	99.902	99.986	100.000

The formula for the salt calculated from the above is $Tl_2SeO_4 . MgSeO_4 . 6H_2O$.

THE PREPARATION OF THALLOUS MANGANESE SELENATE

A preliminary study was made as before with the microscope. A small fragment of one of the most perfect crystals of the manganese selenate was dissolved in a drop of water on a glass slide.

—15—

A much smaller fragment of the thallous selenate was then added and the solution slightly warmed. The preparation was then placed under the microscope and the formation of the crystals studied. A new salt, white, opaque, and apparently monoclinic could be distinguished. If these crystals were those of the desired compound, there remained only to find out at what concentration of the two components the double salt would crystallize out. Since Tutton had found difficulty in preparing potassium manganese sulphate, unusual care was used not only in the preliminary work but also in the preparation of the thallous and manganese salts which were to be used.

It was found that the new salt crystallized best from a solution containing .50 grams of the manganese selenate and .048 grams of the thallous selenate.

THE ANALYSIS OF THALLOUS MANGANESE SELENATE
THE DETERMINATION OF WATER

Two samples of salt, finely ground and weighing respectively .2132 and .3110 grams were placed in the oven and kept at a temperature of 100 degrees for three hours. At the end of that time the decrease in weight was very slight. The temperature was raised gradually to 120 degrees and the salt lost weight rapidly. When at last constant weight had been reached the smaller had lost 12.8% and the larger 12.7%.

THE DETERMINATION OF THALLIUM

Thallium was determined in the usual way as the iodide. The manganese iodide, which was formed at the same time, being quite soluble made the separation of manganese and thallium complete.

THE DETERMINATION OF MANGANESE

The filtrate from the determination of the thallium contained the manganese and selenium. The manganese was precipitated from this solution as maganese ammonium phospate, filtered into a tared Gooch crucible, ignited and weighed as $Mn_2P_2O_7$. The selenium was determined as before after the removal of the metals.

The results of the complete analysis are tabulated below.

	Sample .2132	Sample .3110	Average	Calculated
	%	%	%	%
Tl	47.51	47.30	47.405	47.59
Mn	6.54	6.34	6.440	6.41

—16—

H_2O	12.80	12.70	12.750	12.60
SeO_4	33.25	33.60	33.420	33.40
	100.10	99.94	100.015	100.00

The formula of the new salt, based on the average percentage composition was found to be $Tl_2SeO_4 . MnSeO_4 . 6H_2O$.

THE CRYSTAL FORM AND ANGLES OF THE DOUBLE SELENATES

The crystal system of the five double selenates of the general formula $Tl_2SeO_4 . R''SeO_4 . 6H_2O$ is monoclinic, and the crystal class is monoclinic-prismatic. The crystals are highly refractive, and invariably lighter in color than the salt of the divalent metal. Two angles of each salt were measured on the goniometer and compared with the results obtained by Werther[1] on the double sulphates and by Tutton[2] on the thallous zinc selenate.

$FeSO_4 . Tl_2SO_4 . 6H_2O$	70°	38'	109°	24'
$ZnSO_4 . Tl_2SO_4 . 6H_2O$	70°	48'	109°	12'
$NiSO_4 . Tl_2SO_4 . 6H_2O$	70°	54'	109°	6'
$MgSO_4 . Tl_2SO_4 . 6H_2O$	70°	54'	109°	6'
$ZnSeO_4 . Tl_2SeO_4 . 6H_2O$	71°	32'	108°	28'
$MnSeO_4 . Tl_2SeO_4 . 6H_2O$	71°	17'	108°	48'
$CuSeO_4 . Tl_2SeO_4 . 6H_2O$	71°	50'	108°	54'
$MgSeO_4 . Tl_2SeO_4 . 6H_2O$	71°	85'	108°	25'
$CoSeO_4 . Tl_2SeO_4 . 6H_2O$	71°	28'	108°	32'
$NiSeO_4 . Tl_2SeO_4 . 6H_2O$	71°	34'	108°	26'

Tutton claims that the difference in the angles of isomorphous compounds should not be over two degrees. These differences are but a few minutes.

It is interesting to note that the substitution of magnesium for nickel in the double sulphates causes no change in the angles, and approximately none in the double selenates, in spite of the fact of the difference in the atomic volumes of magnesium and nickel.

The substitution of selenium for sulphur in the double salts causes an increase of about 40' in the acute angles and a corresponding decrease in the obtuse angles, an approximate constant as it should be.

1. Journal fur praktischi Chemie, 92, p. 128, (1864).
2. Proceedings of Royal Soc., 83 A, p. 216, (1910).

APPENDIX VIII

DR. CHAMOT OF CORNELL

GEORGIA STATE COLLEGE
FOR WOMEN
DEPARTMENT OF CHEMISTRY
MILLEDGEVILLE, GA. May 6, 1930

Friend Chemist,

Unless you obtained a copy of "Industrial Microscopy" for the chemical library from some dealer of whom we have no record, yours is one of the very few larger institutions in the United States without a copy.

Since its appearance in November it has been accepted as authority in the research laboratories of 47 states and 9 for _____ The edition is fast becoming exhausted. In order that you might have an opportunity to examine a copy before they are all gone we are sending you one by prepaid express. If you find it too specialized for the present or future needs in the laboratory return it to us by express collect. The opportunity to examine it costs you nothing.

If library funds are running low it will not inconvenience us to wait for payment until next session.

You will find a postal enclosed to inform us of your pleasure.

Yours truly,
R C Lindsley

CORNELL UNIVERSITY
DEPARTMENT OF CHEMISTRY

ITHACA, N.Y.

Nov. 25, 1929

Dr. L. C. Lindsley

Milledgeville

Georgia

My dear Lindsley:

Many sincere thanks for the copy
of your very interesting book. Heartiest
congratulations. You have compiled much
valuable data that should be very useful
to the analyst. I trust that you will
keep up the good work.

Very sincerely yours,

E. M. Chamot

EMC/MB

APPENDIX IX

ADVERTISEMENTS FOR INDUSTRIAL

MICROSCOPY

"First In Field, Classroom and Laboratory"

Industrial Microscopy

By

L. C. LINDSLEY, Ph. D.
(*Cornell University*)

Formerly Head of Department of Chemistry at the College of William and
Mary in Virginia; Professor of Industrial Microscopy, Department
of Chemical Engineering Columbia University Summer
School; Industrial and Research Chemist.

Industrial Chemists and Students will discover that this manual is the first of its kind to combine text matter with elaborate photomicrographs of crystalline precipitates used for the detection of traces of the elements. ¶ Besides presenting systematic procedures for the identification of most of the elements, the text includes the procedures as applied to common starches, alkaloids, industrial woods and pulps, papers and textiles, minerals and rocks. Photomicrography, and micrometry also are fully described. ¶ Dr. Lindsley's clear and concise treatment of the subject, based upon varied experience in the classroom and in the industrial field, makes the work invaluable as a textbook and laboratory manual for schools and colleges. ¶ Ready reference tables, and numerous laboratory exercises are among the outstanding features of the volume.

INDUSTRIAL MICROSCOPY is the result of a demand made by Dr. Lindsley's professional students at Columbia University for a permanent record of classroom and field technic that would draw attention to the Microscope as the powerful, though often neglected, aid to a broader understanding of industrial chemistry. ¶ Through personal preparation of all the material, and financing the printing and distribution the author is able to offer the work for $4.00. 143 illustrations and charts. Copies 10 days on approval. Special discount to former students if purchased before October 15. Copies may be obtained from the author, at Williamsburg, Virginia, or

—◇—

THE WILLIAM BYRD PRESS, INCORPORATED
RICHMOND, VIRGINIA

Send me at best library discounts to
THE PUBLIC LIBRARY,
JACKSONVILLE, FLORIDA

TYPE OF ILLUSTRATIONS CARRIED IN CHAPTER
DEVOTED TO STARCHES

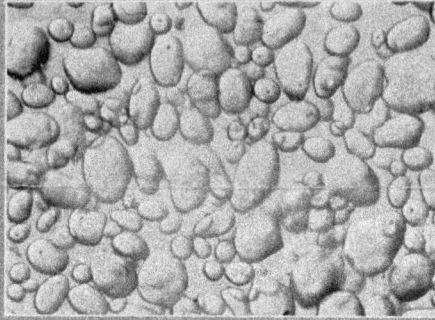

German potato, with hilum

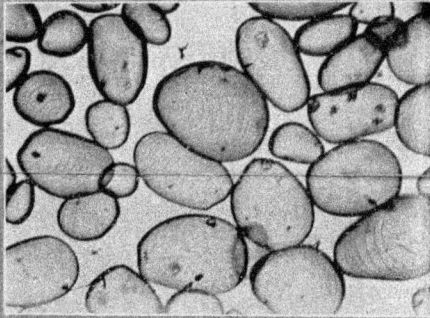

Hawaiian canna, with lamellae

Photomicrographs Showing Common Characteristics of Starches.

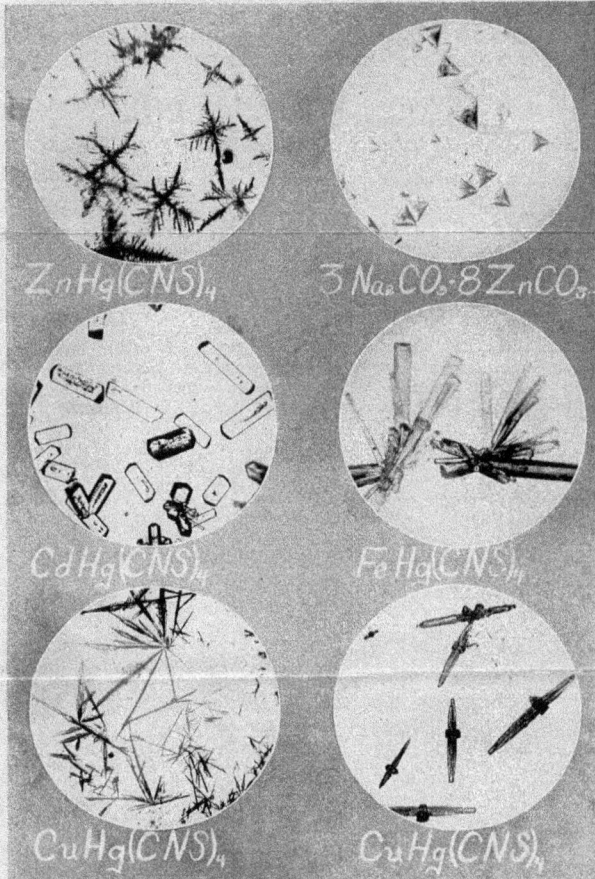

TWO OF THE MANY PHOTOMICROGRAPHS INCLUDED IN
INDUSTRIAL MISCROSCOPY

$ZnHg(CNS)_4$

$3Na_2CO_3 \cdot 8ZnCO_3$

$CdHg(CNS)_4$

$FeHg(CNS)_4$

$CuHg(CNS)_4$

$CuHg(CNS)_4$

Showing Minute Traces of Zinc, Cadmium, Copper and Iron.

Sketch of Author

Dr. Lindsley brings to the subject of Industrial Microscopy a fund of practical experience acquired in the field, as well as the theory of the classroom. Since he graduated at the College of William and Mary in Virginia, in 1907, he has alternated between research work in the field and teaching appointments.

In preparation for his degree of Doctor of Philosophy at Cornell University—in 1922—it was the author's privilege to be a student under Dr. E. Chamot, who more than anyone else is responsible for the development of Chemical Microscopy in this country.

During the past decade Professor Lindsley has devoted much of his time and thought to experiments with the microscope, building up step by step the data contained in this work, making over five thousand experimental preparations.

Coincident with his post-graduate work, Dr. Lindsley was associate Professor of Chemistry at the College of William and Mary in Virginia. From 1923 until 1925 he was head of the department of Chemistry in this famous institution. In 1926, following this period of teaching, he was Chemist for the Royster Guano Works, Norfolk, Virginia. From 1925 until the past year he has held the chair of Professor of Industrial Microscopy, Department of Chemical Engineering in the Summer School of Columbia University. Besides these activities, Dr. Lindsley has specialized in industrial and research problems since 1927, doing special research for the Royster Guano Company and acting as research Chemist for the Archeological Department of one of the world's largest museums. Dr. Lindsley has won an international reputation in the field of archeological chemistry.

—◇—

Scope of the Volume

Some idea may be obtained as to the scope of Industrial Miscroscopy by reference to the following Table of Contents:

Luther had two versions of this four-page flyer. Some were as shown above. Others substituted the page below for the second page showing illustrations of starches. He also printed the page below as a separate sheet, perhaps as an insert for the flyer showing the two pages of photomicrographs.

A decided advance in the field of microscopy. A splendid manual for college and industry.

D. D. JACKSON, CHEM. ENGINEERING
Columbia Univ.

The "get up" is fine, paper and print show up wonderful. The photomicrographs are splendid.

PROF. T. L. KELLY
Holy Cross College.

It is a fine book and about as well gotten up as any I have ever seen.

THOS. C. HERNDON
George Peabody College.

I have gone through it several times, each time with renewed interest. I like the precise practical tone.

A. G. WOODMAN
Mass. Inst. Tech.

I have occassion to examine your book and enjoy it more and more.

V. W. MELOCHE
Univ. of Wisconsin.

The book shows the author has a thorough knowledge of the subject.

A. H. GRIMSHAW
State College, Raleigh, N. C.

You have compiled much valuable data that should be very useful to the analyst. I trust that you will keep up the good work.

E. M. CHAMOT
Cornell Univ., Ithaca, N. Y.

Dad also had another typed and printed page that he used to advertise his book. The copy had no date, but from the last line, we know it was after Luther began his summer school classes at Columbia University.

I have endeavored to make my book on CHEMICAL MICROSCOPY different from Chamot's in the following points:

1. It is not primarily a catalog of the optical companies.

2. It should be written so that it has a wider industrial application.

3. It gives tables for identification of minerals—entirely absent in Chamot's.

4. It includes tests for the most common alkaloids—entirely lacking in Chamot's.

5. It gives a better background on crystallography and polarized light than Chamot's.

6. It includes tests for more of the elements than found in Chamot's.

7. It includes approximate sensitiveness of the tests (a modified table of Behrens) not included in Chamot's.

8. It includes photomicrography—not found in Chamot's.

9. It includes about 160 photomicrographs, many of which have been published for the first time. The German writers and the Dutch have used drawings almost entirely.

In order for any book of this kind to be a success it must be profusely illustrated so that the beginners working without assistance everywhere in the country can check their results against standard illustrations. They cannot do this from Chamot's book; many cannot read German, therefore development of this field of chemistry has lagged.

Such a book can be used for reference work as well as a test. The chapter on alkaloids should appeal to every physician. The mineral industries could use the book to advantage and also the paper chemists.

Courses in chemical microscopy are at Colorado, Pittsburg, Western Reserve, Cornell, Columbia, William & Mary, Alabama Polytechnic Institute. Research work was being done at Yale last year. Last summer, ten of the professors attending the summer school at Columbia were hoping to start the work in their colleges.

A few copies left of

$4.00 Industrial Microscopy Write

L. C. Lindsley, Ph. D., Milledgeville, Georgia

30 DAYS APPROVAL

Two hundred and eighty-six pages with 148 illustrations and photomicrographs of tests for the elements, acids, alkaloids, and many materials.

Used in 48 states and 15 foreign countries. It is the first edition of such a book so illustrated in the English language. A part of the essential equipment of every Industrial and University laboratory.

APPENDIX X

MAPS OF WESTOVER AND SURROUNDING

AREA

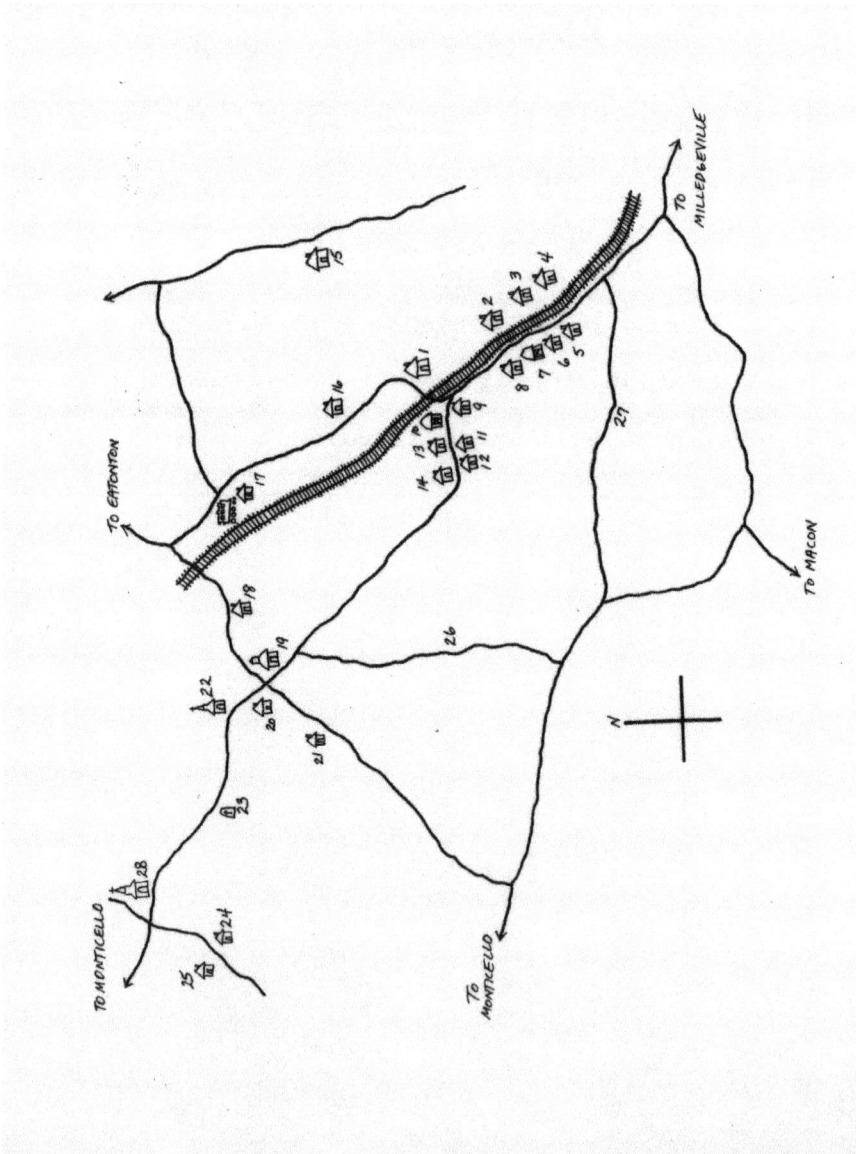

Places and Names: Map Legend

1. Westover Home site (Meriwether Road)
2. Old house site, unknown (GA Hwy 212)
3. Comp's/Manuel's/The Old Place
4. Uncle Dave's
5. Missy's/The Nelson Place (GA Hwy 212)
6. The White House/Candler Place
7. Tin Shed
8. Phil Foster Place
9. Sam Avery home
10. Barn
11. Ida Mae's (spring)
12. Preacher's
13. Farr Place/Ida & Roger's
14. Log Cabin
15. O'Connor's/Andalusia (US HWY 441)
16. Lowe Place
17. Mixon's/Meriwether RR Sta.
18. Tippie's (Little Rd.)
19. Meriwether Schoolhouse (GA Hwy 22 & Nelson Rd.)
20. Gus Myrick's home
21. John Myrick Place (Nelson Rd.)
22. Bethel Church
23. John Myrick grave
24. Dovedale home & post office (Stiles Cemetery Rd.)
25. Dovedale camp place
26. Scoggins' Hill Road (now Avery Store Rd.)
27. Original Monticello Road
28. County Line Primitive Baptist Church
NOTES: Ida and Roger also lived on the north-east corner
of the junction of what is now Little Road and Highway 212.
The road at the bottom of the map is GA Hwy 22 to Macon.

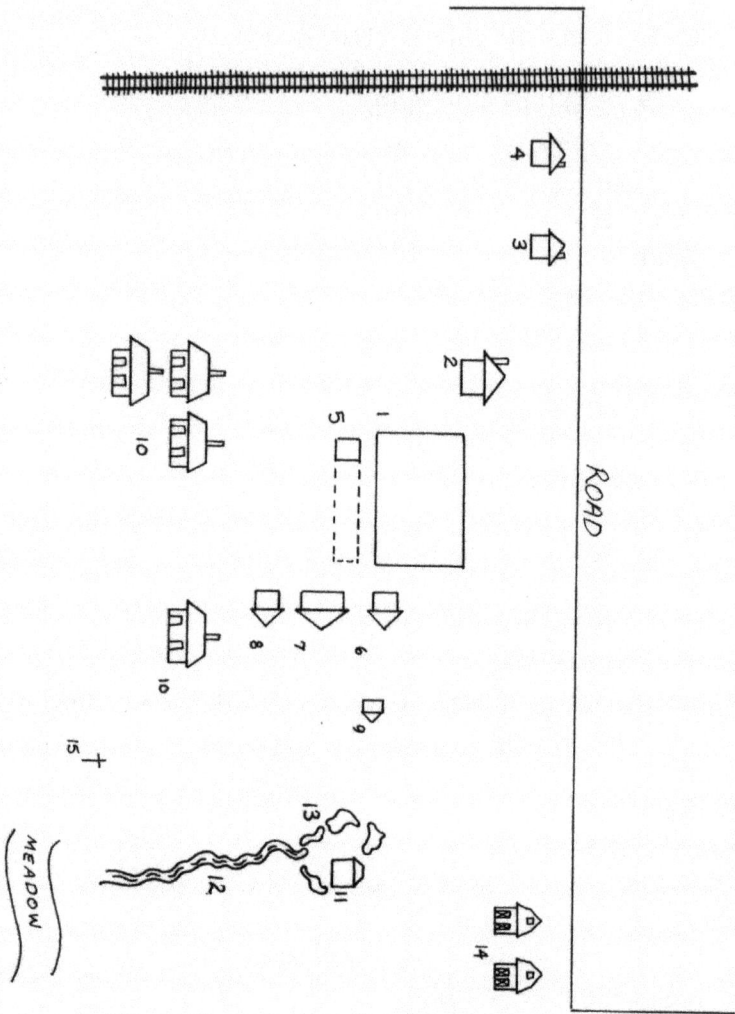

Map Legend
Westover Home Place on Meriwether Road

1. Main House
2. Brick House
3. Cottage
4. Willie's House
5. Play House (Kitchen)
6. Commissary
7. Wash housel
8. Smoke House
9. Outhouse
10. Slave Houses
11. Spring House
12. Stream
13. Fish Ponds
14. Barns
15. Graveyard

APPENDIX XI-A

WESTOVER ARTICLES

Perhaps the last tribute to Westover before she burned came from Colonel Edwin T. Bowden, Allie's husband (and thereby Lillas's brother-in-law).

WESTOVER

Modern, all gray, hurries away the road to tomorrow,
Olden, so red, wends to the right the road we must follow.
Slow! There's the field of clover.

Gate turned gray, office coral pink in the bright sunlight.
Dark shine old magnolias, hovering birds so shy and white.

See! There lies Westover.

Old house! White columns! Pale Dreamer
Aged green box amid shrubs breathing days of past,
The faint imprint that carriages once circled:
Now tell me, what visions past hold you fast?

No, don't! Just let me love you as you are,
Let dreams say what you did.

This tribute to old Westover and its plantation at Milledgeville, Georgia, we also intended as one to Doctor Luther Campbell Lindsley, its owner and lover, a man who has successfully combined a love of modern science, modern practicality and a reverence for things of the past.

Edwin T. Bowden
Washington, D.C
12 April 1953

* * *

We do not have the date or the source of the article below, but it was probably in the Macon paper.

Old Home's Owner Is Busy Restoring It

The garden party at Westover, which Dr. Lindsley himself is restoring, was a lovely affair, Westover being the most fascinating place to have such a to-do.

Built about 1830 (sic) by Ben Jordan, one of the states' wealthiest planters, this home, outstanding for its cornices, stairway, plaster work and perfect symmetry, had been occupied for only a few years since Sherman left in 1864 until Dr. Lindsley acquired it several years ago.

The present owner, carefully doing most of the work himself, has done a great deal toward restoring the house and grounds to their former beauty since he obtained the plantation and he has plans for continuing further the restoration of the building and gardens.

About 20 years after the house was erected the banquet room was built and marble mantels replaced the wooden ones in the downstairs rooms, and the woodwork was painted to harmonize with these. There mantels were removed about 20 years ago, and now the mantel in the parlor is one of the original ones that was found in an old slave house and the other two are from other old dwellings.

Broken panels in the door tell a story, showing where Sherman broke into the house in 1864, and at the top of the stairs is a hole in the wall where the Union soldiers broke into the place where the family treasures were hidden.

At the rear of the house were the kitchen and domestic work room, but they burned in 1929. However, a few of the old slave cabins are still standing and will be reclaimed. The sites of the old carriage house, gin, and stables and blacksmith shop can be seen and the old wash house, dairy and smoke house which remain are to be restored. At the front of the house is a small brick office building and it used to be balanced on the opposite side of the yard by the orangery. In the brick house is the old bell that was in 1822 "the capitol bell of Georgia."

By the gardens with their wonderful old boxwood (there are about 600 plants remaining) the crytomaria japonica, photina, cherry laurel and other interesting plantings, as much as by the whole house itself, are thoughts of antebellum days brought to mind, and wandering about them, one can almost see hoop skirts brushing against the boxwood's deep, fragrant green, or swishing down the walks toward the garden gate. That gate is now the front gate and (I believe) in other days the berry and vegetable gardens were in front of the house. Portions of the old picket fence still stand, and part of it is to be rebuilt. Plans are being made to build lily pools at the rear; several hundred pieces of shrubbery have been placed to outline the gardens, terraces will be made where gullies are now and the slaves houses are to be converted into laboratories, museums and guest houses. It is hoped by the owner that by next year the banquet hall will have a big chimney and fireplace.

The gullies referred to here are now the daffodil field behind the playhouse and tool house. When Dad bought the place, he said, he could have buried a mule standing up in the site of that daffodil field. We believe the date of original construction was 1822. From the date 1852 etched in mortar on the southeastern chimney, visible only after the original house burned, we know that the ballroom, the side porch and the southeastern room were added then.

*   *   *

Susan Myrick, sister of Lillas, wrote a feature article about Westover that ran in the *Macon Telegraph*. Date is about 1945.

Stairway Called One of Loveliest in the Country

By SUSAN MYRICK

Known for many years as the Jordan Place, the handsome, two-story frame house six miles from Milledgeville was named Westover by its original owner, Col Ben Jordan, and is still so called by its present owner, Dr. L. C. Lindsley, Professor of Chemistry at GSCW.

Built about **1830** (1822), the house was one of a number planned and constructed by Daniel Pratt in Central Georgia in the early parts of the nineteenth century. Lowther Hall, home of Dr. and Mrs. Frank Jones at Clinton (destroyed by fire some years ago) and the Blount Place, near Haddock, are two others which Pratt built. Dr. Lindsley is now restoring the Blount Place, which he acquired recently.

The gardens of Westover are among the handsomest in Georgia; they are, today, of the same plan as when they were begun more than a hundred years ago. The boxwood stands in groupings that are fifteen feet in circumference and the plants are eight feet or more in height in many places on the front lawn. A circular driveway, leading from the road, is bordered with red cedars, magnolias, ancient elms, is further enhanced in beauty by the many crepe myrtles. Other crepe myrtles, standing near the house, are taller than the second story of the house and an overnight guest at the Lindsley house in midsummer looks from his bed into a sea of pink blossoms.

Four Doric columns, in pairs, are two stories tall; a balcony is finished in slender white banisters. The frieze of the gable is plain but the deep eaves are decorated, here, as well as around the entire house.

Seldom may one see handsomer fan lights or side lights than those at the front doors, both upstairs and down, at Westover. Nor may one find a more graceful, curving, freehanging stair than that which reaches from the first floor to the attic, with a handsome medallion in acanthus leaf pattern at the top.

With more restraint than he showed at the Blount place, Daniel Pratt nevertheless went in for gold paint and "marbleizing" at Westover, too. In the parlor at the right of the wide hallway, the trims of windows are elaborate; the painting is in delicate shades of green and lavender and rose, finished at the top of the decorative pilasters with gold in a feathery design.

Gold, too, is used for the trim on the stringer of the stairway; the baseboard and the risers of the stairs are "marbleized."

Originally, the house had four rooms, one up and one down on each side of the front hall. A porch occupied the right rear of the house. But somewhere in the fifties (1852) the owners of the house decided a ballroom was needed; so, it was added at the rear of the right-hand parlor. The effect produced is unusual, for the windows of the parlor at one side now open upon the ballroom instead of upon the out-of-doors.

The ballroom is elaborately decorated with painted woodwork similar in design to that in the parlor. But it is in the parlor that the cornice and medallion design reach their greatest beauty.

Originally the house had handsomely carved mantels of wood; but at that stage of America's life when marble mantels were considered the last word in beauty, the wooden mantels of the first floor were replaced with marble ones, imported from Italy and considered among the finest in the country.

Some time in the late 1890s the house was sold, the mantels taken out and sold to others. When Dr. Lindsley bought the home, some 15 years ago, he began searching for mantels of the periods and had the good fortune to find one of the originals in an old slave house in the back yard. That one is now in the parlor; a handsome mantel of the Adams type.

Other mantels of the home are handsomely carved and handmade; they have been acquired by the owner in various places.

The floor boards of the house are wide and made of heart pine. The baseboards throughout the house are "marbleized," the doors are painted to resemble a variety of woods. The original paint remains in the house; Dr. Lindsley's only treatment of the fine old paint was a good scrubbing with a pure soap and plenty of water.

Plaster walls, so often found in homes throughout the South in the antebellum days, are white, and the spacious rooms are cold and airy with their many windows and high ceilings.

The fire places of the house have not been converted for coal and the dancing flames of the wood fires add to the effect of the long-ago, when cold winter days are here.

A number of houses that were quarters for the slaves that worked in the house, as well as other outbuildings, still stand. But some 12 years ago, a fire destroyed the kitchen and the old workhouse where slaves did the laundry and the sewing.

The present owner hopes to restore the old wash house and the other houses in the yard; and to rebuild the kitchen and furnish it as in the old days, with Dutch oven and huge fireplace and crane and kettles.

CLARIFICATIONS: The "wash house" survived into the 1970s, when it finally was pushed apart by elm trees growing up in the foundations. The "workhouse" used for laundry and sewing must have been used for ironing and sewing, and may have been the eastern end of the kitchen. The wash house had two huge pots set over fireplaces with a joint chimney for boiling clothes, one pot for washing and the other for rinsing. Three or four rows of dove cotes lined the upper walls. It had a dirt floor.

Thulia, Susan and Lil

*   *   *

Michael W. Kitchens, author of *Ghosts of Grandeur,* has presented
one of the most accurate portraits of Westover that we have seen

published. With his permission, I have excerpted the portion of his book that deals with the house, the gardens and the crops. I have given his footnotes in the text and listed them at the end of this section.

For those who wish more information, his book is:

Kitchens, Michael W., *Ghosts of Grandeur: Georgia's Lost Antebellum Homes and Plantations*, The Donning Company Publishers, 2012. Westover section: pp. 166-174

WESTOVER
Baldwin County

The story of antebellum Westover is, in many ways, the story of antebellum Georgia. Established in the early years of the nineteenth century, on land that was then close to Georgia's frontier, Westover was built in Baldwin County, approximately five miles from Georgia's still new capital city, Milledgeville. Built with the vast wealth gained by the acquisition and sale of large quantities of land, cotton, and slaves, Westover's plantation home exhibited the finest and best that money could obtain both for the comfort of its occupants and the entertainment of the state's leading citizens who traveled to Milledgeville each year to conduct the state's business. For more than thirty years, Westover stood as a gleaming example of the best the plantation system could offer. ---

---When it was built in 1822, Westover had few rivals in middle Georgia. Adopting designs from popular architectural pattern books available at the time, Pratt designed a manor house practically dripping with classical detailing both inside and out. Its portico was supported by pairs of fluted Doric columns, a departure from Pratt's penchant for using single columns at each edge of the portico (ft note 37). At each corner of the home were fluted pilasters, which were uncommon to country houses at the time. Perfectly portioned semicircular fanlights crowned both front and balcony doors. Rather than employing the gable roof so common to other Federal-style homes of the period, Pratt employed a hipped roof that enhanced the scale and balance of the structure. ---Brick end chimneys covered with plaster and scored to simulate stone blocks added emphasis to the classical design of the facade.

Inside, perhaps the home's most striking feature was its graceful, curving three-story stairway in the back of the broad central hall (Ft note 38). Drawing the eye upward was a beautiful carved acanthus-leaf ceiling medallion centered on the third floor ceiling and framed by the spiraling mahogany handrails of the staircase. Grapevine- and acanthus-carved plaster ornamentation abounded in the cornices and medallions of the public rooms on the first floor. Windows and doors were surrounded by fluted pilasters of carved wood, in some places Ionic, and in other Corinthian, which were surmounted by entablatures with classical urns in relief. With the exception of the mantels, all the woodwork was grained to simulate dark exotic woods and provide stark contrast to the light color of the plaster finished walls. To add further contrast, many of the wood or plaster carvings were high-lighted in gold. Beneath each window were wood-grained panels that enhanced the regal effect (ft note 39). More detailing was found on wide baseboards that were marbleized to simulate marble veining, an expensive process requiring the hand of a skilled artisan. Mantels were decorated with carved sunbursts, fluted pilaster topped by acanathus leaf capitals, and paneling. Virtually every surface on the first floor was carved or molded into intricate classical patterns.

Westover was known throughout Georgia, if not the South, for the beauty of its gardens, which were just as awe-inspiring as the home itself (ft note 40). The front gardens alone occupied four acres, all of which were enclosed by white spearhead picket fences (ft note 41). The circular pattern seen in the entryway fanlights and spiraling stairway were repeated in the front gardens. From the front gate, a large circular carriage drive was bisected by a wide walkway and bordered with a boxwood hedge. The drive was lined with elms, magnolias, and cedars. Immediately in front of the residence were small circular, parterre gardens edged with dwarf boxwood and centered with tea olives, a favorite of southern gardeners for generations because of the year-round green foliage and highly fragrant flowers. Crepe myrtles were planted at the edges of the parterres close to the front portico so their heady fragrance could be enjoyed from inside the home. On one side of the round carriage drive was a small brick building used as a plantation office, and on the other side was an orangery, used as a sort of greenhouse (ft note 42). The plantation complex also included large vegetable gardens and fruit orchards. Jordan even had an environmentally controlled greenhouse dedicated to producing winter grapes (ft note 43). —

—Large acreage at Westover was dedicated to growing crops other than cotton, such as sweet potatoes, grains, and large quantities of peas and other vegetables (ft note 46).

Between the crops grown at Westover and the array of livestock Jordan raised, virtually everything the family and their servants needed for day-to-day living was produced on the plantation.

Footnotes to Kitchens' article:
37. Linley, John, *The Architecture of Middle Georgia: The Oconee Area.* (Athens, University of Georgia, 1976), pp. 46-47.
38. Linley, *Georgia Catalog*, (Athens: University of Georgia, 1982), 314
39. Linley, *Georgia Catalog*, p.314
40. Linley, *Architecture of Middle Georgia*, 47
41. Anonymous. "Westover," n.d. , in file of Old Governor's Mansion archives, Milledgeville, Georgia
42. Rainwater, Hattie E., ed., *Garden History of Georgia 1733-1933* (Atlanta: Peachtree Garden Club 1933). Anonymous.
43. Rainwater, ibid.

APPENDIX XI-B
BIBLIOGRAPBY AND SUGGEASTED
READING

In her research of the history of Westover and the Jordan family who originally owned the house and plantation lands, Thulia Bramlett has assembled or researched a number of sources. Susan has added others that refer to Westover. Many of these are quoted in this book.

Berdendt, John, *Midnight in the Garden of Good and Evil*, Random House, 1994, pp. 299-300.

Conyngham, Captain David P., *Sherman's March Trough the South*, Sheldon and Company, 1865, pp. 250-252.

Dunkelman, Mark H., *Marching with Sherman*, LSU Press, 2012.

Garden History of Georgia 1733-1933, Peachtree Garden Club, 1933.

Hair, William Ivy; Bonner, James C.; et al., *A Centennial History of Georgia College*, Georgia College, 1979, pp. 108-109.

Hutto, Richard, *A Peculiar Tribe of People*, Globe Pequot Press, 2011.

HABS Historic American Building Survey, Library of Congress.

Kitchens, Michael, *Ghosts of Grandeur—Georgia's Lost Antebellum Homes and Plantations*, Donning Company Publishers, 2012.

Ladd, James Royal, "From Atlanta to the Sea," *American Heritage*, Vol. 30, No. 1, December 1978.

Lindly, John M., *The History of the Lindley-Lindsley-Linsley Families in America 1639-1930*. Vol I, (Reprinted) Higginson Book Company, Salem, MA 2011.

Linley, John, *Architecture of Middle Georgia*, UGA Press, 1972.

Nichols, Frederick Doveton, *The Early Architecture of Georgia*, UNC Press, 1957, pp. 117, 124-126, 128, 130, 134-139, 159-161.

Perkerson, Medora Field, *White Columns in Georgia*, Rinehart & Co., Inc., 1952, pp. 65, 68, 318.

NOTE: Mrs. Perkerson refers to Major Henry Hitchock's published diary titled *Marching with Sherman.* (Same title as Dunkelman's book).

APPENDIX XI-C

THE HISTORIC AMERICAN BUILDING SURVEY REPORT ON WESTOVER

The Historic American Building Survey (HABS) was established by President F. D. Roosevelt during the Great Depression to provide work for architects and others in related fields. The Westover file contains photographs and architectural drawings from 1934

To find these files, search HABS Westover, GA

The file title is HABS GA 5-MILG.V. 1

These photographs were taken by Branan Sanders in March 1934.

View showing side porch added in 1852, where Lillas taught her three daughters "summer school" classes. Note chair on front porch, and the height of the boxwoods. Note the fence also. In the 1950s, when the house burned, these hedges were 5-6 feet high.

View from the south side. Luther planted the young cedars.

Back porch. Small boxed area on right side of lower roof an added-on full bathroom A half-bath was located in the downstairs back hall. The kitchen window is "pointed to" by the front cedar tree. Luther planted the Spanish bayonet, which by the 1950s grew out of control and became a nesting site for the yard chickens.

**Luther brought the Windsor chair seen on this porch from Williamsburg.
Two of them sat on the front porch as long as the house stood.
Good view of side porch and the original fence.**

Typical ceiling decoration

Parlor. On the western side, across the hall from the "sitting room." In 1934, the family still had no curtains or furniture here and was probably still living in the "cottage" next door.

View upon entering front door. Opening under stairs goes to the ballroom. Table is in possession of daughter Susan Lindsley; it was damaged—probably tossed out—during the fire. Note painting in the window. Window originally opened into the back yard, and was closed when the ballroom was built (1852). The cloud over the sailboat was supposed to be the silhouette of Ben Jordan, original builder of the house.

Stairs from the second floor landing. At top, the stairs ended in a plaster wall, where Luther left a hole showing that the Yankee soldiers had searched the attic for silver. The entrance to the attic was a small hole in the ceiling of the hallway that led to the upstairs bath from both bedrooms on the east side of the house.

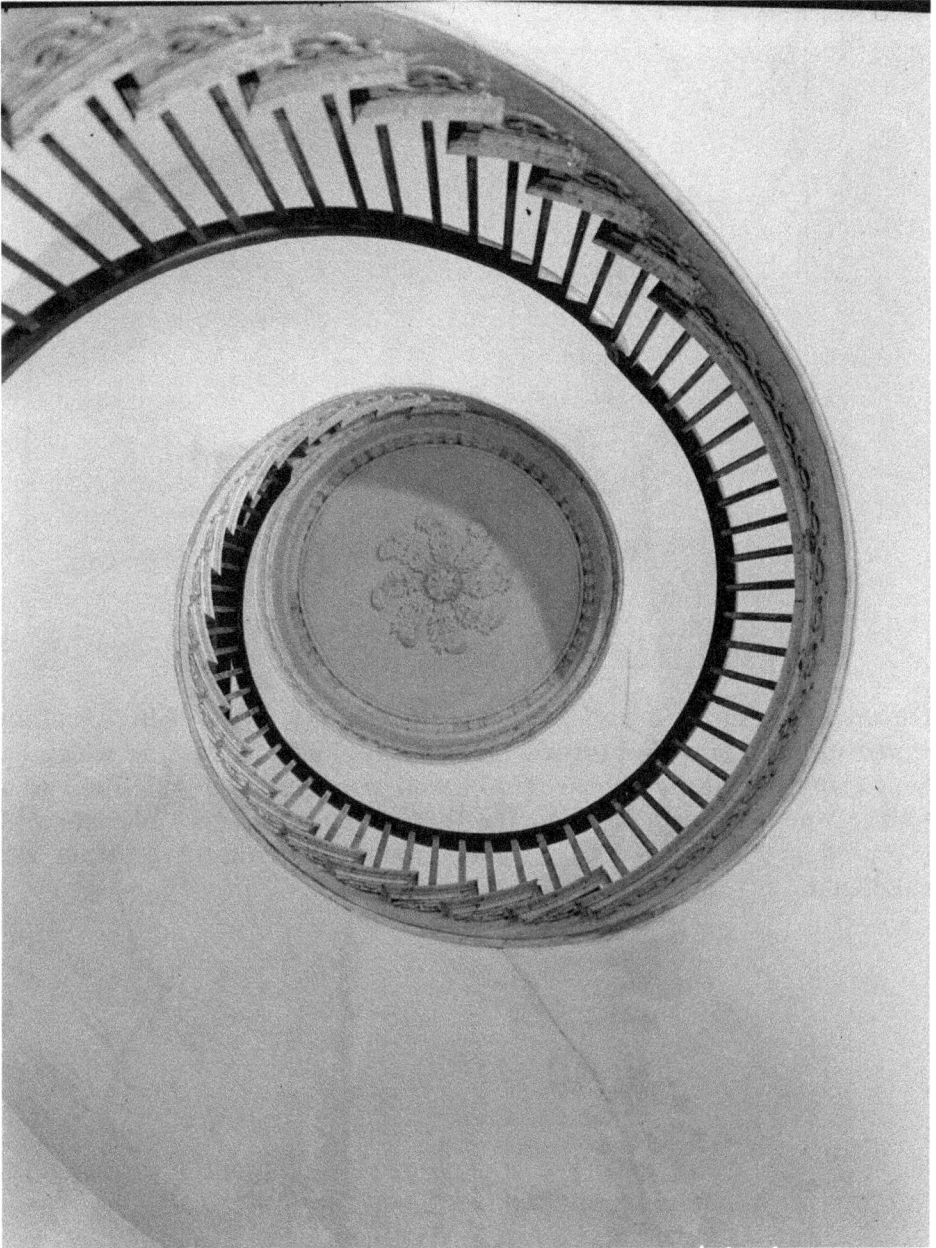

View up, from first floor hallway.

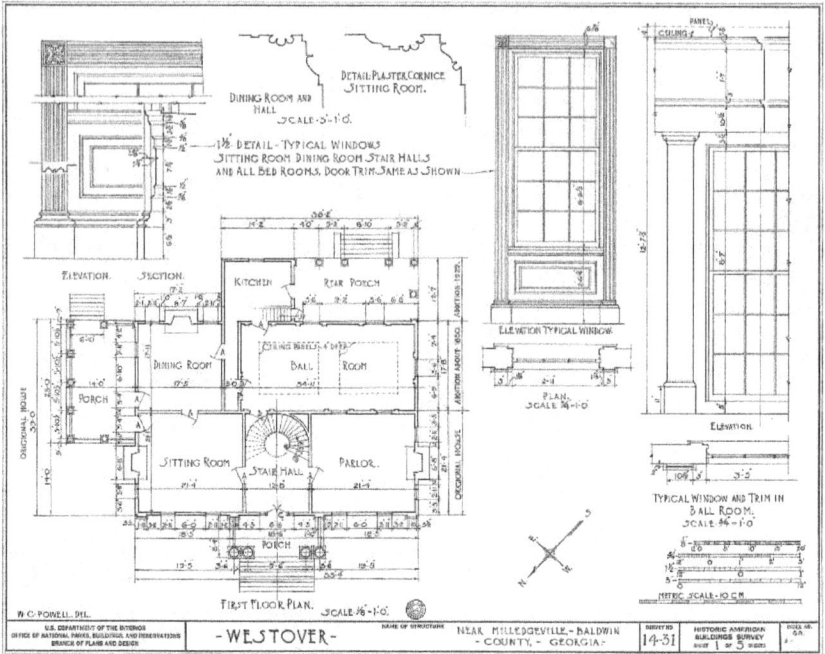

On this diagram, a door leads from the kitchen to the ballroom. Dad closed up that door and turned the space into a book case, in which he kept many old history books. One I well remember was the diary of a soldier who was present when the Indian chief Mangus Colorado was captured and murdered. The books were years out of print in my childhood.

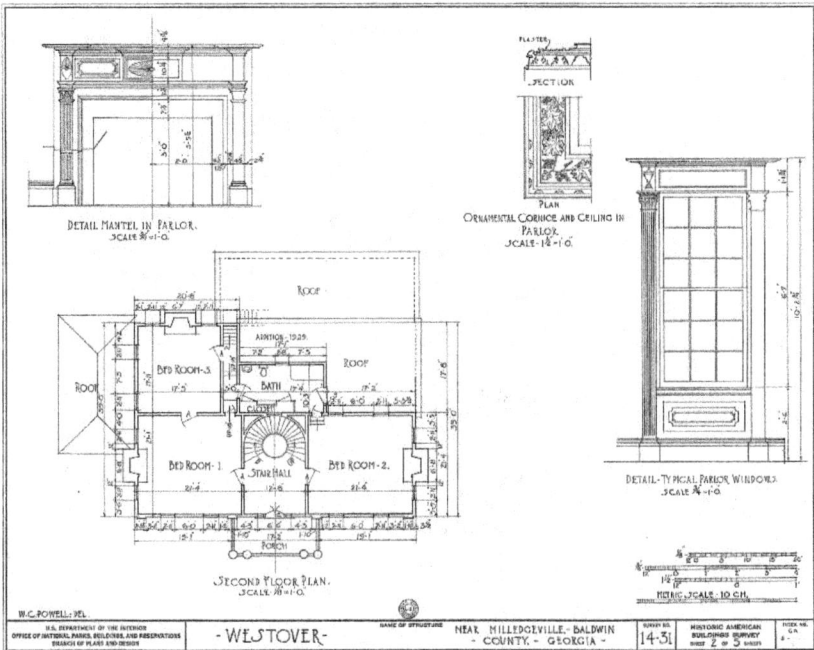

DETAIL MANTEL IN PARLOR.
SCALE ¾=1'-0".

ORNAMENTAL CORNICE AND CEILING IN
PARLOR.
SCALE 1½=1'-0".

DETAIL-TYPICAL PARLOR WINDOWS.
SCALE ¾=1'-0".

SECOND FLOOR PLAN.
SCALE ⅛=1'-0".

ROOF

BED ROOM-3

BATH

CLOSET

BED ROOM-1

STAIR HALL

BED ROOM-2

ROOF

ROOF

PORCH

METRIC SCALE: 10 CM.

W.C. POWELL: DEL.

U.S. DEPARTMENT OF THE INTERIOR
OFFICE OF NATIONAL PARKS, BUILDINGS, AND RESERVATIONS
BRANCH OF PLANS AND DESIGN

-WESTOVER-

NAME OF STRUCTURE
NEAR MILLEDGEVILLE.-BALDWIN
- COUNTY, - GEORGIA -

SURVEY NO.
14-31

HISTORIC AMERICAN
BUILDINGS SURVEY
SHEET 2 OF 5 SHEETS

INDEX NO.
GA.
2.

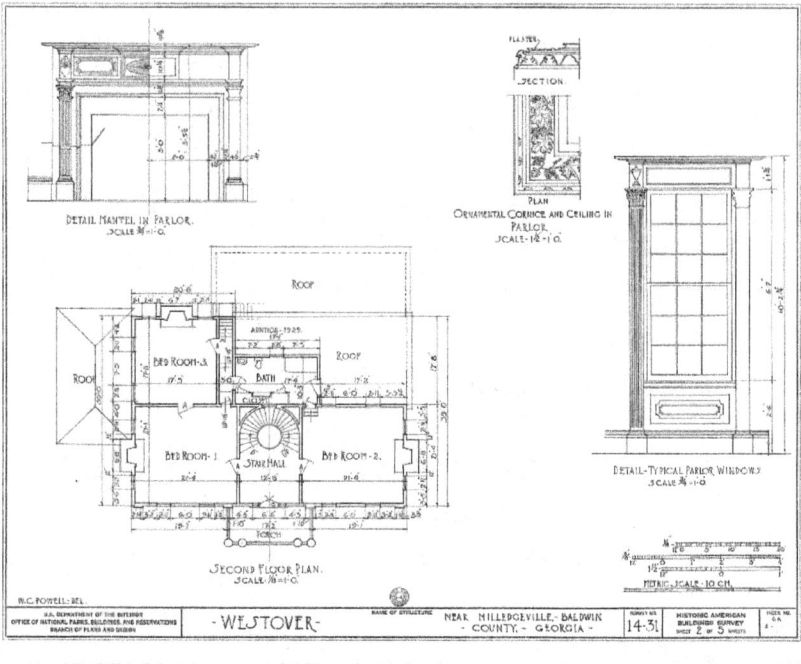

DETAIL MANTEL IN PARLOR.

ORNAMENTAL CORNICE AND CEILING IN PARLOR.

DETAIL - TYPICAL PARLOR WINDOW.

SECOND FLOOR PLAN.

- WESTOVER -

NEAR MILLEDGEVILLE - BALDWIN COUNTY - GEORGIA -

14-31

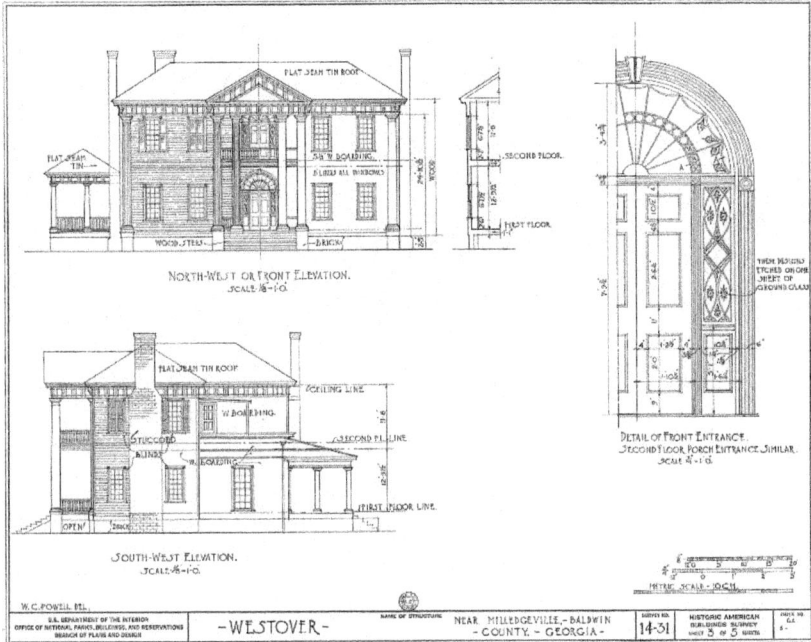

NORTH-WEST OR FRONT ELEVATION.
SCALE ⅛=1·0.

SOUTH-WEST ELEVATION.
SCALE ⅛=1·0.

DETAIL OF FRONT ENTRANCE.
SECOND FLOOR PORCH ENTRANCE SIMILAR.
SCALE ¾=1·0.

—WESTOVER—

NEAR MILLEDGEVILLE,—BALDWIN
—COUNTY,—GEORGIA—

- NORTH-EAST ELEVATION -

- SOUTH-EAST ELEVATION -

WESTOVER

NEAR MILLEDGEVILLE - BALDWIN - COUNTY - GEORGIA -

14-31

SOFFIT MAIN CORNICE.
SCALE 1½"=1'-0"

STAIR DETAIL AT "A".

STAIR ELEVATION.

ELEVATION

JAMB SECTION.

3" SCALE DETAIL OF WINDOWS IN
PARLOR - SEE SHEET NO. 2.
FOR ELEVATION.

PLAN.
DETAIL-START OF
STAIR-FIRST FLOOR.
SCALE ¾"=1'-0"

- DETAIL OF FRONT NORTH ELEVATION -
SCALE 1½"=1'-0"

METRIC SCALE: 10 C.M.

WM. B. HARPER DEL.

U.S. DEPARTMENT OF THE INTERIOR
OFFICE OF NATIONAL PARKS, BUILDINGS, AND RESERVATIONS
BRANCH OF PLANS AND DESIGN

- WESTOVER -

NAME OF STRUCTURE
NEAR MILLEDGEVILLE - BALDWIN
- COUNTY, - GEORGIA -

SURVEY NO.
14-31

HISTORIC AMERICAN
BUILDINGS SURVEY
SHEET 5 OF 5 SHEETS

INDEX NO.
GA.
5 -

Note that Luther's middle initial is given as "E" rather than "C" in the first of these HABS documents:

WESTOVER
Near Milledgeville, Baldwin County
Georgia

Owner: Dr. L.E.Lindsley.

Date of Erection: Before 1830 (see following page); 1830 (drawings).

Architect: Daniel Pratt (?).

Builder: Daniel Pratt (?).

Present Condition: Good.

Number of Stories: Two.

Materials of Construction: Wood.

Other Existing Records: See text; see Gardens of Colony and State,
                        vol. 2, pp. 322-324.

Additional Data: See following pages.

WESTOVER
Near Milledgeville, Baldwin County
Georgia

HISTORICAL NOTES:
    The exact date of construction of this mansion is un-
certain. It was built prior to 1830 by Colonel Ben Jordon, who
had already acquired in 1822 this extensive plantation on the
old Eatonton Road about four miles from Milledgeville.

    Tradition states that the building was designed by Daniel
Pratt, and architect and builder, of Temple, New Hampshire.

    The similarity of details with those of "Lowther Hall",
Clinton, Georgia, designed by Pratt in 1822, and of the Blount
House at Haddock, Georgia, said to have been designed by Pratt
in 1828, would indicate the correctness of this tradition.

    A man of extensive public interest, Colonel Jordon found
this home a convenient meeting place for the discussion of
political questions, and in 1852 he made an addition of a banquet hall. The home was occupied by the Jordon family for many
years and is now owned, occupied and well maintained by Dr. L.E.
Lindsley.

                                    P.Thornton Marye
                                    District Officer HABS

                        (Revised at HABS Headquarters,
                            1936, H.C.F.; original sheet
                            in field notebook).

```
                    WESTOVER
              Near Milledgeville
                 Baldwin County
                    Georgia
```

ARCHITECTURAL NOTES:

A two storey high Doric and pedimented port-
ico stands on the main façade. A frieze of triglyphs extends
all the way around the house. The width of the architrave has
been reduced to a minimum. The brick chimneys are stuccoed, with
joints to appear like stone.

The interior of the house is decorated with
some interesting wood and plaster carvings. The parlor windows
are flanked by fluted pilasters of the composite order and the
frieze above is decorated with urns. Three sunbursts are carved
on the mantel-piece. The plaster cornice has the grave-vine
motif.

Behind the circular stairway is the ballroom,
thirty-five by seventeen feet in area, with its two large ceiling
panels.

by *Henry Chandlee Forman*
March 1936

The signature on the last page of these documents is Henry
Chandlee Forman, the architect who prepared the blueprints. He was
active in historic preservation and worked as an archaeologist for the
National Park Service and as a art professor at Wesleyan College
(Macon) and Agnes Scott College (Decatur, Georgia).

APPENDIX XII

FICTION BY LILLAS STANLEY MYRICK

This story was handwritten on lined paper that seemed to have been torn from a note pad. Three sets of initials had been written at the end, each set the same LSM (Lillas Stanley Myrick). It appears to have been written in her childhood. The handwriting is vastly different from her adult writing, which showed the need to "hurry" in taking notes during post-graduate lectures. This first-person story is narrated by one of the boys, not a girl.

A TRUE STORY

Dean Newman, a boy about nineteen years old, was overseeing a farm for his aunt while she with her husband went to the Springs. I had a friend Alec Keith visiting me then and Dean asked Alec and me with another boy Pat Ward to spend the night with him one Saturday night. Of course we were glad of the invitation and accordingly Saturday evening we "hitched up" and drove to his house, about three miles from ours. Pat was there when we arrived.

Before I go any further I must tell that Dean had ridden twelve miles on horseback at about ten o'clock on this June day and when he reached his destination he had a glass of iced coca-a-cola and a dish of ice cream.

That night we had a very nice time. There were just we four boys and we had a jolly good time. About nine o'clock we made "pallets" on the floor by placing a mattress on the floor and putting a sheet on it.

At about ten o'clock Pat, who was sleeping with Dean, arose and went to the pallet where Alex and I slept and said Dean was hitting him and talking in his sleep and Pat wanted to sleep with me. He lay down by us and all was peace till about twelve o'clock when Dean suddenly arose, grabbed a shotgun, and exclaimed "I've got you now. I'll kill you." I butted for a small lounge in one corner of the room and got under it. As I went under one end Pat went under the other and our heads met together. (The stars we saw are not to be mentioned.) Alec went into the dining room and got under the table. Dean heard Pat and me under the bed and started for us. We ran out the front door and I went toward Pat's home and he went toward mine. I ran through briers that were up to my waist and Dean shot just as I got out of sight. This frightened me more than ever and I looked back and saw an old white dog. I could scarcely see the dog so I thought it was Dean. Just then I struck the cow-pen and five cows. I jumped the fence and slid over three cows' backs in a hurry. Looking back I saw that the object was getting over the fence and I drew a long breath of relief. It was the dog.

Meanwhile Pat had run toward my home and met some Negroes. He frightened the Negroes very much. They thought he was a "haint" and ran from him as fast as possible. Pat and I both heard Dean calling just then and I crept up behind Dean and grabbed his arms behind his back and took the gun away from him. I called Pat and I turned Dean over to him while I hunted for Alec.

When we left the house Alec was under the table, scared nearly out of his wits. Dean came back into the house after shooting at Pat and me. He was (several words illegible) Alec thought he (Dean) was laughing because he had Alec hemmed up in the house. Dean, though, stumbled over something just then and awoke from his unnatural sleep and went out of the house to call us and Alec slipped out of the house and got out under a wagon body. I went all though the house holding Dean and searching for Alec. Finally I called till he came and we "hitched up" and came home.   Nobody ever knew what was the matter with Dean. Pat expressed it thus: "That fool had a fit."

LSM

APPENDIX XIII-A

LILLAS'S COLLEGE EXAM AND THESIS

Lillas Myrick's Blue Book (Exam) (date unknown)

The school, year and class are unknown. Lillas received an 8.5 score on this exam. Note that "1" is given second, and the first answer/section is not numbered. The exam is given here in the order given in her Blue Book.

The chemical elements essential to human nutrition are: carbon, hydrogen, oxygen, nitrogen, sulfur, phosphorus, sodium, potassium, calcium, magnesium, iron, chlorine, iodine, fluorine (trace) silicon.

Of these iron, calcium and phosphorus receive special attention. While there is on(ly) a small amount of iron in the body its functions are most important as it makes up haemoglobin which carries oxygen to the tissues. Since iron is not stored (small amounts in liver, spleen and bone marrow) as calcium and phosphorus, when it is lacking in our food, anemia conditions result to a more or less degree.

Housemann, doubting the ability of inorganic iron to be used by the body working in Bunge's laboratory experimented with animals and found that no more iron was stored in the body of the rats receiving inorganic iron than those receiving no iron in the diet, except in one case where the experiment was continued for a long time. Abderlalden found that inorganic iron had more influence the more organic iron present, but that it did not aid by forming sulfides but rather as a stimulant. Tartakowsy and Smidt's experiences proved that inorganic iron could be used by the body, when given to a "iron free" rat the anemic conditions were overcome. It is still an open question as to the use of inorganic or medicinal iron but there is a incline toward organic. The diet of potato and rice—iron free—was also inadequate in vitamins. It is believed that the radicals of the organic iron may be used in the haemoglobin so in that way organic iron is necessary.

The body requires 15 mg. per day. This can be obtained from

eggs, whole grain cereals, fruits and vegetables, especially green vegetables as spinach.   Since anemic conditions and excessive intestinal putrefaction often go together, the bulkiness and laxative tendency of fruits and vegetables together with their high iron content are advantageous in combating the conditions which are caused from excessive intestinal putrefaction and at the same time add iron to the diet.

Phosphorus, another important element, is essential, structurally as bone builder, sexual element, in glandular tissue, and in nerve stimulant;   functionally in cell multiplication, all movement, control actions of enzymes, stimulant to nerves, liquid movement thru osmotic pressure, liquid content of soft tissue, alkalinity of the organism, secretion and absorption.   Surely any element that plays such an important part must be furnished to the body. The requirement, .88 gm per day for the average man.

Experiments have shown that the body can use inorganic phosphates as well as the phosphatized proteins or fats tho' the organics may be more favorable. This is furnished to the body in eggs, milk, milk products and whole wheat.

The body requires .45 gm of calcium per day. Calcium is used as a bone builder, to maintain neutrality, influence the heart action and muscular control.   There must be a balance maintained between calcium, sodium, and potassium to prevent irritability, and calcium aids in the clotting of the blood.

Growing children need calcium to build the body. This is best obtained thru milk. Children should drink a quart of milk daily until twelve or fourteen years of age. Milk furnishes more calcium per quart than lime water. The body is able to absorb less iron when there is a liberal supply of calcium.

The pregnant woman or nursing mother should have a liberal amount of calcium and iron in their diet to keep from drawing on the calcium stored and yet furnish sufficient for the child. If the iron isn't furnished before birth then it must be furnished after. Children contain about three times as much iron as when older.

Calcium is also furnished by whole wheat, carrots, cabbages and oat meal.

The amounts of iron, calcium and phosphorus given are the required amounts but it is best to have more to insure a sufficiency.

1. There are three types of proteins: The complete, as casein or edestin, which when fed maintains normal growth. The partially complete, as gliadin, which maintain life but growth is very slight. The incomplete, as gelatin or zein (?), which do not maintain life. If casein is fed as the sole protein in a diet where it constitutes 18 % of the protein growth is normal. If this amount is lowered to 9% it becomes partially complete protein and cystine must be added to the diet. When gliadin is fed as sole source of protein there is no growth until lysine is added. When (illegible) is fed as sole protein death occurs in short time. Gliadin, which contains tryptophan, must be added, or tryptophan, for life and the lysine before growth is normal. The protein requirement has been estimated as 44 gm per day. The protein metabolism is influenced by kind and amount of food and water, and not by muscular exercise as the energy metabolism. Thus an increase in calories does not necessarily mean an increase in protein, altho it usually is as the usual kind of food is simply increased. The protein requirement must not only be met by the amount of proteins but by the kind of proteins. Milk furnishes complete proteins, which is about 10 %. Whole grains furnish complete but in such small amounts that they are really incomplete. Eggs furnish a complete protein. Since cells are continually breaking down protein into simple substances which are eliminated from the body, they must be replaced in the diet.

*　　*　　*

INSULIN AND DIABETES

This paper is either her bachelor's or her master's thesis, for she received her Bachelor of Science on February 25, 1925, and her Master of Science degree in October 1925, from Columbia University.

Diabetes was of tremendous interest to Lillas because her father died of its complications and her sister-in-law Chan Myrick (wife of Fullilove) suffered from the disease and was a volunteer in the research studies of insulin.

INSULIN AND DIABETES

Lillas Myrick
Chemistry 175
Jan. 6, 1925

Introduction.

No medical discovery of the past fifty years and perhaps few medical discoveries in history compare with insulin in its importance to the welfare of humanity. Insulin is a name applied to substance obtained from the pancreas of animals, which has the power of increasing the combustion of carbohydrates in diabetes. It was discovered about three years ago and is probably one of the most notable achievements in the treatment of any disease in the twentieth century. At last we have an effective weapon with which to combat diabetes, a disease which is one of humanity's greatest scourges.

History of diabetes.

Diabetes occurs thru out the civilized world and is common to all classes and ages of people. It was known to the ancients. Aretaeus, the Cappadocian, gives the following descriptive account: "The nature of the disease then is chronic, and it takes a long period to form but the patient is short lived if the constitution of the disease be completely established, for the melting is rapid; the death, speedy. Moreover life is disgusting and painful; thirst, unquenchable   excessive   drinking   which   however   is disproportionate to the large quantity of urine passed."

The foundation of modern knowledge on the subject was laid by Von Mering and Minkowski who extirpated the pancreas in dogs. Glycemia and glycosuria conditions resulted, and finally death. If a part of the pancreatic gland remains there is no diabetes. If a piece of pancreas is ingrafted under the skin when the entire pancreas is removed from the body no sugar appears in the urine in two months.

Nature and symptoms.

The cause of diabetes is not fully understood. It is a disease of particular interest since it is a departure from the physiological conditions of the body to care for sugar in the normal manner. All the symptoms, the excessive quantities of sugar in the blood and urine and finally acidosis, are due to this one fact. The islands of Langerhans in the pancreas furnish a secretion into the blood stream giving a substance which causes carbohydrates to be utilized by tissue. When this function is lost it is believed that sugar is not changed to inactive form and instead of being used by the body, stored in the liver as glycogen and oxidized (it) remains in the blood and is given off in the urine. As a result protein is called upon as glucose supply. Since carbohydrate is necessary for normal fat metabolism, combustion of fats is incomplete, causing diabetic acidosis. "Diabetes must therefore be considered a disease of metabolism in which carbohydrate is not efficiently utilized by the body therefore causing a derangement of the normal metabolism of proteins and fats, as well as carbohydrates." This is recognized by voracious appetites, hyperglycemia and hyperglycosuria.

When a person is fed more than two hundred grams of glucose the power of liver to store glycogen is exceeded. Blood sugar increases so above normal the excess passes into the urine, glycosuria resulting. In this case alimentary glycosuria, the assimilation limit for glucose has been exceeded. The assimilation limit for sucrose is about two hundred grams varying with individuals and when there is a tendency toward diabetes the sugar tolerance is low. Glucose in the blood is about 0.1%. The respiratory quotient of diabetic animals show little or no carbohydrate is burned. The body is incapable of storing glycogen in the liver (shown by autopsies of diabetics), however, there may be some glycogen formed in its muscles. This is probably due to the fact that the glycogen is broken down as fat as it is formed. The sugar-hungry cells are constantly calling for sugar. The formation of fats from carbohydrates does not occur in diabetes as in normal animals possibly because of lack of glycogen in (the) liver.

In severe cases there is more sugar in the urine than can be accounted for by carbohydrate of food. Some of this must have synthesized from protein or from fat. It has been found that feeding protein causes an increase in the amount of sugar excreted. Stiles and Lusk have shown that this sugar is formed by animals from certain amino acids which are present in the protein molecule. It has been determined from the elementary composition of proteins that 80% of the protein molecule might be transformed into sugar. Urine of a totally diabetic animal will contain nitrogen and glucose produced in protein metabolism. This glucose production from protein is expressed in terms of D:N ratio. In diabetes this D:N ratio has a value of 2.8.

Acidosis.

The dangerous part of diabetes is the formation of acetone bodies. In a normal person a temporary formation of acetone bodies occurs when carbohydrate food is omitted from the diet. In starvation acetone bodies are formed and in diabetes acetone bodies are formed. These are diminished slightly if some sugar can be oxidized. Acetone bodies fed to normal persons in moderate amounts are oxidized to carbon dioxide and water, but in diabetes since they can not be oxidized they produce acidosis.

If a normal animal is fed organic acids as malic, citrus or tartaric unless excessive, they are oxidized to carbon dioxide and water. We find the potassium salts of these acids in fruits which when oxidized yield an alkaline ash consisting of potassium bicarbonate and consequently make the urine more alkaline.

The acetone bodies with the exception of acetone itself, which is not an acid are poisonous because they unite with the bases in the body forming salts. For the transportation of carbon dioxide from tissue to the lungs it is necessary for sodium bicarbonate to be in blood. When this is used up excess carbon dioxide occurs in the tissues. The patient then passes into a state of coma. With increasing losses of alkaline reserve there comes a time when so little sodium bicarbonate (is) left that no amount of respiration is possible.

The body combats acidosis in three ways. First, oxidizing acids when possible; second, producing a more acid urine; and third, forming ammonia to neutralize acids.

The kidneys can remove weakly acid substances from the blood, acid phosphates and weak organic acids, but more acid substances cannot be eliminated by kidneys with out previous neutralization. A small amount of urea can be changed into ammonium carbonate to be used for neutralization. Benedict claims this is done by the kidneys. In acidosis considerable amount is done in this way.

Normally phosphoric acid and sulfuric acid are formed by the sulfur and phosphorus of proteins. The body produces ammonia to neutralize, so that ammonium salts are present in the urine from 3% to 5% of total nitrogen present. In severe acidosis the ammonia nitrogen may be high as 40% of total nitrogen. The body is not able to produce enough ammonia to neutralize all the acid produced in acidosis.

Discovery of Insulin.

For many years the existence of a substance supplied by the pancreas which regulated carbohydrate metabolism was known. Von Mering and Minkowski in 1889 demonstrated that the removal of the islands of Langerhans from animals caused fatal diseases; and a few years later Oslen predicted that the pancreatin hormone controlling blood tissue would be discovered in the near future. In 1919 Joslin expressed the confident hope that the extracts from the islands of Langerhans would some day be used in the treatment of diabetes.

The secret for the pancreatic hormone was unavailable for thirty years after the discovery of Von Mering and Minkowski. As a result of their experiments work was begun by Banting and Best under Macleod of (the) University of Toronto to obtain this product from the islands of Langerhans.

It was believed the pancreas furnished two secretions: one an external secretion, trypsinogen; the other an internal secretion from the islands of Langerhans affecting the carbohydrate metabolism. To obtain this internal secretion the pancreatic duct of a dog was ligated so that the tissue containing trypsinogen would degenerate. After eight weeks the dogs were killed, and while the acinsar cells had degenerated the islands of Langerhans had not. Extracts were prepared and injected in a depancrenized dog. There was a lowering of sugar in blood and removal of sugar in urine. By insulin injections the degree of blood sugar could be accurately controlled and the animals fed sufficient carbohydrate to keep them in physiological condition.

Before this time they had failed on account of simultaneous

extractions from pancreas of trypsin which destroyed the hormone as well as had a toxic effect on animals when injected. Since the process of tying the pancreatic duct and waiting for degeneration was a slow process, other means of obtaining insulin were sought. Collip who was invited to join the work succeeded in preparing active extracts of insulin from fetal or adult undegenerated pancreas, by the use of alcohol, then, obtaining the insulin of the pancreas from animals from slaughter houses.

The lessening of glycemia and removal of glycosuria after an insulin injection supports the view that the islands of Langerhans in the pancreas contain a substance which lowers blood sugar and diminishes or abolishes sugar in the urine. A special type of glycosuria is caused by phlorhizin injection as was discovered by Von Mering. The blood looses its power to retain sugar therefore the sugar (passes) thru the kidneys leaving the blood in a hypo-glycemic condition.

Lush found that the injection of a large quantity of glucose to a phlorhizin dog in no way affects the respiratory quotient, showing that the power to oxidize glucose is completely lost. The protein metabolism is here identical with that observed in diabetes where the pancreas is removed from the dog, which is analogous to dia-betes in men. Thus, the animal may be given diabetes by depan-crenizing or by phlorhizine. Nash and Benedict (J. Biol. Chem. 55. 765) do not agree with Lush (Sc. of Nutrition) that the failure to burn sugar under phlorhizic conditions is due to acidosis since frequently the acidosis is not as marked as in diabetes of man where a partial sugar capacity may be retained.

Unit Measure.

The great variability of resistance of rabbits to insulin has made the quantitative study of a unit uncertain. Rabbits fresh from the country are more resistant than after they have been kept in the Laboratory.

One-third of the amount of insulin injected in a two-kilogram rabbit having fasted twenty-four hours, which lowers the blood sugar from normal (0.118%) to 0.045% over a period of five hours, is the official insulin unit adopted by the Insulin Committee of the University of Toronto.

Chemical Nature .

As to the chemical nature of insulin, although it has not been isolated in pure form, there seems to be no doubt that it is protein in nature. Preparations refined to the place where 0.1 mg of dry substance represents one rabbit unit still contains a high percent of ash and therefore is far from pure. H. A. Shonle and J. H. Waldo in article in Journal Biological Chemistry "...conclude that pancreatic substance containing insulin appears to be a complex mixture of proteomes, which it has been as yet impossible to isolate a simple substance."

Source and preparation.

The most important factor in insulin production is the use of absolutely fresh glands. The amount varies from 1,500 to 2,200 rabbit units per kilo of fresh glands. The average yield approximates 1,800 units from cattle, dogs and sheep. While insulin was originally extracted from the pancreas of dogs, sheep and cows Dr. Macleod states now that the glands from fish have been found to contain large amounts of insulin and a substance capable of producing an insulin of like effect has been extracted from the kidneys, spleen and muscles of dogs and cattle. That this substance is produced in the pancreas and stored in the tissue is indicated by the fact that no insulin action can be demonstrated in the extracts prepared from the organs of depanceanized dogs. Insulin is also obtained from plant tissue and is known as glucokinin.

Originally alcohol was used as extractive for insulin, a later method was to separate the material by absorptive charcoal. To increase the unit per kilo of pancreas or to introduce a cheaper extractive yet obtain a pure product and lower the cost is desirable.

Cases requiring insulin.

The mild diabetic whose blood sugar can be kept with in normal range of from 50 to 120 milligrams per 100 c.c. on a diet that will keep him well nourished does not need insulin. Insulin is needed:

(1) The coma cases in which, if given early enough, insulin will give almost certain relief.

(2) The severe or mild cases that have dropped low in weight and

are in a state of debility.

(3) Severe cases with tendency toward acidosis.

(4) The tubercular diabetics.

(5) Cases requiring operations for gangrene or other causes in which it is important to remove acidosis as rapidly as possible.

Dosage and diet.

There is no fixed dose for insulin. The amount required depends on the severity of the case, the patient's carbohydrate tolerance, the presence or absence of acid substances in the blood and urine and complicating conditions. The amount required by each patient can be determined with accuracy only by a study of the blood sugar and urine for the total output of sugar, acetone, diacetic acid etc.

If sugar is present in the urine and the patient is receiving sufficient calories, carbohydrate is reduced until the urine is sugar free, or insulin may be increased if carbohydrate is below 30 gm per day.

The first dose of insulin is usually one unit, before the second meal two units, before the third, three and so on up to five units. Then this quantity is given three times per day and decreased or increased as needed. During this time the diet is being changed.

The first diet should be relatively the same as the diet the patient is accustomed to with the number of calories reduced by less fats; and protein limited to one gram per kilogram of body weight, and it is desirable to begin with about 200 grams of carbohydrates. Once the urine is sugar free, the noon dose is stopped by shifting the carbohydrate in diet to breakfast or supper. The doses are given ¼ to 1 ¼ hours before meals, depending on rapidity of absorption of carbohydrates.

By testing the urine before and after meals they can determine whether the relation between carbohydrate and insulin is satisfactory. Blood sugar tests are desirable but Benedict tests on urine are easier made and less expensive. Intelligent patients can be taught the use of diet and insulin and in two weeks time become free of acid and sugar.

Methods of Administering.

Insulin has no effect when given by mouth for there are certain digestive juices in the stomach and intestines which destroy it. It is given intravenously and not intramuscularly. If given intramuscularly it causes pain and has a slight destructive and irritant effect upon the muscular tissue.

Physiological effects of insulin.

When insulin is ingested in proper doses in a diabetic patient the blood sugar returns to normal and sugar does not appear in the urine; the respiratory quotient rises, showing carbohydrate is being burned; and acetone and B-oxidation products are no longer formed. The patient feels better unless too much insulin is given. In diabetics receiving determined doses for a long time, the amount required gradually decreases, which shows that in a good portion it is an actual cure, the pancreas increasing its power.

Insulin shock.

If an over dose of insulin is given, insulin shock develops. The symptoms are trembling, weakness and nausea. When nothing is done for it, more severe symptoms occur—convulsions, unconsciousness and low pulse rate. It is not dangerous if one knows how to treat it. All symptoms can be rapidly overcome by giving a little orange juice, sugar or some form of quickly absorbable carbohydrate.

Conclusion.

Patents are held on the manufacture of insulin by the University of Toronto, the object being to insure a product of uniform quality and potency at the least possible cost. The price now charged per unit is below the cost of production. Banting, the discoverer of insulin, has not and will not profit one cent by its manufacture.

We cannot yet call insulin a cure for diabetes, but since the functions of the islands of Langerhans may possibly be revived and regenerated, there is no reason why the temporary relief afforded by insulin might not finally affect a cure. Dr. Banting's dream has at last come true. Human diabetes is at last under control.

Convincing proof of this was furnished at the meeting of the Association of American Physicians when doctors from all over the country reported upon the striking success of insulin in the treatment of diabetes.

REFERENCES.

C. H. Best and D. A. Scott. Insulin in tissue other than pancreas. JAMA 81: 382-383 (1923).

Insulin Committee, University of Toronto. Insulin: its action, its therapeutic value in diabetes and its manufacture. JAMA 80: 1847 (1923).

E. P. Joslin. Routine treatment of diabetes with insulin. JAMA 80: 1581 (1923).

Special Article – The Status of Insulin. JAMA 80: 1258 (1923).

H. A. Shonle and J. H. Waldo. Insulin and diabetes. J. Biol. Chem. 58: 731-736 (1924).

T. P. Nash, Jr. and S. R. Benedict. On the mechanism of phlorhizin diabetes. J. Biol. Chem. 55: 757-767 (1923).

M. Somogyi, E. A. Doisy, and P. A. Shaffer. On preparation of insulin. J. Biol. Chem. 60: 31-58 (May 1924).

Edward Tolstoi. Glycolysis in blood of normal subjects and of diabetic patients. J. Biol. Chem. 60: 69-75 (1924).

Charles Best and D.A. Scott. Preparation of Insulin. J. Biol. Chem. 57: 709-723 (1923).

L. B. Winter and W. Smith. On the nature of the sugar in blood. J. Physiol. LVII: 100 (1922).

W. Dennis and Upton Giles. On glycolysis in diabetic and non-diabetic blood. J. Biol. Chem. 56: 739-744 (1923).

F. Fenger and R. S. Wilson. The amount of available insulin in the pancreas of domestic animals. J. Biol. Chem. 59: 83-90 (1924).

Lush. "Science of Nutrition."   G. The elements of the science of nutrition, 2nd Edition, 1909. W. B. Saunders Co.

APPENDIX XIII-B

LILLAS'S RESEARCH PAPERS

From *Chemical Abstracts*, Vol. 25, p. 4306 (1931)

Ovarian hormone and metabolism. J. F. McClendon, Lillas Myrick, Claire Conklin and I. H. Wilson. Am. J. Physiol. 97, 82-5 (1931). —The basal metabolic rate for 23 women during the post-menstrual period was 98.88 ± 0.15; and for the pre-menstrual period 101.41 ± 0.27. A hormone or hormones from the corpus luteum may cause the change noted.

The entire article from *The American Journal of Physiology*, Volume 97, No. 1, April 1931 is given on the next few pages.

Reprinted from THE AMERICAN JOURNAL OF PHYSIOLOGY
Vol. 97, No. 1, April, 1931

OVARIAN HORMONE AND METABOLISM

J. F. McCLENDON, LILLAS MYRICK, CLAIRE CONKLIN AND I. H. WILSON

From the Laboratory of Physiological Chemistry, University of Minnesota Medical School, Minneapolis

Received for publication September 29, 1930

In studying the relation of ovarian hormone to metabolism it is important to note what hormone is being considered. There seem to be three hormones in the ovary and the data on normal women would be influenced by these three hormones collectively. In the assay and injection experiments, the *follicular* hormone was the one used because at the time the work was done it was the only one we had means to assay or we could obtain. It had been repeatedly reported by Frank and others that the follicular hormone occurs in the blood of women in the pre-menstrual period and is absent or deficient in the post-menstrual period, and we have confirmed this finding to the extent that some samples of 40 cc. of pre-menstrual blood produced an abundantly cornified vaginal smear in an ovariectomized mouse, whereas all samples of 40 cc. of post-menstrual blood failed to do this. After 400 days of work on the assay of the follicular hormone, we ruled out all results unless there was a *great abundance* of cornified cells in the vaginal smear. (It seems to us more logical to take out the ovary from the dorsal side without cutting into the peritoneal cavity.)

Laqueur, Hart and deJongh (1926) reported an increase in the basal metabolic rate of ovariectomized mice on injection of the follicular hormone. McClendon and Burr (1929) reported a slight rise in basal metabolic rate of a woman who apparently had been devoid of ovarian function since birth (absence of menstruation and puberty-growth), on the injection of 1000 or more mouse-units of follicular hormone during a day. We have repeated this experiment on another woman who had never menstruated although she was thirty-five years old. She was also sterile and had only vestiges of nipples. On injecting 30,000 mouse units of follicular hormone in oil (which was given to us by Doctor Laqueur) there was a rise in basal metabolic rate during the day and it continued high the second day. Although Laqueur claimed the potency was as great as that of Doisy's crystals of "theelin," since it was dissolved in oil we did not consider it pure. We obtained some pure "theelin" from Doctor Kamm but were not able at the time to find a proper subject for the metabolism experiment. We therefore injected this at the rate of 50 units every half-hour for ten doses into a man and determined the basal metabolic rate every half-hour. There was no consistent rise in metabolism with the accumulation of the hormone. This is the same result as reported by Laqueur for male mice and normal female mice and by Kunde, D'Amour, Carlson and Gustavson (1930) for normal female dogs. It is not clear why the hormone should raise the basal metabolic rate of ovariectomized females or those with congenital lack of ovarian function and not that of normal females or males. Certainly the males show lack of ovarian function. One might suppose that the rise in basal metabolic rate was due to the growth of the endometrium, but time was not sufficient for very much growth, and, according to Corner and Hisau, the *follicular* hormone does not cause a growth of the endometrium. We are forced to leave these injection experiments in this unfinished state and pass on to the cyclical changes in normal women.

Since the follicular hormone increases in the blood during the inter-menstrual period, if it caused an increase in basal metabolic rate, there should be such an increase in metabolism during this period. Benedict and Finn made such a study on one woman and we have averaged the cubic centimeters of O_2 per minute for the pre-menstrual and for the post-menstrual weeks. For the post-menstrual weeks there were 178.8 cc. of O_2 per minute and for the pre-menstrual weeks 179 cc. of O_2 per minute. The slight increase indicates that statistical methods must be used to find out its significance. A number of writers have reported a greater increase. Some of them are Snell, Ford and Rowntree (1920), Rowe and Eakin (1921), Wakeham (1923), Hafkesbring and Collett (1924), Collett and Liljestrand (1924), and Conklin and McClendon (1930). On the other hand a number of writers have denied this, the latest being Sandiford, Wheeler and Boothby (1931). The data of the latter show a slight rise, however, the average of the pre-menstrual week being slightly higher than the post-menstrual week. The average for the post-menstrual week is 32.9 ± 0.2 and for the pre-menstrual week 33.3 ± 0.2. This careful work combined with that of Benedict and Finn (1928) recalls the necessity of statistical methods. We have made prolonged series of determinations on twenty-three women, varying in age from nineteen to thirty-five years, with a mean of 21.2 years. The average of the post-menstrual period was 32.5 calories per square meter per hour and for the pre-menstrual period was 33.7 calories per square meter per hour. The grand average of the basal metabolic rate was 33.6 calories per square meter per hour, which corresponds closely to the average given by Sandiford, Wheeler and Boothby (1931) for a normal woman during her 34th to 41st years, which is 33.1 ± 0.06. It should be noted that these are trained individuals and cannot be used as standards for clinical work.

We believe the spread of the curve and the probable errors will be more evident if results are put in percentages of the mean values of these women. The basal metabolic rate during the post-menstrual period for these twenty-three women was 98.88±0.15, and for the pre-menstrual period 101.41±0.27. The determinations were as follows: Post-menstrual period, 82 (once), 87 (once), 88 (once), 90 (four times), 91 (twice), 92 (5 times), 93 (3 times), 94 (12 times), 95 (12 times), 96 (11 times), 97 (17 times), 98 (14 times), 99 (18 times), 100 (8 times), 101 (19 times), 102 (16 times), 103 (11 times), 104 (4 times), 105 (4 times), 106 (7 times), 107 (4 times), 108 (twice), 109 (twice), 110 (once), (n = 179); pre-menstrual period, 86 (once), 88 (once), 90 (once), 91 (once), 92 (once), 93 (twice), 94 (4 times), 95 (7 times), 96 (9 times), 97 (8 times), 98 (11 times), 99 (11 times), 100 (12 times), 101 (18 times), 102 (9 times), 103 (11 times), 104 (12 times), 105 (14 times), 106 (8 times), 107 (6 times), 108 (5 times), 109 (twice), 110 (twice), 111 (twice), 112 (3 times), 116 (once), 120 (once), (n = 163). The difference between the post and pre-menstrual periods is a rise of 2.53 per cent and the probable error is 0.15 for the post and 0.27 for the pre-menstrual period so we have here a significant rise in the metabolic rate during the inter-menstrual period, based on 342 determinations. These individuals were not selected except that only women who would thoroughly coöperate and who did not show nervousness or complain of menstrual pain, were utilized. The average number of determinations on each woman was less than in the work of Conklin and McClendon and the difference between the post and the pre-menstrual periods was not quite so great but the probable errors were very much smaller owing to the larger number of determinations.

Since it has been shown by Frank (1929) Steinach (1925) Hartman (1926) and others, that the ovarian hormone causes an increase in the mammary gland and nipple, an attempt has been made to study the volume of the nipple in the post and pre-menstrual periods. In this case the volumes of the nipples are recorded in per cent of the average volumes for the women studied. The volumes during the post-menstrual week measured on thirteen women were 93.9±0.693, and the volumes during the pre-menstrual week were 106.3±0.8. The individual determinations were of the post-menstrual period: 82 (once), 84 (once), 85 (once), 86 (3 times), 88 (twice,) 89 (twice,) 90 (once), 91 (once), 92 (4 times), 93 (once), 94 (3 times), 95 (3 times), 96 (once), 97 (twice), 98 (once), 99 (3 times), 100 (once), 101 (twice), 102 (twice), 103 (once), 108 (once), (n = 37) and for the pre-menstrual period: 93 (twice), 96 (once), 98 (once), 100 (once), 101 (twice), 102 (twice), 103 (4 times), 104 (6 times), 106 (twice), 107 (4 times), 108 (once), 109 (3 times), 110 (twice), 111 (3 times), 118 (once), 119 (twice), 120 (once), 121 (once), (n = 39). The increase in volume of the nipples from the post to the pre-menstrual week was 12.8 per cent, and is many times larger than the probable error.

APPENDIX XIV

LILLAS RECEIVES PUBLICITY RE RESEARCH

Lillas received general publicity for her research. She would have continued this research and published in a scientific journal had she not married. Note the spelling of "goitre" in the 1930s.

The *Macon Telegraph*, Sunday Magazine, May 18, 1930 page 4:

IODINE IS GEORGIA'S SIDE CROP

High content of Valuable Vegetable Element in Georgia Products Pointed Out by Georgia Chemistry Professor Now Studying in Minnesota -- "Not a Goitre in a Gallon" May be New slogan

"Not a goitre in a gallon" may be adopted as Georgia's slogan with regard to her corn, if the recent analyses of the iodine content of Georgia vegetables are an indication.

Georgia carrots, broccoli, and tomatoes have been analyzed by Miss Lillas Myrick of Milledgeville, who is studying at the University of Minnesota, and they are found to contain a high percentage of iodine, when compared with those of the middle west or the far western states.

It is well known to both scientists and laymen that the presence or absence of iodine in the food supply is responsible for the action of the thyroid gland. Throughout the middle west, where iodine is lacking both in vegetable and fish, the prevalence of goitres is many times higher than in our section.

Some months ago, the vegetables of South Carolina were examined for iodine content and were found to be high in this valuable element. The people of the state, realizing the importance of this discovery, have advertized extensively. It is a matter of importance, as well as from the standpoint of the health of South

Carolina's inhabitants, for vegetables grown and canned in that state may have a sale value far ahead of others.

Carrots grown in California show 170 parts of iodine per billon, while those grown in Chatham County, Georgia, show 407 parts per billon, an increase of more than 200 parts per billon over South Carolina's carrots. The same vegetable grown in Oregon contains only two and three tenths parts of iodine per billon. Tomatoes grown in California show 17.5 parts of iodine per billon, and those from Georgia contain 71.

Since the Pacific Ocean contains much less iodine than the Atlantic, it is easy enough to realize that the vegetables grown on the Pacific coast should show the low proportion.

Sea salt, and therefore the spray which evaporates in the air at the seashore, is relatively rich in iodine and as this sea salt dust is carried inward by the wind, it gives iodine to the rain water, the soil water, the soils and the crops of nearby regions.

Therefore, in our section of the country we are fairly well protected from goitre if we eat liberally of vegetables grown in our state, drink milk from cows which feed on grass grown in soil where the sea spray has produced iodized soil and water and if we eat salt water fish.

The amount of iodine present in sea animals is much higher than in plants or land animals. There is a variation in amounts found in different fish, but iodine contents is high in all of them. Mackerel contains 300 parts per billion, herring 1,800; shrimp, 700; salmon trout 100; mullet, 600; mussel, 1,900; Portuguese oysters, 1,300. A large amount of the iodine is leached out in the cookery, even as high as 800 per cent.

It is proven that a region high in goitre is low in iodine. South Carolina has very little goitre, as has Georgia. The vegetables of South Carolina show a very high content as against those of Oregon, for instance: Spinach in South Carolina contains 424 parts of iodine as against 19.5 parts in Oregon. String beans compare 429 parts as against 29 in Oregon, and carrots 135 against two and three-tenths.

Cereal grains are poor in iodine regardless of their habitat, so we cannot depend upon them for protection, no matter in what soil they may be grown. The tops of turnips, beets and carrots contain more iodine than the roots. Only the potato—the Irish—contains any appreciable amount of iodine among the root vegetables.

Miss Myrick, who is former head of the department of chemistry at the Georgia State College for Women in Milledgeville and who is on leave of absence, writes interestingly concerning the method employed in determining the content of iodine in vegetables.

"I first weighed the carrots, then sliced them thin, put them and the broccoli in wire racks that stack and sent hot air through them until they were dry. It took three days for the broccoli to dry. I boiled the tomatoes down as low as I could and then put them in a low oven for about ten days. I then ground them till they were as fine as flour, ending up with three colors, a green, a red and an orange (the broccoli, the tomato and the carrot).

"Then the real analysis began. I weighed 100 grams, then put a low flame under it, when it started burning, I removed the flame and the burning continued for about two hours, till it all was charred. Then it was put into a muffler and heated to a temperature of 800 degrees, all this time being done in a silica dish, so that the heat would not affect it. It remained at the 800 degree temperature for 24-48 hours until there was nothing left but a white ash.

"The ash was then extracted with alcohol twice, in a ball mill (to keep it shaken and make the alcohol come in contact with it all). The alcohol was then evaporated and the solid left, burned; the gases being drawn into an iodium sulfite solution by means of suction. The sulfite was then boiled down to 5cc and phosphoric acid and sodium azide added.

"I next transferred it to a separatory bulb, made up to 10cc and added 1cc of chloroform and sodium nitrite. The chloroform takes the iodine out, giving a pinkish violet color. This is compared with the iodine chloroform solution, of a known strength in a colorimeter.

"This may not mean much to a layman, but it gives some idea of how long it takes for one analysis and if you do not check yourself you keep doing the experiment till you do check. The amount present is so small that it is expressed as so many parts per billion.

"Dr. J. F. McClendon, head of the Physiological Chemistry department here, is regarded as an authority on iodine, that is why they sent all the way to Minnesota to have Georgia vegetables done. He had analyzed water from every state and has found that the region high in iodine is the region low in goitre."

Some of the large cities of the middle west have been experimenting with the placing of iodine in the drinking water in order to offset the prevalence of goitre. Chocolate iodine tablets are in use in the school systems of Michigan; the use of iodized salt is recommended in some middle western states. But it is generally conceded that the use of food which contains iodine is preferable to artificial methods.

As far back as 1896, the presence of iodine in the normal thyroid gland was demonstrated by the German chemist Bauman. It occurs not only in the thyroid, but also in the tissues, in relatively small amounts. It is relatively high in the spleen, the suprarenal and the salivary glands. It is estimated by Von Vellenberg that the thyroid gland contains only about one percent of the total iodine in the body, but since the lack of iodine shows such a prompt reaction in the thyroid we have come to talk of this gland, primarily, in discussing the need for iodine.

The thyroid gland is a ductless gland—that is, it pours its secretions directly into the blood stream instead of sending it through a duct or tube as other glands may do. For instance, the liver secretes a substance called bile, which it pours directly into the intestine, through a short duct or tube, and the food in the intestine is acted on by the digestant in the bile. Likewise, the pancreas secrets a material called pancreatic juice which is sent through a duct into the intestine to help with the transforming of food.

But the so-called ductless glands, such as the thyroid, the pituitary, the adrenals and so on, manufacture certain substances which they pour directly in the blood as it passes through them, bringing nourishment and taking away waste products. The blood then carries the secretions of the glands directly to the parts where it is needed.

The secretions of the ductless glands contain hormones, substances which are chemical in nature and which being carried to an associated organ by the blood excite in the latter organ a functional activity.

The hormone or active principal of the thyroid gland is called thyroxin and it is secreted in the proper amount and proportion only when the body receives a normal amount of iodine. The iodine is a stimulant to the gland and causes it to produce its secretion.

When the thyroid gland is not functioning in the proper way, the disturbance is spoken of as a goitre. These are of varying types and degrees of dangers. The goitre, which strangely enough seems to cause no harmful results in the system and which a person may have for years without any danger or disturbance of the other functions of the body, is called a colloid, and it is merely an enlargement of the gland—a swelling, producing a lump on the front of the neck, which is perhaps unsightly but does not actually affect the general health.

This type of goitre is not the rule, however, and any disturbance of the gland should receive medical attention. The other classes of goitre usually result in about two out of a thousand, while in the Far and Middle West, they reach the number of 21 or 27 to 1,000 people.

Thyroid disturbances may take the form of lack of energy, excess weight and cloudy brain, if there is a lack of secretion. On the other hand, too much thyroid secretion may bring about a highly nervous condition, with inability to put on weight and a quick, jumpy temperament.

Since the thyroid gland is concerned with growth of the body and with metabolism—the breaking down and the building up of the cells of the body, the changing of food into energy and tissue, it is easy to understand that the lack of this gland is conducive of much bodily harm. When the mother is lacking in iodine or had a greatly disturbed thyroid function, the baby many be born a dwarf or a cretin. Dwarfs may be treated with thyroid extract and attain natural growth if taken in the early stages. Giants also may be the result of abnormal thyroid secretion. The freaks in the side shows, giants and dwarfs, are usually the result of abnormal thyroid secretion and the condition is congenital. Experiments had been made in laboratories with tadpoles. The thyroid gland was removed in baby tadpoles, and growth and development was stopped outright.

In Switzerland, which is remote from the sea and where goitre and cretinism are prevalent, the giving of iodine has been found to prove of inestimable value. In three Swiss cantons, where iodine was given all school children, during the three years 1918-1922, the increase of goitre was diminished from 87 percent to 13 percent.

The effects of iodine on the growth of children has not been studied very carefully, but it has been proven that in the case of abnormal thyroid which produced dwarfs, the giving of iodine or of thyroid extract had been effective in procuring growth if the case were taken in its early stages.

Ellenberger and Hunziker, two scientists, gave potassium iodine for 40 weeks to children, a group of 339 of them, and kept accurate records of height and weight. The boys who received the iodine grew on an average of seven-tenths of a centimeter more than the boys who were untreated and they put on two-tenths of a kilogram more weight. The girls gained four-tenths of a centimeter in height and put on one-tenth of a kilo more weight.

The first modern experiments in the treatment of goitre were those of Marine and his co-workers on trout reared under artificial conditions for commercial purposes. The mortality of the fish from goitre was so high that the industry was threatened with extinction. Marine found that traces of iodine prevented the trouble. In younger fish the appearance of goitre was prevented.

Marine made his first experiments on humans in Akron, Ohio. Two thousand one hundred ninety school children, who had no goitre, were given iodine and at the end of the year, only five had developed goitre. Of 2,305 who had no goitre and received no iodine, 495 had developed goitre by the end of the year. At the same time, 1,152 children who already had goitre were treated with iodine and of these 773 showed reduction in the size of the gland at the end of the year. While 1,048 who had goitre but were untreated, only 145 showed reduction at the end of the year.

From other experiments, it has been shown that in the vast majority of cases, administration of iodine arrests the growth of a goitre and reduces its size. The effect is greater the earlier the treatment is applied. After the age of puberty, the efficacy of the treatment is reduced and after the age of 20 gives little or no response.

APPENDIX XV

LILLAS AND HER TRIP HOME FROM U. MINNESOTA

TINKER BELL

Lillas S. Myrick
1929

Lillas and Tinker Bell

Her traveling companions

Wanted: A passenger. Driving to Georgia or Florida in Pontiac roadster. Desire someone for company and to share expenses. Leaving middle of June. P. O. Box 4485.

"Interested in driving with you if you go anywhere near Baltimore. Jack. P.O. Box 6872."

"Would like to go to Alabama with you. Have made trip before and could help with driving. I'm a female. Hope you are same species. Julie. P.O. Box 2684. Phone: Dismore 2795."

"Am a widower, 25 years old. Going to Miami and would like to go with you as far as you go. Phone MI-6687."

"I'm a P.E. major, junior. If you'll take me to Memphis, I'll go with you. Come to see me at 1268 Fourth Avenue."

Such were the answers received from my want ad posted on the bulletin board in the post office of the University of Minnesota. Only a week before I would leave for home, and all these applicants to be interviewed! Alas! None of them proved successful. Consequently, I jumped at the idea when one of my professors said he was going to Chicago and would be glad to accompany me that far.

Exams, last minute parties, and, in the midst of good-byes, I began packing Tinker Bell. That was the name I gave the Pontiac, since it flies around everywhere. It seemed to possess everything except a kitchen stove and a piano. With much assistance and struggling, however, I managed to tie everything that wouldn't go into the trunk and rumble seat on top of them. I then parked Tinker Bell by the side of Sanford dorm, ready to leave early in the morning.

The old alarm clock sounded fifteen minutes after my head hit the pillow. In less time than that, I crept down the stairs while it was not quite light. The prof joined me, and then homeward bound. We were away from the city just as it was waking. I talked intellectually for miles and miles. On across Wisconsin, and the close of the first day found us in Chicago after 500 miles more or less.

I was cordially received by friends and forgot hot dusty roads and detours. Yet, with the dawn of another day, maps and more maps were unfolded, routes and more routes traced, suggestions and more suggestions received. Finally it was decided that I should take Nation No. 41. So manfully and fearlessly, I started out, accompanied by two French dolls. Toodles was stylishly dressed in high heels and long skirt, while Flatateena wore pajamas. By sitting on top of the portable Victrola on the seat, they had a ringside view.

Chicago traffic on Sunday morning seemed, at first, impenetrable, but Tinker Bell stayed on Route 41 and was soon speeding on toward Indianapolis, then away from Indianapolis. Sunset found us at Frankly, Indiana, a tourist town. We made 260 miles.

A bell ringing jarred me awake and someone said, "You asked to be called at five o'clock." Half awake and half asleep, I headed for Louisville.

M-I-N-N-E-S-O-T-A
Minnesota! Minnesota!
Yes, Gopher!

No longer was I sleepy or lonesome, for I had the University of Minnesota band with me.

Minnesota, hail to thee!
Hail to thee, our College dear!
Thy light shall ever be
A beacon bright and clear;
Thy sons and daughters true
Will proclaim thee near and far
They will guard thy name;
And adore thy name;
Thou shall be their Northern star.

The Alma Mater, and I couldn't stand! No chance of getting lonesome, for when the band left, I had Rudy Vallee and the Boob-Boop-A-Doop girl along, for I found that I could crank the portable Vic on the seat beside me and have music as I rode along.

At last, in the blue grass region of Kentucky. It was again time to feed Tinker Bell. I never gave her more than five galloons of gas at a time, so I could have an excuse to stop often and talk to someone. Having had little chance to see a newspaper, I was dumbfounded to see the extreme drought. At a Louisville filling station, I inquired, "It is this dry all over Kentucky?"

He replied, "Why, lady, it ain't dry. I kin git you ten gallons in ten minutes."

Later I was advised that going through Stanton and Ashville, instead of Nashville and Chattanooga, would shorten my route considerable. Willingly, I accepted the advice and started out in that direction.

After going about thirty miles, I thought I should be somewhere near a town so I stopped the first person I met and asked, "How far to Shelbyville?"

"You're going the wrong way. It's on the other side of Louisville."

Realizing I took the right highway but had gone the wrong direction, I asked, "Well, where does this road go?"

"To Elizabeth."

"And on to Nashville?"

"Yes."

"Thanks," I said. "I'll just go to Nashville."

The man looked at me and shook his head, as though I needed more assistance than he could give me. But after all, what difference did it make which way I went?

I drove on.

After leaving Nashville, I soon reached the Appalachian Mountains. Just a gradual incline, around curves, and more curves, and then down, and soon I was across one mountain and ready to start the next. With the car top back and the windshield down in the late afternoon, it was "boop, boop, a doop." If the curve was just right, the Vic played double quick time; if the curve turned the other direction, it played backwards.

When I reached the Georgia line, I felt as though I were really home. The first person I talked to noticed my Minnesota license plate and said, "You sho' are a far way from home. Going to Florida?"

Finally at home, I pitched bags and baggage into the house, and at 4:30 a.m. I started out for Daytona Beach to join my family. On through Jacksonville and to St. Augustine, where I took the ocean boulevard. At last, after miles and days, I arrived at the end of a 440-mile day.

I drove from one end of Atlantic Avenue to the other and half way back before I found number 353. Just as I stopped, my five-year-old red-headed nephew ran out and shouted, "Here's Lil," at the top of his voice.

The first question was, "Who came with you?"

Then I couldn't tell it fast enough—company for the 550 miles to Chicago in one day; but the rest of the trip alone (apologies to Toodles and Flatateena). The next day, 260 miles, starting out after 10 a.m., then 340 miles the next, 250 to Atlanta, and another 100 to Milledgeville, and then 440 to Daytona. Only 1500 miles!

The most famous beach in America, a playground for all. The baby in his sunsuit (as the prof who rode with me to Chicago would say, "activates his ergosterol"), granddad in his bathing suit and sis in her beach pajamas. Here for a month I frolicked, rode the waves, bathed in the sun and rode up the beach to the lighthouse where the crabs were thickest, across to the inlet where the big fish bite, and back to the cottage to eat and sleep.

I started for home early one morning. This time my mother was with me. When we reached the Florida line, we were stopped by uniformed men "to be inspected."

"For bugs?" I asked.

"Do you have any fruit or plants?"

"Yes," I said hesitatingly. Feeling like a bootlegger, I confessed and handed over my tree orchids I had found in the woods after a day's hunt. I also handed over a bag of oranges.

"Would you mind getting out, lady?" he asked as he pitched my orchids, which I treasured so, and my fruit onto the ground. Then he searched under the seat and actually opened the suitcases as though I had more hidden away.

"All right," he called out as he put on the inspection seal.

"Hope you enjoy the orange juice," I called out as I drove off, and then wondered why I hadn't just stayed and eaten some.

I began a rapid conversation with Mother, lest she should realize I was somewhat disgruntled with having to part with the orchids. Then the landscape began to show Georgia around us, and when I saw a roadside stand with baskets running over with peaches, I felt the thrill of home, my native land as the words came to me.

Second stanza:

When you see the cotton blooming and the fields of waving grain,
Then you know you're down in Georgia land.
When the wind sighs through the pine trees as you stroll down lovers' lane,
When you hear the banjos thrumming and all the pickaninnies dance,
In the moonlight near the cabin doors
And you feel so free and happy, then you know you've reached the Land,
Georgia Land,
Where milk and honey flows.

Chorus:

> *Oh, Georgia with your hedges of Cherokee a bloom*
> *Your watermelons, peaches and goldenrod's tall plume.*
> *You're dearest and the nearest, in my heart your beauty glows.*
> *Oh, Georgia Land, my Georgia, where milk and honey flows.*

The quotation is from "Georgia Land," by Nellie Womack Hines, from her book *Home Keeping Hearts*, pages 42-43, © 1929. The title is from a quote by Longfellow. The song, written in 1923, was adopted by the Georgia Congress of the PTA in 1925.

*   *   *

On another trip, she landed in Vicksburg, Mississippi on Tuesday, the 8th, but her note did not give year or month. She had traveled 431 miles, and on the letterhead of Vicksburg Motor Company (Buick) she wrote:

The fourth tire is now being fixed. Just so much heat...165 miles to Gladwater and mail and breakfast. On to the Delta and 2 hours wait for the ferry (illegible) **the moon shining and every star up in the sky seemed to wink as we went by.**

APPENDIX XVI

NOTES FOR POTENTIAL WILL IN LUTHER'S

HANDWRITING

These notes were found in a small flip-over pad. They were written in Luther's hand sometime after the death of Pattie Love in 1933 and before his marriage to Lillas in 1934.

To Mrs. Mildred Beale, Manassas, Va, $500.00 and the Lindsley furniture inherited from my family, provided the state does not (want or) desire it for museum purposes (illegible)

To Mrs. Hugh _____ , Rockbridge Baths, Virginia, $500.00 toward the education of her daughter.

$500.00 for Glenwood Cemetery, Washington, D. C. for upkeep of the lot where my sister (and her son) Grover Hoxton and her mother are buried.

To W. T. Jones, Boydton, Virginia (amount not legible)

To Mrs. J. Thos. Goode of Boydton, Va $100.00

To Mrs. D. H. Jones of Boydton, Virginia, mother of my wife $15.00 a month during her lifetime.

To J. Henry Jones, his pick of ten white-faced calves or their equivalent in money.

To Jeff Watson, colored man on the plantation, (struck out: my black mare Maude or) **$100.00**

To Ida May Watson, colored, _____chickens or $50.00 as she desires.

To Dr. Sam Anderson _____in cash or the Phil Foster Place 10 acres during his lifetime.

To Miss Lena Martin of GSCW any chemical magazines and my 1928 Chevrolet. (Lena Martin was later recruited by the Department of Defense to work on the Manhattan Project.)

To Miss Jessie Trawick my microscope and accessories

To Miss Lillas Myrick my 1932 Chevrolet and my dog Penny

and my cockerel "Ripley."

To the Department of Chemistry of GSCW all title to my book "Industrial Microscopy" and uncollected bills for same to be used for the further endowment of the Herty medal.

To the Department of Biology at William and Mary the farm I purchased from George Jones in Powhatan District, James City County, Virginia, to be kept as a place for wild flowers and particularly Mountain Laurels. This may be used if necessary in trade for an area of laurels near the College on left of Capitol Landry Road near Queen's Creek.

My house (known as Nicholson) and lots in Williamsburg, Virginia, are to be sold to best advantage to either the Rockefellers or some private individual and a marker erected in the yard or house to Mrs. (Pattie Love Jones) Lindsley who was the inspiration behind its restoration.

I desire that my black mare Maude have a home on the plantation until her natural death.

Westover Plantation Home I give to the State of Georgia as a home for the Faculty of the Chemistry Department of the Georgia State College for Women for their lifetime and at their death to their successors.

To each of the following colored families on the plantation, $50.00

Rev. Josiah Watson

Parker Waller

Charlie Sanford

The balance of the cash from insurance and from various kinds of paper, I leave in trust for the upkeep of the Plantation and for the purpose of Cancer Research (illegible) Lillas Myrick of the Department of Chemistry of the Georgia State College for Women cooperating with the Medical College at Augusta and the State Sanatorium.

See Appendix XXIII for information on the burial site of Pattie Love Jones and her grave stone that shows the front of both the Nicholson House and Westover.

APPENDIX XVII

WHEN GSCW FAILED TO PAY HER SALARY

Lillas Myrick was hired on a nine-month contract for the school term 1933-1934, for the amount of $2400.00.

The contract below is for the previous school term, and is probably the same as the one for the school term in question.

June 13, 1932

Miss Lillas Myrick,

You are hereby officially notified that you have been elected by the Board of Regents of the University System of Georgia as Asso.Prof.Chem. in the Georgia State College for Women for the regular session of 1932-33 at a salary of $2400 with this proviso: "Election shall carry with it liability for the salary attached only to the extent that State Appropriations and other sources of current revenue are available therefor, after supply bills shall have been met."

J. L. Beeson,
President.

She had been teaching for several years, and the contracts were simply a typed notice signed by the president, that the teacher was being hired for the school term, for a certain amount. The payments extended for twelve months, with the monthly pay $200.00

Student enrollment had been declining since the start of the depression, just when Luther had come to GSCW in 1929, raising the chemistry faculty from three to four. In 1934, when the college learned that she planned to get married, Dr. Beeson, the president, asked her to leave the department at the end of the spring quarter. They had too many chemistry teachers for the number of students.

So Lillas agreed to not ask for a position the next fall. The college then cut off her salary and refused to pay her the next two months' $400.00 due.

Although she and Luther fought for more than two years, she never received her pay. Apparently the State of Georgia decided that it lacked the funds to pay a woman who was getting married.

The two single female teachers in the department, Jessie Trawick and Lena Martin, however, received their full salary that year.

Lillas retained documents relating to her claim. In a draft of a letter Luther accused the State of Georgia of illegally borrowing money from some faculty members. Of course, the "loans" he referred to were never paid. A court judged that the Board of Regents could not be sued, even if they without cause cut a professor's salary.

Here are Lillas's documents. Note the wording of the contract's final sentence, used to protect the State when it declined to pay her (and others).

M ___Chancellor Philip Weltner_____ ___19___
                    Atlanta, Ga.

  *Bought of*_____

*Terms:*_____

	Balance of salary for 1932-33 Georgia State College for Women		$400
	This claim was presented in January through President Wells and I hope you will find time to give it your consideration before the end of this fiscal year. You will recall that I was asked to leave the department last year, by Dr. Beeson, because the department was overmanned and you had asked him to economize.		

Jan. 1935 __19__

*M*___ Regents University System of Georgia, Atlanta, Ga.
~~Georgia State College for Women, Milledgeville, Ga.~~

Bought of to Mrs. Lillas Myrick Lindsley
(nee Lillas Myrick)

*Terms:*___ Milledgeville, Ga.

Balance due for services rendered as a member of faculty of Georgia State College for Women for session 1932-33. My contract being for nine months service at $2400 on which only $2000 was paid.	$400.00
Personally appeared before me the under signed who under oath says the above account is just, due and still owing.	

THE UNIVERSITY SYSTEM OF GEORGIA

STATE CAPITOL

ATLANTA, GEORGIA

OFFICE OF
PHILIP WELTNER
CHANCELLOR

May 8, 1935

Mrs. Lillas Myrick Lindsley
Milledgeville, Georgia

My dear Mrs. Lindsley:

It has been our uniform practice to deny claims such as yours where the relationship continued beyond the end of the school year 1932-33.

If you wish to make an appeal from this decision you are at liberty to follow the procedure adopted by the Universith System, an outline of which you can get from President Wells.

Yours truly,

pw/tp

Nov. 14, 1935 —

Miss Florence Barnett,
Milledgeville, Georgia.

Dear Miss Barnett:

We have your letter of November 12th. There is a
suit pending in the Superior Court of this county in favor of
Miss Vera Alice Paul against the Regents involving the same
questions which would be involved in your case. That suit was
brought by Erwin, Erwin & Nix of Athens, and is being defended
by the Attorney General. The question has been raised in that
case as to whether or not the Regents at this time can be sued.
That case, like yours, arose before the act of the legislature
referred to in our former letter.

Under the circumstances, we think that it is best
for you to await filing suit until the question is determined
in the case above referred to, because if the court in that
case should determine the Regents are suable you could then
bring your case; or, in all likelihood, it would then be settled without a suit. On the other hand, if it should be held
that the Regents are not suable, you would be liable for the
costs. On the whole, therefore, we think that it is best to
await the decision on that question in the case above referred
to.

With regards,

Yours very truly,

BRANCH & HOWARD,

By J. A. Branch

Copy

*I wrote him that we would
"sit pat" and see what
happens in the case of
Miss Paul. F.B,*

F. B. is probably Frank Bell, local attorney who had done previous
work for Luther.

APPENDIX XVIII

MONEY MATTERS

LUTHER'S SPENDING

Banks used to return checks to the account holder. Luther and both of his wives saved some of their checks, which throw light onto the husband-wife relationship as well as give us other information.

The most notable revelation is that he wrote multiple checks to "Mrs. L. C. Lindsley," to Pattie Love and to Lillas Myrick. "For" tells us that some of these were for "cash" and some for "grocery." One to Lillas was for "Tax acct of Mrs. L. C. Lindsley," probably for taxes on the land. Pattie Love wrote checks made out to "My self"—two survived: One for $2.00 and one for $2.50. She also paid $1.60 for "King's Daughter's dues."

They paid the washer-woman $1.75.

He bought four books (0.60, 1.00, 1.80, and 4.00, total $7.40) from the "college shop" for "Mrs. LCL" on June 18, 1929, apparently while still in Williamsburg.

In July 1929, he paid $3.00 "tuition for college." No indication as to whose tuition the check was for.

Luther had fire insurance on the Nicholson House, as shown by a check for the "balance on fire insurance" for $14.60 on his Williamsburg bank in July.

Cancelled checks in 1929 on the First National Bank of Williamsburg show that he arrived in Georgia in August; he paid $25.00 to Katherine Scott on August 7 for the first month's rent on a nine-month lease for an apartment. On the 19th he cashed a check for $2.50 for "fishing, etc." On September 3, he cashed a check for $75.00 for "Georgia."

Money must have become a problem in August 1929, for he and Pattie Love both signed a note to the First National Bank of

Williamsburg for $500.00, and on October 1 renewed a note for $2,500.00 from the same bank, with "renewal secured by deed of trust" stamped on this note. Collateral must have been the Nicholson House. He had paid 37 days interest on the note in August, $15.54.

A check made out to Sears Roebuck that September shows he purchased furnace grates for $3.00 to be sent to Mrs. Murphy in Williamsburg. Perhaps it was for the Nicholson House.

He bought five watermelons for $1.00 that September.

A statement from The Peoples' Hardware Company for October 1936 shows his purchase of plows (2.25), planter (1.40), plaster of Paris (.76), roofing (1.25), beams (1.90), 2 bu. peas (4.50), 1 doz 2-qt jars (.93), peas (1.40), horse shoes (.40), horse shoes & nails (1.65), cement (.90), slat brick (.65).

Some of these materials may have been used to build his barns. The support posts (cedar tree trunks) were embedded in cement.

Some checks show purchases to restore or repair houses. In May 1955, he bought a fanlight from Trader Bob Harper for twenty dollars, "for rebuilding house" (Westover).

*   *   *

This is a random listing of some checks Luther wrote in late 1929 and 1930 after he arrived in Milledgeville. The ones relating to his work are listed in **boldface.** Copies of the checks relating to Westover/the Jordan Place are given below also.

> 1929 January 1 $15.00 Am Chem Society (dues?)
> 1929 April 19 $3.50 Culver & Kidd for Easter
> 1929 November 9 $7.20 W. T. Little, Deputy Collector Auto
>   license tag for Georgia
> 1929 November 5 $3.71 Cornell Coop Soc.
> 1929 November 14 $1.00 D. F. Montgomery for groceries
> 1929 November 22 $1.00 Red Cross

1929 November 15 $3.00 William Byrd Press for copyright, U.
S. Library etc.

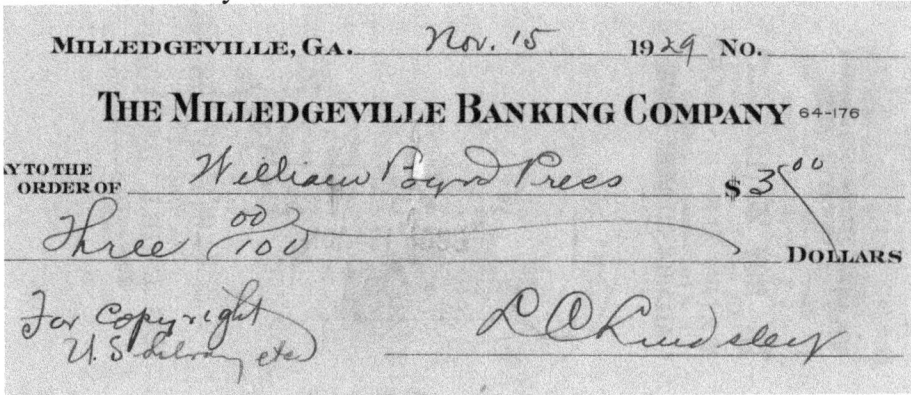

MILLEDGEVILLE, GA. *Nov. 15* 19*29* No.

THE MILLEDGEVILLE BANKING COMPANY 64-176

Y TO THE ORDER OF *William Byrd Press* $3 00

Three 00/100 DOLLARS

*For Copyright
U. S. Library etc.* *R. C. Lindsley*

1929 December 30 $4.75 Wm. Byrd Press for 1,000 copies
Reagent Block key
1929 December 30 $6.53 Ward. Nat. Science for **minerals for GSCW college**
1929 December 20 $3.95 Eastman Kodak Co. **Chemicals for GSCW**
1930 March 1 $2.20 to Kathryn Duggan for reading to Mrs.
LCL
1930 Feb 17 $25.99 Miss Katherine Scott, rent
1930 March 8 $14.00 Mr. G. T. Brooks Insurance on Nicholson
Street house
1930 January 8 $12.00 Geo. H. Carswell, Sec. of State for
license tag
1930 January 21 $2.55 John Wiley & sons for Holmes Colloids
1930 February 8 $3.60 Daily Press, 6 month subscription
(Virginia paper)
1930 November 1 $10.40 William Leakey Repair Roof, 141
York Street, Williamsburg (the Nicholson House)
1930 April 5 $4.75 Treasurer City of Williamsburg for water
and sewer
1930 February 4 $1.28 Railway Express Agency for 8 books
1930 January 9, $4.25 *Union-Recorder*, printing
1930 February 28 $1.50 Miss Bettie Ferguson, Balance, Music
Club dues
1930 February 11 $11.50 William Byrd Press, Balance due on
500 circulars

1930 February 25 $2.00 George Brown for **making chem. box**
1932 January 13 $1.00 Culver & Kidd for **chem. GSCW**
1930 November 3 $14.57 Ga. State College for Women

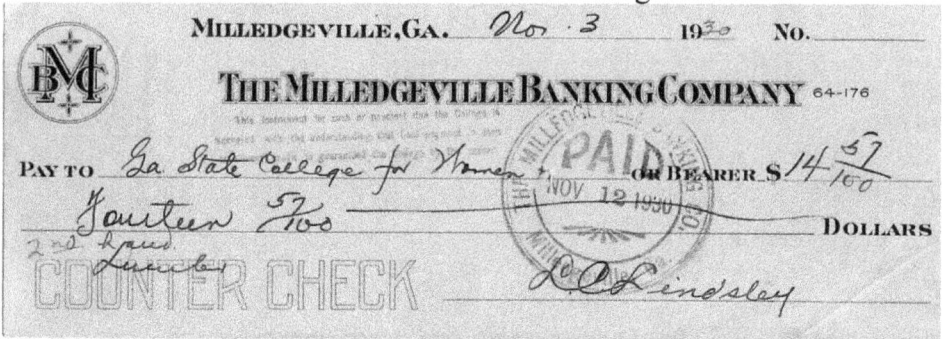

1930 October 23 $2.50 Mr. Fowler (Bursar, GSCW) for
  Lyceum tickets
1930 March 2 $5.00 Mr. Frank Bone, Treas, Episcopal Church
1930 March 3 E. A. Tigner for dentistry
1930 March 1 $1.60 Elizabeth Fort for reading to Mrs. LCL
1930 March 12 $11.84 E. Leitz & Co for **eyepiece etc**
1930 June 20 $8.00 Shine Mason for labor, for Shine and boy,
  Jordan Place

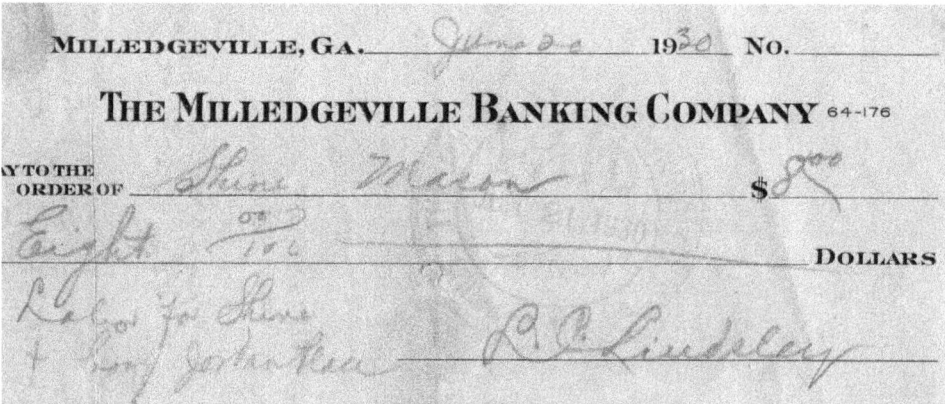

1930 July 13 $9.00 J. E. Stevens for pigs
1930 April 2 $4.50 John Wiley & Son for **Chamot Chem.
  Microscopy**
1929 October 5 $32.75 Kiwanis Club
1930 October 4 $2.00 Robert Densley, Mowing

1930 October 6 $25.00 Miss Katherine Scott for Rent, Sept 6-Oct 6

1930 October 4 $1.28 D. Van Nostrand & Co. (publishers) for Silverman Lab Manuel

1930 June 17 $5.00 M. F. Davis for shoes

1930 July 7 $33.00 Hatcher Hdw on act. Jordan repairs

1930 April 13 $1.00 Mr. Frank Bone (atty) for foreign work

1930 April 15 $20.00 for suit

1930 date illegible $4.50 Atlantic Ice and Coal Co. for coal

1930 January 27 $5.00 Treasurer General N. S. D. A R. for dues for Mrs. LCL

1930 November 20 $10.00 cash for Chemistry Club picnic

1930 November 22 $1.00 Henry Vinson for oranges

1930 November 22 $3.00 Charlie Sanford for labor

1930 June 9 R. H. Hatcher $13.45 for hardware for Jordan Place

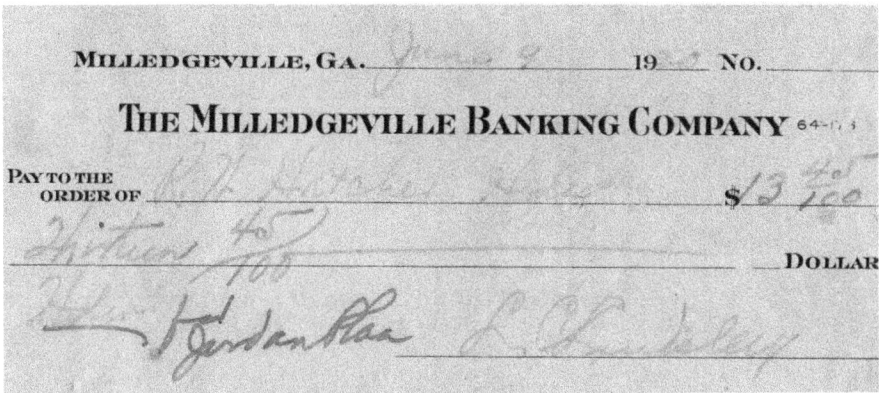

1930 September 9 $1,279.16 Mrs. Ophelia Wall or Bearer for first note on Jordan Place.

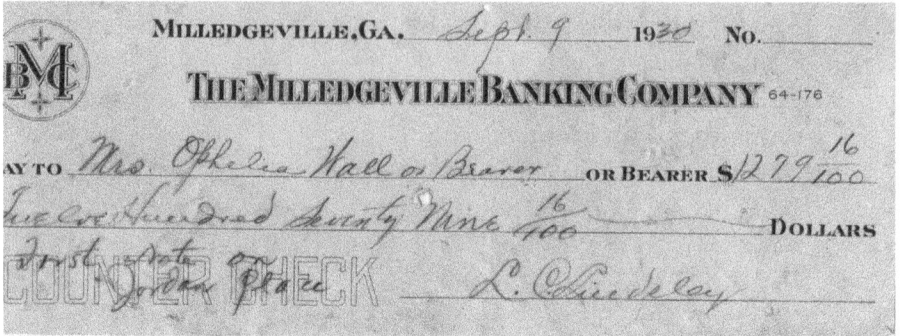

1930 October 29 $5.00 Shine Mason for advance on painting house

1930 September 4 $13.60 Mr. W. H. Gore for Jordan Place
1930 September 17 $26.89 D. M. Rogers Agent C. of GA. Railroad for freight on furniture from Williamsburg, Va.

1930 November 1 $68.60 Mrs. Ophelia Wall for "int. at 6% on 1st mortgage of $2750 on Jordan place by Aetna Life Ins. Co., being assumed by me since June 3."

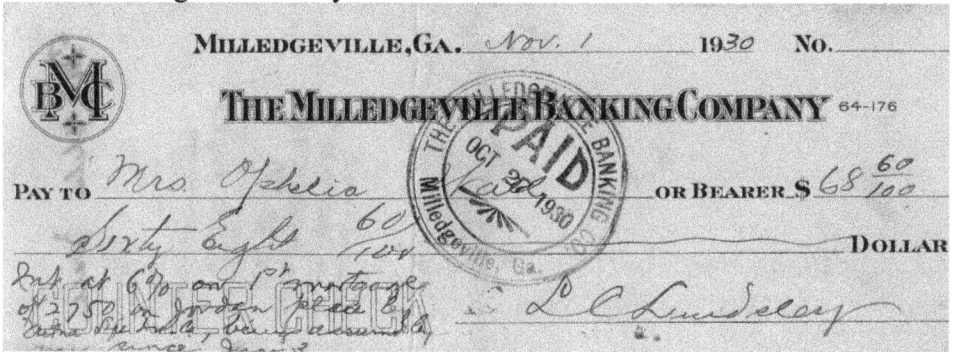

LILLAS'S MONEY MATTERS

PURCHASES

This section gives a look at the checks she wrote for various purposes, to the hired help, to the hardware store and other institutions and companies. Many of the people are remembered as workers at Westover. Most of the businesses have long been closed. But these listings will give a sample of costs for everything from laundry to land.

A look at some of her cancelled checks from the 1930s gives us a view of banking as well as how she spent her funds, from buying clothing to home repairs and dry good purchases, as well as names of the people who worked at Westover.

The earliest check we have from her is on the Merchants & Farmers Bank, Milledgeville, for $100.00, payable to the University State Bank, Minneapolis, dated October 2, 1930.

One example of banking in the 1930s is a check made out to the Merchants & Farmers bank, to pay for interest on her note, and signed "Lillas M. Lindsley by Emolte G. Doole." (The "by" name is almost illegible.)

Two checks, each for $500, in 1933 seem to be payment for the section of Dovedale that belonged to Jim Myrick (the section now owned by Susan Lindsley). One check is to J. D. Myrick, dated September 26, 1933, endorsed by "J. D. Myrick, agent." the other check, dated October 30, 1933, to J. C. Cooper, is "For purchase of 135 acres of land, 318th dist. Baldwin Co., Ga.; part Myrick Place conveyed by Mrs. Lena R. Myrick, Est. of J. D. Myrick."

Checks to officials, such as Cooper, the State Revenue Commission (income tax, 1934, $10.23) bear a stamp in red "Federal Tax 2¢."

Several checks, ranging from $2.00 to $20.00, to Phalack (also spelled Phalox) Myrick indicate that he was one of the hired men in the late 1930s. In 1935 he paid $40.00 rent for the segment of Dovedale Plantation called "Miss Katie's Place," which had to be Katie Lowerre's land since Guy Humphries lived on the "Home Place" of Dovedale.

Shine Mason is remembered by her children as one of the farm workers; checks for him ranged from $2.00 to $7.00. He lived at one time in a house that stood between the "cottage" and the railroad. (The cottage was the house the family lived in when the children were small and again years later, after Westover burned.) Shine Mason's home was also called "Willie's House."

Dave Waller was paid $2.00 in April 1937. He lived at "Uncle Dave's," the most southern and eastern house on the lands, along Hwy 212. (The house was later occupied by Little Sam Avery and his family.)

Sam Avery, father of Little Sam, lived at the junction of what is now Highway 212 and Meriwether Road. He worked for Luther, was paid by Lillas, in the 1930s and for many years thereafter. Two checks for him paid $5.00 and $1.25. His daughter Alice and her husband Robert live on Highway 212 today.

"Sherman" (John) Calhoun was a most beloved worker at Dovedale Plantation when Lillas was a child. He told the children stories of Brer Rabbit, Brer Fox, and other mythical creatures of African folklore at a time that Joel Chandler Harris was collecting the stories to preserve the African heritage. A December 1939 check by Lillas shows that he was a part of Westover also.

Daisy Grimes might have been a house worker or a washerwoman, for her only surviving check is for $1.60.

Lillas purchased clothing from Sears and from Lane Bryant, and dry goods from E. E. Bell Dry Goods and from the Union Department Store. Her sister Allie proclaimed her an excellent seamstress, and Lillas made her daughters' clothes for many years. During the Depression and the Second World War, a good source of cloth was the cotton bags that livestock feed came in. Luther had instructions to purchase feed in matched bags so there would be enough cotton in one pattern to make a dress.

In January 1936, she wrote a check to W. E. Bass Company for $192.00, for the "Henderson Reeves note." Two notes signed by Reeves (also spelled Reaves) to W. E. Bass were for mules and horses, and one of them was also for a "two-horse Thimbleskein hackney wagon."

Other Dovedale tenants included J. J. Bledsoe and David Parham. One lease was $50.00 cash for 45 acres; the other, $150.00 for 135 acres.

Her contract with Edward Monday was written out by Luther:

This rent contract entered into this 18th day of January 1940 between Lillas M. Lindsley and Edward Monday   Witnesseth that Lillas M. Lindsley agrees to rent to Edward Monday the farm on Dovedale Plantation formerly used by Fred S— Myrick for (500 lb) one bale of cotton (lint?)   The said Lillas Myrick agrees to waive the rent up to $70.00 and Edward Monday agrees to furnish corn or labor to pay any balance due on the 1940 rent. Lillas M. Lindsley agrees to furnish nails etc for repairs and Edward Monday will furnish labor.
 X Edward Monday   Lillas M. Lindsley

Note that Luther wrote her name once as Lillas Myrick.

In December 1938, she closed out her mother's estate with a payment of $50.00 estate taxes. A draft letter in her papers indicates that she had trouble collecting rent; with "five months rent due" the tenant was probably not a resident of the Liberty Street House. Lillas and Sue Myrick inherited the house, and a number of checks from Lillas to Susan indicate that Lillas collected the rent. Lillas later purchased Susan's half of the house.

After Westover burned, Lillas was the one who signed many checks to replace lost items. She purchased a cradle from Trader Bob Harper for $14.00 to replace the one hand-made by one of Luther's Lamb ancestors. Thulia Bramlett has the check and the cradle.

Lillas also paid by check for the color picture of Lt. L. C. Lindsley and for many of the porcelains and coins they purchased after the fire.

These three bills from hardware stores show that even before she married she was involved in home repair as well as maintaining her parcels of Dovedale Plantation. She supervised roofing, fencing and anything else that needed doing.

SALES MADE STRICTLY F. O. B. CARS MINES, BASED ON R. R. SCALE WEIGHT NEAREST INITIAL POINT OF SHIPMENT AND SUBJECT TO CAR SUPPLIES, STRIKES AND OTHER UNAVOIDABLE CONTINGENCIES

LEWIS FLEMISTER, President   JOHN T. DAY, Vice President

Milledgeville, Ga., _____ 3/31 1933

Miss *Lillas Myrick*

To - FOWLER-FLEMISTER COAL CO. - Dr.
WHOLESALE AND RETAIL DEALERS IN
COAL, WOOD AND BUILDERS' SUPPLIES

Feb.	13	3 sqs. Syau Comp. Shingles · Red.	16	50	
"	"	10# roofing nails	1	00	
"	"	24 linft. Strip cap		50	
"	"	1 frmz. 1x8 - 8 - D4S - B.		25	
"	"	1 " 1x8-16 " "		50	
"	22	1 Glass 15 x 36	1	00	
"	"	5 # Roofing nails		50	
			20	25	
Apr	1	Credit by 2 bdls. shingles (¼ sq.)	1	37	18 88

THE PEOPLES' HARDWARE COMPANY
HARDWARE, GAS RANGES AND HEATERS
GUNS AND SHELLS
LYNCHBURG PLOWS, GALVANIZED AND FELT ROOFING

MILLEDGEVILLE, GEORGIA

2/1 _____ 193 4

Sold To _Miss Lilla Myrick_

TERMS: Due 1st of Month following purchase. If not paid by 15th of Month account will be closed.

1933

Nov	25	Nails .106 Lime .50 24# nails 1.20		2	75
"	"	Lime .50 (1/2") 6 pr. Hgs. .210 (wagon)		2	60
		Nails .55 (1/2) 40# nails 2.00 (14) 3 Rolls B. wire 8.75		12	30
Dec	14	Staples .26 40 pcs 12 ft 5 V 45.90		46	15
"		9 pcs 10 ft .5 V 7.47 46 ft R. roll 2.25		9	72
"		13# roof nails 1.95 10- L & B wire 27.50		29	45
"		Dye 2.50 1 pr. 12 ft roofing 1.18 5# nails .26		3	93
		1 pr lines .30			30
Jan	17	6 door locks 3.50 10# Staples .70 3# nails .16	3	85	111 05
					37 25
					73 40

The People's Hardware Company
DEALERS IN
EVERYTHING IN HARDWARE
Lynchburg Plows, Poultry and Wire Fencing

Milledgeville, Ga., 4/16 1935

Sold To _Mrs L. C. Lindsley_

TERMS: Due 1st of Month following purchase. If not paid by 15th of Month account will be closed.

Feb 1934	19	30 ft well rope .30 bucket .50 whirl .75	1	55
Dec	10	nails .26 rope+ bucket .85	1	10
		2 rolls wire + staples	7	15
		rope + bucket .85 1 pr shears 2.50	3 36	13 16

INTANGIBLES

In her 1940 intangible tax files, Lillas showed ownership of:
    a checking account in the amount of $125.00
    10 shares of Black and Decker stock valued at $75.00
    10 shares of New Amsterdam Casualty Company valued at $74.00
    One bond with Beneficial Loan valued at $500, with 6% income and due in 1956.

She always spoke of being land poor—all income was invested in the land, which was taxed higher than intangibles.

APPENDIX XIX

HERTY DAY GUESTS

The invitation list for the Herty Day tea includes all the social, financial and political leaders in the town and county at the time, as well as faculty and staff of the college itself and the associated teachers' practice school (Peabody).

The celebrities given in the news article were in addition to the local invitees.

LOCAL INVITEES

Dr. and Mrs. E. W. Allen
Dr. and Mrs. H. D. Allen, Jr.
Mr. and Mrs. L. H. Andrews
Mrs. And Mrs. J. E. Bell, Sr.
Mr. and Mrs. Miller R. Bell
Mr. and Mrs. E. Bell
Mr. and Mrs. Frank Bone
Mrs. Jennie Brooks
Miss Emma and Miss Carrie Carrington
Mr. and Mrs. Otto Conn and Mrs. Morrison
Mrs. David Ferguson
Mr. and Mrs. L. C. Hall
Dr. and Mrs. T. M. Hall
Mrs. Frank Hancock
Mrs. Cora Holt
Rev. and Mrs. F. H. Harding
Mrs. R. W. Hatcher and family
Miss Elizabeth Jones
Mr. H. W. Little
Mrs. G. C. McKinley
Father Kind
Mr. and Mrs. Rufus Oakey
*Mrs. L. D. Rozar
*Miss Nannette Rozar

Mr. and Mrs. J. W. Shinhoster
Rev. and Mrs. James Teresi (and visitors)
Rev. and Mrs. Pierce
Mr. and Mrs. Steve Thornton
Mrs. Lucy P. Walker
Mrs. Dixon Williams
Mr. and Mrs. R. H. Wooten
Mr. and Mrs. Terrance Treanor
Mr. and Mrs. Charles Whitfield
Mr. and Mrs. Frank Bell
Mrs. Richardson
Mrs. Miller
Mr. and Mrs. Cotton
Miss Gertie Treanor
Mrs. C. P. Crawford
Mr. and Mrs. Sallee
Mrs. Mattie Bivins
Mrs. Griner
Mr. Harper
Miss Annie Harper
Erwin Sibley
Mr. and Mrs. C. B. McCullar
Dr. and Mrs. E. A. Tigner
Dr. and Mrs. Dennis Turner
Mrs. Ed Napier and Miss Elizabeth Napier
Dr. and Mrs. W. E. Ireland
Mrs. M. M. Parks
Dr. and Mrs. Andrews
The Jenkins

*Aunt Josey, sister of Lillas's mother, and her daughter Nannette.

The two-page list of faculty included not only GSCW but also faculty of the Peabody School:

7 GSCW Administration
8 Music department
6 Secretarial training
12 Home Economics

9 Teacher training
24 Peabody school
8 English department
5 Foreign languages
6 Math department
24 Office workers/house mothers, dietitians /engineers
3 Biology
8 Health and PE
2 Chemistry (excludes LCL)
7 Social sciences/Geography/History
4 Library
1 YWCA
1 Alumnae office
3 Art department
1 Physics

HERTY DAY OUT-OF-TOWN CELEBRITIES: 1936

The *Union-Recorder* always gave extensive coverage to the Herty Day events. Dr. Walter H. MacIntire of the University of Tennessee received the award in 1936, and the *Recorder* not only gave his educational and professional background but also gave the history of the Medal.

Herty Day brought the elite of the scientific world to Milledgeville.

At the afternoon tea held at Westover, the visiting celebrities included: Mr. Whatley and two students from Bessie Tift College, Dr. H. F. Kurtz of Bessie Tift; Miss Elise C. Shover, Atlanta; Mr. and Mrs. Claude V. Bruce, Macon; Miss Catherine Moore, Augusta; Miss Minnie Yetter, Macon; Dr. G. H. Boggs, Georgia Tech, Atlanta; Dr. and Mrs. William S. Taylor, Georgia Tech, Atlanta; Dr. and Mrs. Burt P. Richardson, Mercer University, Macon.

Miss Grace Wyatt, Shorter College, Rome; Miss Vaidee Gurry, Shorter College; Dr. and Mrs. J. E. Boyd, Atlanta; Mr. and Mrs. John Bretz and guest, Atlanta; Dr. Paul Weber and guests, Georgia Tech; Miss Evangeline Papageorge and guests, Emory University; Mr. Philip Shuey and Miss Shuey, Savannah; Mr. and Mrs. Robert

Hold, Agnes Scott College; Dr. and Mrs. George T. Lewis, Emory University; Dr. John L. Daniel and Miss Daniel, Georgia Tech; Dr. and Mrs. T. H. Whitehead, University of Georgia; Mr. G. P. Shingler, Lake City, Florida; Dr. Harrold Friedman, Georgia Tech; Dr. and Mrs. W. H. MacIntire*, Knoxville, Tennessee; Dr. and Mrs. William H. Jones, Emory University; Dr. and Mrs. Sam Guy, Emory University; Dr. and Mrs. Almand, Wesleyan College, Macon; Miss Sara Bunch, Atlanta; Dr. Osburne Quayle, Emory University.

*Dr. MacIntire was the Herty Medal recipient.

APPENDIX XX

THE NICHOLSON HOUSE

HABS has no other picture of the house, and none of the inside. HABS VA-48-WIL, 42—1. Note the overgrowth of vines and shrubs.

The deed transferring ownership of the Nicholson House to Luther and Pattie Love is dated July 5, 1923.

They borrowed $3,000.00, the entire cost, for the purchase: $1,000 from the Dey family (owners) and $2,000 from the local bank. The note to the Dey family was due and payable in 60 days, the bank note on or before January 15, 1924. The deed states that the land is the security for this note and for any future renewals.

The bank's note had priority over the seller's note. Failure to pay interest, taxes, insurance, etc., would result in public sale of the property.

The loan was renewed on January 15, 1924, for $2,500.00.

When Luther and Patti Love moved to Georgia in 1929, they must have rented out the house. This shows how it looked when the Historic American Building Survey photographed it, after the couple moved to Georgia and before it was sold in 1938.

Luther told his children that because Pattie Love had no will, at her death in 1933 her share of the property went to her mother, by Virginia law.

On March 23, 1938, Pattie Bugg Jones (Pattie Love's mother) "conveyed all of her right, title and interest" in the property to Luther.

On May 16, 1938, Luther and Lillas signed a deed to transfer the Nicholson House and its land to Channing M. Hall, of Williamsburg, "hereinafter called the Trustee." He apparently was trustee for the bank that held the note. The deed states that the property is to be sold at auction either at the courthouse or at the property itself.

The property did not sell for two years. One report found on-line stated that the house was overgrown and becoming dilapidated when it was sold. The deed of sale, dated August 19, 1940, shows that it was purchased by James L. Cogar of Williamsburg.

For other information on the house, search HABS VA-188, the file code for the Historical American Building Survey in the Library of Congress.

DEED: NICHOLSON HOUSE FROM MRS. JONES TO LUTHER

This deed, made this 23rd Day of March 1938, between

PATTIE BUGG JONES, widow, of Mecklenburg County, Virginia, as party of the first part, herein-after designated as the grantor, and LUTHER C. LINDSLEY of Milledgeville, Georgia, as party of the second part, hereinafter designated as the grantee:

WITNESSETH: That for and in consideration of the sum of One Dollar and other good and valuable considerations in hand paid by the grantee to the grantor at and before the sealing and delivery of these presents, the receipt whereof is hereby acknowledged, the grantor doth grant, bargain, sell and convey to the grantee with Special Warranty the following property, to-wit:

All of the right, title and interest of the grantor as the mother and heir at law of the late Pattie Love Jones Lindsley in and to the following Parcels of real estate:

<u>PARCEL ONE</u>

(The Nicholson House)

An undivided one-half interest in and to a certain lot of land, together with the buildings and improvements thereon, lying on the north side of York Street in the city of Williamsburg, Virginia, the said lot being known as the Slaughter Lot, and being the same lot of which Bascom Dey died seized and possessed, and bounded as follows: on the south by York Street, on the east by the lot now or formerly owned by W. A. Gore, on the west by the lot now or formerly owned by P. G. Powell, and on the north by land now or formerly owned by L. W. Lane. The said lot of land hereby conveyed consists and is composed of two adjacent lots or parcels of land, one of which the said Bascom Dey, deceased, heired from his father, John B. Dey; and the other lot or parcel being the same conveyed to Bascom Dey by deed from John H. Lawson and Margaret N. Lawson his wife, dated December 14, 1894, and recorded in City of Williamsburg Deed Book No. 2, page 595, and being the same lot conveyed to John W. Lawson by deed from H. B. Warren, Special Commissioner, dated September 16, 1885, and recorded in Williamsburg DB 2, page 168. The property above described is the same as that conveyed to Luther C. Lindsley and Pattie Love Jones Lindsley, husband and wife, as joint grantees, by deed from Hetty L. Dey and others, as the widow and all the children and heirs at law of Bascom Dey, deceased, dated July 5, 1923, and recorded in Williamsburg Deed Book 10, page 65.

PARCEL TWO

All that certain tract of land, together with the buildings and improvements thereon, situated in Powhatan Magisterial District, James City County, Virginia, containing twenty (20) acres more or less, but sold and conveyed in gross and not by the acre, and being bounded on the north by the road leading from Wilkinson's store to Yarmouth Island, on the east by the public road, on the south by the land of Willie Taylor and on the west by the land of Clifton Williams. Being the same land conveyed to Georgia A. Jones by deed from Clarence Vaiden dated May 28, 1900, and recorded in James City County DB 7, page 392, with the exception of 6 1/2 acres conveyed to Willie Taylor and Laura Taylor and 8 acres conveyed to Clifton Williams. Said Parcel No. Two being the same property conveyed to the late Pattie Love Jones Lindsley by deed from George A. Jones and Mary Jones, his wife, dated December 30, 1931, and recorded in James City County Deed Book No. 26, page 342.

This conveyance is subject to the life estate of the said Luther C. Lindsley as surviving husband of his deceased wife, Pattie Love Jones Lindsley, who died intestate on October 3, 1933, leaving surviving her, her said husband, who is the grantee in this deed, and leaving as her heir at law the grantor herein, who is the mother of the said Pattie Love Jones Lindsley. The said grantor is the only surviving parent of Pattie Love Jones Lindsley, and the grantor covenants that Daniel H. Jones, husband of the grantor, and father of Pattie Love Jones Lindsley, died on the 1st day of March, 1918.

WITNESS the following signature and seal:

Pattie Bugg Jones

STATE OF VIRGINIA
COUNTY OF MECKLENBURG, to-wit

I, J. Henry Jones, a J. P. for the County of Mecklenburg in the State of Virginia, do certify that Pattie Bugg Jones, widow, whose name is signed to the writing hereto annexed bearing date on the 23rd day of March, 1938, has this day acknowledged the same before me in my County and State aforesaid.

Given under my hand this 26th day of May, 1938.

J. Henry Jones, J. P.

State of Virginia,
City of Williamsburg and County of James City, to-wit:

In the office of the Clerk of the Court for the City and County afore said, on the 8th day of June, 1938, this deed was presented with the certificate annexed, admitted to record at 10:30 A.M.

Teste:

Virginia Blanchard, Clerk

APPENDIX XXI

LAST DEED WITH LUTHER IN PRINCE

WILLIAM COUNTY

DEED BOOK 76, PAGES 133-135:

This deed transferred six acres of land belonging to the deceased Willie Johnson and Hannah Lamb Lindsley Johnson to Hannah's surviving children; the two grandchildren, Luther C. Lindsley (then at Cornell) and wife received $250.00 as did Virginia Lindsley Hoxton (who had divorced her husband).

George W. Johnson, whose will was probated October 5, 1914, left his son Willie L. Johnson 14 acres of land, and his wife Hannah the house and six acres of land. Hannah died intestate in 1921, and still owned the house. She was heir at law of her son, and so owned his 14 acres also at her death.

This deed apparently was to transfer any claim the grandchildren might have made to these two properties to George and Hannah's surviving children.

The deed stated that

...also agrees to deliver the Douglas Hill furniture, boxed and crated and billed collect at the So. Ry. Depot at no cost to said parties of the first part, at their request.

APPENDIX XXII

BURIAL INFORMATION

HANNAH LAMB LINDSLEY JOHNSON

The Prince William County Burial Index shows that Hannah is buried in the Manassas City Cemetery, Lot 52

ERNEST L. LINDSLEY

Ernest is also buried in the Manassas City Cemetery, Lot 52.

The lot map shows that by entering the cemetery from Main Street, Manassas, and taking the road that angles to the left, you will find the lot the seventh on the right.

FRANCES VIRGINIA LINDSLEY HOXTON AND HER SON FRANCIS

Frances Virginia Lindsley Hoxton is buried at the Glenwood Cemetery in Washington, D. C., in Section O, Lot Number 37. The south entrance to the cemetery is located on Lincoln Road, which borders the SE and E sides. Franklin Road forms the N border and Girard Street the NW border; the SW side adjoins other lands. The cemetery is irregular, and there is another entrance, on the NW corner.

Photo by W. Edgar Marshall. His note on the back reads:
The wreath is in alignment (horizontal) with the tombstone of
Virginia, her mother and son.
The marker in rear (left of the two) is Uncle Sam and Aunt Rena.
The stone in rear of wreath and in alignment with Uncle Sam is for
Grandmother and Papa before we moved him.

Tall Monument reads:
    Elizabeth Lindsley 1861-1885
    Francis L. Hoxton 1909-1917
    Frances V. Hoxton 1881-1922

The wreath was laid by Edgar at Luther's request.

Plat of the Marshall Lot:

In Plot 4:
    Bettie (Bessie) Lindsley 1892
    Francis Hoxton 1917
    Virginia Hoxton 1922
In Plot 5:
    Lillie Lindsley 1892 (Luther's mother)
    Willie Lindsley 1892 (Luther's infant brother)

A handwritten note on the back of this page reads:
    Elizabeth Lindsley 1861-1885
    Francis L. Hoxton 1909-1917
    Frances V. Hoxton 1881-1922

The Glenwood Cemetery
2219 Lincoln Road
Washington 2, D. C.

NORTH 7-1016

Perpetual Care - $100.00 for first site and $25.00 for each additional site.

Includes Regrading, sodding when needed, seeding when needed
         Fertilizer and Liming
         Cutting and trimming   Includes Planting of bushes, etc.
         Filling in when needed
         Cutting lawn

         Does not include taking care of monument.
         Does not include watering.

APPENDIX XXIII

MARKER FOR PATTIE LOVE JONES

LINDSLEY

Presbyterian Church Cemetery
Boydton
Mecklenburg County, Virginia

The Boydton Presbyterian Church is no longer used as such, and sits on a knoll above Cemetery Street across a side street from the Baptist Church cemetery. A sign announces the Baptist Church cemetery but not the Presbyterian one, although they are across the side street from each other.

Close-up of plaque at front of the church.

Facing the church, look to your left. Patti Love's grave shows in the picture below, to the left of the forked tree. The marker is a "slab" rather than a vertical marker. Susan Lindsley visited the cemetery on November 2, 2014, and took some of these photographs.

View of the entire grave stone.*

The Nicholson House as on the marker.*

WESTOVER PLANTATION
MILLEDGEVILLE, GEORGIA

———

A GRACIOUS LADY WHO DIED
THAT OTHERS MIGHT LIVE

1886 — 1933

Westover as on the marker.*
*Photographs of the markers by Margaret Gagliardi, from a web site created by Margaret C. Cowles.
Those without the asterisk were taken by Susan Lindsley, November 2, 2014.

www.ingramcontent.com/pod-product-compliance
Lightning Source LLC
Chambersburg PA
CBHW021154160426
42812CB00082B/3043/J